The
COMPLETE
LANGUAGE
of BIRDS

The

COMPLETE
LANGUAGE
of **BIRDS**

A Definitive & Illustrated History

Randi Minetor

wellfleet
press

© 2024 Quarto Publishing Group USA Inc.

Text © 2024 by Randi Minetor

First published in 2024 by Wellfleet Press, an imprint of The Quarto Group,

142 West 36th Street, 4th Floor, New York, NY 10018, USA

(212) 779-4972   www.Quarto.com

Wellfleet Press titles are also available at discount for retail, wholesale, promotional, and bulk purchase. For details, contact the Special Sales Manager by email at specialsales@quarto.com or by mail at The Quarto Group, Attn: Special Sales Manager, 100 Cummings Center Suite 265D, Beverly, MA 01915 USA.

10 9 8 7 6 5 4 3 2 1

ISBN: 978-1-57715-374-0

Digital edition published in 2024

eISBN: 978-0-7603-8305-6

Library of Congress Cataloging-in-Publication Data

Names: Minetor, Randi, author.
Title: The complete language of birds : a definitive & illustrated
    history / Randi Minetor.
Description: New York, NY : Wellfleet Press, an imprint of the Quarto
    Group, 2024. | Series: Complete illustrated encyclopedia | Includes
    bibliographical references and index. | Summary: "The Complete Language
    of Birds offers stunningly illustrated profiles of nearly 400 bird
    species, covering both their physical and mystical qualities"-- Provided
    by publisher.
Identifiers: LCCN 2024005116 (print) | LCCN 2024005117 (ebook) | ISBN
    9781577153740 (hardcover) | ISBN 9780760383056 (ebook)
Subjects: LCSH: Birds--Encyclopedias. | Birds--Identification. |
    Birds--Folklore--Encyclopedias. | Birds--Nomenclature (Popular)
Classification: LCC QL672.2 .M56 2024 (print) | LCC QL672.2 (ebook) | DDC
    598.03--dc23/eng/20240229
LC record available at https://lccn.loc.gov/2024005116
LC ebook record available at https://lccn.loc.gov/2024005117

Group Publisher: Rage Kindelsperger
Editorial Director: Erin Canning
Creative Director: Laura Drew
Managing Editor: Cara Donaldson
Editor: Elizabeth You
Cover and Interior Design: Verso Design

Printed in China

CONTENTS

INTRODUCTION

Birds have fascinated human beings since the first people walked the Earth, dazzling us with their brilliant feathers, their wide variety of shapes and sizes, their unusual skills, and, most of all, their ability to fly. In that way that people have of trying to make sense of the world based on their own uses for the resources around us, people began to define birds' influences on our experiences even before they developed a way to record their ideas. Many of the stories told in this book were passed down verbally through the millennia, through extended families gathered around cooking fires, or through tribes meeting at kivas to trade tales as well as wares.

From drawings on cave walls, hieroglyphs inside tombs, and myths told and retold, we learn that birds played a role in the pantheons of Greek, Roman, Egyptian, Norse, Māori, and Aboriginal mythologies. Heroes and villains may vary, but the messages are often the same: Birds serve as familiars or alternate forms of gods and goddesses, adding to deities' powers or allowing them to rescue victims of wrongdoing. In Indigenous cultures in the Americas, birds' involvement explained everything from the change of seasons to the transition from day to night. Birds even contribute to creation myths, often nudging the process into motion by rolling a stone, diving through deep water to bring up a beakful of mud, or laying an egg that contains the whole planet.

The gift of flight makes birds mysterious as well as remarkable, a skill that many cultures interpret as necessary for their communication with other realms. Thousands of years of folklore underscore a common theme: Birds fly so high and so far because they must carry messages to other planes of existence—the worlds of gods and goddesses, each culture's heaven or hell, or the spiritual realm of long-dead ancestors. What were deeply held beliefs in days of old may seem quaint today, but even in these modern times, we can't help but wonder if the cardinal cocking its head at us from a backyard bird feeder might truly be an ancient relative with an important message.

This book looks at 387 bird species from all over the world, providing many of the stories passed down through history, as well as facts that bird lovers at every level will enjoy—whether you toss out seed to pigeons in the park, hang bird feeders in your yard, or travel far and wide to see birds you've never seen before (what avid birders call "life birds"). Whether you find mythology and folklore intriguing or preposterous, you are likely to come away with a new understanding about the ways that birds have helped people make sense of their complex, infinitely varied world, and their own place within it.

How to
USE THIS
BOOK

The birds in the body of the book are listed alphabetically by their scientific names, and are numbered starting with 001. Beneath the Latin name is the official common name of that bird, according to the International Union for Conservation of Nature (IUCN) and the International Ornithologists Union (IOU). If you do not know the scientific name of the bird (most people do not), but you do know its common name, you can find that name in the Index of Common Bird Names at the end of the book. You can then find the bird's number, and look it up easily in the sequence.

Many birds have subspecies: birds that are very similar biologically but that have slightly different characteristics from the main species. Subspecies are usually isolated geographically, like the Cuban Sandhill Crane, a subspecies of the Sandhill Crane that only appears in Cuba. When a bird's subspecies have common names, they are included in the species' main entry in the Other Common Names to help direct people to the right bird even if they know it only by its subspecies name. Where you see the term *Subspecies* in the Common Names, everything that follows is a subspecies of that bird.

Each bird's entry has an icon that tells you the bird's current conservation status throughout its range, according to the IUCN. This organization examines the status of the bird's population throughout the world, rather than in one place, so some birds that are endangered or even extirpated from one region may still be ranked "Least Concern" because of a healthy population elsewhere.

You will also see Collective Nouns for each species. These are more suggested than hard-and-fast rules, as no official arbiter of grammar determines which collective nouns should or should not be used. Some of these date back to the fourteenth or fifteenth century (a nide of geese, for example, or a tok of capercaillies), but many are more modern and facetious, pressed into use by linguistic acrobats who enjoy drawing ironic parallels and have some skill with the internet (a Durante of toucans, for example, making reference to a large-nosed movie star of the mid-twentieth century).

No. 000: (cross-reference number to use when searching from any index.)

Specific primary scientific name

Primary Common Name
Other Common Names | *Other Scientific Names*

BIRD'S CURRENT CONSERVATION STATUS

🦟 **COLLECTIVE NAMES**
Names given for a flock

✳ **SYMBOLIC MEANINGS:** Love; Strength; Power; And so on.

🌀 **POSSIBLE POWERS:** Generosity.

☾ **FOLKLORE AND FACTS:** Tidbits of the factual, fanciful, mystical, magical, and anything else of interest or note.

🏛 **CULTURE:** The country or society in which a mythical bird is celebrated.

CONSERVATION STATUS

- DOMESTICATED
- LEAST CONCERN
- NEAR THREATENED
- VULNERABLE
- ENDANGERED
- CRITICALLY ENDANGERED
- EXTINCT

Accipiter gentilis

Eurasian Goshawk

Blue Darter | Cook's Hawk | Goose Hawk | Gos | Goshawk | Northern Goshawk

● **LEAST CONCERN**

🦅 **COLLECTIVE NAMES**

Cast of goshawks | Flight of goshawks | Kettle of goshawks

✸ **SYMBOLIC MEANINGS**

Justice; Protection; Safety; Self-defense; Strength.

🌀 **POSSIBLE POWERS**

Stealth, especially in forests.

🌙 **FOLKLORE AND FACTS**

Big enough to hunt waterfowl ("gos" is short for "goose") and pheasants, the Eurasian Goshawk has been a favorite among falconers for centuries, especially bird keepers in the genteel middle class of medieval times. This hawk makes its home in the northern and coastal regions of Europe, North Africa, and Asia, where it holds its place as the largest hawk in these regions—and on each continent, it has earned its reputation as a fierce guardian of its nest and young. It's no wonder that this has made the goshawk a global symbol of protection and self-defense since the early days of human civilization.
• Sources speculate that the hawk in a fable by Greek storyteller Aesop might be a goshawk: The goshawk caught a nightingale for its dinner, but the clever nightingale pled for its life, claiming to provide not nearly enough sustenance to satisfy such a large hawk. The ever-practical goshawk, however, noted that the nightingale would do nicely; only a fool would pass up a good meal in hopes of coming across a better one. • Eurasian Goshawks may be most famous for a remarkable honor bestowed upon them by ruler Attila the Hun, who ruled Scandinavia from 434 to 453. Legend has it that Atilla wore a painting of a goshawk on his helmet, taking the bird as his own totem of strength and dominance.

Acridotheres tristis

Common Myna

Calcutta Myna | House Myna | Indian Myna | Mynah | Talking Myna

● **LEAST CONCERN**

🦅 **COLLECTIVE NAMES**

Flock of mynas | Local of mynas | Statutory of mynas

✸ **SYMBOLIC MEANINGS**

Bad luck; Communications; Everlasting love; Intelligence; Messenger.

🌀 **POSSIBLE POWERS**

God's messenger; Harbinger of sorrow.

🌙 **FOLKLORE AND FACTS**

In India, where the gregarious Common Myna originates, spotting a pair of mynas as you go about your daily tasks brings good luck—but encountering just one without its mate can have exactly the opposite effect. This belief is so ingrained in Indian culture that a nursery rhyme lists the various ways a myna sighting can affect human lives:

> One for sorrow,
> Two for joy,
> Three for a girl,
> Four for a boy,
> Five for silver,
> Six for gold,
> Seven for a secret never to be told.

(This rhyme totals up magpies instead of mynas in other cultures, but in India, it applies to either species.)
• The myna's name comes from the Hindu word *maina*, translated by some as "messenger of God," so we can imagine how thrilling it may have been when people first heard these brilliant mimics imitating the human voice and forming actual words. This remarkable skill has undoubtedly saved the lives of many mynas in Southeast Asia, where at least one tribe's members—the Sema Nagas—refuse to eat the chatty birds because they believe they may be reincarnated humans.
• The rest of the world takes a less reverent view. The Global Invasive Species Database includes the Common Myna as one of just three birds in its list of the 100 World's Worst Invasive Alien Species. Mynas became popular as pets, but a significant number of owners, apparently bored with the noisy birds, released them into the wild in Australia, New Zealand, southern Florida, and southern Europe. In Hawai'i, misguided nineteenth-century farmers brought mynas to

O'ahu to control cutworms, and this effort worked at first—but soon the mynas spread to all of the islands, consuming far more than their share of insects and fruit and starving out the native birds. They also prey on other birds' eggs and chicks, and their aggressive egg-hunting in Australia threatens the continent's native parrots. So while two Common Mynas represent joy, large flocks of them can be harbingers of sorrow and strife.

No. 003

Aegolius acadicus

Northern Saw-Whet Owl

Acadian Owl | Pocket Owl | Saw-Whet Owl | Whet Owl

● **LEAST CONCERN**

✼ **COLLECTIVE NAMES**

Group of owls | Hoot of owls | Parliament of owls

✻ **SYMBOLIC MEANINGS**

Change; Good luck; Self-actualization; Transformation.

✺ **POSSIBLE POWERS**

Guide to the afterlife; Predictor of death.

✦ **FOLKLORE AND FACTS**

Centuries ago, when a tiny Northern Saw-Whet Owl gave its *toot-toot-toot* call, early Americans likened the sound to a saw being sharpened against a whetstone. The name stuck, and this 7-inch (18 cm)-high bird took its place as one of the smallest (and cutest) owls in North America. • Make no mistake, however: the Saw-Whet is a fierce predator, diving silently from its hidden perch near a conifer trunk to nab a mouse or shrew. This stealth made the Northern Saw-Whet Owl a contributor to the mystery and superstitions surrounding all species of nocturnal owls. • It's highly unlikely that this owl of dense northern forests will show up at your home while you or a relative lie ill, but some Indigenous Peoples believe that such a visit would signal the sick person's impending death. This is not necessarily a malicious gesture, though—the Ojibwa believe that owls arrive to help bring the dead person's spirit over the Owl Bridge to the afterlife. • The Menominee people of America's Midwest tell the creation story of Wabus the rabbit and Totoba the Saw-Whet Owl, who met at dusk and argued over the amount of light in the sky. "Why must it be so dark?" Wabus asked Totoba. "I don't like it, so I will make it light again." Totoba, doubting the rabbit's power over light and dark, said, "Let's test our powers. Whoever wins will decide whether it will be light or dark." As other animals gathered to watch, Wabus began repeating at a quick pace,

"Light! Light!" while Totoba countered with "Dark! Dark!" If one of them became tongue-tied and repeated the other's word, he would lose the battle. This went on for some time until, finally, Totoba's tongue stumbled and he said, "Light!" Wabus, a sporting fellow, decided that light would dominate, but that dark also should have its time. Thus the rabbit and the Saw-Whet created day and night.

No. 004

Aegolius funereus

Boreal Owl

Richardson's Owl | Tengmalm's Owl

● **LEAST CONCERN**

✼ **COLLECTIVE NAMES**

Group of owls | Hoot of owls | Parliament of owls

✻ **SYMBOLIC MEANINGS**

Bad luck; Death; Foreboding; Funeral.

✺ **POSSIBLE POWERS**

Bad omen; Predictor of death.

✦ **FOLKLORE AND FACTS**

The best time to look for a Boreal Owl in the forests of Alaska, Canada, and far northern Europe is also the most difficult time: February through early April, when the birds are most active in their mating season. This elusive, 10-inch (25 cm)-high bird prowls boreal (spruce and fir) forests, roosting throughout the day against the trunk of an aspen, birch, or conifer. • In folklore, Boreal Owls are bad omens that may even signal death. Even its two-part taxonomic name means "ill omen" in Greek and "boding ill" in Latin, giving this bird a double whammy of dark portent. The Cree people, for example, believed that the spirits of the dead inhabit Boreal Owls, so if the owl calls, they must answer with a whistle. If the owl does not respond to a person's whistle, it's a silent message from the spirit that the person will soon die. • The Inuit of Alaska tell this story: A Boreal Owl discovered a lemming taking a nap, giving the bird the perfect opportunity to take it unawares. He dove from a branch and tackled the lemming, pinning it to the ground with its sharp claws. The lemming, however, proved to be clever. "Look what a great hunter you are!" he said. "You should make this known to everyone. You should soar into the sky while I sing your praises." The owl let go of the lemming and flew straight upward . . . and the lemming ran off. The moral: Don't be swayed by pretty but insincere words that mask a darker motive.

No. 005
Aerodramus fuciphagus

Edible-Nest Swiftlet

Brown-Rumped Swiftlet | Sea Swallow | White-Nest Swiftlet

● **LEAST CONCERN**

✣ **COLLECTIVE NAMES**
Colony of swiftlets | Flock of swiftlets

❋ **SYMBOLIC MEANINGS**
Good health; Prosperity; Refinement.

❂ **POSSIBLE POWERS**
Kidney health; Lung health; Slowing of aging.

☾ **FOLKLORE AND FACTS**
The small, acrobatic Edible-Nest Swiftlet spends much of its life either swooping through the air to catch insects on the wing, or constructing the hard, white, half-bowl-shaped nests that several Southeast Asian cultures consider a culinary delicacy. Whether or not the nest—constructed entirely of the bird's saliva—appeals to your sensibilities, its popularity since the fifteenth century as the key ingredient in bird's-nest soup has pushed this remarkable little bird into endangered status in regions of India and Malaysia. • The origin story goes that Chinese navy captain/diplomat Zheng He (1371–1433) and his men anchored their ship off the coast of an uninhabited island in the Malay Archipelago to wait out a storm. Low on food and in danger of starvation, they came across a colony of swiftlets and their nests in a cave. How they determined that these nests might be tasty (or even edible) is anyone's guess, but they gathered the nests, boiled them, and consumed them. In a few days, all of the men appeared healthier than they had ever been—and as they'd had nothing to eat but bird nests, they attributed their health to them. Zheng He brought some of these nests to the emperor of China, launching an industry that continues to this day. • Today the soup is credited with keeping kidneys healthy, clearing congestion from the lungs, curing asthma and tuberculosis, and slowing the aging process. The startlingly high cost of a bowl of this soup, however—the equivalent of $380 USD in 2023—makes it a treat only for the wealthy. • Bird's-nest soup is so much in demand in Southeast Asia that Edible-Nest Swiftlets live in colonies in "house farms" inside buildings constructed for this purpose.

No. 006
Aethopyga siparaja

Crimson Sunbird

Goulpourah Sunbird | Scarlet-Breasted Sunbird | Scarlet-Throated Sunbird

● **LEAST CONCERN**

✣ **COLLECTIVE NAME**
Flight of sunbirds

❋ **SYMBOLIC MEANINGS**
Risk-taking; Speed.

❂ **POSSIBLE POWERS**
Perpetual motion; Spellbinding.

☾ **FOLKLORE AND FACTS**
With its flaming red throat, deeper-red head and back, curved bill, and bright blue tail, the Crimson Sunbird can stop birders in their tracks to watch in wonder as it darts from flower to flower, drinking all the nectar it can. To see this 4-inch (10 cm)-long feathered jewel, bird lovers must travel to the Asian tropics, where Nature Society Singapore has been working for nearly two decades to have the Crimson Sunbird officially named the national bird of Singapore. In a survey conducted by the society, 38 percent of respondents chose the tiny red-and-olive bird for this honor. • Why is it the frontrunner? The sunbird has come to represent the "Little Red Dot," a term first used in 1998 by Indonesian president B.J. Habibie to dismiss Singapore as nothing more than a little red dot on the world map, and not worth the region's attention. A few years later, in 2003, Singapore's then-Deputy Prime Minister Lee Hsien Loong embraced Habibie's disparaging remark, noting that "the little red dot has entered the psyche of every Singaporean, and become a permanent part of our vocabulary, for which we are grateful." Logically, the Crimson Sunbird has become a symbol of the Little Red Dot—very small, brilliantly colorful, and perpetually in motion. • Gamers, please note: The actual Crimson Sunbird bears no resemblance at all to the rooster-like creature of the same name in the *Yu-Gi-Oh!* manga series and card game.

A

Agarponis swindernianus

Black-Collared Lovebird

Cameroon Black-Collared Lovebird | Emin's Lovebird | Ituri Black-Collared Lovebird | Swindern's Lovebird

● **LEAST CONCERN**

COLLECTIVE NAMES
Cleaving of lovebirds | Orgy of lovebirds

✳ **SYMBOLIC MEANINGS**
Companionship; Everlasting love; Fidelity.

POSSIBLE POWERS
Commitment; Love; Monogamy.

FOLKLORE AND FACTS
Most small parrots in the *Agarponis* family are so attractive to exotic bird collectors that these birds struggle to maintain their wild populations, their fledglings falling prey to poachers every year. Luckily, lovebirds are so strongly monogamous and so attached to their mates that most of them do breed fairly easily in captivity, so the legal pet trade in Europe and the western hemisphere does not need to venture into the wilds of central Africa to capture birds. Even poachers, however, avoid trapping the Black-Collared Lovebird, because of a quirk in their diet that makes them nearly impossible to keep as pets. • Black-Collared Lovebirds require the seeds and flesh of a fig that is native to equatorial Africa as the center of their everyday diet. The bird has evolved a symbiotic relationship with this fig, eating the fruit and defecating the seeds in other places in the forest, where new fig trees then grow. This keeps the bird's major food item plentiful in its range. Pet owners generally do not keep groves of native African figs in their gardens, especially on other continents, so this bird perishes quickly in captivity.

Agelaius phoeniceus

Red-Winged Blackbird

Subspecies: Bicolored Blackbird

● **LEAST CONCERN**

COLLECTIVE NAMES
Grind of blackbirds | Merl of blackbirds

✳ **SYMBOLIC MEANINGS**
Change; Good fortune; Inner strength; Justice; Protection.

POSSIBLE POWERS
Inspiration; New start; Positive change; Valor.

FOLKLORE AND FACTS
Long ago, says a legend of the Chitimacha people of Louisiana, a man reached the end of his tolerance with his lot in life. He decided to lash out at the world that had done him so little good and given him so much suffering. He stepped outside his home and went to a nearby marsh, where he managed to ignite the foliage and set the whole thing to burning. A blackbird—at the time solidly black as midnight—flew up out of the marsh and into the nearest Chitimacha village. "The world is burning!" the little bird called at every door, awakening the townspeople. "The whole world will be destroyed!" • The townspeople rushed to the bird's aid and began to squelch the fire, but this only further angered the man, who set the world ablaze. In his rage, he picked up a shell and threw it at the blackbird, hitting its wing and cutting it at the shoulder. Once the fire was out, the people went back to their usual lives, but the bird continued to wear his bright red badge of honor on both shoulders, a fitting reminder of his heroic call to action. • Today the Red-Winged Blackbird is one of the most common birds in North and Central America, filling wetlands with their song and coming readily to backyard feeders. The appearance of this striking bird (or the more muted female, which looks like a large sparrow) is considered a sign of positive change on the horizon, or the need for us to believe in our own abilities and take steps toward making change in our own lives. Several Native American tribes take this association even further, suggesting that the blackbird comes to remind people to let go of their feelings of loss, remorse, or anger, and to move past these burdens and start anew.

Aix galericulata

Mandarin Duck

Oshidori (Japanese) | Yuanyang (Chinese)

● **LEAST CONCERN**

COLLECTIVE NAMES

Badelynge of ducks | Plump of ducks | Raft of ducks (when on water)

✳ **SYMBOLIC MEANINGS**

Devotion; Enduring love; Fidelity.

✿ **POSSIBLE POWERS**

Blessing of marriages; Everlasting love; Fidelity; Partnership power.

☾ **FOLKLORE AND FACTS**

Some call the Mandarin Duck's plumage "ornate," while others might say "extravagant," but there's no denying that this little East Asian waterfowl is the top candidate for the most beautiful duck in the world. Even its own female mate does not attempt to compete, maintaining gray-brown plumage with only a hint of a white streak extending from the eye to the ear. • For centuries, East Asians believed that these birds pair-bonded for life, making it only logical that they should become the avian symbol for fidelity and eternal love. A Chinese saying calls a loving couple "two Mandarin Ducks playing in water," an expression that dates back to a seventh-century poem: Lu Zhaolin's *Changan: Poem Written in an Antiquated Form*, which includes a line about lovers who "wished to be mandarin ducks more so than immortals." The truth, ironically, is that these ducks are serially monogamous, pairing up in winter and maintaining a pair bond throughout a single breeding season; once the chicks are hatched, the male moves on and finds a new partner the following winter. • Nonetheless, many Asian homes feature artwork of pairs of these ducks, in hopes that the image will bless and encourage the marriage contained within. Even the practice of feng shui has embraced Mandarin Ducks as a tool for activating the "partnership area" of a home, the space that supports love and harmony. Feng shui practitioners direct families to the back right corner of the floor plan, and recommend placing an object with the motif of a pair of Mandarin Ducks in this area to bring positive energy into this corner. One pair of Mandarin Ducks is quite enough—more will not result in additional partnership strength.

Aix sponsa

Wood Duck

Carolina Duck | Squealer | Summer Duck | Swamp Duck | Woodie

● **LEAST CONCERN**

COLLECTIVE NAMES

Flight of ducks | Flock of ducks | Flush of ducks | Raft of ducks | Team of ducks

✳ **SYMBOLIC MEANINGS**

Courage; Duty; Loyalty; Protection.

✿ **POSSIBLE POWERS**

Bravery; Messenger of the Creator.

☾ **FOLKLORE AND FACTS**

The Mandarin Duck's only direct relative in North America, the Wood Duck sports equally flamboyant plumage with its strikingly marked green head, red eye, and colorful green, brown, and gold body plumage. Wood Ducks are plentiful throughout much of the United States and southern Canada. • Some Native American tribes saw a connection between the Wood Duck and the spirit of the Family Creator, who made this duck its messenger of choice in communicating with mortals. The Wood Duck's ability to thrive both on water and on land made it a particularly versatile message carrier, one that Indigenous Peoples revered for its flexibility and adaptability. Oddly enough, this ability to move between environments made the Wood Duck a Christian symbol as well, its crest and bright white facial markings thought to represent the halo in paintings of Jesus and the saints. • While the Book of Genesis does not specify a list of animals that Noah admitted to his ark, several interpreters of the story of the forty-day flood have suggested that the Wood Duck was the first animal to depart from the ark (after the dove that Noah released himself). Noah was so impressed with the plucky duck's courage that he decorated the duck's head with a gorgeous crown of colors, so everyone would know from that day forward of the creature's bravery and its commitment to God.

A

Alauda arvensis

Eurasian Skylark

Northern Skylark | Skylark | *Subspecies:* Japanese Skylark

● LEAST CONCERN

✿ **COLLECTIVE NAME**
Exaltation of skylarks

✴ **SYMBOLIC MEANINGS**
Freedom; Hope; Joy; Spirit of God.

🌀 **POSSIBLE POWERS**
Cure for colic; Messenger from the gods; Pleasant voice (from drinking eggs).

☾ **FOLKLORE AND FACTS**
We need only listen to the Eurasian Skylark's orgiastic song to understand why it is associated with joy, freedom, and the divine spirit. It's easy to miss this little brown bird when it scurries across the ground in a plowed field or darts around shrubs in a heath, but its continuously trilling song brings it into focus for birders from London to Kamchatka. Even bird enthusiasts in Australia, New Zealand, and Hawai'i can enjoy populations of introduced birds singing in the bush country or on plantations. • "Hail to thee, blithe spirit!" begins Percy Bysshe Shelley's 1820 poem "To a Skylark," rhapsodizing for twenty-one stanzas on the bird's good fortune in enjoying an "ignorance of pain": "With thy clear keen joyance / Languor cannot be: / Shadow of annoyance / Never came near thee." William Wordsworth, Frederick Tennyson, James Hogg, and a number of other poets attempted to capture the song's spirit as well. • Many cultures believe skylarks carry messages directly from the gods, making a skylark singing in your backyard a joyous omen indeed. Interpreting that song is quite another matter, of course, though spiritualists encourage listeners to think deeply about their own situation and the obstacles holding them back, and to consider which of these the bird—and hence, the gods or God—may be telling you to change. • If none of that works, it is said in rural England that if you drink three skylark eggs, you can improve the timbre of your voice. • In very ancient times, eating a skylark was said to cure colic.

Alcedo atthis

Common Kingfisher

Cobalt-Eared Kingfisher | Halcyon Bird

● LEAST CONCERN

✿ **COLLECTIVE NAMES**
Clique of kingfishers | Concentration of kingfishers | Crown of kingfishers

✴ **SYMBOLIC MEANINGS**
Beauty; Happiness; Virtue.

🌀 **POSSIBLE POWERS**
Calm; Happiness; True love.

☾ **FOLKLORE AND FACTS**
The gorgeous Common Kingfisher is the only small, bright blue kingfisher in its range (Europe, Southeast Asia, and parts of Asia). More than 100 species of kingfisher around the world play a role in local mythology, just about always bringing good tidings. • Greek mythology brings us the tragic tale of Ceyx and Alcyone. These two beautiful people attracted the gods' admiration, making their marriage a much-celebrated event—and so happy were they in wedlock that they began to refer to themselves in jest as Zeus and Hera, the most powerful gods in the Pantheon. Zeus was not amused. • One day, when Ceyx boarded a ship to Ionia, Zeus kicked up a storm, and his wrath created a massive wave that swallowed up the ship. Ceyx drowned, his body descending to the depths of the sea. • Hera, however, knew how devastated Alcyone would be if she never knew for certain what had happened to Ceyx, so she caused his body to wash up on the shore near where Alcyone waited for word of him. Alcyone, anguished by her loss, threw herself into the sea and drowned. • Now Zeus felt remorse for the revenge he had exacted. He turned the two lovers into "halcyon birds"— what we know today as Common Kingfishers. For two weeks out of every year, the winds grow calm, so kingfishers nest on the beach and bring a brood into the world. These are the "halcyon days," a period of calm and happiness.

No. 013

Alectoris barbara

Barbary Partridge

Perdiz Moruna

● **LEAST CONCERN**

COLLECTIVE NAMES

Bevy of partridges | Brace of partridges | Clutch of partridges | Covey of partridges | Warren of partridges

✳ **SYMBOLIC MEANINGS**

Courage; Fertility; Plenty.

✴ **POSSIBLE POWERS**

Duplicity; Fertility.

🌐 **FOLKLORE AND FACTS**

The national bird of Gibraltar is so revered in its native country that it appears on the one-pence coin there—and Gibraltar provides a safe haven for the otherwise aggressively hunted game bird. Even with this safeguard, however, just a handful of these round, chubby, gray, and rufous birds remain on the Rock of Gibraltar, the lone survivors of military exercises, stray cats, dog-walkers, and hunting (no longer allowed). Today, the Gibraltar Ornithological and Natural History Society leads a project to help the species recover, working to breed partridges in captivity, meanwhile clearing vegetation on the upper rock to create more suitable habitats for the remaining birds. • The Barbary Partridge is also native to Morocco and Tunisia, where hunting resorts breed the birds and release them as game—allowing a hunting party to take as many as 500 birds daily. This practice sustains itself, however, because the birds lay sizeable clutches of eggs—sometimes as many as 30 in a single season—making it a folkloric symbol of fertility. • Aesop tells us of a partridge ensnared by a hunter. "Please let me live, and I will bring you many partridges," says the bird. The hunter shakes his head. "Now you give me good reason to kill you, as you would readily sacrifice your friends." The moral: Plotting against your friends means putting yourself in danger.

No. 014

Alectoris chukar

Chukar

Chakora | Chukar Partridge | Chukker | Indian Chukar | Keklik

● **LEAST CONCERN**

COLLECTIVE NAME

A covey of chukars

✳ **SYMBOLIC MEANINGS**

Good luck; Unrequited love.

✴ **POSSIBLE POWERS**

Good fortune; Granting of insight.

🌐 **FOLKLORE AND FACTS**

This Asian member of the pheasant family has been imported into North America and often escapes from game farms, making them a frequent sight in the northeastern and western United States. In their native range, Chukars puzzle onlookers by standing with their heads raised, gazing upward, as if contemplating the sky. This has led philosophers to speculate that the Chukar is in love with the moon, staring up at it in unrequited love. • Hindu mythology tells tales of a bird called Chakora, a cross between a partridge and a crow. Seeing this mythological bird brought the viewer good luck, as a man named Kuchela discovered one day (at least, according to the *Mahabharata*—this story is told differently in other texts) when he began a journey to see his childhood friend, the Hindu god Krishna. Kuchela lived in abject poverty and hoped that Krishna would show him a way to change his fortune. On the way, Kuchela happened to spot a Chakora bird. When he reached Krishna's home, his old friend received him with such generosity and honor that he felt ashamed to ask for his assistance. Even without prompting, however, the omniscient Krishna quickly deduced that his friend suffered in poverty. By the time Kuchela returned home, he had become a rich man, and his crumbling hut had become an estate, complete with a palace and everything he and his family needed in abundance. The *Mahabharata* implies that Kuchela's brief encounter with the lucky Chakora made the difference for the shy pauper, perhaps opening Krishna's eyes to the truth about his old friend's life.

A

No. 015

Alectoris graeca

Rock Partridge

Common Rock Partridge

● **NEAR THREATENED**

🐾 **COLLECTIVE NAMES**

Bevy of partridges | Bew of partridges | Brace of partridges | Clutch of partridges | Covey of partridges | Warren of partridges

✸ **SYMBOLIC MEANINGS**

Circumspection, Fertility; Watchfulness.

🌀 **POSSIBLE POWERS**

Fertility; Positive energy.

🌛 **FOLKLORE AND FACTS**

Not so long ago, the Chukar and Rock Partridge were considered to be one species, but eventually they were split into two distinct species—one (Rock Partridge) with a whiter throat and grayer back, and one (Chukar) with a yellowish throat and a brown back. It's not as hard as you may think to tell these two birds apart in the wild, as you are not likely to encounter both in the same range. The Rock Partridge's native lands include Germany, France, Italy, and Greece, some distance from the Chukar's southern Asian range.

• The deities of Greek mythology had very strong opinions about various birds, but Athena, goddess of wisdom and war, considered the partridge—probably the Rock Partridge, as it is native to Greece—to be a sacred animal imbued with fertility and positive energy. She held the bird in such high esteem, in fact, that when she saw the Greek tutor Daedalus push his nephew, Peradix, off a cliff out of jealousy for the boy's superior talent in the mechanical arts, Athena swiftly turned Peradix into a partridge. The boy lived out his life as a ground bird, avoiding the heights that had nearly led to his death. Some see a moral in this story: Recognize your own limitations and work within them—in this case, if you are not a strong flyer, stay away from high places.

No. 016

Alectoris rufa

Red-Legged Partridge

Frenchman | French Partridge | French Redleg Partridge | Redleg

● **NEAR THREATENED**

🐾 **COLLECTIVE NAMES**

Bevy of partridges | Bew of partridges | Brace of partridges | Clutch of partridges | Covey of partridges | Warren of partridges

✸ **SYMBOLIC MEANINGS**

Adaptability; Cowardice; Vigilance.

🌀 **POSSIBLE POWERS**

Self-preservation; Tenacity.

🌛 **FOLKLORE AND FACTS**

The dominant partridge of western Europe, the Red-Legged Partridge may be the most striking of the four *Alectoris* partridges. Its red bill, white face, red-ringed eye, and black-and-white striped neck bands differentiate it cleanly from its three close relations, and its dominance on the Iberian peninsula makes it fairly easy to recognize as a covey of several birds runs along a roadside or field edge. • In the United Kingdom, game farms raise millions of Red-Legged Partridges annually for sport hunting, giving them the unflattering nickname of "Frenchmen"—some say because the birds originated in France, others because their red legs resemble the bright red pants of the French infantry uniforms worn before World War I. The least-charitable hunters claim that the Red-Leggeds gained the nickname because they run away from guns, unlike English Grey Partridges that stand still and face gunfire. (The discussion omits whether the English partridges do this out of bravery or a simple lack of comprehension.) • These plucky little partridges were imported into England in the 1600s by King Charles II to give his soldiers a moving target for marksmanship drills. They finally became established in England in the late 1700s, and soon they became a popular game bird. New Zealand game farms brought in these birds in the 1980s and have had good enough results to land the bird on the country's annual Fish and Game Council stamp.

No. 017

Alopochen aegyptiaca

Egyptian Goose

Great Honker | Nile Goose

● LEAST CONCERN

✤ **COLLECTIVE NAMES**

Corps of geese | Flock of geese | Gaggle of geese | Nide of geese | Plump of geese |
Trip of geese | Wedge of geese

✳ **SYMBOLIC MEANINGS**

Fertility; Linking Earth to Heaven; Rebirth.

🌀 **POSSIBLE POWERS**

Creating the world; Fertility.

🌙 **FOLKLORE AND FACTS**

One of the most sacred of all animals in Egyptian mythology,
the goose known in ancient times as the Great Honker, or
Gengen-Wer, carried and protected the egg from which
all life on Earth came into being, according to one of the
Egyptian creation myths. Another version tells us that this
divine egg came from Geb, the god of earth—also known as
the Great Cackler—who actually laid the golden egg from
which the sun itself hatched, and forever wore an Egyptian
Goose on his headpiece to remind all of this great deed.
• A third creation myth tells us of Amun, Lord of the
Thrones of the Two Lands, who could appear in a number
of different incarnations, one of which was a primeval goose
known as the Great Shrieker—so named because its honk
of victory was the very first sound heard on Earth. While
in his goose incarnation, Amun laid an egg that contained
the entire mortal world. • The presence of an Egyptian
Goose in all of these myths lets us know that this flamboyant
waterbird—actually not a goose at all, but related to the
shelduck—played a significant role in the daily lives of
ancient people of the Middle East. • Thousands of years
after the myths attempted to explain creation as a series of
goose eggs, the Egyptian Goose's distinctive plumage remains
unmistakable on waterways throughout eastern and southern
Africa. Egyptian Geese that have escaped from exotic bird
collections are also well established throughout Europe
and the southern United States—one more testament to the
fertility ancient
Egypt held in such
high regard.

No. 018

Amazona guildingii

Saint Vincent Parrot

Saint Vincent Amazon | Vincie | Vincy Parrot

● VULNERABLE

✤ **COLLECTIVE NAMES**

Company of parrots | Pandemonium of parrots | Prattle of parrots | Psittacosis of parrots

✳ **SYMBOLIC MEANINGS**

Good luck; Intelligence; Prosperity.

🌀 **POSSIBLE POWERS**

Energy; Protection from evil spirits; Vitality.

🌙 **FOLKLORE AND FACTS**

When a bird relies on a single island for its livelihood and
survival, it lives in a state of perpetual peril, with each
change in its habitat or food supply a direct threat to its very
existence. Such is the case of the Saint Vincent Parrot, the
national bird of the West Indies island of Saint Vincent, and
a bird that relies on the island's tropical fruit supply. The
pale-faced, brown-bodied bird's population has dwindled
to just about 750 birds in the wild. • Why is this parrot so
threatened? Loss of forests to large banana plantations, the
bird's popularity in the illegal exotic bird trade, hurricanes
that strip the islands of natural foliage, and the April 2021
eruption of the La Soufrière volcano all threaten the parrots'
survival as a species. • The vincie is more than a national
symbol on Saint Vincent, where all parrots are symbols of
good luck and protection. Having parrots frequent someone's
garden or neighborhood wards off evil spirits. Parrots'
bright colors represent vitality and life's energy, and the
birds' ability to mimic speech shows that they are intelligent
animals. • The Botanical Garden of Saint Vincent runs a
breeding program for Saint Vincent Parrots to protect them
from extinction, but birds living in the wild need direct
assistance. Conservation organizations work together to
provide fresh, ripe fruit on high platforms in forest areas,
find and rescue weak or injured birds, and assess damage
to habitats. Survival of the national bird of Saint Vincent
represents a high priority for the island's people.

No. 019

Amazona imperialis

Imperial Amazon

Dominican Amazon | Sisserou | Sisserou Parrot

● **CRITICALLY ENDANGERED**

COLLECTIVE NAMES

Company of parrots | Pandemonium of parrots | Prattle of parrots | Psittacosis of parrots

SYMBOLIC MEANINGS

Communication with the spirit world; Good luck; Wisdom.

POSSIBLE POWERS

Intelligence; Messenger to and from the gods.

FOLKLORE AND FACTS

The bright, colorful Imperial Amazon, also known as the Sisserou Parrot, graces the national flag and the coat of arms of the Commonwealth of Dominica, the tiny country that has made this charismatic bird its national symbol. • In reality, however, the sisserou is one of the most endangered bird species in the world, with just about fifty adults remaining in the wild in 2019. Monogamous and loyal to their mates even after death—often grieving themselves to death when their mate is lost—these parrots further complicate their breeding cycle by choosing a cavity in a rainforest tree to make their permanent nest, returning to the same tree year after year. When stormy weather topples their chosen tree, it may be some time before they choose another. These factors make the Imperial Amazon the parrot with the lowest rate of reproduction of any *Amazona* bird. • Caribbean cultures hold parrots in high esteem, considering them to be highly intelligent and symbols of wisdom. Some believe that parrots can connect with the spiritual realm, carrying messages to those in the afterlife or bringing messages back from them. Some people even believe that parrots speak to the gods, making them critically important in making that connection to the divine.

No. 020

Amazona leucocephala caymanensis

Grand Cayman Parrot

Cayman Brac Parrot (another species, but often confused) | Cayman Parrot

● **NEAR THREATENED**

COLLECTIVE NAMES

Company of parrots | Pandemonium of parrots | Prattle of parrots | Psittacosis of parrots

SYMBOLIC MEANING

National symbol of the Cayman Islands.

POSSIBLE POWERS

Ability to hear the voices of ancestors; Mimicry.

FOLKLORE AND FACTS

A wash of pink on this green parrot's white forehead differentiates it from its close relative, the Cayman Brac Parrot (*Amazona leucocephala hersterna*), which lacks the pink hue but retains the black ear patch, orangey face, and bright blue wings that both parrots share. These two descendants of the Cuban Parrot are found only in the Cayman Islands, making them prime candidates for preservation efforts by the island's government. • For centuries, Cayman Islanders kept these plentiful parrots as house pets, training them to repeat English phrases and giving the birds the attention and affection that they demanded in captivity. When hunters from other places began capturing the birds for the black market trade in exotic pets, selling them for thousands of dollars each, Grand Cayman Parrots dwindled on the island . . . and a series of hurricanes that destroyed the trees they used for nesting hastened their decline. Road construction and residential development plowed over thousands more acres of parrot habitat, leaving little for these brilliantly colored birds. Some experts predict that the birds could reach extinction by 2040. • Parrots are brilliant mimics, and this talent comes from an extraordinary ability to listen to sounds and pay attention to what they hear. Islanders believe that this teaches us a lesson about listening ourselves, taking in what we can from our surroundings, and hearing the voices of ancestors—as well as our inner voice, our own consciousness. This, they believe, helps us move closer to achieving true spirituality.

No. 021

Amazona versicolor

Saint Lucia Amazon

Jacquot | St. Lucia Parrot

● **VULNERABLE**

🐾 **COLLECTIVE NAMES**

Company of parrots | Pandemonium of parrots | Prattle of parrots | Psittacosis of parrots

✸ **SYMBOLIC MEANINGS**

Communication; Cultural diversity; Spiritual guidance.

🌀 **POSSIBLE POWERS**

Messenger to and from the gods; Mimicry.

🌙 **FOLKLORE AND FACTS**

West Indies island nations are especially fond of their parrots, elevating them to honored status as their national birds and placing their images on flags and in coats of arms. Saint Lucia's population of Saint Lucia Amazons have become a symbol of diversity for this tiny island, the birds' blue head, red bill, green body and wings, and brilliant patches of yellow and orange plumage working together to represent the many human cultures that dwell here. • The Saint Lucia Amazon was declared the national bird in 1979, and not a moment too soon—at that point, just 100 Saint Lucia Amazons remained on the island, a small population holding its own deep in the rainforest. Proclaiming the parrot the national bird bestowed upon it a system of protections that made trapping and exporting the birds illegal, eliminating one of the most destructive forces to threaten the endangered parrot. Today an estimated 2,000 birds populate the island, an impressive comeback from the brink of disaster. • At least some credit for this remarkable recovery must go to Paul Butler of Rare Conservation, who has made it his life's work to educate children about the Saint Lucia Parrot and its importance to their home island. Butler asked the World Parrot Trust for a bus outfitted with toys, displays, and videos about the azure-faced national symbol, to take to schools, parks, and other venues to teach children about the parrot and its plight. Today it's safe to say that no child on the island would dream of harming the bird, and many are engaged in the cause of protecting it.

No. 022

Anas acuta

Northern Pintail

Koloa māpu (Hawaiian) | Pintail | Sprig

● **LEAST CONCERN**

🐾 **COLLECTIVE NAMES**

Flock of pintails | Knob of pintails | Parliament of pintails | Plump of pintails

✸ **SYMBOLIC MEANINGS**

Adaptability; Speed.

🌀 **POSSIBLE POWERS**

Endurance; Speed in flight.

🌙 **FOLKLORE AND FACTS**

Some call it the "greyhound of the air," this slim duck with its long profile in flight and its elegant plumage, including its tapered tail held at a roughly 45-degree angle from the water. The Northern Pintail's dark head, slender bill, white neck, and wisp of a white stripe extending from chest to head make it an especially striking bird, even at rest on a pond or lake. • Perhaps because of their widespread range—including North America, all of Europe, northern and eastern Africa, southern Asia, and northernmost Russia—Northern Pintails have more than their share of interesting nicknames. In addition to "greyhound," "nomad of the skies," for example, refers to its long migration flight of up to 1,800 miles (2,897 km) from its far northern breeding grounds to the tropics. "Sprig" refers to the male duck's long, upward-pointing tail. • Awareness of the Northern Pintail as a species dates back thousands of years. Archaeologists in Egypt have found 5,000-year-old drawings of pintails inside tombs—specifically, depicting these slender ducks caught in nets. Indeed, hunters today claim that pintails are particularly tasty birds, making reference to their "unusually mild flavor" and their excellence in gumbos and stews, so they may have been one of the poultries of choice for pharaohs in ancient times.

No. 023

Anas platyrhynchos

Mallard

Greenhead | Puddle Duck | Red
Legs | River Duck | Wild Duck

● LEAST CONCERN

🐾 COLLECTIVE NAMES

Flock of mallards | Flush of mallards | Paddling
of mallards | Plump of mallards

✴ SYMBOLIC MEANINGS

Abundance; Change; Hope; Starting over.

🌀 POSSIBLE POWERS

Adaptability; Prosperity; Tolerance.

☾ FOLKLORE AND FACTS

When we say that someone takes to a new activity "like a duck to water," we celebrate the easy-looking life of the Mallard, the world's most widespread duck. Mallards contribute a great deal of simile and metaphor to our vernacular: a person trapped in an untenable situation is a "dead duck;" an obvious target is a "sitting duck;" and when we shrug off a slight or an insult, we treat it "like water off a duck's back." • Mallards' plentiful population has given them a role in many folk tales, from Aesop's fables to the *Jataka*, stories from the past lives of the Buddha. In Aesop's story, a Mallard and a Woodcock fed together one day in a marshy area. "What a beastly way you have of eating!" the Woodcock said. "You will eat anything: Snails, toads, any kind of filth you come across!" The Mallard, in turn, scoffed at the Woodcock's criticism. "Who are you to tell me what to eat, with your delicate sensibilities?" he said. "Isn't it proper that I be pleased with whatever food nature offers me?" The two birds parted, but a moment later, Mallard ate something that turned out to be bait, and found himself impaled on a fisherman's hook. Woodcock, in turn, flew off into a glade and sailed right into a net. The moral: Criticize others' life choices at your own risk; your fortunes can turn at any time. • The *Jataka* tells us of one of Buddha's incarnations as a Brahmin, whose wife bore him three daughters. When the Brahmin died, he was reincarnated as a Golden Mallard with a special power: When he freely gave his feathers to humans, the feathers turned to actual gold. The Mallard chose to give one feather to his wife for her to sell for enough money to pay the family's expenses. He did this several times over the course of months. Over time, however, the Brahmin's wife grew more and more distrustful that he would continue to come and bring them a feather. "The next time he comes, let's capture him and pluck all

of his feathers," she said. • Sure enough, the next time the Mallard arrived with a feather to give them, the wife and daughters grabbed him and plucked out all of his feathers. As soon as they did so, the feathers ceased to be gold and turned into ordinary duck feathers. The wife tossed the denuded bird into a barrel and kept him fed until his feathers grew back, but they were no longer golden—now he was just a Mallard like any other.

No. 024

Anas platyrhynchos domesticus

Domestic Duck

Buff Duck | Pekin Duck

● DOMESTICATED

🐾 COLLECTIVE NAMES

Badelynge of ducks | Dropping of ducks | Plump of ducks | Waddling of ducks

✴ SYMBOLIC MEANINGS

Balance; Family; Forgiveness; Loyalty; Parenthood; Trust.

🌀 POSSIBLE POWERS

Bringer of riches; Protector; Sacrifice.

☾ FOLKLORE AND FACTS

Ducks have a place in just about every culture's mythology, from the Mandarin Ducks that represent true love in Chinese folklore to the flock of ducks that rescued Penelope, the wife of Odysseus, from almost certainly drowning at sea after her own father cast her into the waves. Perhaps ducks' ubiquitous presence makes it easy to attach meaning to them, or maybe, as scientists at the University of Hertfordshire in England determined, ducks are simply amusing—their careful research found ducks to be the funniest animal on the planet (just ask Daffy, Donald, or Scrooge McDuck), making every story about them just a bit more delightful. • Christians tell the story of a little boy playing in his grandmother's front yard, testing his own ability to hit objects with his slingshot. He pulls back the sling and lets a rock fly . . . and the rock hits his grandmother's favorite duck, killing it instantly. The little boy panics, knowing that his grandmother will be sad to lose the duck and angry with him, so instead of owning up to the mistake immediately, he hides the duck's body. He's not stealthy enough, though, and his spiteful sister sees him. Now she grabs an opportunity for her own mischief. She threatens to tell their grandmother about the duck, whipping her brother into a frenzy, and then says she'll keep his secret if he pays a price: He has to do all of her chores.

He agrees, but as his sister heaps more and more work on him, he finally decides that telling his grandmother what he has done will be less painful. When he owns up and apologizes, his grandmother hugs him and says she knew all along! Grandma had simply waited to see how long it would take him to rustle up enough courage to tell her. Christians say that the duck in this story represents all the sins that God will forgive, and the boy's hesitancy demonstrates the work of the devil in stoking the boy's fears, keeping him from doing the right thing. • A Russian fairy tale combines a variety of folk themes. In "The White Duck," a king has married a fair maiden whom he loves very much, but he must leave her for a time to journey through his kingdom. He instructs her to stay in the women's quarters of his estate, and to avoid those who may give her bad advice. Once he has taken his leave, however, the new wife becomes curious about all that the estate has to offer. She ventures outside, where she encounters a wicked witch. The witch brings her close to a pond, where she transforms the young maiden into a white duck. She then shifts into the maiden's own shape, taking her place and awaiting the king's return, so that all of his riches will be hers. • The white duck builds a nest and lays three eggs, and soon they hatch into three ducklings. The white duck warns them to stay away from the wicked witch, but the ducklings wander, and when the witch realizes what they are and to whom they belong, she kills them instantly. When the white duck finds the bodies of her children, she breaks down and weeps—and this sound attracts the attention of the king, who has returned to the estate. Marveling at a weeping duck, he orders his servants to capture the duck and bring it to him. The duck eludes the servants handily. This brings the king out to the pond to see the strange duck for himself, and as soon as she sees him, she flies into his arms and becomes his young maiden once again. Now she can tell him everything, most importantly that the three dead ducklings are his children. He summons a magpie to bring him magic water that he sprinkles over the ducklings, and they spring to life as the human children she promised. Overjoyed at this turn of events, the king summons his guards to capture the wicked witch and put her to death … and he, his bride, and their three children live happily ever after. • Russians also tell the tale of Abrosim and Fetinia, an impoverished couple, and their fifteen-year-old son Ivan, who found themselves in a tussle with a trickster over a crust of bread. Abrosim begs the trickster to give him the bread, for he and his family have nothing to eat, but the trickster says that if he lets her keep the bread, she will tell him where to find a duck that lays a golden egg every day. He agrees, and she gives him directions to the promised duck in a nearby pond. Abrosim goes to the pond and, sure enough, a duck waits there for

him. He brings it home and he and Fetinia wait … and the duck lays a golden egg. • Abrosim takes the egg to market and sells it for 100 rubles, with which he buys plenty of food to last the family for weeks. The next morning, the duck lays another golden egg, and each day it lays another. Soon the family is quite well off, building a big house and opening a shop in town to continue to sustain them. While tending to the shop, Fetinia befriends another young shop owner. She does not tell him about the duck's special power, but one day he picks up the duck and looks it over, and discovers written in gold under one wing, "Whoever eats this duck will become a Tsar." The shop owner does not tell Fetinia what he has seen, but he begs her to roast the duck, with the intention that he will eat it. Fetinia refuses, but he persists—and eventually, she relents. She wrings the duck's neck, plucks its feathers, and pops it into the oven to roast. • While she is out of the kitchen, Ivan comes home from his own activities and, being very hungry, he eats the duck. Abrosim comes home soon after, discovers what his wife and son have done, and flies into a rage. He throws Ivan out of the house. • Ivan begins walking, and soon finds himself out of town and on a long road. He keeps walking until he comes to a big, beautiful city, where a crowd of people have gathered in the square. As he passes through the gate, they throw up a great cheer of joy. The people tell him that their Tsar has died and they did not know how to choose a successor, so they decided that whoever walked through the gate next would become the new Tsar. The duck's prophecy has come true! Ivan becomes the Tsar and rules for thirty years, and even brings his parents to live with him and share his riches … so they, too, live happily ever after.

Anhinga anhinga

Anhinga

Darter | Devil Bird | Snakebird | Water Turkey

● **LEAST CONCERN**

✢ **COLLECTIVE NAME**

Flock of anhingas

✳ **SYMBOLIC MEANINGS**

Mystery; Patience; Secrets.

✺ **POSSIBLE POWERS**

Dark magic; Faith; Forgiveness; Self-sacrifice; Trickster.

☾ **FOLKLORE AND FACTS**

Bird lovers recognize the Anhinga easily in their subtropical habitats, both for their long necks and for their unique stance, spreading their wings while standing to dry their feathers. While other water birds produce an oil in a special gland and use it to waterproof their wing feathers, Anhingas do not have such a gland. This is both a boon and a problem for this bird, as the Anhingas totally submerge themselves to fish, so their wing feathers become soaked through. This allows them to sink down into the water completely, but the birds must take time after fishing to dry their wings thoroughly if they want to move about on land comfortably or take flight. • Perhaps it's no surprise that the classic Anhinga stance has been interpreted by Christians as an imitation of the crucifix. Christians attribute the qualities of self-sacrifice, faith, and forgiveness to this bird—in direct contrast to the Indigenous Tupi people of Brazil, who named the bird "anyinga," or "devil bird," after an evil forest spirit who terrorizes villages with dark magic and mean tricks. The Tupi gave the bird this name after seeing it swim, its neck jutting out ahead of the mostly submerged body like a water snake. While Anhingas are no more dangerous than ducks or pigeons, we can see how the Tupi people could mistake the birds for something sinister.

Anser anser

Graylag Goose

Greylag Goose | Wild Goose

● **LEAST CONCERN**

✢ **COLLECTIVE NAMES**

Flock of geese | Gaggle of geese | Nide of geese | Trip of geese

✳ **SYMBOLIC MEANINGS**

Holy Spirit; Patience; Telling the future.

✺ **POSSIBLE POWERS**

Association with the gods; Fertility; Foretelling of the future.

☾ **FOLKLORE AND FACTS**

While many variations on the Graylag Goose exist throughout its range in Europe and southern Asia, certain standard features tell us that a goose is a graylag: an overall tawny brown body, pure white rump, and bright pink legs and bill with a white ring around the bill's base. This is the goose in the timeless nursery rhyme "Goosey Goosey Gander": "Goosey goosey gander / Whither shall I wander? / Upstairs and downstairs / And in my lady's chamber. / There I met an old man / Who wouldn't say his prayers, / So I took him by the left leg / And threw him down the stairs!" The goose in this rhyme represents "my lady's" fertility, which the bird will do its best to make more potent by actually entering her chamber. ("Goose," it turns out, once served as British slang for prostitute, adding even more sexual undertone to this innocent-seeming rhyme.) • Long before the graylag descended into bawdy poetry, however, it associated with gods and goddesses in several mythologies. Aphrodite, Greek goddess of love, is depicted in ancient art riding sidesaddle on what appears to be a Graylag Goose. Eating a goose was *de rigeur* for the Christian festival of Michaelmas, for the express purpose of getting the wishbone—a tool used to access the foretelling power of the Oracle. This tradition played a key role in turning the graylag from a free bird to a domesticated one, as it required untold thousands of geese to be harvested every September to allow citizens to try to get a glimpse of their own future.

No. 027
Anser caerulescens

Snow Goose

Blue Goose (morph) | Greater Snow Goose |
Subspecies: Lesser Snow Goose

● **LEAST CONCERN**

🦢 **COLLECTIVE NAMES**

Flock of geese | Gaggle of geese |
Nide of geese | Trip of geese

✳ **SYMBOLIC MEANINGS**

Endurance; Hope;
Perseverance; Renewal.

🌀 **POSSIBLE POWERS**

Authority; Energy; Fresh starts;
Practicality.

🐦 **FOLKLORE AND FACTS**

The pure white Snow Goose, with its black wingtips and bright pink bill, plays an important role as one of the twelve totems in Native American astrology, placing it in the Medicine Wheel where the Greek zodiac places Capricorn (December 22 through January 19). This time slot represents renewal and rebirth, so these traits have become part of the Snow Goose's power as a birth totem animal. If the Snow Goose is your totem, it imbues you with practicality, the skills needed for positions of authority, and the energy to make fresh starts. • While white geese appear in a great deal of folklore around the world, most of these are about domestic geese rather than the wild and free Snow Goose. Novelist Paul Gallico may have best established the Snow Goose as a creature of extraordinary resilience in his short story, "The Snow Goose," published in 1940 in *The Saturday Evening Post*. In his simple tale of an artist living on his own in a dilapidated lighthouse in England's marshlands and his friendship with a young local girl, Gallico inserts a wounded Snow Goose that the friends nurture back to health together. Gallico turned this award-winning parable into a novella, and a long list of recorded readings, musical interpretations, and films followed, including the 1975 instrumental album by the rock group Camel, which led to a classic recording with the London Symphony Orchestra.

No. 028
Anthropoides paradisea

Blue Crane

Paradise Crane | Stanley Crane

● **VULNERABLE**

🦢 **COLLECTIVE NAMES**

Herd of cranes | Sedge of cranes | Siege of cranes

✳ **SYMBOLIC MEANING**

Bravery.

🌀 **POSSIBLE POWERS**

Bestower of authority; Strength in struggle.

🐦 **FOLKLORE AND FACTS**

South Africans love their Blue Cranes, the balletic birds that execute fascinating acrobatic dances to attract a mate, but their bravery attracts the most admiration from all quarters. The Ndebele people, for example, know the bird as Mxololo and tell stories of the crane catching a venomous snake by grabbing it with its bill, flying high into the sky with it, and then dropping it from a dizzying height so it would die on impact. • Becoming the national bird of South Africa gave the Blue Crane special protections, but many cultures throughout the country already forbade the hunting or eating of this tall, elegant bird. The Xhosa culture knows the crane as Indwe, and their chiefs present warriors with the feathers during the ceremony of *ukundzabela* after a battle. Zulus call the bird Udoyi, and royalty wear Blue Crane feathers in their headdresses; a well-known drawing of King Shaka portrays him with a single curved crane feather rising from his headband. Those who achieve the status of *isitwalandwe*, or "the one who wears the plumes of the rare bird," are recognized by Zulus as the bravest of warriors—and in 1955, this custom led to the creation of the Isitwalandwe/Seaparankoe, a highly esteemed award given by the African National Congress to "those who have made an outstanding contribution and sacrifice to the liberation struggle."

No. 029

Anthropoides virgo

Demoiselle Crane

Koonj | Kurjan | Zaanray

● **LEAST CONCERN**

✦ **COLLECTIVE NAMES**

Flock of cranes | Herd of cranes | Sedge of cranes | Siege of cranes

✺ **SYMBOLIC MEANINGS**

Beauty; Long journeys.

✹ **POSSIBLE POWERS**

Stamina; Strength in deprivation.

☾ **FOLKLORE AND FACTS**

Marie Antoinette, wife of King Louis XVI of France, took it upon herself to give Demoiselle Crane its refined moniker. Seeing these statuesque, gray-mantled creatures, she called them *demoiselle*, or "young lady" in French. • India's native crane may look small and delicate, but this mighty bird proves its outstanding stamina twice annually when it crosses a continent to complete its migration. Cranes move from their breeding grounds in western Eurasia to winter in northern Africa, and from their spring and summer home in Mongolia and Kyrgystan to spend the darker months in India, crossing the Himalayan mountains at altitudes above 16,000 feet (4,877 m). • Many cranes might not survive this perilous journey without assistance from a town called Khichan in northwest India, where residents provide the cranes with a large area to stop, rest, and eat plenty of grain for their continued journey south. Once townspeople have filled the town square with grain, some 25,000 cranes make this town their stopover site—and their visit has become so much a part of the town's culture that they have even removed utility lines to make certain that the birds can land safely.

No. 030

Antigone antigone

Sarus Crane

Greater Indian Crane | Serious Crane

● **VULNERABLE**

✦ **COLLECTIVE NAMES**

Flock of cranes | Herd of cranes | Sedge of cranes | Siege of cranes

✺ **SYMBOLIC MEANINGS**

Devotion; Marital fidelity; Unconditional love.

✹ **POSSIBLE POWERS**

Fidelity; Good luck.

☾ **FOLKLORE AND FACTS**

Nicknamed "the bird that dips its head in blood" in some areas of Australia because of its bright crimson face and neck, the Sarus Crane has another notable distinction: it is the tallest flying bird in the world. It also has a special friend in the founder of Buddhism, Prince Siddhartha.
• While Siddhartha sat in the garden of his father's palace one morning, a Sarus Crane fell out of the sky and landed, clearly wounded, at his feet. Siddhartha examined the bird and found it had been shot by an arrow, so he took it inside the palace, removed the arrow, and gently cared for the bird until it was healthy again. As the bird began to heal, Siddhartha's cousin Devadatta arrived at the palace. Siddhartha showed him the crane and the arrow, and Devadatta immediately recognized the arrow as one of his own. He demanded that Siddhartha hand the bird over to him, because he was the one who shot it. Siddhartha refused, and in minutes they began to fight, but they could not resolve which of them should have the bird. They took the case to the king, Siddhartha's father, who instructed his court to hear it right away. The court determined that the boy who had saved the bird's life, not the one who had tried to kill it, should have the bird. • The Hindu *Ramayana* tells the story of Valmiki, a sage, who witnesses the death of a Sarus Crane along the Ganges River when a hunter shoots the bird before his eyes. As these cranes mate for life, Valmiki's grief for the bird and its mate becomes overwhelming, and he writes poetry in which he curses this hunter for destroying the bird. This tale has come to represent the worst possible sorrow to Hindu people, the soul-rending loss that a loved one's death means for the living. • Today Sarus Cranes are protected throughout their range in northern India and southwestern Nepal, as well as in Myanmar, where a healthy population recently came to light and appears to be growing.
• Even beyond their association with Prince Siddhartha,

Sarus Cranes have become legendary for their lifelong pair bond with a single mate—so much so that in the Indian state of Gujarat, families often take newly married couples to see a pair of Sarus Cranes, a tradition that brings good fortune and fidelity to the marriage.

help. The girl was never seen again, but the cranes continue to circle and call before they migrate to this day. • The crane also represents one of the seven original tribal clans of the Chippewa tribe; they call the Sandhill Crane the "echo-maker," reminding them to communicate with honesty.

No. 031

Antigone canadensis

Sandhill Crane

Subspecies: Canadian Sandhill Crane | Cuban Sandhill Crane | Florida Sandhill Crane | Greater Sandhill Crane | Lesser Sandhill Crane | Mississippi Sandhill Crane

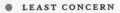

● **LEAST CONCERN**

❊ **COLLECTIVE NAMES**
Herd of cranes | Sedge of cranes | Siege of cranes

✴ **SYMBOLIC MEANINGS**
Balance; Discretion; Fairness; Family; Purity; Wisdom.

🌀 **POSSIBLE POWERS**
Calling out lies and duplicity; Warning of evil deeds.

☾ **FOLKLORE AND FACTS**
Few sights are more spectacular in North America than the migration of Sandhill Cranes through the Midwest, with tens of thousands of birds landing on the banks of the Platte River in Nebraska or in Bosque del Apache National Wildlife Refuge in New Mexico. These statuesque, neutrally colored birds with their bright red and white caps migrate from their wintering grounds in New Mexico, Texas, Florida, and northern Mexico all the way to islands above the Arctic Circle—and 80 percent of these birds stop along the Platte River on their way north. • Myths abound about the cranes' migration journey. One comes from nineteenth-century correspondents who believed that the cranes carried smaller birds on their backs for the long trip. "Apart from their squawking, I could distinctly hear the twittering of small birds, sparrows of some kind," a man in Alberta wrote to American naturalist Ernest Ingersoll. "The chirping grew louder as the cranes drew towards me, and grew fainter as they drew away." This theory has long since been dismissed. • An Inuit story attempts to explain why the cranes fly in circles and cry out before they head south. One clear autumn day, migrating cranes spotted a beautiful young girl standing alone outside her village. They found her beauty irresistible, so they surrounded her, lifted her up and flew off to bring her with them. Other cranes joined the kidnappers and called loudly to cover the girl's entirely understandable screams for

No. 032

Antrostomus vociferus

Eastern Whip-Poor-Will

Whip-o-Will | Whip o' Will | Whippoorwill

● **NEAR THREATENED**

❊ **COLLECTIVE NAME**
Dirge of Whip-Poor-Wills

✴ **SYMBOLIC MEANING**
Impending death.

🌀 **POSSIBLE POWERS**
Bad luck; Bringer of death; Knowledge of soul leaving the body.

☾ **FOLKLORE AND FACTS**
Few birds are as dreaded a sight as the Eastern Whip-Poor-Will, named for the high-pitched lament that splits the night. This secretive bird has been linked to centuries of beliefs that seeing or even hearing a whip-poor-will can bring bad luck. Lucky for humans, whip-poor-wills are among the most expertly camouflaged of all North American birds, so only a handful of even the most ardent birders can claim to have actually laid eyes on one. The bird's plumage blends so seamlessly with a forest floor's leaves, twigs, needles, old logs, and other detritus that a whip-poor-will could be sitting at a hiker's feet and still be invisible. • While whip-poor-wills sing at night throughout their mating season, Indigenous Peoples were the first to decide that those who hear the bird's call should prepare for the imminent death of a loved one. This superstition has enflamed the imaginations of a wide range of writers, from H.P. Lovecraft in his book *The Dunwich Horror*—in which the whip-poor-will knows when a soul leaves a human body after death, and captures this disembodied spirit—to humorist James Thurber, whose story "Whip-Poor-Will" tells of a man so tortured by the nightly call of the bird that he murders everyone in his home. The bird clearly sparks creativity in all kinds of writers: it plays a minor role in stories, poems, and songs by Elizabeth Barrett Browning, Washington Irving, William Faulkner, Stephen Vincent Benét, Robert Frost, Emily Dickinson, Hank Williams, Bernie Taupin, George A. Whiting and Walter Donaldson, Oscar Hammerstein, Kurt Vonnegut, and many others. • As far back as ancient Greece, Aristotle penned a

A

patently absurd observation about the bird: "Flying to the udders of she-goats, it sucks them and so it gets its name." All Whip-Poor-Will species, once known collectively as goatsuckers because of this concept (reinforced in writings by ancient Roman author Pliny 400 years later), eat nothing but insects and never approach goats.

No. 033

Apteryx

Kiwi

Great Spotted Kiwi | Little Spotted Kiwi | North Island Brown Kiwi | Okarito Brown Kiwi | Southern Brown Kiwi

● **ENDANGERED**

✿ COLLECTIVE NAME
A raft of kiwis

✹ SYMBOLIC MEANINGS
Collaboration; Community; Sacrifice.

✪ POSSIBLE POWERS
Selflessness; Service to others.

☾ FOLKLORE AND FACTS
When the Māori people first landed on New Zealand in the thirteenth and fourteenth centuries, they found a land uninhabited by humans—but also entirely without mammals. The only animals on the islands were insects, bats, and birds, especially a round, wingless and tailless creature they called "kiwi." So peculiar was this little critter as it dug with its lengthy bill into the ground for insects and grubs that it soon became part of Māori mythology. • Tane-mahuta, the Māori god of the forest, became worried about the trees on the island, because insects and birds had stripped them of their leaves and fruit. He asked his brother Tane-hokahoka, god of the birds, to help him solve the problem, so Tane-hokahoka bade his children to come down from the forest canopy and live on the floor. Every bird objected to this: Tui feared the dark, others didn't care for the wet ground or didn't want to dirty their feathers. But Kiwi, which had beautiful, colorful plumage at the time, considered the request and agreed to give up his wings, his gorgeous feathers, and his ability to fly, and live on the forest floor. Tane-hokahoka demonstrated his gratitude by making Kiwi the most beloved bird on the island—a status the bird maintains to this day as the national animal of New Zealand. Later, Tane-mahuta asked all of the birds if they would help him clean up the fallen leaves from the giant kauri tree, and once again all the birds refused except Kiwi, who said he would be delighted to help. In return, Tane-mahuta gave Kiwi his long bill, to help him reach into the ground more easily for food.

Apus apus

Common Swift

Subspecies: Devil's Bird | Martlet

● **LEAST CONCERN**

✿ COLLECTIVE NAME
Scream of swifts

✹ SYMBOLIC MEANINGS
Arrival of summer; Fair weather; Work of Satan.

✪ POSSIBLE POWERS
Yet to be discovered.

☾ FOLKLORE AND FACTS
As one of the last birds to arrive in Europe and Asia with the onset of spring, Common Swifts are a welcome sight to many, especially those who may not be aware of their darker mysteries. These birds have been shrouded in a lack of understanding for hundreds of years, with farmers and townspeople of the seventeenth and eighteenth centuries convinced that the birds did not migrate at all, but simply disappeared into the mud below ground until spring—because they were in cahoots with the lord of the underworld. One farmer in Hampshire, England, the story goes, claimed that he shot seventeen swifts for the fun of it one day, and the next day seventeen of his most prized cows died. Surely these birds brought bad luck with them, further evidenced by their high-pitched, screeching calls, which people in medieval times decided were the anguished cries of a soul condemned to hell. • The greatest mystery concerned whether Common Swifts have feet, as they seemed to have no need for them. Often in flight for months at a time, the birds rarely revealed their roosting places, so people who would never see the bird up close assumed that it did not have the ability to land. Swifts do indeed have feet, of course, which becomes evident at many landmarks made of stone throughout Europe, Africa, and Asia, as swifts nest in cracks in these edifices (in particular, the Wailing Wall in Jerusalem is a well-known Common Swift nesting site).

No. 035

Aquila chrysaetos

Golden Eagle

Subspecies: Asian Golden Eagle | Berkut | European Golden Eagle | Himalayan Golden Eagle | Iberian Golden Eagle | Japanese Golden Eagle | Kamchatkan Golden Eagle | North American Golden Eagle | Siberian Golden Eagle

● **LEAST CONCERN**

✥ **COLLECTIVE NAMES**

Aerie of eagles | Brood of eagles | Congregation of eagles | Exaltation of eagles

✺ **SYMBOLIC MEANINGS**

Endurance; Power.

✺ **POSSIBLE POWERS**

Dominance; Messenger to the gods; Power.

☾ **FOLKLORE AND FACTS**

Golden Eagles have been prominent figures since mythology began, appearing in the Greek canon as Aetos Dios, Zeus's personal messenger, and even earning a place in the heavens as the constellation Aquila. Jupiter, the Roman god of the sky, also revered the eagle and made it his sacred animal, and the Roman army used the bird as a symbol of its own power. The Golden Eagle appeared on both Greek and Roman coins, usually holding a thunderbolt in its claws.
• The Old Testament of the Bible makes frequent mentions of eagles, though largely as a metaphor for power—except in Deuteronomy, which lays down the kashrut dietary laws followed in Judaism, and specifically lists the eagle as an unclean animal that should not be eaten. • Four countries celebrate the Golden Eagle by making it their national animal: Albania, Germany, Austria, and Mexico. Many others use a symbol of an eagle within their coats of arms or other symbols, passed down to their governments from an era when they were part of the Roman Empire. • Not all of these uses are benevolent, however: The Nazi Party under Adolf Hitler's command used the Golden Eagle as a more tangible symbol than a swastika, with statues and monuments of the bird all over Germany to encourage solidarity with the Nazi cause.

No. 036

Aquila nipalensis

Steppe Eagle

Egyptian Eagle of Saladin | Saladin Eagle

● **ENDANGERED**

✥ **COLLECTIVE NAMES**

Aerie of eagles | Brood of eagles | Congregation of eagles | Exaltation of eagles

✺ **SYMBOLIC MEANINGS**

Power; Strength.

✺ **POSSIBLE POWERS**

Authority; Bestowing of rank.

☾ **FOLKLORE AND FACTS**

Large, brown, and soaring over grasslands, deserts, and other open areas, the Steppe Eagle has seven distinct "fingers" on the ends of its wings, making it easier than you might expect to tell it apart from Golden Eagles and other large birds of eastern Africa and southern Asia. Unlike most eagles, it preys almost exclusively on ground squirrels and a few other small mammals, and it nests close to or right on the ground, making its nest vulnerable to predation. If this were the only threat to its survival, Steppe Eagle might not be on the endangered species list, but fires that scorch its flat, open habitats have forced a decline in its numbers as well, and electrocution from collisions with electrical wires also takes its toll. Becoming the national bird of Egypt does not appear to have led to greater protection for this bird. • Arab governments have employed images of the Steppe Eagle since the twelfth-century reign of Saladin, the first sultan of Egypt and Syria, who chose the emblem of the eagle as a symbol of his power. Legend has it that Saladin carried a yellow flag with a stylized, double-headed eagle painted on it in red as his personal standard. The Eagle of Saladin continues today to be an icon of Middle Eastern countries, with illustrations of the eagle on Egypt's coat of arms since that country's 1952 revolution. The same eagle later became part of the current coats of arms of Iraq, United Arab Emirates, Yemen, and Palestine.

No. 037

Ara macao

Scarlet Macaw

Macau | North Central American Scarlet Macaw |
Subspecies: South American Scarlet Macaw

● **LEAST CONCERN**

✥ **COLLECTIVE NAMES**

Cry of macaws | Endangerment of macaws |
Family of macaws

✴ **SYMBOLIC MEANINGS**

Fertility; Power of the sun;
South; Summer.

◉ **POSSIBLE POWERS**

Boldness; Communication;
Messenger to the gods; Mimic.

☾ **FOLKLORE AND FACTS**

Just about every culture from the American Southwest to
the rainforests of Brazil has a myth or legend about popular,
charismatic Scarlet Macaws. This Mayan story is particularly
apropos of the birds' return to Palenque National Park in
Mexico. • Before civilization came to be, another world had
preceded the Mayans, but a massive flood swept it away and
the waters lingered for a very long time. Only a few people
survived, but their lives were filled with perils, including a
macaw named Vucab-Caquix that terrorized them at every
opportunity. "I am the Sun and the Moon, and the sky
between them," he informed his victims. "If you question
this, I will attack and eat you." A handful of dissenters tested
this claim and did not survive the experience. • A pair of
twins, Hunahpu and Xbalanque, grew very weary of the
presumptuous macaw and angry about the way he treated
them. They knew that Vucab-Caquix roosted in a huge, dead
tree, so they hid under it, camouflaged by the tree's giant
roots. When Vucab-Caquix came to roost for the night, they
shot darts at him and lodged them in his face, blinding him.
This only made him angry, however, and he attacked the
twins, ripping off one twin's arm. The twins fled for their
lives and managed to survive, but they did not give up: They
convinced an older couple to pretend to be healers and
bring the wounded bird a tasty potion of maize, spiked with
poison. The couple made their way to Vucab-Caquix's roost,
found the ailing bird there, and after complimenting his
gorgeous red feathers, they urged him to drink the healing
potion. The macaw downed it in a gulp, and almost instantly
began to weaken. In moments he was dead, and his reign of
terror came to an end.

No. 038

Aramus guarauna

Limpkin

Crippled Bird | Crying Bird | Lamenting Bird

● **LEAST CONCERN**

✥ **COLLECTIVE NAME**

Hobbling of limpkins

✴ **SYMBOLIC MEANINGS**

Grieving; Relief.

◉ **POSSIBLE POWERS**

Grief; Guilt; Release of emotion.

☾ **FOLKLORE AND FACTS**

Despite their strange-looking gait, Limpkins do not limp.
This bird makes its methodical way along freshwater
marshes, mangrove swamps, and streams in Florida, Mexico,
and much of South America, looking for its preferred giant
apple snails. • Brown overall with a scattering of white spots
over the neck, back and wings, the well-camouflaged bird
tends to attract human attention with its rattling calls and its
keeeer flight song. So exotic are these sounds that they were
used as jungle sound effects in the Tarzan films of the 1930s,
and more recently as the voice of the hippogriff in the movie
version of *Harry Potter and the Prisoner of Azkaban* (2004).
• Argentine folklore gives us a story of how the Limpkin
came to be such a dark bird with a screechy voice. A mother
fighting a terrible illness sent her son to the village for
medicine that she needed to survive. The son set out,
but on his way to the village he came to a country dance,
where a very pretty girl caught his eye. He asked the girl to
dance and stayed throughout the evening. In the wee hours
of the morning, a friend arrived at the dance and took his
arm. "I am so sorry to hear of the death of your mother,"
he said. "I am very sad for you." The son shrugged him off.
"What of it?" he said, "I will have plenty of time to grieve
later. Right now I am having a good time." The pretty girl
stepped back from him in shock. "I am done with you," she
said. "I would never spend time with someone who has so
little love for his mother!" • This was enough to snap the
young man out of his foolishness. He began to weep for
his mother, and started for home. But God felt he needed
further punishment, so he turned him into a bird shrouded
in mourning colors, and only able to speak by uttering a
plaintive cry of grief. To this day, the Limpkin cries in the
wetlands, a reminder to all to honor their parents.

Archilochus colubris

Ruby-Throated Hummingbird

● LEAST CONCERN

✿ **COLLECTIVE NAMES**
Charm of hummingbirds | Chattering of hummingbirds | Hover of hummingbirds | Shimmer of hummingbirds

✳ **SYMBOLIC MEANINGS**
Hope; Joy; Luck.

❂ **POSSIBLE POWERS**
Courage; Daring; Polygamy.

☾ **FOLKLORE AND FACTS**
A Cherokee legend puts the Ruby-Throated Hummingbird front and center as a mighty hero in a tiny package. When the world began, just one tobacco plant, Tsa'lu, fulfilled the needs of all people and animals—until one day, when the evil Dagul'ku geese swooped in and stole it, flying off with it to the east. This had a profoundly negative effect on the health of many people, especially one old woman who became weak and frail without her tobacco. The people realized that she would die unless they got Tsa'lu back. Large animals offered to go east to get the plant, but the Dagul'ku geese dove down and killed them. Smaller animals, thinking themselves stealthier than the larger ones, also attempted to sneak through the understory to reach the plant ... but the geese saw them and killed them before they could get close. At last, a tiny Ruby-Throated Hummingbird came to the people and said, "I can do it." The people shook their heads, but the little bird insisted, and they finally decided to let him try. • The hummingbird flew off to the place where the Dagul'ku kept the captive plant. The geese surrounded the plant and watched in every direction, but the hummingbird zipped right past them, nipped off the top of the plant with its leaves and seeds, and vanished before the geese could even see what had outsmarted them. • The hummingbird flew back to the people, gave them Tsa'lu, and they lit a leaf and blew smoke into the nostrils of the now-unconscious old woman. Instantly her eyes flew open, and she recovered quickly. The hummingbird was the hero of the day.

Ardea alba

Great Egret
Common Egret | Great White Egret | Large Egret

● LEAST CONCERN

✿ **COLLECTIVE NAMES**
Colony of egrets | Congregation of egrets | Skewer of egrets | Wedge of egrets

✳ **SYMBOLIC MEANINGS**
Good luck; Grace; Patience; Purity; Transformation.

❂ **POSSIBLE POWERS**
Good luck; Patience; Peacemaking.

☾ **FOLKLORE AND FACTS**
Tall, bright white, long-necked, and yellow-billed, the Great Egret is unmistakable in the wild, making it the perfect bird for the logo of the National Audubon Society. • In Hungary, the bird appears on the five-forint coin, and in New Zealand, the two-dollar coin is embossed with an egret. In 2008, the Belarusian treasury chose the Great Egret for a one-ruble coin, to commemorate it as the country's Bird of the Year. • The Great Egret brings luck to people who are fishing, so a flyover can signal an excellent catch. • Several Native American tribes believe that Great Egrets are peacemakers, making it prudent to wear or carry an egret feather when you need to engage in potentially contentious negotiations. • The demand for egret feathers in women's fashion in the late 1800s—especially the luscious plumes called aigrettes that emerge during the breeding season—became so acute that poachers in the southern United States nearly wiped out the entire population of Great and Snowy Egrets in their zeal to cash in on the lucrative plumage trade. It took two Boston socialites, Harriet Hemenway and Minna Hall, holding tea parties and lecturing their friends on the near-extinction of these beautiful birds, to put an end to feathers as fashion. These women went on to form the inaugural chapter of the National Audubon Society, and their work saved entire species from being eliminated.

No. 041

Ardea cinerea

Gray Heron

Grey Heron | Old Nog

● **LEAST CONCERN**

✢ **COLLECTIVE NAMES**

Flight of herons | Scattering of herons | Sedge of herons | Siege of herons

✳ **SYMBOLIC MEANING**

Foretelling and shaping the future.

✿ **POSSIBLE POWERS**

Patience; Predicting the future.

☾ **FOLKLORE AND FACTS**

The Gray Heron has played an important role in Eastern creation mythology. The Egyptian deity Bennu portrayed himself as a Gray Heron, and flew over the great abyss of Nun to land on a rock, let forth a loud, raucous call, and directed the rest of creation. • Contrast this with the Gray Heron's value as a delicacy on the medieval English banquet table, so much so that one celebration featured four hundred herons served up to the king's guests. All herons were the king's property, so if a peasant dared to poach one of the birds, the court would exact a crippling fine. The penalty worsened in Scotland—having the audacity to bag a heron resulted in amputation of one of the poacher's hands. • Fishermen of old observed Gray Herons standing patiently waiting for fish to swim by at just the right distance, and decided that something about the heron's feet must attract fish. They carried a heron's foot to improve their luck, and some coated their fishing lines with a brew made from heron's fat and feet. As this practice has faded, we can assume that it was not effective. • Aesop tells us about a heron and a fox who inexplicably decide to dine together. The fox hosts first, but serves the heron a plate of soup, something the bird can't possibly eat with his long bill. When the heron hosts, he serves food in a bottle with a narrow neck, so the fox can't get at the meal. The moral: A nasty trick just begets more nastiness.

No. 042

Ardea herodias

Great Blue Heron

Blue Heron | Great White Heron (white phase) | Shitepoke | Wüdermann's Heron

● **LEAST CONCERN**

✢ **COLLECTIVE NAMES**

Flight of herons | Scattering of herons | Sedge of herons | Siege of herons

✳ **SYMBOLIC MEANINGS**

Patience; Self-determination; Self-reliance; Solitude.

✿ **POSSIBLE POWERS**

Peacemaking; Self-reflection.

☾ **FOLKLORE AND FACTS**

The largest of the western hemisphere's long-legged waders commands considerable respect throughout a wide range of cultures. Native American folklore says that herons are birds of brotherhood, making peace between other birds and maintaining a quiet dignity. In particular, the Mi'kmaqs have a name for this majestic creature: *dum-gwal-ee-gun-idge*, meaning "his neck is broken"— not a reference to the bird's ability to compress its neck into an S shape, but to the challenges of conflict resolution. In this tradition, those who choose mediation as a calling are said to go "the way of the heron." • While many stories speak with great admiration for the heron's patient, solitary hunting practice, the Cherokees see a different reason for this. Cherokee Little People—small folks who live in gardens, wooded areas, and marshes— worried about encountering Great Blue Herons because the birds were larger than they were, so they might think the Little People were food. A Cherokee hunter taught them to make bows and arrows, so they were prepared should the herons come after them. One day, a flock of Great Blue Herons landed in the marsh. Everyone fled screaming, except for the well-armed warriors, who stood their ground and protected their families; their courage came to the attention of the Great Spirit, who admired their tenacity and decided to punish the herons. The birds were sentenced to a life of hunting and dining alone, not in flocks; their current message to all living things is one of self-reflection, solitude, and good works.

No. 043

Ardeotis kori

Kori Bustard

Christmas Turkey | Kalahari Kentucky

● **NEAR THREATENED**

🐾 **COLLECTIVE NAMES**

Flock of bustards | Wake of bustards

✹ **SYMBOLIC MEANINGS**

Aggression; Competition;
Courtship; Parenthood.

🌀 **POSSIBLE POWERS**

Communication between realms;
Union of Heaven and Earth.

🌙 **FOLKLORE AND FACTS**

The first thing anyone notices about the male Kori Bustard is its size: as the largest bird in Africa, it weighs in at almost 42 pounds (19 kg) and grows to as much as five feet (1.5 m) tall. Once an observer has absorbed this staggering information, another fact quickly comes to light—this massive bird can fly. In fact, it may be the heaviest living animal to be able to lift itself off the ground. This bird prefers the ground, though, so if you spot one, chances are it will remain earthbound for your viewing pleasure. • Females do not achieve the same bulk as the males, coming at about a quarter of the male's size, so don't be fooled into thinking that a flock of smaller birds are not bustards. • Such an unusual bird could not help but have a place in mythology. The KhoiSan people of South Africa have a number of different creation myths, but one of them gives the Kori Bustard a supporting role: The creator god ignited a great fire to bring all of the various traits that animals might have out of the ether and into reality. The god then gathered these traits and baked them into the shapes of animals, creating order from the chaos—and as he did this, a trusty Kori Bustard used its great wings to fan the flames and keep the fire burning hot.

No. 044

Arenaria interpres

Ruddy Turnstone

'Akekeke (Hawai'i)

● **LEAST CONCERN**

🐾 **COLLECTIVE NAMES**

Cluster of turnstones | Time-step of turnstones

✹ **SYMBOLIC MEANINGS**

Faithfulness; Tenacity.

🌀 **POSSIBLE POWER**

Messenger between Earth and the gods.

🌙 **FOLKLORE AND FACTS**

Few things are as delightful as coming across a group of Ruddy Turnstones on a sandy beach. Plump, brightly colored, and larger than many sandpipers, this turnstone is easy to differentiate from the other birds on the sand. • This turnstone's Latin name translates to "sand-living interpreter," a phrase that seems to imply a good story. It turns out, however, that Carl Linnaeus, the Swedish zoologist who in 1735 created the taxonomy system still in use worldwide, actually got the name wrong. While visiting the island of Gotland in Sweden in 1741, he did not know that the word *tolk*, the Swedish word for "interpreter," actually meant "legs" in the local dialect. He heard the locals use it while talking about a redshank on the beach—so they were not even talking about the turnstone. The error has never been corrected. • The Ruddy Turnstone does distinguish itself in Hawaiian mythology—and as a messenger, oddly enough. The spunky turnstone and other cliff-nesters, including Wandering Tattler, two species of tropicbirds, and plovers, are all sent out by the divine chiefs to scout for them and bring back information, and to fly from one island to another to carry messages.

No. 045

Arini

Macaws

Macau | Guacamaya

●● **THREATENED OR ENDANGERED**

🐾 **COLLECTIVE NAMES**

Cry of macaws | Endangerment of macaws | Family of macaws

☀ **SYMBOLIC MEANINGS**

Fertility; Guardian of the south;
Summer.

🌀 **POSSIBLE POWERS**

Communication with the afterlife;
Connection with the sun; Happiness in
marriage; Healing; Messenger for the gods.

🌙 **FOLKLORE AND FACTS**

The largest members of the parrot family, Macaws are spread
throughout the rainforests of Central and South America,
with seventeen living species and two that are known to be
extinct. Three more species are considered "hypothetical,"
as their appearances were recorded in centuries past, but no
physical evidence proves their existence conclusively. • Most
every Indigenous civilization from the southwestern United
States to the southern tip of South America considered the
brightly colored, gregarious Macaws to have a sacred place in
their culture. When various tribes came together at central
meeting places to trade their wares, macaw feathers were a
favorite item that shamans tied to prayer sticks, and healers
used them in ceremonies and rituals. Many bought the birds
to keep as pets as well, seeing them as guardians with the
power to bring healing energy through the relationship
between their brilliant colors and the sun that made them
sparkle. • Several tribes also believed that the Macaws were
messengers to the gods, the perfect bird to get
the deities' attention as it rose up through
the sky. The Bororo tribe in Brazil extended
this even further, believing that the birds
could communicate with their ancestors in the
afterlife. • Those who were not chiefs or healers
saw benefits to maintaining a relationship with a
macaw as well. The birds' legendary longevity—
some live as long as eighty years—brought good
luck and long life to their households, and their lifelong
pair bonds in the wild became symbols of fidelity and
happy marriages.

No. 046

Athene cunicularia

Burrowing Owl

Shoco

● **LEAST CONCERN**

🐾 **COLLECTIVE NAMES**

Company of owls | Parliament of owls |
Stare of owls | Wisdom of owls

☀ **SYMBOLIC MEANING**

Guardian of fires and the underground.

🌀 **POSSIBLE POWER**

Protection for the brave.

🌙 **FOLKLORE AND FACTS**

Burrowing Owls maintain a respectfully distant relationship
with prairie dogs and ground squirrels, taking over their
burrows when these mammals have finished with them.
This alone makes these little yellow-eyed owls particularly
fascinating, but the fact that they live on the ground, raise
their young in these burrows, hunt for small rodents and
insects at eye level, and then store much of their food in the
burrow to guard against tougher times, all combine to create
an even more intriguing picture of a unique bird. • Modern-
day birders are not the only ones who find these birds so
appealing. The owls' peculiar behavior drew awe from the
Hopi people, who believed the owl in the ground was their
god of the dead, as well as the protector of all things under
the ground—including the growth of seeds into crops. They
called their Burrowing Owls Ko'ko, or "watcher of the dark."
• The Hidatsa tribe elevated the Burrowing Owl to the status
of a protector of warriors, helping these fighting men survive
and come home from battle. • The Zuni people tell us how
the Burrowing Owl got its white-spotted plumage: The owls,
busy performing a ceremonial dance, were distracted by the
antics of a coyote and laughed so hard that they spilled foam
(presumably from a drink) all over themselves.

A

No. 047

Athene noctua

Little Owl

Owl of Athena | Owl of Minerva

● **LEAST CONCERN**

🐾 **COLLECTIVE NAMES**

Company of owls | Parliament of owls | Stare of owls | Wisdom of owls

✷ **SYMBOLIC MEANINGS**

Impending death; Knowledge; Wisdom.

🌀 **POSSIBLE POWERS**

Bad luck; Predictor of death; Preventer of alcoholism.

🌙 **FOLKLORE AND FACTS**

The Little Owl is indeed little, but at 8–9 inches (22 cm) high, it is not the world's littlest owl (the Elf Owl at 5 inches, or 13 cm, high is much smaller). Nonetheless, throughout its range across Europe and Asia, the sight of this small owl with its bright white, furrowed eyebrows peeking out of a tree cavity delights birders from all over the world. • Apparently Athena, Greek goddess of wisdom, found the Little Owl a charming sight as well, as stories say that she kept one as a companion. So, too, did Minerva, Athena's counterpart on the Roman side, making this tiny owl indispensable to the Mediterranean deities. A bronze statue of Athena from the fifth century BCE depicts her holding a Little Owl in her hand. • The folklore of Bulgaria and Romania mentions the Little Owl as well, but in a less benevolent light: Both cultures see the bird as a harbinger of death. They are not the only ones to hold this superstition—in fact, historic records suggest that the murder of Julius Caesar may have been preceded by the call of a Little Owl. In Iran, the appearance of a Little Owl is believed to bring bad luck. • A perplexing bit of folklore in Yorkshire, England, leads some residents to believe that a meal of Little Owl, complete with plenty of salt, will cure gout. Devouring their raw eggs, the Yorkshire folks continue, will cure alcoholism—and feeding the raw eggs to children, no matter how much the kids resist, can protect them from the ravages of alcohol for their entire lives. The owl eggs could even cure epilepsy, making it a miraculous egg indeed! None of these tricks holds any actual merit, of course, which must be a relief for the children who risked being force-fed raw eggs.

A

No. 048
Baeolophus bicolor
Tufted Titmouse

● **LEAST CONCERN**

✢ **COLLECTIVE NAMES**
Banditry of titmice | Dissimulation of titmice

✴ **SYMBOLIC MEANINGS**
Good luck (Plains people); Liar (Cherokee).

🌀 **POSSIBLE POWER**
Deception.

☾ **FOLKLORE AND FACTS**
Tidily marked with a gray mantle, a white underside with rosy flanks, and a bright black eye, the Tufted Titmouse readily comes to bird feeders filled with sunflower or safflower seed, making it one of the most popular feeder birds in the eastern United States. Its plaintive *peter-peter-peter* call and scolding hiss announce the bird's approach even in the dead of winter, making it easy to see and identify among flocks of Black-Capped or Carolina Chickadees, its close cousins.

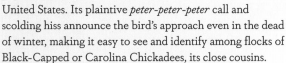

• It's hard to imagine how the plucky little Tufted Titmouse earned a bad reputation among Cherokee people. The Cherokee story tells us that they caught the titmouse in a string of lies about Spearfinger, a monster that had attacked them repeatedly. The titmouse told them a tale about the best way to kill this monster, but the chickadee, hearing the titmouse's fabrications, flew in and told the people that his cousin's words were nothing but lies. The people believed the chickadee because he had a long history of honest dealings with the Cherokee—and then the chickadee flew to Spearfinger's breast and landed exactly where her heart was, so they could aim an arrow at the right spot.

• The Cherokees killed the monster, further cementing the chickadee's heroism. This also became an important lesson for Cherokee children about telling truth from lies: The titmouse and the chickadee have very similar songs, but one is honest and one is not. The moral: It can be very difficult to be certain who is telling the truth, so we must listen carefully to sort out the messages.

No. 049
Balaeniceps rex
Shoebill
Shoe-billed Stork | Whalebird | Whale-Headed Stork

● **VULNERABLE**

✢ **COLLECTIVE NAMES**
Flock of shoebills | Pair of shoebills

✴ **SYMBOLIC MEANING**
Bad luck.

🌀 **POSSIBLE POWERS**
Bad omen; Predictor of hard times.

☾ **FOLKLORE AND FACTS**
Most of us will never encounter this large, stork-like bird with its oversized bill, but those who have often declare it the scariest bird they have ever seen. Nicholas Lund, writing for *Audubon*, suggested that "Death Pelican" would be a better name for this bird of Africa's eastern tropical region—though it has no intention of harming humans, instead snapping up fish, reptiles, and even baby crocodiles and splitting them in half with a single clap of its knifelike bill. • Beyond delivering a quick death to its prey, the Shoebill has another use for its bill: scooping up water from its surrounding swamp and pouring it over its own eggs. Shoebills incubate their eggs during the hottest part of the African summer, so they keep their eggs from cooking in their shells by cooling them with water. • This bird looks as if it can take care of itself in the wild, but it falls prey to poachers in its native South Sudan, Uganda, Democratic Republic of the Congo, and Zambia. Shoebills have long been considered a bad omen, so killing the birds serves as one way to deplete the bird's power over human fate.

B

Balearica pavonina

Black Crowned-Crane

Borin Tunke | Dark Crowned Crane | Sudan Crowned Crane | West African Crowned Crane

● **VULNERABLE**

✻ **COLLECTIVE NAMES**

Herd of cranes | Sedge of cranes | Siege of cranes

✻ **SYMBOLIC MEANINGS**

Peace; Language; Thought.

◈ **POSSIBLE POWERS**

Good will; Messenger of peace; Thoughtfulness.

☾ **FOLKLORE AND FACTS**

Watch where the hyphen belongs in this bird's name. The emphasis here is on the Black Crowned-Crane's glorious burst of golden feathers atop its head, made even more wondrous by the fact that each feather spirals upward, combining white and gold sides with a black tip for dramatic effect. • The Black Crowned-Crane has served as one of the national birds of Nigeria since 1985 (the other is an eagle), but the crane's lofty position has been questioned in recent years as dams change the landscape and drive the bird into other countries. Today the birds live in the grassy savannas south of the Sahara Desert in Chad and Senegal, with few actually living in Nigeria. These cranes can be found for sale in cages along roadsides in Nigeria, making the country's ornithologists decry the lack of protections for this bird.

• Perhaps because of the way the bird stands for long periods as if lost in thought, people throughout its range associate the Black Crowned-Crane with contemplation, thoughtfulness, and language. As with most cranes, this one is seen as a messenger of peace, bringing good will and good fortune to those who see one.

Balearica regulorum

Gray Crowned-Crane

Subspecies: African Crane | African Crowned Crane | Crested Crane | East African Crane | East African Crowned Crane | Eastern Crowned Crane | Golden Crested Crane | Golden Crowned Crane | Kavirondo Crane | South African Crane

● **ENDANGERED**

✻ **COLLECTIVE NAMES**

Herd of cranes | Sedge of cranes | Siege of cranes

✻ **SYMBOLIC MEANINGS**

Longevity; Peace; Wealth.

◈ **POSSIBLE POWERS**

Adaptability; Generosity; Patience.

☾ **FOLKLORE AND FACTS**

Africa's splendid crowned-cranes are among the oldest animals on Earth, with fossils that date back as far as 56 million years. This means that they have survived two ice ages, one of them ending just 11,500 years ago—but current conditions threaten to end their long sojourn on the planet. • How the birds received their gorgeous golden crowns is the subject of African folklore: Long ago, an African king on a hunting expedition found himself alone in the grasslands. He had no idea how to get back to the oasis where his servants had set up court. Desperate, he asked some nearby zebras for help. "You hunt us, so we will not help you," the zebras replied. The king asked the elephants and the antelopes for assistance, but they, too, turned him down. Finally, he asked a group of gray cranes for help—and instead of shunning him, they brought him water and showed him the way to the oasis. In gratitude, the king had crowns made for them, but when the other animals became jealous and stole the crowns right off the cranes' heads, he had them remade as feathers that could not be removed. The Gray Crowned-Crane wears this crown to this day. • The national bird of Uganda, pictured on the country's flag and featured in its coat of arms, has adapted to many adverse circumstances, using its willingness to eat many kinds of plants, seeds, and animals to find sustenance in dwindling open land, and following herds of gazelles and antelopes to devour insects and small rodents kicked up by the animals' hooves.

No. 052

Bombycilla cedrorum

Cedar Waxwing

Forehead Up | Silky-Tail

● **LEAST CONCERN**

✤ **COLLECTIVE NAMES**

Earful of waxwings | Museum of waxwings

✹ **SYMBOLIC MEANINGS**

Family; Gender equality; Harmony with others; Unity.

✺ **POSSIBLE POWERS**

Building communities; Functionality while tipsy.

☾ **FOLKLORE AND FACTS**

The exquisite Cedar Waxwing gets its name from the drops of a waxy, bright red substance on the edge of its wings, just one of the many field marks that makes this bird so elegant. Always traveling in flocks, sharing resources, and drawing no lines between male and female birds, these scavengers descend into fruit-filled trees together and feed voraciously, keeping in contact with one another with their near-constant, high-pitched calls. The dapper waxwing has much to teach us about cooperation and getting along in a world filled with other people who want the same things that we do. • During its breeding season, the male waxwing joins the female on a branch and brings her a berry, and the two pass the berry back and forth between them to indicate that they have made a pair bond. The female ends the courtship by eating the food item, and the mates remain together for the rest of the season. This makes them role models for gender equality. • Cedar Waxwings have one more trait that delights birders: They wait until winter to devour berries that they find in trees, like serviceberry, winterberry, mountain ash, and holly. By winter, the berries have fermented, turning them into tiny vessels of alcohol—and the waxwings swallow up to a thousand of these every day. Many backyard birders report finding flocks of the birds apparently staggering drunkenly on the ground under their berry trees, or struggling to keep their balance on branches. Waxwings, then, have the most winter fun of just about any bird in the animal kingdom.

No. 053

Bombycilla garrulus

Bohemian Waxwing

Forehead Up | Silky-Tail

● **LEAST CONCERN**

✤ **COLLECTIVE NAMES**

Earful of waxwings | Museum of waxwings

✹ **SYMBOLIC MEANINGS**

Family; Gender equality; Harmony with others; Unity.

✺ **POSSIBLE POWERS**

Building communities; Functionality while tipsy; Luminosity.

☾ **FOLKLORE AND FACTS**

Luminous waxwings? That's what people believed back at the beginning of the Common Era, when Roman naturalist Pliny the Elder wrote that the feathers of what would later be called the Bohemian Waxwing "shine like flames" in the darkness of European forests. • Three centuries later, Latin geographer Gaius Julius Solinus made note of a story he had heard: Germans captured waxwings to use as lanterns when they traveled at night, because the birds shone so brightly in the dark. • It took until the late 1500s before Ulisse Aldrovandi of Italy performed an actual experiment to tell truth from fiction: He captured a waxwing and took it into his home, and tended to it for three months. The bird never lit up in the dark, not for a moment. • When Bohemians do get lit, however, is in winter, when they devour berries that have clung to trees until they have fermented, raising their alcohol content exponentially. Bohemians join their Cedar brothers in tippling their way through the winter, perhaps becoming the most relaxed birds in the neighborhood. • Bohemian waxwings are slightly larger and a little bit grayer than the Cedars with which they often fraternize, but the easiest way to tell them apart from Cedars is to look for the rusty patch at the base of their underside, just under the tail. As most waxwings are seen from below, this becomes a quick way to sort out one species from the other.

B

Bonasa umbellus

Ruffed Grouse

Drummer | Thunder-Chicken

● **LEAST CONCERN**

🐾 **COLLECTIVE NAMES**

Brace of grouse (two birds) | Brood of grouse | Covey of grouse | Drumming of grouse

✳ **SYMBOLIC MEANINGS**

Justice; Revenge.

🌀 **POSSIBLE POWERS**

Concealment; Guidance in seeking vengeance.

🌙 **FOLKLORE AND FACTS**

It's hard to know whether being named the state game bird of Pennsylvania is a good thing or a bad thing for the plump, chunky Ruffed Grouse, as this makes it a prime target for hunters—but the grouse serves as challenging prey, hiding in dense brush, picking its way through thickets, even burrowing in snow to create its own shelter. • The one way a male Ruffed Grouse gives away his vicinity is with his legendary drumming behavior, standing on a rock or log and beating his wings in the air to build up a vacuum. This produces a booming sound that increases in speed as the bird persists, telling any potential mate exactly where to head to hook up. • It seems only natural that Native American legends would spin tales about Ruffed Grouse, but the grouse is notably absent from this history. Scholars believe that "grouse" was mistranslated into English as "partridge," though partridges are not native to North America and did not arrive on the continent until the late 1800s. Reviewing the old translations, then, suggests that the great hero Pulowech from Mi'kmaq legend is not of the partridge totem after all, but that it's most likely his totem is a Ruffed Grouse. Pulowech's story is complex and lengthy, but he sets out to find the marauders that murdered his wife, and has quite an assortment of vengeful adventures until he confronts and kills the last of them. This story alone is enough to imbue Ruffed Grouse with meaning as a symbol of vengeance and justice.

Botaurus lentiginosus

American Bittern

Mire Drum | Stake Driver | Sun Gazer | Thunder Pumper | Water Belcher

● **LEAST CONCERN**

🐾 **COLLECTIVE NAMES**

Prettying of bitterns | Sedge of bitterns | Siege of bitterns

✳ **SYMBOLIC MEANINGS**

Harbinger of doom; Water and rain.

🌀 **POSSIBLE POWERS**

Disguise; Predictor of rain; River builder.

🌙 **FOLKLORE AND FACTS**

When the only sound you can make is a low, guttural "whunk-a-chunk," and this odd noise overshadows everything else about you, it stands to reason that you're going to get a bad rep in the bird world. This was the plight of the American Bittern, a fascinating creature with the ability to stand stock-still for long periods with its head raised and its bill pointed skyward, making itself look like just another reed in the marsh. Colonists in New England found the bittern's spring call so eerie that they decided it was an affront to the Sabbath, and they went out into their wetlands to hunt and kill the birds. Chances are that we only have bitterns in New England today for two reasons: first, their uncanny camouflage, and second, there weren't a lot of New Englanders to hunt them down. • Indigenous Peoples have a more benevolent view of bitterns. While the bird does not play a leading role in any Indigenous mythology, bittern symbols turn up in silhouette to indicate the presence of water. Athabaskan stories portray bitterns as helping to end the Great Flood by swallowing large amounts of water and regurgitating it in specific places to form rivers. Aztecs actually looked forward to the strange call of the bittern in their marshes, believing that it heralded steady rains, which would produce more fish in the rivers. If a bittern only called every three days or so, Aztecs knew that only light rains were coming, so fishing would not be very productive.

No. 056

Botaurus poiciloptilus

Australasian Bittern

Brown Bittern | Bunyip Bird | Matuku Hūrepo

● **VULNERABLE**

✸ **COLLECTIVE NAMES**

Prettying of bitterns | Sedge of bitterns | Siege of bitterns

✸ **SYMBOLIC MEANINGS**

Harbinger of doom; Water and rain.

✸ **POSSIBLE POWERS**

Concealment; Scaring children.

☾ **FOLKLORE AND FACTS**

Pity the poor Australasian Bittern, a bird that has become the physical manifestation of an old Australian legend—one whose main purpose in life is to frighten little children. Dreamed up by the Australian First Nations peoples to coerce children into behaving themselves, the bunyip lurks in wet places like watering holes, billabongs, swamps, and wetlands, waiting for bad children to cross its path so it can leap out of the shadows and devour them. This creepy swamp bogie managed to make its way from ancient Aboriginal mythology into the legends of European folks as they arrived in Australia, so now the story is as ingrained in local culture as Santa Claus is in American life. • So where does the Australasian Bittern fit in? Like its American counterpart, the bittern Down Under makes a deep, plunging, booming sound so ominous that it could easily be construed as something wicked coming this way. While the Bunyip Bird is rarely more than 25 inches (66 cm) tall, remains secreted among the reeds and grasses along the edges of wetlands and mangroves, and means no harm to anyone but the fish and eels it eats, its voice has married it to the Sasquatch of the southern hemisphere—a fate just slightly better than living in complete obscurity.

No. 057

Branta bernicla

Brant

Atlantic Brant | Black Brant | Brent Goose | Dark-Bellied Brant

● **LEAST CONCERN**

✸ **COLLECTIVE NAMES**

Blizzard of brant | Chevron of brant | Knot of brant | Plump of brant

✸ **SYMBOLIC MEANINGS**

Courage; Righteousness; Truth.

✸ **POSSIBLE POWER**

Transmutation (disproven).

☾ **FOLKLORE AND FACTS**

We know so much about birds and their movements today that it's hard to imagine a time not so long ago when no one had discovered that birds migrate. In Europe in the 1500s, the people exploring science groped for explanations of where birds went when the weather turned colder, and how they materialized back in the northern climates when sun and warmth returned. One of these theories involved the reappearance of the Brant, the smaller, darker geese of the northern seas. John Gerard, who published his *Generall Historie of Plantes* in 1597, thought he had discovered how these geese returned to England in spring: They dropped from the blossoms of "certaine trees, of a white colour, tending to russet," in northern Scotland and its adjacent islands. If the blossoms dropped into the water, the Brant would emerge—and this discovery was borne out by eyewitness accounts of flowers falling into coastal bodies of water, and the Brant swimming in the same body of water when it had not been there the day before. • Today we know, of course, that Brants breed in the high Arctic and migrate south to quiet open waters along beaches and in bays in the southern United States, Mexico, and southern Europe. Their preference for coastal habitat separates them from most other goose species that prefer inland waters and plowed fields, making it not uncommon to see a large flock of Brants with no other ducks, geese, or seabirds invading their personal space.

No. 058

Branta canadensis

Canada Goose

Canadian Goose

● **LEAST CONCERN**

COLLECTIVE NAMES

Corps of geese | Flock of geese | Gaggle of geese | Nide of geese | Plump of geese | Trip of geese | Wedge of geese

SYMBOLIC MEANINGS

Focus on personal goals; Staying true to one's path.

POSSIBLE POWERS

Focus; Transformation.

FOLKLORE AND FACTS

Thanks to efforts in the 1960s and 1970s to bring the Canada Goose back from the brink of extinction from overhunting and habitat loss, northern regions around the world now enjoy healthy populations of this large, easily seen bird. In fact, the efforts to repatriate these geese were so successful that Canada Geese have become a nuisance in urban areas, clustering in large numbers in parking lots and city parks, on ponds, and in agricultural fields. These geese generally do not fear humans and are quick to approach them, either for food or to defend their young with aggressive raised-wing displays and truly intimidating hissing. For this and for leaving their droppings in the middle of sidewalks, the Canada Goose has fallen out of favor with many municipalities, some of which now have lethal culling programs to keep goose numbers in check. • People up around the Arctic Circle tell the tale of a flock of Canada Geese that fly to a lake, alight on land, shed their goose skins, and become women. They have come to bathe, so they leap into the lake … but a hunter, out to take down a goose for his dinner, sees the geese land and shed their skins, and watches these women from behind the trees. As the women immerse themselves in the lake, the hunter creeps forward and steals one of the goose skins. The women spot him and clamber out of the lake to re-clothe themselves in the skins, but one of the women finds her goose skin is gone. Exposed in her nudity to the hunter, she now has no choice but to become his wife. She bides her time with him until she can steal away to the Land of the Birds, where she recovers her feathers and becomes a goose once again.

No. 059

Branta leucopsis

Barnacle Goose

Clack Goose | Clag-Goose | Claik Goose

● **LEAST CONCERN**

COLLECTIVE NAMES

Corps of geese | Flock of geese | Gaggle of geese | Nide of geese | Plump of geese | Trip of geese | Wedge of geese

SYMBOLIC MEANING

Metamorphosis.

POSSIBLE POWER

Transmutation (disproven).

FOLKLORE AND FACTS

So many origin myths surround the Barnacle Goose that it would take a whole book to sort them all out. Despite observations recorded in ancient times by Aristotle and Pliny of birds flying southward as the weather changed, human acknowledgment of migration would not emerge until the late 1700s, when sea captains saw swallows flying northward from Africa in early spring and finally put two and two together. • In the meantime, European observers struggled to understand why they never saw Barnacle Goose chicks or evidence of nesting and breeding. They decided that Barnacle Geese must emerge fully formed from the aptly named goose barnacles, shelled animals that attach themselves in great clusters to rocks and driftwood along the edge of the ocean. Gerald of Wales claimed in the 1200s to have seen this phenomenon with his own eyes, watching barnacles "hatch" on the Atlantic seashore. • In the 1400s, Pope Pius II visited Scotland and claimed he saw a tree on a riverbank that produced flowers shaped like ducks; when the flowers dropped from the tree into the river, they turned into Barnacle Geese. • The myth got another boost in the 1600s, when author Hector Boece claimed to have pulled a piece of driftwood from the ocean and found it covered with barnacles—and when he pried them open, they contained tiny birds. • Eventually, Charles Darwin's work put an end to the idea that one species could transmute into another one, and the Barnacle Goose myth finally waned. Discovery of the extensive bird breeding grounds in Greenland rendered the myth even more ridiculous, dismissing it once and for all.

Branta sandvicensis

Nēnē

Hawaiian Goose | Nene

● **ENDANGERED**

✿ **COLLECTIVE NAMES**

Corps of geese | Flock of geese | Gaggle of geese | Nide of geese | Plump of geese | Trip of geese | Wedge of geese

✹ **SYMBOLIC MEANING**

Guardians of the land.

✺ **POSSIBLE POWERS**

Communication with spirits of ancestors; Protection.

☾ **FOLKLORE AND FACTS**

Hawai'i's state bird has the dubious honor of being the rarest goose in the world, brought back from the brink of extinction by captive breeding efforts launched in the 1950s. Today, with just 2,500 birds living in the wild, the Nēnē's future continues to be precarious as non-native animals including mongooses, feral pigs, and house cats freely prey upon these birds. • The Kumulipo, the great chant of creation, mentions the Nēnē as one of the animals created, and also speaks of the bird as a link between sea and land—a direct reference to its migratory path. Indigenous Hawaiians consider the Nēnē to be an 'aumakua, a spirit of a Hawaiian ancestor who has taken the form of an animal to help protect the people and the land. This is at least part of the reason that Nēnē are endemic to Hawai'i, living only on these islands and nowhere else in the world; the 'aumakua have powers that can only be invoked by Hawaiians who have the skill to do so, and who honor and respect the spirits.

• The remarkable Nēnē has evolved to be perfectly suited to life on the volcanic islands, eating ohelo berries that grow on lava fields, as well as grasses, flower buds, and other plant matter found on the islands in abundance.

Bubo bubo

Eurasian Eagle-Owl

Eagle Owl | Hubro | Uhu

● **LEAST CONCERN**

✿ **COLLECTIVE NAMES**

Group of owls | Hoot of owls | Parliament of owls

✹ **SYMBOLIC MEANINGS**

Knowledge; Wisdom.

✺ **POSSIBLE POWERS**

Foreteller of riches; Good luck; Predictor of wickedness.

☾ **FOLKLORE AND FACTS**

At 28 inches (71 cm) tall and weighing as much as 9 pounds (4 kg), the Eurasian Eagle-Owl holds the title of the heaviest owl on Earth, so birders need not be concerned that they won't recognize it in the wild. Its habitat stretches from Europe all the way across Asia, with sixteen different subspecies—but with its preference for rocky, often inaccessible terrain, this widespread owl may be particularly hard to see (and its generally nocturnal lifestyle doesn't help). • While owls of all kinds have been a symbol of knowledge and wisdom as far back as ancient Grecian times, they are no more intelligent than any other bird—but that hasn't stopped people from attributing all kinds of powers to them. In Norway, for example, people once believed that when a Eurasian Eagle-Owl let out its piercing cry in the forests, something wicked was about to happen. People of ancient Rome saw the Eurasian Eagle-Owl's arrival inside the city as a sign of bad tidings to come. In olden times in Japan, the owl represented good luck instead of bad: If a Eurasian Eagle-Owl sat on a perch above someone, and that person walked under the branch and heard the sound of falling rain, the person would soon become very rich. The circumstances of this are so specific that it would be hard to prove or disprove this belief, giving it lasting power for generations.

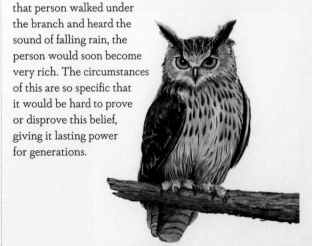

No. 062

Bubo scandiacus

Snowy Owl

Arctic Owl | Ghost Owl | Great White Owl | Night Eagle | Oopik

● **LEAST CONCERN**

🐾 **COLLECTIVE NAMES**

Group of owls | Hoot of owls | Parliament of owls

☀ **SYMBOLIC MEANINGS**

Higher knowledge; Insight.

🌀 **POSSIBLE POWERS**

Bringer of wisdom from the spirit world; Messenger to the elders; Revealer of secrets of the Great Mystery.

🌙 **FOLKLORE AND FACTS**

Pure white, generally silent, and able to glide low and slowly over open fields in pursuit of prey, the Snowy Owl cannot help but spark the imagination. Snowy Owls have feet insulated with extra feathers, more feathers than other birds around the bill, and the ability to stay still and vanish into their snow-covered surroundings, making them stealthy hunters with superior endurance in even the most frigid conditions. • Indigenous Peoples of the Arctic believe this bird to be a messenger who carries terrestrial wisdom to the Elders—and a human favored by the Snowy Owl receives the words of the Elders through intuition, and translates them to share with the community. They also believe that snowy owls can glide into the spirit world to bring back ancient wisdom from the void of Great Mystery, revealing secrets that have been hidden to humans for ages. • An Inuit story tells us of Snowy Owl and Raven, who both began their existence as pure white birds. They decided to find a way to add some more color to their plumage, so Raven very carefully painted gray crescents on each of Snowy Owl's feathers, creating a very striking pattern. When it was Raven's turn to be painted, however, he squirmed and would not hold still. Finally, Snowy Owl upended an entire lamp full of oil on Raven, turning him jet black. The Snowy Owl remains the brightest white bird in the Arctic.

No. 063

Bubo virginianus

Great Horned Owl

Hoot Owl | Tiger Owl

● **LEAST CONCERN**

🐾 **COLLECTIVE NAMES**

Group of owls | Hoot of owls | Parliament of owls

☀ **SYMBOLIC MEANINGS**

Courage; Strength.

🌀 **POSSIBLE POWERS**

Adaptability; Connection to the spirit world; Hearing messages from the beyond; Sense of purpose; Truthseeking.

🌙 **FOLKLORE AND FACTS**

The Great Horned Owl, the western hemisphere's most widespread owl, is easily recognized by its large size, the feathery horns at the top of its head (which are not ears, and have nothing to do with hearing), and its ability to turn its head a full 180 degrees to look directly backward. This highly adaptable owl can be found in a wide range of habitats, from forests to deserts, as well as in suburban settings. • In some Native American cultures, the feather horns give the Great Horned Owl the ability to connect with the beyond, whatever the observer may believe that to be. The owl's superior hearing certainly does give the impression that it can hear whispers from the spirit world, and its silent flight, its ability to sit still for long periods, and its otherworldly hoot in the night all convey a sensibility for things well outside of human experience. • The owl serves as a totem in the Native American zodiac, coinciding with the Greek zodiac's Sagittarius. People born under the owl totem love honestly, seek truth in all things, and serve as messengers for the Great Spirit. They may be so tenacious that they are seen as stubborn, but this comes from utter determination to accomplish goals or to complete a task. Overall, the owl totem inspires a sense of purpose that may turn into a lifelong journey or quest for these self-motivating people.

No. 064

Buceros rhinoceros

Rhinoceros Hornbill

Kenyalang

● **VULNERABLE**

✢ **COLLECTIVE NAMES**

Flock of hornbills | Party of hornbills

✳ **SYMBOLIC MEANING**

Chief of all worldly birds.

✺ **POSSIBLE POWER**

Leadership.

☾ **FOLKLORE AND FACTS**

Honors abound for the Rhinoceros Hornbill, a revered bird of Southeast Asia and the Thai peninsula and one of the oddest creatures in the bird world. Coal black except for its white abdomen and tail, the bird sports a large, heavy, downward-curved bill, and an enormous, bright orange and yellow casque atop the bill, as if protruding from its forehead. The Rhinoceros Hornbill dwells in mountain rainforests in Borneo, Java, the Malay Peninsula, and Sumatra, as well as in southern Thailand. Malaysia has honored it twice, making it the official bird of the state of Sarawak and the country's national bird. • What is the casque for? It amplifies the hornbill's call, serving to increase the call's resonance so it booms throughout the forest. The bird also uses this strange appendage to knock fruit out of a tree, to dig through vegetation in a search for food, and in courtship displays.

• The Iban, Sarawak's largest Dayak tribe, considers the Rhinoceros Hornbill to be the chief of all birds the world over. They use carvings of the bird to welcome Sengalang Burong, the bird god, to festivities during Gawai Kenyalang, the Hornbill Festival, a ceremonious occasion that the tribe held originally before headhunting raids against its enemies. With those days long behind them (and banned at the highest level), the Hornbill Festival precedes the rice harvest instead. A totem pole of Kenyalang birds is just one of the ornaments used in the celebration.

No. 065

Burhinus grallarius

Bush Stone-Curlew

Bush Thick-Knee | Scrub Stone-Curlew | Southern Stone-Curlew | Southern Stone-Plover | Weelo | Willaroo

● **LOCALLY THREATENED**

✢ **COLLECTIVE NAMES**

Curfew of curlews | Herd of curlews

✳ **SYMBOLIC MEANING**

Messenger of death or loss.

✺ **POSSIBLE POWERS**

Concealment; Guide in grieving.

☾ **FOLKLORE AND FACTS**

This bird of the open Australian plains wears cryptic plumage that blends into its surroundings by day and makes it virtually invisible at night, a sound strategy for evading predators while skulking along on the ground. • The Bush Stone-Curlew can fly, but most of the time it chooses not to, instead freezing into rigidity if it knows something is watching it. Most birders hear it long before they lay eyes on one, its *weee-lo* call piercing the night as more and more individuals join the conversation.

• This eerie call inspired a number of stories in Australian First Nations circles about the bird's connection with loss and death. One of these tells the story of how death originated on the Tiwi Islands: Purrukapali and Bima, two of the first people on Earth, had a baby son named Jinani. One day Bima went off to have an affair with her husband's brother, leaving the child in the care of Japara, a young man in the village. Japara left the baby out in the blazing sun while he did other things, and when he returned, the baby had died. Purrukapali, discovering this, flew into a rage and beat Japara senseless. He then picked up his son and walked backward into the sea, proclaiming, "As I die, so must all of you." This brought death into the world for the first time. Bima, returning and finding her son and her husband dead, became Wayiyi, the curlew that forever roams the forests at night, its *weeee-lo* cry her lament of remorse for her lost child.

B

No. 066
Buteo buteo
Common Buzzard

Subspecies: Brown Buzzard | Buzz-Hawk |
Steppe Buzzard | Tourist's Eagle

● **LEAST CONCERN**

🐾 **COLLECTIVE NAMES**
Pack of buzzards | Wake of buzzards

✳ **SYMBOLIC MEANINGS**
Freedom; Purification; Renewal.

🌀 **POSSIBLE POWERS**
Bringer of renewal; Harbinger of death; Relaxation.

🌒 **FOLKLORE AND FACTS**
Let's be clear: This entry is about a bird of prey with a wide range in the eastern hemisphere, not the large, carrion-eating bird (actually the Turkey Vulture, No. 84 in this book) of the western hemisphere. The Common Buzzard is a mostly brown, barrel-chested raptor that roams all over Europe, in much of Africa, and across Asia, with some individuals showing more white underneath as they fly, and others more rufous-colored. Like many raptors, it lives where woodlands meet open land, giving it plenty of perches from which to observe the ground, and plenty of ground on which to find and capture live prey. Carrion only becomes part of its diet in the lean winter months, when there are no other choices. • The Common Buzzard's laconic hunting style makes it appear sluggish and even lazy to some raptor fans, leading William Yarrel to disparage it in his *A History of British Birds*, calling it "a lazy, sleepy, cowardly fellow who [dozes] away half his time on some old rotten stump." The truth, however, is that this bird can hunt with the best of them, so much so that landowners in the United Kingdom blamed it for declines in the game birds they raised for hunting. Buzzards are a protected species in the UK, but this did not keep game farmers from shooting them off their perches in trees on their land. This aggression has ended, but it has taken some time for Common Buzzards to return to their historic numbers. • Despite their general disdain for carrion, these buzzards are associated with death and renewal, the clearing of old strife and the birth of new beginnings. That is, when they are not being mistaken by first-time UK visitors for Golden Eagles, a much larger bird with a huge wingspan. That's how these birds gained the nickname "Tourist's Eagle."

No. 067
Buteo jamaicensis
Red-Tailed Hawk

Chicken Hawk | Harlan's Hawk | Redtail

● **LEAST CONCERN**

🐾 **COLLECTIVE NAMES**
Boil of hawks | Cast of hawks | Kettle of hawks

✳ **SYMBOLIC MEANINGS**
Clear vision; Courage; Power.

🌀 **POSSIBLE POWERS**
Courage; Majesty; Protection.

🌒 **FOLKLORE AND FACTS**
North America's most common hawk, the Red-Tailed Hawk is also the easiest to identify as it soars past or over birders observing it, mainly because of its namesake red tail. When it sits on a fencepost, utility pole, or tree limb, the hawk's white chest and the jagged, dark brown band across its belly provide even more confirmation that this large hawk could only be a red-tail. • Cherokees see the Red-Tailed Hawk as their protector spirit, admiring the courage the birds demonstrate in attacking and devouring rattlesnakes, even though the snake's venom is dangerous to them. The bird's tail feathers are much prized, but the Cherokee would never harm the sacred birds—instead, they use bait (a rodent tethered to a post in an open space) to bring the bird in close, then catch the bird and collect a few feathers from it before releasing it. These feathers adorn headbands and are used in ceremonies. • Residents of New York City became fascinated with a Red-Tailed Hawk that nested on the edge of Central Park for more than thirty years. "Pale Male" became the subject of a movie documentary and an episode of the *Nature* television series. Over the course of his sojourn on a ledge of a Fifth Avenue apartment building, Pale Male had five mates and raised a successful brood just about every year. His life ended in May 2023 at thirty-two years old, but he had outlived the vast majority of Red-Tails, whose lifespan is usually about fifteen years.

No. 068

Buteo platypterus

Broad-Winged Hawk

Subspecies: Antigua Broad-Winged Hawk | Antillean Broad-Winged Hawk |
Cuban Broad-Winged Hawk | Dominican Broad-Winged Hawk |
Puerto Rican Broad-Winged Hawk

● **LEAST CONCERN**

✿ **COLLECTIVE NAMES**

Boil of hawks | Cast of hawks | Kettle of hawks

✴ **SYMBOLIC MEANINGS**

Exploration; Freedom.

🌀 **POSSIBLE POWERS**

Messenger to the gods; Messenger to the spirit world.

☾ **FOLKLORE AND FACTS**

Hawks soar to great heights, and the Broad-Winged Hawk
is one of the highest flyers, with large migrating flocks
ascending until they become tiny specks against the blue
or vanish above the cloud cover. It's easy to see why many
Native American cultures see this altitude-loving bird as
a messenger between Earth and sky, able to carry word of
what's happening below to the gods themselves, or even
beyond to the spirit world. • This hawk of the western
hemisphere spends the breeding season in the eastern United
States or as far north as southern Canada, then migrates in
huge, high flocks to Central and South America, often in
kettles of more than 30,000 birds at a time. Broad-Wings
prefer to migrate over land rather than water, bringing them
inland on the Atlantic Flyway and making them a welcome
sight at mountaintop observatories. • To sort them out from
other migrating hawks, keep in mind that Broad-Winged
Hawks are smaller and browner than other *Buteo* species of
the eastern United States, with a brown-barred or rufous-
barred chest. If you miss it during migration, it can be hard
to find in breeding season as it secretes itself and its nesting
location in dense forests of mixed deciduous and coniferous
trees. Listen for its high-pitched whistle in
spring season—a sound quite unlike
the Red-Tail's hearty
screech—as it
performs its
sky-dancing
display in an effort
to attract a mate.

No. 069

Cacatua alba

White Cockatoo

Ayab | Umbrella Cockatoo

● **ENDANGERED**

❋ **COLLECTIVE NAMES**
Chattering of cockatoos | Crackle of cockatoos

✹ **SYMBOLIC MEANINGS**
Good luck; Hope; Purity.

✺ **POSSIBLE POWERS**
Warning of trouble; Watcher.

☾ **FOLKLORE AND FACTS**
Snow-white with a hint of yellow visible on its underwings and tail in flight, the White Cockatoo comes from the rainforest on the islands of North Maluku, Indonesia, but it is much more widespread as a pet throughout the United States, Europe, and Asia, where breeders produce their birds in captivity. • The more localized passion for the pure-plumaged bird had driven its numbers in the wild nearly to the point of collapse, as poachers trapped live birds in their natural habitat to sell in markets in Surabaya and Jakarta, Indonesia, or in the Philippines. The cockatoos are protected by a 1990 law that prohibits poaching, but the birds draw high prices at markets, so the practice continues. • White Cockatoos let the world know when they are surprised, raising a semicircular crest of white feathers above their heads—one of the most endearing aspects of interacting with one. This broad crest earned the bird the nickname "umbrella cockatoo." • It also may have a connection to why Australians call a designated look-out person a cockatoo, especially when that person is keeping watch for law enforcement or others who might disrupt a good time—like the lookout for illegal gambling. No one raises an alarm more quickly or effectively than a rattled cockatoo.

No. 070

Cacatua galerita

Sulphur-Crested Cockatoo

White Cockatoo

● **LEAST CONCERN**

❋ **COLLECTIVE NAMES**
Chattering of cockatoos | Crackle of cockatoos

✹ **SYMBOLIC MEANINGS**
Exploration; Self-sufficiency; Survival.

✺ **POSSIBLE POWER**
Problem-solving.

☾ **FOLKLORE AND FACTS**
The all-white cockatoo with the lemon-yellow crest is one of the most recognizable birds in Australia. Distributed widely through the forests of the Australian continent, Papua New Guinea, Indonesia, and nearby islands, the Sulphur-Crested Cockatoo thrives on seeds, berries, nuts, and leaf buds—and if it stayed in its lane in the abundant forests, it would be a much-loved creature by anyone who spotted one. Its twentieth-century introduction into western Australia's agricultural land changed this, however; now the cockatoos are considered pests by farmers, stripping their grain crops and competing with native birds for nesting territories. • The Aboriginal belief system known as the Dreaming has quite a number of meaningful stories about this cockatoo. In one of these, a woman from the plains moves to the swampland with her husband, but as she came from an area with little water, she never learned to swim. One day while her husband is away, the area floods. She climbs into a hollow tree to escape the water, but soon finds herself trapped by the rising water. Thinking quickly, she turns herself into a cockatoo—not just for flight, but so she can use her sturdy, powerful bill to dig her way through the tree to the top, and then fly out and away from the water. The lesson in this story? If you feel trapped in your situation, find your own way out. • These charismatic birds go for a pretty penny on the black market. Many owners discover later that Sulphur-Crested Cockatoos love to chew on things, especially wood and wire, and their razor-sharp bills can gnaw right through cages or ruin furniture.

C

No. 071

Calamospiza melanocorys

Lark Bunting

Prairie Finch

● LEAST CONCERN

COLLECTIVE NAMES

Decoration of buntings | Mural of buntings | Sacrifice of buntings

SYMBOLIC MEANING

Pride in Colorado.

POSSIBLE POWER

Good luck.

FOLKLORE AND FACTS

It's not a lark and it's not a bunting—in fact, the Lark Bunting is a sparrow, and a flashy one at that. Males in breeding plumage are solid black with bright white wings, easily spotted by passers-by as they flit across the tops of tall stalks in prairies and grasslands. Females present a dimmer picture, with mottled brown back and wings and a streaky underside, and males tone it down to very similar plumage in non-breeding season. • How the Lark Bunting became the state bird of Colorado in 1931 is a classic tale of old-time politics, filled with contention and showmanship. Three birds came up as candidates: the Meadowlark, the Mountain Bluebird, and the Lark Bunting, and the showier, more colorful birds might have won the day if they had not already been selected as symbols in several other states. Despite more than 111,000 school students across the state voting for the Meadowlark, and the Mountain Bluebird's champion going so far as to whistle the bird's song while drawing it in chalk in front of an audience, they both lost out to a grandstanding soliloquy on the state legislature's floor. High school teacher Roy Langdon packed the room with his students and spent fifteen minutes rhapsodizing over the little black bird with the white wings. By the time he finished, the bunting received a unanimous vote.

No. 072

Callipepla californica

California Quail

Subspecies: Owen Valley Quail | San Lucas California Quail | San Quintin California Quail | Santa Catalina Quail | Warner Valley Quail

● LEAST CONCERN

COLLECTIVE NAMES

Bevy of quails | Covey of quails | Flush of quails

SYMBOLIC MEANINGS

Humbleness; Modesty.

POSSIBLE POWERS

Averting disaster; Building communities.

FOLKLORE AND FACTS

Plump and round with a plume of feathers rising up and out from its forehead, the California Quail presents an amusing picture when a covey of these strikingly patterned gray and brown birds transects a field or marches across a road. • The Pima people tell a story about wily quails playing a trick on Coyote. Finding Coyote asleep in the wild, they cut away pieces of his own hind end without waking him. Later, while they cook the meat over a fire, Coyote smells the broiling meat and comes up to them. "Look at that nice meat! Give me some," he says. The quails, no doubt snickering behind their wings, give him some. As he starts to leave, however, one of them calls to Coyote: "You just ate your own flesh." • Coyote moves on, but soon he feels the pain of his wound and discovers that they had indeed cut him. He runs back to the quails, who dive into a hole—but one of them grabs a piece of cholla cactus first. Coyote catches up and begins dragging them out of the hole one by one, asking, "Were you the one who said I ate my own flesh?" Each one says no, and Coyote lets them all go until only the piece of cactus remains, now covered in feathers. Coyote grabs the cactus and asks the question one more time, but the cactus is silent. "Aha!" said Coyote, "You were the one!" He sinks his teeth into the cactus, but the cactus stabs him with its quills, and Coyote dies instantly. • If there is a moral in this story, it might be, "Look carefully before you bite." Or, perhaps, "Don't mess with quail."

No. 073

Callipepla squamata

Scaled Quail

Blue Quail | Cottontop

● **LEAST CONCERN**

✿ **COLLECTIVE NAMES**

Bevy of quails | Covey of quails | Flush of quails

✹ **SYMBOLIC MEANINGS**

Cooperation; Unity.

✺ **POSSIBLE POWERS**

Defense; Scaring off potential danger.

☽ **FOLKLORE AND FACTS**

The Scaled Quail is one of the dominant quail species of the American southwest, found from western Texas to southeastern Arizona and throughout central Mexico. Their preference for low trees like mesquite and cholla, sagebrush, yucca, and shin oak make them fairly easy to see as they perch atop a tree at a tall human's eye level. Their soft brown plumage has the appearance of scales over nearly all of the body, while a bright white "cotton top" crest gives away the bird's location. • When a covey of Scaled Quails comes together in one place, the birds often form a tight circle on the ground with their tails in the middle and their heads facing out. This acts as an excellent defense against predators—a major concern for birds that spend most of their time on the ground. If a predator approaches, the birds all take flight in the same instant, an explosive move that startles the pursuer. • While quails do not play a significant role in Native American legends, some do pop up in stories. In one of these, Thunder appoints Eagle the ruler of all animals, and bids Eagle meet with each animal and ask what they want to be, and grant all the reasonable requests. Eagle meets with Quail, who asks, "Could you make it so when a man sees me fly, he dies instantly?" Eagle answers, "No, but I can make it so when a man hears you fly, he becomes frightened and runs away." This is why the Scaled Quail's wings make a whirring sound when they take flight.

No. 074

Calypte anna

Anna's Hummingbird

● **LEAST CONCERN**

✿ **COLLECTIVE NAMES**

Charm of hummingbirds | Glittering of hummingbirds | Hover of hummingbirds | Shimmer of hummingbirds

✹ **SYMBOLIC MEANINGS**

End of challenging times; Joy; Luck.

✺ **POSSIBLE POWERS**

Cheekiness; Intelligence; Speed.

☽ **FOLKLORE AND FACTS**

Anna's Hummingbird takes its name from Anna Masséna, Duchess of Rivoli, who served as lady-in-waiting to French Empress Eugénie de Montijo in the mid-1800s. French naturalist René-Primevère Lesson named the bird for the beautiful Anna, no doubt as a courtesy to her husband, Duke François Victor Masséna, a naturalist and ornithologist. The Birds Named for Birds project suggests that Lesson intended to attract favor from the royal court, so he used the bird-naming process to honor them even though they had no interest in birds. • A species that breeds in California, Oregon, Washington, and southern Arizona, the male Anna's Hummingbird sports a bright magenta gorget that sometimes sparkles orange in the sun, and wraps all the way to the top of the head. Females lack the full gorget, but they usually have a small pink "soul patch" at the chin. • A creation myth told by the Ohlone people of California places Eagle, Coyote, and Hummingbird at the top of a mountain, waiting for the waters that preceded creation to recede. When the world finally dries, Coyote heads down to investigate and reports that there is only one human below—a beautiful girl. Eagle commands him to go down and marry the girl and begin to restore humans to the Earth, but Coyote hesitates, not knowing where on the girl's body to put children. Hummingbird, exasperated by this talk, says, "Coyote, put it in her belly!" Eagle agrees, but Coyote becomes angry at being embarrassed by this tiny bird, so he takes a swipe at him with a paw. Eagle protects the bird, hiding him from Coyote. Finally, Coyote gives up and heads down to marry the beautiful girl and begin to repopulate the planet. • So we have Hummingbird to thank for all of the people on the planet, descendants of the none-too-wily Coyote and his lovely maiden.

No. 075

Calyptorhynchus banksii

Red-Tailed Black Cockatoo

Banks' Black Cockatoo | Banksian Black Cockatoo | Great-billed Cockatoo | Ngaoara

● **LEAST CONCERN**

✿ **COLLECTIVE NAMES**

Chattering of cockatoos | Crackle of cockatoos

✴ **SYMBOLIC MEANINGS**

Change; Enlightenment; Rain.

✺ **POSSIBLE POWERS**

Guide of the spirits of the dead; Predictor of rain.

☾ **FOLKLORE AND FACTS**

The tale is told in Arnhem Land, in the northernmost part of Australia's Northern Territory, of two people who contracted an affliction that came across the northern seas to their peninsula. So sickened were they by this strange malady that they both suddenly began to grow black feathers. To escape certain death, they transformed into birds and flew high and far, becoming the Crow and Black Cockatoo we know today. • All black with a bright red tail and a full, nearly circular black crest, the Red-Tailed Black Cockatoo must be connected directly with the great beyond—at least, so say the Tiwi people of Bathurst and Melville Islands. Tales from the Tiwis tell us that the Red-Tailed Black Cockatoo serves as a guide to the next world, ushering the recently dead into heaven. Its melancholy call not only persuades the ancestors to open the entrance to their realm, but it also serves people here in the mortal world in a much more mundane way: as a predictor of rain. People who see the black birds circling above them know that their loved ones in heaven are still close by, and perhaps even thinking of them at that moment.

No. 076

Campephilus principalis

Ivory-Billed Woodpecker

Kint Lord God Bird

● **CRITICALLY ENDANGERED**

✿ **COLLECTIVE NAMES**

Descent of woodpeckers | Gatling of woodpeckers | Whirlagust of woodpeckers

✴ **SYMBOLIC MEANING**

Resilience.

✺ **POSSIBLE POWERS**

Healing; Protection.

☾ **FOLKLORE AND FACTS**

Few birds have come back from the dead as many times as the Ivory-Billed Woodpecker, known among southerners of the Louisiana, Arkansas, and Texas swamplands as the "Lord God bird" because of how people react when they see the giant bird swoop into their field of vision. • The largest woodpecker in the United States, the Ivory-Billed Woodpecker stands as much as 20 inches (51 cm) tall with black wings ending in wide white wing patches, a black back with white streaks, black head with a bold, white eye, heavy white bill, and a bright red crest. • Considered to be extinct several times during the twentieth and twenty-first centuries, the bird has nonetheless reappeared near an oxbow of the Trinity River in Texas in 1904; once again in 1935 when it allowed Arthur A. Allen to photograph and film it in Tensas Parish, Louisiana; and in bottom land in northeastern Louisiana in 1944. Since then, *Living Bird* magazine editor Tim Gallagher and passionate local birder Bobby Harrison saw and videotaped an Ivory-Bill in an Arkansas bayou on February 27, 2004, though this sighting remains controversial. • Harrison continues to search for the bird, and he once again caught what may have been an Ivory-Bill on video on October 17, 2020, but his video has not yet been accepted as an official sighting by the American Ornithological Society. Nonetheless, it raised enough questions about whether or not individual Ivory-Billed Woodpeckers may still exist that the U.S. Fish and Wildlife Service backed off their 2021 decision to declare the bird extinct. It is now listed as "critically endangered," and ornithologists continue to seek definitive proof that it lives.

No. 077

Campylorhynchus brunneicapillus

Cactus Wren

● **LEAST CONCERN**

✢ **COLLECTIVE NAMES**
Cabinet of wrens | Chime of wrens | Flock of wrens

✳ **SYMBOLIC MEANINGS**
Family; Preparation; Protection.

🌀 **POSSIBLE POWER**
Passionate protection of family.

☾ **FOLKLORE AND FACTS**
America's largest wren has earned its place as the state bird of Arizona, standing atop cholla or saguaro cacti and singing a song that sounds like a car engine that just won't turn over. A showy wren with a boldly patterned back, orangey underside, and a wide white eyebrow on its brown face, the Cactus Wren does not shy away from making itself seen and heard. • Even with so many characteristics that draw eyes and ears, the Cactus Wren has more surprises to demonstrate. The bird protects its nesting area with a vehemence that belies its size, using its sharp bill and ability to attack from above to fend off other birds, squirrels, and sometimes even people who have wandered into the vicinity of its nestlings. This behavior brings Cactus Wren its reputation with Native American folklorists, who consider the plucky bird a symbol of protection and family loyalty. In the summer, the wren takes this commitment to family another step: As the female bird incubates a clutch of eggs, the male goes off to find a cavity in another cactus and build a second nest for her next brood. When the first clutch hatches, the male cares for the nestlings while the female goes off to the second nest and lays her next clutch. This efficient method virtually guarantees that the birds will raise two (or even three) broods every summer.

No. 078

Caprimulgus europaeus

Eurasian Nightjar
Corpse Hound | Gabbleratchet | Goatsucker | Spinner | Wheelbird

● **LEAST CONCERN**

✢ **COLLECTIVE NAME**
A kettle of nighthawks.

✳ **SYMBOLIC MEANINGS**
Death; Witchcraft.

🌀 **POSSIBLE POWERS**
Concealment; Keeper of secrets.

☾ **FOLKLORE AND FACTS**
It sleeps all day in dead leaves on the ground, virtually invisible and unnoticed, thanks to its cryptic plumage. • At night, it rises in silent flight out of its hiding place and darts this way and that in the dark. Only its voice gives away its location: a long, throaty rattle that changes in pitch with each phrase, or a dry, spooky *pk, pk, pk* as it passes overhead. The Eurasian Nightjar's secretive life takes place out of view of most would-be observers, inviting all kinds of sinister imagery. • Probably the best-known myth is the one that gives nightjars their alternate name: *goatsucker*. Despite millennia of insistence on this by authorities like Aristotle and Pliny, and later by country farmers, nightjars and nighthawks do not suck the milk from cows and goats. How did such a rumor begin? Nightjars fly close to barnyard animals, but only to catch and eat the bugs that gather around the beasts. • The most heinous of the nightjar tales suggests that the birds are actually the souls of unbaptized children, forced to flutter their way through the nights for eternity. This falsehood, circulated by the many medieval Christian denominations, did not persist into modern life. Nightjars are simply insectivores who are adapted to night flight, when bugs are most active. Nothing eerier than that.

C

No. 079

Caracara plancus

Crested Caracara

Caracara Eagle | Mexican Buzzard | Mexican Eagle

● **LEAST CONCERN**

✿ **COLLECTIVE NAME**

A bazaar of caracaras

✳ **SYMBOLIC MEANINGS**

Sky; Sun.

✺ **POSSIBLE POWER**

Indicating the location of the Aztec capital city.

☾ **FOLKLORE AND FACTS**

The Indigenous Tupi culture of Brazil gave all nine birds in the caracara family their onomatopoetic name, basing it on their screechy *carrrrRA-carrrrRA-carrrrRA* call. The distinctive Crested Caracara, with its white and orange face and black cap, is one of the easiest birds to identify along the Texas/Mexico border and farther south—even in flight, when the bright white patches toward the outer end of its wings become a definitive field mark. • The Crested Caracara carries important symbolism for the Aztecs, who built their capital city in central Mexico. Legend tells us that the Aztecs once wandered the countryside, following the food supply of snakes and lizards, battling those who attempted to take what little they had, but claiming no land for their own. One day, the sun god Huītzilōpōchtli spoke to the people, telling them to watch for a sign that would come to them: An eagle with a snake in its bill, perched on top of a cactus. This sign would tell them where to build their capital city and make a permanent home. They waited for this sign, and one day it arrived on an island in the middle of Lake Texcoco, and the Aztecs ended their nomadic ways and built the great city of Tenochtitlán. • Today a Golden Eagle holding a snake graces the Mexican coat of arms in remembrance of this day, but some historians believe that the eagle must have been a Crested Caracara— so Mexico made the caracara its national bird, even though the eagle remains in the place of honor.

No. 080

Cardinalis cardinalis

Northern Cardinal

Common Cardinal | Red Cardinal | Redbird

● **LEAST CONCERN**

✿ **COLLECTIVE NAMES**

College of cardinals | Conclave of cardinals | Deck of cardinals

✳ **SYMBOLIC MEANINGS**

Harmony; Love; Loyalty; Rejuvenation; Vitality.

✺ **POSSIBLE POWERS**

Harbinger of death; Messenger from the spirit world; Predicting arrival of visitors.

☾ **FOLKLORE AND FACTS**

Bright red with a black face and a clear, lyrical song, the male Northern Cardinal may have more symbolism attributed to it than any other songbird. Cherokees believed that if a cardinal sang near their home, visitors were on their way—but if the bird actually came into their dwelling, a death might be imminent. • Cherokees also told the story of how the cardinal got its color: A trickster raccoon played a joke on a wolf, plastering its eyes shut with mud. As the wolf staggered around blindly, a brown cardinal happened along, and the wolf begged it for help. "If you remove this plaster from my eyes, I'll show you where you can get red paint to change your color," he said. The cardinal agreed and pecked off the mud, and the grateful wolf kept his word and brought the bird to a rock with veins of red dye. The cardinal pecked out enough red to coat himself with it, and he and his descendants remained red for eternity. • Which came first, the Catholic cardinal or the bird? The men in red garb had the name first, given to the birds by Linnaeus in the late 1600s as he developed the taxonomic system for classifying species. Christians went on to embrace the red birds, however, making them part of Christmas décor and believing that a cardinal in the backyard is the spirit of a departed loved one paying a visit.

C

No. 081

Carduelis carduelis

European Goldfinch

Goldfinch | Goldspink

● **LEAST CONCERN**

🐦 **COLLECTIVE NAMES**

Charm of goldfinches | Chattering of goldfinches |
Glister of goldfinches | Vein of goldfinches

☀ **SYMBOLIC MEANING**

Association with Jesus and Christianity.

🌀 **POSSIBLE POWER**

Foresight of the Crucifixion.

🐦 **FOLKLORE AND FACTS**

Fans of Italian Renaissance paintings of the Madonna and
Child can't help but note a little buff-colored bird with a
bright red and black face in a surprising number of these
works. The European Goldfinch, these artists believed, had
the dubious honor of knowing that the Crucifixion was on
its way, and the bird somehow conveyed this to John the
Baptist, who holds the bird out to Jesus Christ as a warning
in paintings by Raphael and Barocci. Other paintings place
the bird in Jesus's hand or pair it with Saint Jerome, though
the specifics of that relationship are not clear. • Perhaps this
association with Christianity played a role in the European
Goldfinch becoming one of the most popular exotic birds
in the caged bird trade, so much so that tens of thousands
of them were trapped in Great Britain and sold to bird
enthusiasts around the world. Despite this practice being
illegal, it continues today. • Neighborhoods in major eastern
and midwestern us cities often have small colonies of these
goldfinches, managing to thrive even after being released
from caged life.

No. 082

Carpodacus synoicus

Sinai Rosefinch

● **LEAST CONCERN**

🐦 **COLLECTIVE NAMES**

Charm of finches | Trembling of finches | Trimming of finches

☀ **SYMBOLIC MEANING**

Jordanian national pride.

🌀 **POSSIBLE POWERS**

Adaptability; Tenacity.

🐦 **FOLKLORE AND FACTS**

With a name that includes one of the most sacred sites of
three of the world's major religions, we might assume that
this little pink finch and his sand-colored spouse would have
major symbolic significance. Oddly enough, beyond being
named the national bird of Jordan—and then only because it
lives there in abundance—the Sinai Rosefinch seems to be a
common bird that minds its own business. It lives largely in
nature preserves and hot desert areas in the Sinai Peninsula,
making its home in Egypt, Israel, Jordan, Palestine, and
Saudi Arabia, and it happens to be about the same color
as the stone from which the historic "Rose City" of Petra
in southern Jordan was carved. This made it particularly
appropriate to serve as its national bird.

No. 083

Casuarius

Cassowary

Casuarius | Dwarf Cassowary |
Flightless Bird | Northern Cassowary |
Ratite | Southern Cassowary

● **LEAST CONCERN**

🐦 **COLLECTIVE NAME**

Shock of cassowaries.

☀ **SYMBOLIC MEANING**

Standing firm against adversity.

🌀 **POSSIBLE POWER**

Shutting out negative influences.

🐦 **FOLKLORE AND FACTS**

Yes, it's true that Cassowaries are among the most aggressive
and dangerous birds in the world—but only if you make them
angry. These three species of tall, flightless, fruit-eating birds
usually spend their lives deep in the rainforests of Papua
New Guinea and nearby smaller islands, avoiding humans
and keeping to themselves, so they have little need or reason
to confront people. They do learn to defend their territory
as soon as they reach reproductive age, however, and
females are especially intolerant of one another, exhibiting
aggressive behavior as soon as another female steps into
range. • What makes these birds so frightening? First, their
size: The Southern Cassowary is the third-largest living bird,
dwarfed only by the ostrich and emu. Cassowaries have a
large protuberance called a casque on the top of their heads,
making them appear quite threatening, though the birds
use it to delve through leaf litter and underbrush as they
search for food, not for defense. Some scientists believe the
casque also amplifies the bird's low, deep voice. Folklorists

C

suggest that the casque wards off bad influences, whatever those may be for a bird. • Of all the scary things about these birds, the most frightening of all is the knife-like claw on their middle toe, the weapon that they tend to employ in confrontations with humans. Ornithologist Ernest Thomas Gillard described it in 1958 as "a long, straight, murderous nail which can sever an arm or eviscerate an abdomen with ease." While abdominal injuries from a Cassowary attack are uncommon, they can be deadly. Cassowaries will stand their ground and strike if provoked.

as the third book of the Torah lays out the dietary laws that became the kashrut doctrine, listing the vulture, kite, eagle, osprey, and others: "They shall not be eaten, they are an abomination" (Leviticus 11:14). Deuteronomy underscores this command (14:13), just in case we didn't get it the first time. This dogma gave the vulture its "unclean" label, piling on later in the New Testament (Revelation 18:2) by sentencing the vulture to the fallen city of Babylon as it becomes "the hold of every foul spirit, and a cage of every unclean and hateful bird."

No. 084

Cathartes aura

Turkey Vulture

Carrion Crow | John Crow | Turkey Buzzard

● **LEAST CONCERN**

🐾 **COLLECTIVE NAMES**

Colony of vultures | Committee of vultures | Kettle of vultures | Wake of vultures

✴ **SYMBOLIC MEANINGS**

Death; Rebirth.

🌀 **POSSIBLE POWERS**

Clearing dead animals from the environment; Neutralizing pathogens.

☘ **FOLKLORE AND FACTS**

The circling of vultures serves as instant foreshadowing in dozens of Western-genre films, letting the audience know that the characters plodding across the vast, parched desert look like a tasty meal to the waiting carrion-eaters. The specter of Turkey Vultures actually following

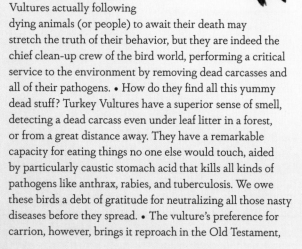

dying animals (or people) to await their death may stretch the truth of their behavior, but they are indeed the chief clean-up crew of the bird world, performing a critical service to the environment by removing dead carcasses and all of their pathogens. • How do they find all this yummy dead stuff? Turkey Vultures have a superior sense of smell, detecting a dead carcass even under leaf litter in a forest, or from a great distance away. They have a remarkable capacity for eating things no one else would touch, aided by particularly caustic stomach acid that kills all kinds of pathogens like anthrax, rabies, and tuberculosis. We owe these birds a debt of gratitude for neutralizing all those nasty diseases before they spread. • The vulture's preference for carrion, however, brings it reproach in the Old Testament,

No. 085

Catharus guttatus

Hermit Thrush

American Nightingale

● **LEAST CONCERN**

🐾 **COLLECTIVE NAME**

Mutation of thrushes.

✴ **SYMBOLIC MEANINGS**

Honesty; Personal renewal.

🌀 **POSSIBLE POWERS**

Communication; Survival.

☘ **FOLKLORE AND FACTS**

The Oneida people of upstate New York tell us the story of the Hermit Thrush: Long ago, birds did not have the ability to sing, but humans did. The Creator, on a visit to Earth, walked through the forest for a time and noted the silence there, when suddenly the people in the nearby settlement began to sing. He saw the birds in the forest stop to listen, and he realized that the birds should be able to sing as well. • The Creator called the birds together from all over the world and told them that the next morning at dawn, they must fly upward as far as they could go. When they had reached the limit of their personal flight, they would find their own song there. The bird that flew the highest would receive the most beautiful song. Then he disappeared. • The next morning, as the little Hermit Thrush stood next to the eagle, he looked at the much larger bird and thought, "I'll never fly higher than he will." Suddenly he had an idea—while the eagle was busy preening, the thrush jumped onto the eagle's head and hid in its feathers. • The sun rose and the birds took flight. Soon the smaller birds began to run out of strength, and they received simple songs of just one set of notes. The thrush's eagle, however, kept flying with just a few other birds, and they flew into the night. When the eagle finally tired and started to turn back, the well-rested thrush hopped off his head and started to fly upward. He soon heard a beautiful song, and he learned it note for note. He rushed back to the Earth's surface to show off his song ... but when he arrived, all the other birds knew what he had done. The little thrush turned tail and flew into the woods. To this day, he hides in the woods, singing alone in shame, even though the other birds all fall silent to listen to his beautiful song.

No. 086

Catherpes mexicanus

Canyon Wren

● **LEAST CONCERN**

COLLECTIVE NAMES
Cabinet of wrens | Chime of wrens | Flock of wrens

✳ **SYMBOLIC MEANINGS**
Confidence; Perseverance; Resilience.

◎ **POSSIBLE POWERS**
Cloud spirit; Courage; Revealing life's secrets.

◉ **FOLKLORE AND FACTS**
Perhaps it's the Canyon Wren's ability to thrive in steep, rocky, seemingly barren places, or maybe the bird's melodious song enchants those who share the deserts with this cheeky little bird. Whatever made it special to the Hopi people of the American southwest and Mexico, the Canyon Wren's likeness became one of the kachina dolls fashioned by the Hopi to help educate young girls about their responsibilities in life. The wren embodies Turposkwa, the war kachina, one of many kachinas that represent birds in the Hopi tradition. Hopi people use bird feathers in the decoration of many of these dolls, honoring familiar birds as cloud spirits. • When wrens appear in Native American stories, they often demonstrate uncommon courage, resourcefulness, and pluck. One story is part of the Hopi emergence myth, the ascent by the Hopi people from three successive underground worlds to the surface, known as the Fourth World. Several different birds attempted to fly to the top of the Third World to find the hole that opened the way to the Fourth World. Crow, Eagle, and others flew as high and as far as they could, but they could not reach the hole. Then a wren stepped up to give it a try, and its speed and small size allowed it to fly all the way to the top, where it found the hole. The people then climbed a reed that a chipmunk had planted for this purpose, and emerged into the light.

No. 087

Centrocercus urophasianus

Greater Sage-Grouse

Sagehen

● **NEAR THREATENED**

COLLECTIVE NAMES
Brace of grouse (two birds) | Brood of grouse | Covey of grouse

✳ **SYMBOLIC MEANINGS**
Adaptability; Family; Justice.

◎ **POSSIBLE POWER**
Warning of environmental changes.

◉ **FOLKLORE AND FACTS**
Birders in the American West crowd into birding blinds before dawn on chilly March mornings to see the crazy mating dance of Greater Sage-Grouse on leks—places where male birds gather to show off for interested females. Males fan their tails, take great gulps of air, inflate two large sacs on their chests, and let out a booming sound that females apparently find irresistible. This can go on for hours until the females choose their mate—and the entire female population may select just one male, making the strongest and most attractive bird the sire of an entire generation of young. • Grouse appear often in Native American mythology, though early English translations usually called the birds partridges, which did not arrive in North America until the 1800s. The symbolism of Greater Sage-Grouse, however, becomes most powerful in present-day America. Greater Sage-Grouse is the only grouse species that eats sage—a difficult plant to bite off, chew, and digest, but that nonetheless serves as the staple of the bird's diet. Recently, invasive cheatgrass has spread throughout sagebrush prairies, crowding out the sage and reducing the birds' food supply. Equally problematic, the arrival of oil wells, mining operations, and wind farms in sage-grouse habitat has driven away birds, as these tall structures become roosting points for birds of prey. • Greater Sage-Grouse is now an "indicator species," warning of impending disaster as its livable habitat disappears. After surviving all kinds of environmental changes for tens of millions of years, fewer than 200,000 birds remain in the wild today, down from 16 million before widespread development took hold in the American West.

C

No. 088

Ceyx erithaca

Oriental Dwarf Kingfisher

Black-Backed Kingfisher | Flying Rainbow |
Rufous Dwarf Kingfisher | Three-Toed Kingfisher

● **LEAST CONCERN**

✻ **COLLECTIVE NAMES**
Concentration of kingfishers | Crown of
kingfishers

✳ **SYMBOLIC MEANINGS**
Fidelity; Good luck; Love; Potential failure.

🌀 **POSSIBLE POWERS**
Good luck; Harbinger of wealth to come; Predictor of failure.

🎔 **FOLKLORE AND FACTS**
Is it one species or two? The Oriental Dwarf Kingfisher
appears to have two very different color morphs: One, the
rainbow of pink, coral, golden, and violet that makes it such a
jewel of Southeast Asia; and two, a more muted plumage with
a black back. A 2010 study suggested that while the two forms
were separated by geography, they were nonetheless the same
bird genetically. • This glittering little bird has no specific
mythology of its own, but kingfishers in general play a role in
the superstitions of their region. In Bengal, for example, if a
person hears a kingfisher's call on their right, they will have
good luck; if the bird calls on their left, whatever project the
person has taken on will fail. Some Southeast Asian cultures
associate kingfishers with love and fidelity, while others
consider it a sign of good fortune and wealth to come.

No. 089

Chaetura pelagica

Chimney Swift

Devil's Bird | Flying Cigar

● **THREATENED**

✻ **COLLECTIVE NAMES**
Flock of swifts | Scream of swifts

✳ **SYMBOLIC MEANING**
Summertime.

🌀 **POSSIBLE POWERS**
Adaptability to human habitat; Continuous flight;
Long-distance migration.

🎔 **FOLKLORE AND FACTS**
For a bird that uses human-made shelter as its primary roost,
we know precious little about the Chimney Swift. We aren't
certain which insects it eats—Chimney Swifts fly all day
without stopping, bobbing and swooping to catch bugs in
the air, and their flight is so swift (hence the name) that they
devour the insects before we can see what they are. We know
that these eastern North American nesters deftly replaced
their preferred nesting habitat—hollow tree trunks—with
human-constructed chimneys and smokestacks when
development wiped out old-growth forests. Perhaps most
significantly, we know that these swifts' legs make horizontal
perching impossible, as they have adapted to grasping
the inside wall of a chimney as they roost overnight.
• The discovery of Chimney Swifts' wintering ground along
the Amazon River in South America has all the makings
of a folk tale, but it's actually true: Scientists struggled to
find where these birds spent the winter until Indigenous
peoples along the Amazon netted themselves some swifts
and served them up for dinner. As they ate, they discovered
tiny metal loops that stuck in their molars—what turned
out to be bands on the birds' legs. Curious about what these
might mean, they took them to a local missionary, who
sent them on to the U.S. Fish and Wildlife Service (USFWS)
in Washington, DC. USFWS tracked down the banding site:
New Haven, Connecticut. The working ornithologists there
connected the dots and filled in the gap in their knowledge,
opening the door to further research on swifts' long-distance
migration to South America.

No. 090

Charadrius sanctaehelenae

Saint Helena Plover

Wirebird

● **VULNERABLE**

✻ **COLLECTIVE NAMES**
Band of plovers | Congregation of plovers | Stand of plovers | Wing of plovers

✳ **SYMBOLIC MEANING**
National pride in Saint Helena island.

🌀 **POSSIBLE POWER**
Resilience.

🎔 **FOLKLORE AND FACTS**
In the middle of the southern Atlantic Ocean, a thousand
miles off the coasts of Africa and South America, a tiny island
once hosted nine bird species found there and nowhere else
on Earth. Today, the Saint Helena Plover is the only one that
remains, so it serves as the island's national bird, appearing

on its flag and coat of arms and on the back of the 5-pence coin (until 1998). • Here the "wirebird," so-called because of its spindly black legs, struggles to maintain its population, falling prey to feral and domestic cats, rats that arrived as stowaways on ships from the mainland, and changes in livestock grazing patterns that have made the birds' habitat inhospitable. Saint Helena Plovers feed on insects, grubs, and caterpillars they find on the ground, and they nest on the ground as well, so cattle hooves become weapons against them. By 2006, just 250 of these birds remained on the island. • Today, significant efforts are underway to save the remaining plovers and allow them to increase their own population. A program to capture cats, as well as changes in livestock grazing areas and signs at the Saint Helena airport that warn drivers to steer clear of birds on the roads all have an impact. • Estimates show that Saint Helena Plover numbers are on the rise, with as many as 350 birds counted in recent years. It's a long way back from the brink, but it's heading in the right direction.

No. 091

Charadrius vociferus

Killdeer

Chattering Plover | Noisy Plover

● **LEAST CONCERN**

☙ **COLLECTIVE NAMES**

Band of plovers | Congregation of plovers | Stand of plovers | Wing of plovers

✺ **SYMBOLIC MEANINGS**

Avoid negative cohorts; Defend at all costs.

✺ **POSSIBLE POWERS**

Creating drama; Skilled at deception.

✺ **FOLKLORE AND FACTS**

Killdeer get their name from their whistling, two-syllable call, a piercing cry of *kill-DEER, kill-DEER* that every beginning birder commits to memory. The only large plover with two wide, dark rings around its neck and a rust-colored rump, Killdeer dominate the open fields and mudflats across North America in spring and summer. • When a bird regularly nests in the middle of parking lots, pastures, and open fields, it needs to have some tricks up its proverbial sleeve to keep its eggs and chicks safe. The Killdeer's method of protection is legendary among common birds: The parent bird flies in front of a potential raider to get the animal's attention, and then feigns an injury to a wing, dragging it alongside its body as the animal notices and starts to follow it. The Killdeer keeps up this deception until the parent bird has lured the enemy well away from its nest, and then suddenly flies off, leaving the animal baffled by the loss of what looked like easy prey. • Given its propensity for pasture nesting, the Kildeer also needs a way to scare off grazing cattle and horses. For this task, the bird puffs itself up, raises its wings and its tail over its head, and rushes toward the cow or horse. Chances are good that the startled animal will turn away from the bird, saving the eggs to hatch another day.

No. 092

Chordeiles minor

Common Nighthawk

Bugeater | Bullbat | Goatsucker | Mosquito Hawk | Nightjar

● **LEAST CONCERN**

☙ **COLLECTIVE NAME**

A kettle of nighthawks

✺ **SYMBOLIC MEANINGS**

Moon; Native American identity; Transitions.

✺ **POSSIBLE POWERS**

Silent flight; Stealth.

✺ **FOLKLORE AND FACTS**

If you are puzzled by the "goatsucker" nickname attributed to nighthawks of all kinds, the explanation for this is almost as bizarre as the name itself. Cattle farmers of old believed that nighthawks visited their cows and goats in the dead of night and drank their milk directly from the animal, the birds' short, wide bills seeming perfectly suited for this. Nighthawks don't do this and never did—in fact, they are insect eaters who catch bugs on the wing. If farmers actually saw these birds near their cattle, they were probably performing a much-needed service by catching the insects that buzzed around their livestock. • The Blackfoot people can explain where nighthawks got their oddly shaped bill and wide mouth. It seems that Old Man, one of the key characters in Blackfoot folklore, got so cold one night that he borrowed a robe from a large rock, and then refused to return it. The rock became angry and began to roll downhill toward Old Man. He called out to the nighthawks for help, and they came and destroyed the rock—but then, in a strange reversal, Old Man decided that he was having fun with the rock and the nighthawks had spoiled it for him. In retaliation, he tore off their bills and split their mouths unnaturally wide, giving them the features that they have today. The nighthawks got back at him, however, by defecating on his bald head as they flew off.

C

Chrysolophus pictus

Golden Pheasant

Chinese Pheasant | Rainbow Pheasant

● **LEAST CONCERN**

✷ **COLLECTIVE NAMES**

Bevy of pheasants | Bouquet of pheasants | Creche of pheasants | Head of pheasants | Nide of pheasants

✹ **SYMBOLIC MEANINGS**

Authority; Beauty; Power.

✺ **POSSIBLE POWERS**

Bestowing of rank; Majesty.

☾ **FOLKLORE AND FACTS**

The word most often used to describe the Golden Pheasant's plumage is "unmistakable"—its crimson chest and underside, golden head and back, and magnificent tail could not belong to any other bird. It's no wonder that this flamboyant creature represents power and majesty in its native China, and that it is one of the most desired species for exotic bird collectors—especially because trapping and transporting them out of their native forest habitat is illegal. • Despite its spectacular plumage, the Golden Pheasant is a shy bird that skulks among the trees and shrubs in northwestern China, dashing away from any disturbance—unless they sense a threat to a female. The Golden Pheasant finds its courage then, fluffing up the ruff around its neck and charging into battle. • Back in the days of the Song Dynasty (960–1279), pheasant feathers decorated the robes of high-ranking women. The Ming Dynasty (1368–1644) changed that tradition, instead having their robes embroidered with emblems of the birds. Emperor Yong Zheng (1725–1735) had the birds painted on porcelain, which brought them to the attention of visiting Europeans; by the end of the emperor's reign, English people brought the birds home with them. Not long after, Golden Pheasants were transported to North America and raised there in captivity as well. • Today several continents have small feral populations of these birds, but most of us have a better chance of seeing them in zoos.

Ciconia ciconia

White Stork

African White Stork | European White Stork

● **LEAST CONCERN**

✷ **COLLECTIVE NAMES**

Flight of storks | Mustering of storks | Phalanx of storks

✹ **SYMBOLIC MEANINGS**

Birth; Fertility; Happiness; Peace.

✺ **POSSIBLE POWER**

Bridge between material and spiritual world.

☾ **FOLKLORE AND FACTS**

Few birds are as welcome a sight to people on four continents as the White Stork, a pure-white, long-legged wading bird with black wing tips, a bright red bill, and red legs. As the unofficial national bird of Ukraine, it has risen to prominence there in the days of war with Russia, with flocks of them dotting open fields and farmlands. White Storks are a fixture in the entire Eastern European region, with large populations gracing hillsides and pastures. • Stork symbolism goes back to the earliest mythologies of Egypt, where a White Stork represents Ba, a bridge between the material and spiritual worlds, sometimes interpreted as the soul. In ancient Greece, storks were said to take care of their own, with young birds looking after the elders and making certain they were fed. One story even suggests that a young stork will carry an aged stork on its back, a gesture of the birds' commitment to honoring their ancestors. • Aesop tells us of a stork that makes the mistake of landing among a group of cranes that a bird catcher is trying to trap. When the stork begs him to release her, claiming that while the cranes are destructive to his crops, she is harmless, the bird catcher scoffs. "If you are so harmless, why do you land here among the wicked?" he asks. He does not spare her, associating her with her companions. The moral here is clear: Stay away from people with whom you do not want to be associated, or their misdeeds will be attributed to you.

No. 095

Cinclus cinclus

White-Throated Dipper

British Dipper | Central European Dipper | Dipper | European Dipper | Irish Dipper |
Northern White-Throated Dipper | Water Ouzel | Wee Water Hen

● **LEAST CONCERN**

✿ **COLLECTIVE NAME**

Ladle of dippers

✴ **SYMBOLIC MEANINGS**

Hardiness; Norwegian pride.

✺ **POSSIBLE POWERS**

Adaptability; Ingenuity.

☘ **FOLKLORE AND FACTS**

How does an unassuming
little brown bird with a white
throat become the national bird
of Norway? The White-Throated
Dipper represents many qualities

that Norwegians admire and respect: Its ability to withstand
cold temperatures in northern Europe's rivers and streams;
its extra protections that allow it to open its eyes underwater
and to nourish its body and lungs with oxygen as it swims; its
fearlessness in diving headfirst into chilly waters. Using the
harsh conditions around it to its best advantage, the White-
Throated Dipper typifies what it is to live through a winter
in Norway. • While the Norwegians have staked their claim
to this swimming songbird, English and Irish sources wax
eloquent about the dipper's tenacity in its nesting habits.
Dippers love to nest in human-made structures close to
water, choosing bridges, weirs, embankments, cowsheds, and
in one case, on the wheel of an active mill. Nesting dippers
have been found in an abandoned car partially submerged
in a river, inside a fish hatchery building, and on the edge
of a waterway even after the nest, eggs, and bird had been
inundated with flood waters. Whether this behavior makes
them a symbol of hardiness or stubbornness, however, may
be up to the individual observer.

No. 096

Cinclus mexicanus

American Dipper

Water Ouzel | Water Thrush

● **LEAST CONCERN**

✿ **COLLECTIVE NAMES**

Ladle of dippers

✴ **SYMBOLIC MEANINGS**

Decisiveness; Hidden talent; Individuality.

✺ **POSSIBLE POWER**

Adaptations for swimming underwater.

☘ **FOLKLORE AND FACTS**

So much about the American Dipper is fascinating and
unusual that it hardly needs folklore to give it nearly magical
powers. The five species of dippers found around the world
are the only songbirds that can immerse themselves in
water and swim, thanks to several evolutionary adaptations:
An extra eyelid closes when they are submerged, allowing
them to see underwater. Scales across their nostrils close
as they dive, keeping water out while they swim. Even
more remarkable, dippers' blood retains more oxygen than
any other songbird's circulatory system, allowing them
to hold their breath and remain underwater for several
minutes. Finally, they have adapted to cooler climates—in
the American Dipper's case, to areas west of the Rocky
Mountains, the Pacific Northwest, and Alaska. • This
nondescript gray bird's astonishing talents drew great
admiration from naturalist John Muir, who wrote an entire
chapter of his 1894 book *The Mountains of California* to
the little swimmer. About the bird he called Water Ouzel,
he wrote, "No cañon is too cold for this little bird, none too
lonely, provided it be rich in falling water. Find a fall, or
cascade, or rushing rapid, anywhere upon a clear stream,
and there you will surely find
its complementary Ouzel,
flitting about in the
spray, diving in foaming
eddies, whirling like a leaf
among beaten foam-bells; ever
vigorous and enthusiastic, yet self-
contained, and neither seeking nor
shunning your company."

C

No. 097
Cinnyris
Sunbird

Hummingbird

● **LEAST CONCERN**

🐾 **COLLECTIVE NAME**

Flock of sunbirds.

☀ **SYMBOLIC MEANINGS**

Freedom; Movement.

🌀 **POSSIBLE POWERS**

Control of the sun; Speed.

☾ **FOLKLORE AND FACTS**

Tiny, nectar-eating birds that resemble the hummingbirds of the Americas, the fifty-six species of sunbirds in this genus usually have bright-colored bibs with a band of feathers in a contrasting color, making them especially stunning in sunlight. They have many of the same abilities as hummingbirds, hovering to feed at cup-shaped flowers, dipping into specific flowers with a bill evolved for that flower's shape, and flying at high speed to elude potential predators. • Sunbirds appear in the mythology of Zimbabwe's Shona people. Dzivaguru, goddess of the cycle of day and night, released two golden sunbirds every morning so the sun would rise, and brought the sunbirds back at the end of the day to lower the sun. The people loved Dzivaguru and worshipped her for her kindness and benevolence, but one day Nosenga, the son of the sky god, became jealous of Dzivaguru's wealth and her beautiful palace, and he decided to unseat her. Dzivaguru caught on to his plan, however, and created fog so he could not see his way to her lands. Nosenga outsmarted her: he acquired a magic ribbon that allowed him to see through the fog. Once he arrived in her land, Nosenga trapped her two sunbirds and brought up the sun, revealing all to him. He took her wealth and lands and sent her packing. • Dzivaguru had one more trick before she departed: she took her lake with her, maintaining control over water and rain throughout Africa. "You stole my sunbirds, so you will have nothing but sun," she said to him. "Now I will withhold the rain. Your land will be parched and dry, and the water will dry up. The people will hate you." So she vanished, and her promise came true: There is almost no rain in her lands, and Dzivaguru has not shown her face there again.

No. 098
Circus approximans
Swamp Harrier

Australasian Harrier | Australasian Marsh Harrier | Harrier Hawk | Kāhu | Swamp-Hawk

● **LEAST CONCERN**

🐾 **COLLECTIVE NAMES**

Cast of harriers | Harassment of harriers | Swarm of harriers

☀ **SYMBOLIC MEANINGS**

Boldness; Cleverness; Discernment.

🌀 **POSSIBLE POWER**

Speed and accuracy in hunting.

☾ **FOLKLORE AND FACTS**

By some measurements, the Swamp Harrier is the largest living harrier in the world—but that may be based on a few particularly large individuals, so other species may make the same claim. This does not make the Swamp Harrier's low, slow hunting glide over a marsh any less impressive, however, its wings held above its body at a slight dihedral as it watches for small mammals, ground birds, and reptiles to devour. • New Zealanders and Australians share an ambivalence about this bird because of its rapier-like ability to kill and eat domestic chickens, ducks, and pheasants. The Swamp Harrier has also been known to raid the nests of New Zealand Falcons; while this may be undesirable in the eyes of falcon lovers, it has not seriously affected falcon numbers within that nation. • Māori mythology of New Zealand tells us how the Swamp Harrier, known as Kāhu, came to have its reddish underside. Māui, a demigod in Māori mythology, brought fire to the world by stealing it from the fingernails of Mahuika, the goddess of fire. This enraged Mahuika, and she threw a burning toenail to the ground and ignited a fire on the mountain. Māui managed to escape the flames by transforming himself into Kāhu, the Swamp Harrier, and flying above the fire—but he flew so close to the flames that the underside of his wings were singed, and forever remain a warm, glowing rufous color.

No. 099

Clangula hyemalis

Long-Tailed Duck

● **VULNERABLE**

🎋 **COLLECTIVE NAMES**

Badelynge of ducks | Plump of ducks |
Raft of ducks (when on water)

☀ **SYMBOLIC MEANINGS**

Chattiness; Friendliness.

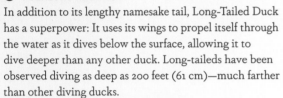

🌀 **POSSIBLE POWER**

Deepwater diving.

🐦 **FOLKLORE AND FACTS**

In addition to its lengthy namesake tail, Long-Tailed Duck has a superpower: It uses its wings to propel itself through the water as it dives below the surface, allowing it to dive deeper than any other duck. Long-taileds have been observed diving as deep as 200 feet (61 cm)—much farther than other diving ducks.

No. 100

Coccyzus americanus

Yellow-Billed Cuckoo

Rain Crow | Storm Crow

● **LEAST CONCERN**

🎋 **COLLECTIVE NAMES**

Chorus of cuckoos | Deceit of cuckoos | Flight of cuckoos

☀ **SYMBOLIC MEANING**

Marital infidelity.

🌀 **POSSIBLE POWER**

Forecaster of rain.

🐦 **FOLKLORE AND FACTS**

The knocking *ka-ka-ka-ka-ka-kow, kow, kow, kow, kowp, kowp,* call of a Yellow-Billed Cuckoo on a hot, humid summer day can only mean one thing: it's about to rain. Heard but much more rarely seen, this cuckoo sits quietly in one place for hours at a time as it belts out its descending, rapid-then-slow call through the still woods. On such a day, it doesn't take a folkloric forecaster to tell us that rain is imminent—chances are we can figure that out on our own—but more often than not, the cuckoo's prediction comes true, so the superstition persists. • Brown-mantled, white-chested, with a yellow bill and a distinctively long tail marked underneath with wide white

ovals, the Yellow-Billed Cuckoo is a much-coveted sight among birders. This secretive bird feeds on tent caterpillars and the larvae of spongy and brown-tailed moths, as well as hopping insects like cicadas, locusts, and katydids, so the best way to find one is to seek out areas where these tasty treats are in abundance. This guarantees nothing, however, as cuckoos shroud themselves deep in leafy oak, ash, hawthorn, willow, and beech trees and build nests as much as 90 feet (27 meters) up. Birders' best bet is patience, finding a place with plenty of insects on the ground, and waiting for the birds to reveal themselves with furtive movements. If you're very lucky, a cuckoo will drop to the dirt to feast on a grasshopper, giving you an unobstructed view.

No. 101

Coereba flaveola

Bananaquit

Beany Bird | Honey-Creeper | See-See Bird | Sikyé-bird | Sugar Bird | Yellow-Breast

● **LEAST CONCERN**

🎋 **COLLECTIVE NAME**

Flock of bananaquits

☀ **SYMBOLIC MEANINGS**

Joy; Love; Sweetness.

🌀 **POSSIBLE POWERS**

Good luck; Happiness; Romance.

🐦 **FOLKLORE AND FACTS**

Lots of birds love sweets, but few are named for the sweets they love. The Bananaquit takes its name in part from its partiality to ripe bananas, a fruit it can usually find in abundance in its native West Indian and South American habitats. It also comes readily to nectar feeders and to bowls of granulated sugar, so residents who can stomach the ants that a bowl of sugar draws can enjoy plenty of little yellow birds at their feeders. • The Bananaquit's name is further validated by its banana-yellow-colored breast and underside, topped with a black mantle and set off by the bird's gray (or white) throat, downward-curving bill, and dark head with a wide white eyebrow. Its plumage varies widely with whatever region the bird may be found—no less than forty-one subspecies exist, with one that's almost completely black from head to tail. • As common and widespread as this bird is, the Bananaquit has surprisingly little folklore or mythology associated with it. In some Caribbean cultures, a Bananaquit visit can mean good luck and happiness for the household. Its fondness for sugary nectar also brings a connection to romance, love, and all the sweetness that comes with this.

C

No. 102

Colaptes auratus

Northern Flicker

Red-shafted Flicker | Yellowhammer |
Yellow-Shafted Flicker

● **LEAST CONCERN**

✤ **COLLECTIVE NAMES**

Guttering of flickers | Menorah of flickers

✹ **SYMBOLIC MEANINGS**

Authenticity; Healing;
Individuality; Self-expression.

✺ **POSSIBLE POWERS**

Good fortune in battle; Protection for warriors.

☾ **FOLKLORE AND FACTS**

The widespread and much-loved Northern Flicker has
a place in many different Native American traditions,
serving as a symbol of good luck and individuality in several
cultures. • The Lenape people tell a story of a maple tree that
became infested with insects, so the tree found itself feeling
very itchy in places it could not reach. The tree called on all
the creatures in the forest for help, but each noted that if they
started digging in the tree's bark, the tree would be damaged
and probably die. At last a flicker came to the tree and said,
"I will bring all of my cousins, and we can use our bills to
eat the insects, and you will not be harmed." This gave the
maple some relief, and it was very grateful. Then a drought
came, and all the animals called on the maple tree for help.
The tree called to the flicker again and said, "Peck deep into
my bark, and I will send out sap for the animals to drink."
The flicker did so, and the animals had sap to drink until the
next rain. • In the American West, the red undertail shafts of
the Northern Flicker have significance to many Indigenous
Peoples. Some say that finding one of these feathers means
that good tidings are on their way, especially among a group
of friends. • The Pueblo used these feathers as symbols of
war, while Indigenous Peoples in Taos placed red flicker
feathers in the mountains as an offering to the Red Bear, the
protector of warriors.

No. 103

Colinus virginianus

Northern Bobwhite

Bobwhite Quail | Virginia Partridge

● **NEAR THREATENED**

✤ **COLLECTIVE NAMES**

Covey of bobwhites | Name dropping of bobwhites

✹ **SYMBOLIC MEANINGS**

Family; Parental care of children.

✺ **POSSIBLE POWERS**

Inspiring maternal/paternal instinct.

☾ **FOLKLORE AND FACTS**

The song rises up from an open grassland, agricultural field,
or shortgrass prairie: A simple, clear, two-syllable *bob-white,
bob-white*. Just one bird sings this song: The Northern
Bobwhite, a roly-poly-looking game bird with a bright black
and white face in males. • It hides itself in tall grasses and
stays still for hours at a time. • Only a few Native American
tribes tell stories about this little quail—and then only as a
player in another animal's story. The Ojibwa call the bird
mush-do-da-sa, "the meadow bird," and note its involvement
in the buffalo getting its hump. The buffalo ran with the
foxes across western prairies, paying no attention to where its
hooves fell—crushing countless bobwhite nests. Nanabozho,
a shape-shifter in Ojibwa mythology, blocked the buffalo and
made it stop running, and then hit the animal hard on
its back, producing a pronounced hump. "For treating
the bobwhite the way you have, you will always have a
hump on your shoulders," he informed the buffalo.
The foxes, meanwhile, feared what Nanabozho would do
to them, so they dug holes in the ground and hid from him.
He saw this and said, "You will always live in the
ground in holes, because you mistreated the bobwhite."
• The discovery of the remains of four Northern Bobwhites
in an earthlodge firepit at an archeological dig suggested
that the bobwhite played a role
in Pawnee religious ceremonial
practices. Anthropologists at the
site speculate that the bobwhite
represented family and the need to
care for children.

Coloeus monedula

Western Jackdaw

Eurasian Jackdaw | European Jackdaw | Jackdaw

● **LEAST CONCERN**

✿ **COLLECTIVE NAMES**

Clattering of jackdaws | Darkening of jackdaws | Train of jackdaws

✺ **SYMBOLIC MEANINGS**

Foolishness; Impending death; Rain; Vanity.

✺ **POSSIBLE POWER**

Good luck for a wedding.

☾ **FOLKLORE AND FACTS**

Black birds that look like small crows ("jack" is a synonym for small) with shorter bills, Western Jackdaws are widespread and numerous across Europe and throughout western Asia and northern Africa. Perhaps because they are so familiar to people in many locations and cultures, folklore about them abounds. • The ancient Greeks and Romans were fond of saying, "The swans will sing when the jackdaws are silent," meaning that the wise will speak only when the foolish run out of words. Greek folklore also tells us that if we put out a dish of oil, the jackdaw will see his reflection in it and fall right into it, a casualty of its own vanity. • Aesop took the jackdaw to task on many occasions, including in this fable: A starving jackdaw sat for days on the branch of a fig tree, looking at the green figs. A fox observed the bird sitting still for some time, so he asked, "Why do you sit there? I can see that you are hungry." The jackdaw replied, "I am waiting for the figs to ripen." The fox shook his head. "You're sitting there just hoping they will ripen. You are living on hope. Hope feeds illusions, but not the stomach." The moral: Appreciate what you have, and use it to sustain yourself.

Columba livia

Rock Pigeon

City Pigeon | Feral Pigeon | Rock Dove | Street Pigeon

● **LEAST CONCERN**

✿ **COLLECTIVE NAMES**

Flight of pigeons | Kit of pigeons | Loft of pigeons

✺ **SYMBOLIC MEANINGS**

Peace; Serenity.

✺ **POSSIBLE POWERS**

Carrying messages; Good fortune; Opportunism; Peace; Resilience.

☾ **FOLKLORE AND FACTS**

Today we may see the Rock Pigeon as a nuisance, gathering in massive flocks in a public square or messing up our monuments with their leavings. In times before cities became the pigeon's home, however, the Rock Pigeon served as a harbinger of peace and good fortune, whether it appeared in its gray mantle with its iridescent ruff, or in the pure white of the domestic variety (or in many variations). Rock Pigeons were released at coronations, and given as gifts of peace at negotiations. • Native to Europe, Africa, and Asia, the Rock Pigeon became one of the first domesticated birds, raised as food in Europe thousands of years ago, and eventually trained to be homing pigeons to transport messages during wartime. Many pigeons received the PDSA Dickin Medal in the UK for their service during World War II. • Pigeons first arrived in North America on colonists' ships in the early 1600s, and again as cities grew throughout the 1700s. Many of these escaped and formed colonies, populating cities as buildings provided high places to nest and people provided food scraps. Their omnivorous nature and adaptability soon made pigeons one of the commonest birds on the continent. • Aesop saw the Rock Pigeon's eagerness to forage particularly apropos in his tale of the thirsty pigeon. The pigeon saw a pail of water in a painting, but she could not understand what a painting was, so she dove head-first into it to try to drink the water. Instead of slaking her thirst, however, she broke her wings. The moral: Do not be carried away by passion; rash judgments can lead to ruin.

C

No. 106

Columbidae

Dove

344 species including Cuckoo-Doves |
Ground Doves | Pigeons

● **LEAST CONCERN**

✥ **COLLECTIVE NAMES**
Bevy of doves | Covey of doves | Dole of doves |
Paddling of doves | Piteousness of doves

✹ **SYMBOLIC MEANINGS**
Freedom; Love; Peace.

✺ **POSSIBLE POWERS**
Bringer of peace; Dependability; Fertility; Love; Loyalty;
Monogamy.

☙ **FOLKLORE AND FACTS**
No bird family is more storied and exalted than the Dove,
a bird whose mythological references date back to the
beginning of mythology itself. Doves are part of early
imagery in ancient Mesopotamia, where they served as
symbols of Inanna-Ishtar, goddess of love and war. In Syria,
one of the many legends of the enigmatic Semiramis suggests
that when her husband Nimrod died, a pair of doves brought
her milk and cheese until she could once again take care of
herself. • The Greek pantheon places doves in the myths of
Aphrodite, goddess of love, whose imagery often includes
doves because of their fertility and monogamous nature.
Roman goddesses of love Fortuna and Venus also associated
with the gentle, affectionate birds. From these early match-
ups between goddesses of love and their doves, we get the
expression "lovey-dovey." • A Dove played a central role
in the Old Testament story of Noah (Genesis 8:11). Noah
released a Dove as the waters receded at the end of the flood,
hoping that the bird would find land; sure enough, the Dove
returned with an olive leaf in its bill. The baptism of Jesus
features a Dove as well, in the leading role of God himself:
"And Jesus when he was baptized, went up straightway from
the water: and lo, the heavens were opened unto him, and
he saw the Spirit of God descending as a dove, and coming
upon him." (Matthew 3:16). Thanks to this passage, a white
Dove has become a symbol of the Holy Spirit.

No. 107

Copsychus saularis

Oriental Magpie-Robin

Dayal | Doel | Doyel Pakhi | Polkichcha

● **LEAST CONCERN**

✥ **COLLECTIVE NAMES**
Charm of magpies | Congregation of magpies | Tribe of magpies

✹ **SYMBOLIC MEANING**
Joy.

✺ **POSSIBLE POWER**
Adaptability.

☙ **FOLKLORE AND FACTS**
The black-and-white bird, with its melodious song and
its tail held erect, has captured the hearts of the people of
the Indian subcontinent and Southeast Asia. It became
the national bird of Bangladesh because it can be seen
anywhere in the country, especially in urban gardens—
making it an accessible symbol of national pride. Locals
call the bird *dayal* or *doel*, even naming a square in the city
of Dhaka "Doel Chattar" (Doel Square). • For centuries,
Oriental Magpie-Robins were trapped and kept as cage
birds throughout the region, and they continue to be sold in
Southeast Asia as pets—though an even more objectionable
practice of using these birds to fight one another for sport
has come to an end. Today the Magpie-Robin appears on
Bangladeshi currency, and its likeness shows up in many
places throughout the nation.

C

No. 108

Coracias caudatus

Lilac-Breasted Roller

Fork-Tailed Roller | Lilac-Throated Roller | Mosillikatze's Roller

● **LEAST CONCERN**

⚘ **COLLECTIVE NAME**
Flock of rollers

✴ **SYMBOLIC MEANINGS**
Joy; Optimism; Playfulness.

🌀 **POSSIBLE POWERS**
Fire magic; Multitasking; Optimism; Wisdom.

☉ **FOLKLORE AND FACTS**
When the multicolored burst of energy that is the Lilac-Breasted Roller comes into view, we can't help but attribute all kinds of happy omens to its presence. Folklorists, symbologists, and spiritualists all heap lots of different meanings on this stunning little bird, from fire magic to playfulness, from multitasking to mental acrobatics, and from wisdom to optimism and joy. • This jewel-like bird of sub-Saharan Africa feasts on crawling things including insects, spiders, centipedes, millipedes, snails, scorpions, lizards, small snakes, and even some birds, making it a scrapper that's not afraid of a struggle if it will end in getting what it wants. • The roller perches high up on top of trees to scan the ground for its prey, swooping in when the time is right and grabbing its target in its small bill. African tradition says that this ability to score on the wing teaches us how to get things done "on the fly," accomplishing much and solving problems as we encounter them. • Unmistakable with its bright purple throat and chest, aqua underside and undertail, aqua wings with a bright blue trailing edge, and long black streamers on its tail, the Lilac-Breasted Roller is often seen at the edge of brush fires, watching for all kinds of prey as it runs from the flames and grabbing it as the opportunity presents itself. The lesson the roller teaches, then, is to seize the day—no matter the circumstances, as even a bad situation can yield good results for someone.

No. 109

Coragyps atratus

Black Vulture

American Black Vulture | Gallinazo | Mexican Vulture | Urubu | Zopilote

● **LEAST CONCERN**

⚘ **COLLECTIVE NAMES**
Colony of vultures | Committee of vultures | Kettle of vultures | Wake of vultures

✴ **SYMBOLIC MEANINGS**
Change; Rebirth; Renewal.

🌀 **POSSIBLE POWERS**
Clearing of old issues; Neutralizing pathogens.

☉ **FOLKLORE AND FACTS**
Seeing a Black Vulture often frightens people who do not know much about these ominous-looking creatures, especially if they circle above in a "kettle" formation as they ride air thermals upward. The arrival of vultures need not signal an impending death—in fact, it's much more likely that their message is change and renewal, the clearing away of old issues (carrion, in the most literal sense) and making room for something new. • The Black Vulture's featherless gray head can seem particularly dismal, like a shriveled body rising from the dead, and a less-lifelike skin shade than the red head of its closest American relative, Turkey Vulture. It's important to keep in mind the good work that both of these vultures do throughout their range, from the United States down to Peru: They eat vast amounts of decaying flesh of dead animals on roadsides, in forests, and across the plains and deserts. This important service removes microscopic pathogens from our environment that can make humans very ill, but that digest harmlessly in a vulture's stomach, thanks to a supply of particularly caustic stomach chemistry. • Native American symbolism suggests that seeing three vultures at once has special significance: It may mean the universe itself is sending us a message of transformation. Three vultures can signify mind, body, and spirit; or past, present, and future, either of which calls for a hard look at the big picture that is a person's life. It may be time to explore an entirely new avenue, or to let go of the past (or other baggage) and move on to whatever is ahead.

C

Corvus brachyrhynchos

American Crow

Crow

● LEAST CONCERN

✦ COLLECTIVE NAMES

Caucus of crows | Congress of crows | Murder of crows

✦ SYMBOLIC MEANINGS

Bad luck; Death; Thievery.

✦ POSSIBLE POWERS

Bad or good omens; Making plans; Unmasking deception.

✦ FOLKLORE AND FACTS

Common, widespread, dark, and crafty-looking, the American Crow is one of the most intelligent birds studied to date, with the ability to make and use tools, develop object permanence, recognize human faces, demonstrate long-term episodic memory, and provide for its own future needs. Crows have been known to scold people they know for wearing masks or disguising themselves. Scientists believe that when two or more crows in one place are cawing to one another, they may well be talking about the humans in their proximity and planning around their presence.

• It's no wonder, then, that people anthropomorphize so much of crows' behavior. We believe them to be sneaky, to be looking for opportunities to cascade droppings on us, and to be ready to attack us if we happen to park in the vicinity of their overnight roosting areas. Many cultures believe that if a crow follows an individual or stares at them, it may be a warning for that person to pay more attention to their intuition than to what others have to say. • Crows are not always bad omen-bringers—they are just as likely to supply good news as bad, according to folklore. That watchful crow may actually be a guardian, helping you along your chosen path. Crows may warn of danger ahead, advising you to change your direction. The number of crows you see may also have meaning: A pair can bring good news, and three may bestow excellent health ... but five may warn that illness may soon take over your entire family.

Corvus corax

Common Raven

Raven

● LEAST CONCERN

✦ COLLECTIVE NAMES

Congress of ravens | Conspiracy of ravens | Crime of ravens | Parliament of ravens

✦ SYMBOLIC MEANINGS

Bad omens; Good omens.

✦ POSSIBLE POWERS

Communication between realms; Predicting the future.

✦ FOLKLORE AND FACTS

Common Ravens are among the most widespread bird species in the world, appearing throughout the northern hemisphere. This makes the large, all-black, croaking raven a symbol of many different things, from their association with the sun god Apollo in the Greek pantheon to their appearance in the Old Testament as one of the birds Noah released to find land after the flood. (The raven never reported back, leading some rabbinical scholars to believe the bird found corpses and was feeding on the dead.) The Jewish are forbidden to eat the "unclean" birds in Leviticus and Deuteronomy, while the Talmud notes that the raven copulated with its mate on the Ark, and therefore was punished by God. • The Qur'an includes a raven in the story of Cain and Abel—the bird taught Cain how to bury his brother so his murder would not be discovered.

• Slightly more recently, in the fourth century, ravens came to guard the body of Christian martyr Saint Vincent after his execution—and they continue to protect his grave to this day. • A raven stepped in to keep Saint Benedict of Nursia from eating a loaf of poisoned bread. • Viking, Welsh, Irish, and British mythology all include ravens in their legends, and in the mythologies of the Indigenous Peoples of the Pacific Northwest, the raven actually created the world. • Of course, no discussion of ravens can be complete without the foreshadowing bird of Edgar Allen Poe's most famous work, "The Raven," in which the sulky bird answers every question put to it with "Nevermore." This set the Common Raven's pace in the world's modern literature for the foreseeable (pardon the pun) future, leaving us with an involuntary shudder every time this big, black bird comes into view.

No. 112

Corvus frugilegus

Rook

Subspecies: Eastern Rook | Western Rook

● **LEAST CONCERN**

🦅 **COLLECTIVE NAMES**
Building of rooks | Parliament of rooks | Storytelling of rooks

✴ **SYMBOLIC MEANINGS**
Adaptability; Wide view.

🌀 **POSSIBLE POWERS**
Bad omens; Good omens; Scheming.

🐦 **FOLKLORE AND FACTS**
Most of the superstitions and folklore associated with crows actually began with the Rook, a large black corvid with a featherless white face and light-colored bill, who is a resident of Europe and Asia. For example, the expression "as the crow flies," meaning the straightest possible route between two points, actually originated with the direct flight of the Rook. • Scarecrows have been misnamed for centuries, as crows are carrion eaters and don't plunder farmers' crops; Rooks, on the other hand, have long been a nuisance bird of agricultural lands. As fruit eaters, they help themselves to some crops, particularly root vegetables that they dig up as they hunt in the earth for small rodents, worms, and grubs. Despite their long reputation as the bane of a farmer's existence, they actually clean up many pests that can harm crops. So here is just one of the ways that Rooks are both good and bad omens, signaling the preservation and destruction of crops at the same time. • Beyond their effect on cropland, the Rook is known for its scheming tendencies, leading to its name becoming derogatory slang: "rooking" a person out of their money or property. This may come from the bird's very real propensity for stealing nesting material right out of the nests of other birds. Its busy nesting colonies also took on negative connotations in nineteenth-century Britain, when overcrowded slums were known as rookeries.

No. 113

Corythaeola cristata

Great Blue Turaco

Blue Plantain Eater

● **LEAST CONCERN**

🦅 **COLLECTIVE NAME**
Flock of turacos

✴ **SYMBOLIC MEANING**
Good luck.

🌀 **POSSIBLE POWERS**
Guardian of the okapi; Messenger of the gods.

🐦 **FOLKLORE AND FACTS**
A bright royal blue or turquoise bird with a candy-corn bill and a dramatically raised black crest, the Great Blue Turaco attracts attention as soon as it arrives in its equatorial African habitat. • This fruit-eating bird also dines on buds, shoots, and leaves, so it finds all the food it needs in the wild, generally leaving human agricultural areas alone. In much of its habitat, this is probably a wise move for the bird; some local natives see Great Blue Turaco feathers as good luck charms, so they hunt the birds for their feathers (and their meat, an added bonus) and make talismans with them to ward off bad spirits and protect themselves from evil. • Among the native peoples of the Democratic Republic of the Congo, Mbuti members of the clan of the Great Blue Turaco cannot eat this bird. Turaco is one of the *ngini-so* ("things prohibited")—and if they do eat the bird, they believe that their teeth will fall out. This is incentive enough to leave the gorgeous creature alone, but the bird's apparent guardianship over the okapi, a deerlike animal, gives the turaco an even greater value in the wild. According to legend, Great Blue Turacos inform okapis of impending danger by calling vociferously when they spot an oncoming threat, and hovering in the treetops above the animals until the danger passes.

C

No. 114

Coturnix

Old World Quail

Common Quail | Harlequin Quail | Japanese Quail |
New Zealand Quail (extinct) | Rain Quail | Stubble Quail

- ● **NEAR THREATENED (JAPANESE QUAIL)**
- ● **EXTINCT (NEW ZEALAND QUAIL)**

COLLECTIVE NAMES
Bevy of quails | Covey of quails | Flush of quails

SYMBOLIC MEANINGS
Abundance; Contrition; Requited love.

POSSIBLE POWERS
Protection; Speed.

FOLKLORE AND FACTS
Five living quail, one recently extinct species, and perhaps as many as eight long-extinct species make up the genus *Coturnix*. These ground-loving birds do not sit in trees like their New World cousins, despite their ability to fly (and fly very fast). Instead, they spend their time on the ground, searching for seeds, grubs, and other small invertebrates as they scurry through tall grasses and densely packed shrubs.
• These small, round, pleasing birds have a place in mythology on all of the continents in the eastern hemisphere. Ancient Greece brings us the story of Asteria, daughter of Coeus (a Titan) and Phoebe, who managed to get herself turned into a quail to escape the sexual advances of Zeus.
• In Old Testament times, as the Jewish people followed Moses across the desert in search of the promised land, they found themselves without food and called out to God for help. When evening came, "the quails came up, and covered the camp," so the Jewish people had plenty of birds to eat (Exodus 16:13). Later, in Numbers, however, the Jewish incur God's wrath by refusing to take possession of the promised land, grumbling instead about the hardships of the desert—and this time God sends flocks of quails to feed them, but strikes them all down with a plague the very next day (Numbers 11:31–33). • More recently, overhunting of quail in spring has reduced the numbers of these little birds dramatically, with tens of thousands of birds falling prey daily to butchering and sport. Today, quail hunting is relegated to game farms throughout most of the birds' range.

No. 115

Crax alberti

Blue-Billed Curassow

Paujil

- ● **CRITICALLY ENDANGERED**

COLLECTIVE NAME
Stroll of curassows

SYMBOLIC MEANING
Gift of fire.

POSSIBLE POWERS
Courage; Endurance.

FOLKLORE AND FACTS
The large, coal-black Blue-Billed Curassow can only be seen in Northern Colombia, and then only in bird reserves in the lowland rainforest—and only by the very fortunate. In sharp contrast to its numbers when an English zoologist recorded its existence for science for the first time, this curassow's population now is estimated at fewer than one thousand birds—and maybe as few as 150. • At one time in their folkloric history, the Blue-Billed Curassow played an important role in humanity's development: They braved the wrath of the rainforest's jaguars, stole fire from them, and gifted it to the Colombians. In performing this courageous deed, the birds carried a burning log on their backs, and the flames scorched the feathers on their heads into short black curls, a badge of honor that they still wear as an impressive crest. • You might think that this deed would win the Blue-Billed Curassow the right to its own health, but a staggering 90 percent of the birds' natural habitat has been sacrificed to mining, ranching, logging, and coca and marijuana production. Their numbers leveled off during wartime, between 1965 and 2017, as deforestation halted, but today the birds' population continues to dwindle. A captive breeding program hopes to see success in releasing a few birds raised in zoos into the wild.

No. 116

Crypturellus undulatus

Undulated Tinamou

Jaó

● **LEAST CONCERN**

✿ **COLLECTIVE NAME**

Flock of tinamous

✴ **SYMBOLIC MEANINGS**

Overcoming obstacles; Serenity.

🌀 **POSSIBLE POWERS**

Concealment; Reconciliation.

☾ **FOLKLORE AND FACTS**

Found in a wide range of habitats throughout northern South America, this brown-gray ground bird blends so well with the sand or mud around it that it becomes virtually invisible, its presence revealed only by its monotonal three-part whistle. • The Undulated Tinamou is a member of the ratite family, meaning that its ancestors were the first to evolve into birds from the prehistoric creatures that preceded them. While nearly all ratites are flightless, this bird actually can fly—but not very well, so its camouflaging plumage and its ability to find places to hide become its most valuable defense. • According to Brazilian legend, the Undulated Tinamou's best friend was the Red-Winged Tinamou, but one day the two birds began to argue, and their disagreement became so heated that they flew off in opposite directions. The Undulated Tinamou headed into the darkest part of the forest, while the Red-Winged Tinamou hurried off into the grasses of the plains. As is often the case between close friends, the Undulated Tinamou began to miss his constant companion, so he came out to the edge of the forest and whistled a plaintive three-note song, "Let's make up?" The Red-Winged Tinamou replied, "What? Not me, never!" To this day, the two birds call the same messages to one another, but they rarely show themselves outside of their own habitats.

No. 117

Cuculus canorus

Common Cuckoo

European Cuckoo

● **LEAST CONCERN**

✿ **COLLECTIVE NAMES**

Chorus of cuckoos | Deceit of cuckoos | Flight of cuckoos

✴ **SYMBOLIC MEANING**

First sign of spring.

🌀 **POSSIBLE POWER**

Recognizing marital infidelity.

☾ **FOLKLORE AND FACTS**

What a precarious line the Common Cuckoo walks in literature and in the minds of men: On one hand, the cuckoo's call heralds the much-anticipated arrival of spring; but on the other hand, its song in spring may mean that the man hearing it has an unfaithful wife, making him a cuckold—a word with "cuckoo" at its root. As William Shakespeare wrote in *Love's Labours Lost*: "The cuckoo then, on every tree, mocks married men; for thus sings he: 'Cuckoo! Cuckoo, cuckoo!' O, word of fear, unpleasing to a married ear!" • Fortunately, the cuckoo's announcement of spring is the far more popular meaning, giving the bird a place in a thirteenth-century round still sung by children today: "Summer Is Icumen In," for which the refrain is "Sing cuckoo, now sing, cuckoo!" Later, with the invention of the cuckoo clock, some households could bring the sound of spring into their own homes, announcing it every hour on the hour. • These references in charming rhymes and classic poetry mask the more insidious truth about the Common Cuckoo: Its role as a brood parasite, laying its eggs in the nests of other birds and leaving these surrogate parents to raise their young, even though nestling cuckoos can be significantly larger than the birds forced to raise them. In all, nearly 300 bird species have been victims of the Common Cuckoo's abandonment of its own offspring.

C

No. 118

Cuculus micropterus

Indian Cuckoo

Short-Winged Cuckoo, Vishupakshi

● **LEAST CONCERN**

COLLECTIVE NAMES
Chorus of cuckoos | Deceit of cuckoos | Flight of cuckoos

✳ **SYMBOLIC MEANINGS**
Desire; Love; Spring.

✺ **POSSIBLE POWERS**
Distraction; Elaborate deception.

☾ **FOLKLORE AND FACTS**
If you thought the brood parasitism of the Common Cuckoo (see No. 117) could be considered despicable, the Indian Cuckoo's methods will be an eye-opener. These clever birds work as mated pairs, the male distracting the host bird from its nest long enough for the female Indian Cuckoo to remove one of the host's eggs, devour it, and then lay her own. The one saving grace is that the Indian Cuckoo chooses the nests of larger birds—particularly crows and drongos—so at least the host bird's nestlings have a fighting chance of surviving the competition with the hungry interloper. • The Indian Cuckoo lives in forests throughout the Indian subcontinent and Southeast Asia, with a migratory population in the Amur region of Russia. Throughout its range, its whistling, four-syllable call has given rise to all kinds of interpretations, from a dead shepherd asking, "Where is my sheep?" to the Chinese translation, "Go to cut wheat." • Indians believe that their cuckoo is a sacred bird to Kamadeva, the Hindu god of erotic love and desire, who uses a bow made of sugar cane and arrows adorned with flowers. Kamadeva keeps a cuckoo as a companion, along with a parrot, bees, and a light breeze—all symbols of spring.

No. 119

Cuculus poliocephalus

Lesser Cuckoo

Hototogisu (Japan) | Jeopdongsae (Korea)

● **LEAST CONCERN**

COLLECTIVE NAMES
Chorus of cuckoos | Deceit of cuckoos | Flight of cuckoos

✳ **SYMBOLIC MEANINGS**
Mourning; Sadness.

✺ **POSSIBLE POWER**
Inhabited by spirits of the dead.

☾ **FOLKLORE AND FACTS**
More boldly patterned than other *Cuculus* cuckoos, with bold black stripes on its white flanks beneath its dark upper parts, the Lesser Cuckoo breeds in southeast Asia and winters in southern India, Kenya, and other parts of eastern Africa. Its down-sloping, minor-key song makes many cultures see this bird as a harbinger of sadness, so much so that Korean fairy tales often include dead or dying humans transforming into this bird. • In one such story, a mother dies and leaves behind ten children: Nine boys and a girl. Their father remarries and their stepmother takes over the children's care, but she resents the stepdaughter and harasses her continuously, even as the daughter plans her upcoming nuptials. One day the daughter dies, leaving behind a large pile of bridal gifts, which her mournful brothers begin burning in the yard—but when the stepmother discovers this, she tries to stop them so she can keep the gifts. The brothers fly into a rage and push the woman into the fire, but even this does not stop her; instead, she turns herself into a crow and flies off. As the crow-stepmother vanishes into the clouds, the dead stepdaughter returns as a Lesser Cuckoo. Every night after that, she visits her brothers and sings her grieving song. • In another story, a poor farmer marries a woman who lives inside a snail shell. One day, as she brings his noon meal out to him in the field, a messenger arrives from the king and kidnaps the pretty wife for the king's own pleasure. The farmer goes after her, but every plan he comes up with to retrieve her ends in failure. He finally dies of grief, and turns into a Lesser Cuckoo, doomed to sing his song of mourning for the rest of his days.

No. 120

Cyanistes caeruleus

Eurasian Blue Tit

Billy Biter | Blue Tit | Common Blue Tit | Jackie Bluecap | Tom Bitethumb | Tom Tit

● **LEAST CONCERN**

COLLECTIVE NAMES
Banditry of tits | Dissimulation of tits | Murmuration of tits

✳ **SYMBOLIC MEANINGS**
Adaptability; Happiness.

✺ **POSSIBLE POWERS**
Cleverness; Resourcefulness.

Just about every backyard in Europe has had Eurasian Blue Tits pay a visit, and homes with bird feeders (called "tables" in England) enjoy long residencies of this pretty little blue and yellow bird. • Older neighbors who once had bottles of milk delivered to their doorstep remember how blue tits loved to tear the foil top off the bottles and drink the cream that rose to the top. Other bird species learned to do this, but reports from the 1940s tell us that blue tits led the charge, accounting for half of all incidents. When the dairy industry started delivering skimmed milk, the blue tits lost interest—and scientists determined that the little birds are lactose intolerant, so the milk made them sick while the lactose-free cream did not. • "Tit" is a Norse word for tiny, attributed to several small birds in Europe and more around the world. In Eurasian Blue Tit's case, size truly doesn't matter: Backyard birders delight in seeing this bold little bird plunder insects and spiders from the undersides of leaves and branches, and taking full advantage of nest boxes supplied by their fans. Not only do the birds raise their young in these boxes, but they also remain through the winter, roosting in the boxes in groups to keep warm. • In 2010, the Eurasian Blue Tit was one of the featured birds in Great Britain's Birds of Britain stamp series, along with the European Robin, European Goldfinch, English Sparrow, European Starling, and Wood Pigeon.

No. 121

Cyanocitta cristata

Blue Jay

Jaybird | Satan's Bird

● **LEAST CONCERN**

COLLECTIVE NAMES

Band of jays | Party of jays

✳ **SYMBOLIC MEANINGS**

Abundance; Change; Healing; New adventures; Strength.

POSSIBLE POWERS

Communication; Connection to the underworld; Mimicry.

FOLKLORE AND FACTS

North America's most widespread jay has a lot to tell us, and flocks of these birds (appropriately called a "party") tell us all about it every chance they get. Their loud, piercing *peel, peel*, summons their flock to mob a predator or ward off some other foe; they substitute a flutelike warble when many jays are together in a quiet yard or concealed by tree cover. Their varied vocabulary also includes a rusty-hinge squeak and the ability to mimic all kinds of sounds, from

hawks' cries to human car alarms. • Perhaps because of this, Blue Jays have quite a folkloric past. Some early settlers were certain that they never saw a Blue Jay on a Friday, and decided that this was because the bird had been conscripted by Satan to carry sticks and twigs to stoke the fires in hell and bring fire to the wicked on the surface. Others attributed a more Christian fate to the bird, believing that a Blue Jay had misbehaved at Christ's crucifixion, so his slavery to Satan was his punishment. (Never mind that Blue Jays do not live in the Middle East and would not have been at that event.) • The jay gets more respect in modern times as the mascot of Major League Baseball's Toronto Blue Jays, and several minor league teams have chosen the bird as their symbol as well. Universities including Johns Hopkins, Elmhurst, and Creighton all have the Blue Jay as their mascot, and Prince Edward Island in Canada named the Blue Jay as the province's official bird.

No. 122

Cygnus atratus

Black Swan

● **LEAST CONCERN**

COLLECTIVE NAMES

Ballet of swans | Bevy of swans | Drift of swans | Lamentation of swans

✳ **SYMBOLIC MEANINGS**

Connection with Satan; Highly unusual event; Sinister forces.

POSSIBLE POWERS

Bad luck; Gloom.

FOLKLORE AND FACTS

For thousands of years, everyone in Europe knew with absolute certainty that all swans were white. Juvenal, a satirist in ancient Rome, wrote in the year 82, "*Rara avis in terris nigroque simillima cygno*," or "A rare bird in the land, like a black swan." As black swans were mythical to the Romans, people called anything they thought could not possibly exist a Black Swan. • So you can imagine the terrifying moment of truth in 1697, when Dutch explorer Willem de Vlamingh sailed into Australia and found Black Swans on what he instantly named the Swan River. His announcement of this to European authorities probably put him on par with those who sight Sasquatch today, but in 1726, an explorer captured two Black Swans and brought them out of Australia to Indonesia to prove their existence. By 1789, when England had established the convict colony at Botany Bay, its governor wrote that Black Swans were "by no means uncommon" there. • When exotic bird collectors began importing Black Swans into Europe, they expected much attention would be paid to the highly unusual birds. Instead, they found that people associated the black birds with the same forces they attributed to black cats: Bad luck and gloom. Composer Peter Ilyich Tchaikovsky even included a sinister Black Swan in his ballet *Swan Lake*. • Soon interest in the ebony birds faded altogether, with just a few remaining in zoos and special collections around the world to this day. Australia continues to honor the Black Swan with a place on the flag of Western Australia, on various coats of arms, and on postage stamps.

No. 123

Cygnus buccinator

Trumpeter Swan

● **LEAST CONCERN**

🐾 **COLLECTIVE NAMES**
Ballet of swans | Bevy of swans | Drift of swans | Lamentation of swans

✹ **SYMBOLIC MEANINGS**
Beauty; Fidelity; Grace; Serenity.

🌀 **POSSIBLE POWER**
Communication with the Great Creator.

🐾 **FOLKLORE AND FACTS**
The Trumpeter Swan holds the crown for being the largest and heaviest living bird native to North America, its wingspan reaching as much as 10 feet (3 m) across, and an adult bird's weight topping out at about 50 pounds (23 kg). • It's hard to imagine that something so impressive might have been close to extinction, but throughout the nineteenth and early twentieth centuries, the Hudson's Bay Company hunted these birds for their skins, used in the manufacture of cosmetic powder puffs, and for their feathers for fashionable robes. By the 1930s, just seventy Trumpeter Swans remained in the wild. • In the 1950s, however, the bird's trajectory changed: An aerial survey of Alaska happened across several thousand more Trumpeter Swans living unnoticed in the wild. This discovery allowed wildlife agencies to begin a reintroduction program in Montana, Idaho, and Wyoming, renewing the gene pool there and rescuing the swans from the brink of extinction. Today more than 46,000 Trumpeter Swans live in North America, making them one of the great success stories for the conservation community. • The Nanticoke people of northeastern North America perform a dance called the Swan Dance, honoring the animals that can reach the Great Creator. The dancers—always women—

come into the dance circle wrapped in shawls, and use these folds of cloth to "fly," moving the shawls like wings. "They stop and face the four sacred directions, to show respect for the Four Faces of the Earth," the Nanticoke Nation website explains. "Weaving in and around each other at each stop, they finally come together in a circle. When the drum stops, the dancers 'ruffle their feathers' with the fringe on the shawls, and exit to the drum beat."

No. 124

Cygnus columbianus

Tundra Swan
Bewick's Swan | Whistling Swan

● **LEAST CONCERN**

🐾 **COLLECTIVE NAMES**
Ballet of swans | Bevy of swans | Drift of swans | Lamentation of swans

✹ **SYMBOLIC MEANINGS**
Beauty; Grace; Loyalty.

🌀 **POSSIBLE POWER**
Transformation.

🐾 **FOLKLORE AND FACTS**
The Tundra Swan's two subspecies divide rather neatly by geography: The Whistling Swan subspecies lives in North America, while the Bewick's Swan resides in Europe and western Asia. • A German folktale (sometimes attributed to snow geese rather than swans) tells of a duck hunter who encountered seven swans as they landed on a nearby lake. He was about to shoot them when they transformed into seven beautiful women in feathery white robes. They dropped their robes to bathe in the lake, and the hunter crept forward and stole the white robe of the most beautiful maiden. When the women came ashore to dress, they discovered that one robe was missing; they flew off and left the seventh maiden to search for her robe. The hunter stepped forward and gave her his cloak instead of her robe, and he insisted that she marry him. She had little choice but to consent. • Over time, the marriage succeeded, and the hunter and his wife had children and made a happy home. One day, when the children were playing hide and seek, they found their mother's feathered robe. She put it on immediately and flew off. The hunter, discovering this, began a long search for his wife, and finally reached her father's kingdom "east of the sun and west of the moon." Once he recognized his wife among her six nearly identical sisters, the king granted them many riches on the condition that she be allowed to visit him and her sisters. The hunter consented, and they lived happily ever after.

No. 125

Cygnus cygnus

Whooper Swan

Common Swan

● **LEAST CONCERN**

✤ **COLLECTIVE NAMES**

Ballet of swans | Bevy of swans | Drift of swans | Lamentation of swans

✷ **SYMBOLIC MEANINGS**

Beauty; Harmony.

✺ **POSSIBLE POWERS**

Singing at the moment of death; Taking on the souls of dead poets.

☀ **FOLKLORE AND FACTS**

Greek mythology has much to say about the Whooper Swan, the bird from which the legend of the "swan song" emerged. During the birth of Apollo, god of the sun, swans flew around the island of Delos seven times to distract the jealous Hera while Leto, Zeus's lover, gave birth to his son. Much later, when Apollo died, his soul passed into a swan—so from that day forward, all poets' souls pass into swans at the moment of death. • As Socrates lay dying from the hemlock he ingested, he told his friend Plato about the nightingale and the swan: The nightingale sang for sorrow, but the swan sings only once and very beautifully, at the moment of its death. • This quickly became a proverb, reiterated by Aesop in his story of the swan and the goose: A man had a swan and a goose, and planned to eat the goose and keep the swan for its song. When the day came to butcher the goose, the man could not tell the two birds apart, and he grabbed the swan instead of the goose. But the swan began to sing a lament to its own impending death, and the man recognized the voice and let the swan go. • Do Whooper Swans actually sing at the moment of their death? Pliny the Elder wrote in the year 77, "Observation shows that the story that the dying swan sings is false," and science now tells us that the swan does not sing as it dies. Whether it's based in fact or romanticism, the "swan song" remains a metaphor for a last creative work or the last act at the end of a lengthy career.

No. 126

Cygnus olor

Mute Swan

● **LEAST CONCERN**

✤ **COLLECTIVE NAMES**

Ballet of swans | Bevy of swans | Drift of swans | Lamentation of swans

✷ **SYMBOLIC MEANINGS**

Beauty; Harmony.

✺ **POSSIBLE POWER**

Resilience.

☀ **FOLKLORE AND FACTS**

How did the Mute Swan get its name? It's not actually mute—Mute Swans can grunt and call hoarsely, and many unsuspecting people have heard them snort or hiss when they get too close. • Native to Russia and northern Europe, with migratory populations in North Africa, the Mute Swan came to North America toward the end of the 1800s. In the Great Lakes region, Mute Swan populations have multiplied by 10 percent annually over the course of thirty years, classifying them as an invasive species. This reduces protections for them, a controversial move that has met with opposition from some environmental advocates. • Hans Christian Andersen's tale of the Ugly Duckling, in which a gawky cygnet gets shunned by other animals until he grows into a beautiful swan, has remained a classic tale for centuries—especially for children, many of whom see themselves in the cygnet's story. • Of course, the Mute Swan served as the inspiration for *Swan Lake*, Tchaikovsky's classic ballet. Prince Siegfried encounters a flock of swans while on a hunting trip and falls in love with Odette, their queen. However, an evil magician, Baron von Rothbart, casts a spell over her so that she can only take human form from midnight to dawn. The Prince must prove his true love to break the spell. As their love grows, von Rothbart sends his own daughter, Odile, to the Prince as a Black Swan to pretend to be Odette and seduce him. The trick works, and the Prince swears his love for the wrong swan. In the end, both Odette and the Prince give up their lives to escape their fate (although in some modern versions, they triumph over von Rothbart).

No. 127
Dacelo novaeguineae

Laughing Kookaburra

Breakfast Bird | Bushman's Clock | Laughing Jackass

● **LEAST CONCERN**

❉ **COLLECTIVE NAME**
Riot of kookaburras

☀ **SYMBOLIC MEANINGS**
Confidence; Laughter; Light; Mischief.

🌀 **POSSIBLE POWER**
Waking the continent at dawn.

☾ **FOLKLORE AND FACTS**
"Kookaburra sits in the old gum tree / Merry, merry king of the bush is he." Every child knows this round from a 1930s poem by Marion Sinclair, but only Australian and New Zealander children know the bird it describes. The Laughing Kookaburra, a member of the kingfisher family, chortles its rolling belly-laugh call most often at dawn and dusk, earning the nickname "Breakfast Bird" for its dependability as a morning alarm. • Beyond the southern hemisphere, its laugh is familiar around the world because of its use in many movies, especially in the Tarzan movies of the 1930s—though a kookaburra would never have lived in equatorial Africa, where Tarzan roamed the jungle. • According to Australian legend, the Laughing Kookaburra played a key role in bringing warmth and light to the Earth. When only stars lighted the planet, the spirits in the sky decided to build a great fire that would bring light to the creatures below, but they worried that the fire would frighten the animals. The spirits searched for an animal who could call to everyone each morning to tell them the fire was coming. When they posed the problem to the Laughing Kookaburra, he saw the opportunity to become a hero to all creatures, and he agreed to sing every morning to welcome the light and warmth to the Earth. To this day, this devoted bird wakes the continent with its extraordinary call.

No. 128
Dendrocygna arcuata

Wandering Whistling Duck

Djilikuybi | Djirrbiyuk | Guyiyi | Tree Duck | Walkuli

● **LEAST CONCERN**

❉ **COLLECTIVE NAMES**
Flush of ducks | Raft of ducks (on water) |
Skein of ducks (flying) | Waddling of ducks

☀ **SYMBOLIC MEANINGS**
Adaptability; Making the most of a situation.

🌀 **POSSIBLE POWERS**
Communication; Forming communities.

☾ **FOLKLORE AND FACTS**
It looks like a cross between a duck and a goose with its long neck and upright posture, but the Wandering Whistling Duck definitely qualifies as a duck that whistles. Until recently, ornithologists called this bird Tree Duck because of its ability to gather and perch in trees, something many ducks cannot do. Its high-pitched whistling call, often uttered by entire flocks at once, separates it further from ducks that communicate in a much lower register. • One of the best places to see Wandering Whistling Ducks is Kakadu National Park in Australia's tropical north, where they live in the Djirrbiyuk Kakukdjabdjabdi area (which means "Whistling ducks are standing up everywhere"), a sacred site protected by the Aboriginal Areas Protection Authority. Sacred sites have special meaning in the Aboriginal cultural tradition, especially in places connected to the Dreaming as the ancestral beings created the physical world. This particular site protects more than 50,000 years of Aboriginal heritage, as well as rivers, caves, waterfalls, and more than 1,600 plant species. Its abundant water and billabongs (still water from storms and other backfilling events) provide the perfect habitat for the Wandering Whistling Duck and many other waterfowl.

D

No. 129

Dinornis novaezealandiae

Moa

Te kura

● **EXTINCT**

🐾 **COLLECTIVE NAME**
Extinction of moas

✳ **SYMBOLIC MEANINGS**
Food; Potential for cultural extinction.

🌀 **POSSIBLE POWER**
Never to be discovered.

😺 **FOLKLORE AND FACTS**
If the long-extinct Moa had symbolic meaning to the Māori people of the fourteenth century, when these large, wingless birds roamed the New Zealand forests and shrublands, that symbolism has been lost to memory. When Polynesians arrived on the shores of New Zealand between 1320 and 1350, they were the first human habitants on the islands—and the plentiful Moa looked like a terrific food source. People set about hunting these giant, upright birds aggressively … and in less a century, the birds reached extinction, eradicating what may have been 2.5 million birds a few decades before. We can only assume that Moa meat must have been truly delicious to encourage this kind of wholesale slaughter. As an added injury to the island's fauna, the extinction of Moa quickly wiped out the Haast's Eagle, a huge raptor that preyed exclusively on Moa. • Since then, despite claims of Moa sightings as recently as 1993 (which carry the same credence as Sasquatch sightings in North America), the only evidence of this flightless bird's existence has been in fossils discovered around New Zealand's Mount Hikurangi and in some other areas, with the first full skeletons emerging in the 1830s. Thousands of skeletons have emerged since, especially in caves and swamps, and some scientific circles have begun to explore the possibility of using these remains to clone the Moa and restore the species. Whether or not this project goes forward, the Māori people have added a simile to their *whakatuki*, or ancestral sayings: "Dead as the Moa," meaning a person or concept that has no chance of being resurrected.

No. 130

Dolichonyx oryzivorus

Bobolink

Butter Bird | Reed Bird | Rice Bird | White-Winged Blackbird

● **LEAST CONCERN**

🐾 **COLLECTIVE NAME**
Chain of bobolinks

✳ **SYMBOLIC MEANINGS**
Good fortune for travelers; Safety.

🌀 **POSSIBLE POWER**
Survival against odds.

😺 **FOLKLORE AND FACTS**
Nineteenth-century American poet William Cullen Bryant celebrated the Bobolink by turning the bird's onomatopoetic name into a mnemonic device:

> Robert of Lincoln is gaily drest,
> Wearing a bright black wedding-coat;
> White are his shoulders, and white his crest;
> Hear him call in his merry note:
> Bob-o'-link, bob-o'-link,
> Spink, spank, spink;
> Look what a nice new coat is mine,
> Sure there was never a bird so fine.
> Chee, chee, chee.

Emily Dickinson also honored the bird in several of her poems, assuring us that spending time listening to the Bobolink could even replace the need to attend church services. • The North American grasslands fill with the Bobolink's bubbling song every spring, alerting us to its intent to nest. Bobolinks' appeal has never been in dispute, but the birds have faced some human-driven forces that threaten their ability to breed successfully in farm fields. Bobolinks prefer fields of feedstock crops—timothy, alfalfa, and other grasses grown for livestock—and the birds begin nesting in mid-May, just as these crops begin to reach their most potent nutritional value. By the end of May, when the birds have built their nests at ground level, it's time for farmers to harvest these crops by mowing their fields. Entire generations of Bobolinks can fall prey to these mowing machines. • The Bobolink Project in the northeastern us works to reverse this trend, by offering financial assistance to participating farmers who are willing to modify their mowing schedules around the birds' breeding period. It also offers information for landowners who want to manage their grasslands in ways that will sustain these birds for many generations.

No. 131

Drepanis coccinea

‘I‘iwi

Scarlet Honeycreeper

● **THREATENED**

🐾 **COLLECTIVE NAME**

Flock of ‘I‘iwi

✴ **SYMBOLIC MEANING**

Decline of all endemic birds in Hawai‘i.

🌀 **POSSIBLE POWER**

Bestowing status on elders.

🌙 **FOLKLORE AND FACTS**

Why should a gorgeous little red bird with a long, pink, deeply curved bill carry the burden for all endangered Hawaiian birds? Possibly the most beloved and charismatic of the Hawaiian honeycreepers, the ‘I‘iwi attracts the immediate attention of those lucky enough to see one, making it the perfect poster child for the decline of endemic species throughout the Hawaiian islands. • The ‘I‘iwi is one of more than fifty species of Hawaiian honeycreeper that once made these islands their home, but the arrival of exotic bird and animal species from across the Pacific Ocean has led to the extinction of most honeycreepers and other endemic birds. Introduced house cats, mongooses, and exotic mosquitoes carrying avian pox and malaria have devastated Hawai‘i’s birds. • Before all of these hazards, Hawaiian spiritual leaders used ‘I‘iwi feathers in ceremonial rituals. People called Kia Manu, or bird catchers, would capture the birds and carefully remove several feathers from them, and then release them back into the wild. The feathers were used to adorn capes, and to define the high status of the person wearing the gorgeous scarlet plumes. Today red feathers are still important in ceremonies, but ‘I‘iwi feathers have been replaced by dyed feathers taken from common domestic birds.

No. 132

Dromaius novaehollandiae

Emu

Barrimal | Courn | Myoure

● **LEAST CONCERN**

🐾 **COLLECTIVE NAME**

Mob of emus

✴ **SYMBOLIC MEANINGS**

Good planning; Moving forward; Survival.

🌀 **POSSIBLE POWERS**

Kindler of light; Protection of young.

🌙 **FOLKLORE AND FACTS**

When you’re the second tallest bird in the world, you don’t let a lot of things get in the way of what you want or need. The Emu, just a little shorter than their neighboring Ostrich, hails from Australia and figures prominently in Aboriginal culture and rituals. It served as one of the Creator spirits that watched over the Earth, playing such an important role that it became its own constellation in the Australian sky. When the Emu appears in the heavens, Emus all over Australia lay their eggs. • An Aboriginal legend tells us that an Emu named Dinewan and a Brolga named Bralagh sat together on their nests, protecting their eggs in the dark, because this was in the days before light. After sitting peacefully for some time, they began to argue about which of them would bring stronger and cleverer children into the world. The fight became so heated that Bralgah reached into Dinewan’s nest, grabbed one of her eggs, and threw it up into the sky with all her might. The egg flew higher and higher until it crashed into a pile of sticks assembled by the spirits of the sky for a fire they intended to light. The egg broke, and the yolk striking the sticks kindled the flame. Suddenly the sky lit up, bathing the Earth in light, and everyone could see how beautiful the world was. The spirits decided to build a fire every day to bring light to the Earth. (See Laughing Kookaburra, No. 127, for the next chapter of this story.)

No. 133

Dryocopus martius

Black Woodpecker

● **LEAST CONCERN**

✿ **COLLECTIVE NAMES**
Descent of woodpeckers | Gatling of woodpeckers | Whirlagust of woodpeckers

✸ **SYMBOLIC MEANINGS**
Resourcefulness; Thor.

◉ **POSSIBLE POWERS**
Communication; Retribution for sin of selfishness.

☾ **FOLKLORE AND FACTS**
All black with a white bill and a red topknot, the largest woodpecker in Europe appears in every country except the United Kingdom, as well as in the Middle East and across Asia. The Black Woodpecker prefers mature forests of many varieties, where it excavates wide holes in otherwise healthy trees, leaving plenty of evidence that it has visited there.
• This woodpecker may be the bird most closely associated with Thor, the Norse god of thunder. Legend has it that Thor took his red hair from the red head of a woodpecker, making the Black Woodpecker the logical representative for this task. This bird also pounds large holes in wood, just the way Thor does the same with his hammer, and the woodpecker's drumming has been compared with thunder, Thor's trademark. • Norwegian fairy tales tell the story of Gertrude, a red-haired woman who receives a visit from Jesus and St. Peter. Gertrude does not recognize the two holy men, and she balks a bit when they ask her to share some food with them. She takes a small amount of dough and bakes some *lefse* (Scandinavian flatbread), but it expands in size to feed all of them well—and this inexplicably annoys her. She tries again and again to produce just a small amount of *lefse,* but each time the dough expands enough to satisfy everyone's hunger. Gertrude finally tells Jesus and St. Peter that she has no food to share. Jesus becomes angry and turns her into a woodpecker, leaving only her red hair to identify her as Gertrude. She flies up the chimney to escape the men and turns herself coal black with soot and smoke—making her an unmistakable Black Woodpecker.

No. 134

Dryocopus pileatus

Pileated Woodpecker

Carpenter Bird | Wood Hen

● **LEAST CONCERN**

✿ **COLLECTIVE NAMES**
Descent of woodpeckers | Gatling of woodpeckers | Whirlagust of woodpeckers

✸ **SYMBOLIC MEANINGS**
Diligent work; Family; Sense of purpose.

◉ **POSSIBLE POWERS**
Determination; Nurturing; Perseverence.

☾ **FOLKLORE AND FACTS**
Here is the inspiration for Walter Lanz's 1957–1958 cartoon character Woody Woodpecker, the bird with the big personality and mischievous nature. The gregarious Pileated Woodpecker can't help but attract this kind of attention: It's the largest woodpecker in North America, its range extending throughout the eastern half of the continent, across southern Canada, and looping southward once again into the Pacific Northwest and coastal California.
• The Native American zodiac places the woodpecker as the birth totem of those born between June 21 and July 21, or where Cancer falls in the traditional zodiac. Those who have the woodpecker as their totem tend to be nurturing people who are devoted to a cause, proceeding with perseverance and determination. These people put their home and family above all other priorities, just as the Pileated Woodpecker does while raising its young in the hollow of a tree. • Native American tradition links the woodpecker's drumming with the rhythm of the Earth as a whole, reminding those who have the woodpecker totem to maintain balance between thought and emotion, and not to become too intense while pounding away at a task.

No. 135

Dulus dominicus

Palmchat
Tanagra Dominica (archaic)

● **LEAST CONCERN**

✥ **COLLECTIVE NAMES**
Colony of palmchats | Community of palmchats

✳ **SYMBOLIC MEANINGS**
Fertility; Intelligence; Prosperity.

🌀 **POSSIBLE POWER**
Good luck.

☾ **FOLKLORE AND FACTS**
The Palmchat serves as the national animal of the Dominican Republic, and rightly so: This bird is endemic to Hispaniola, the island that includes the Dominican Republic and Haiti. The olive-brown bird with the streaked chest, olive rump, reddish eye, and yellow bill appears on the Dominican coat of arms, flag, and some of its currency, and many believe that seeing one of these common birds brings good luck. • If you're looking for a Palmchat to grant you some good fortune, search in the palm trees from which it takes its name. Any city park or forest will have its share of the little bird, and areas that contain its large nests may have colonies of a dozen or more birds, all sharing the messy bundle of twigs high in a royal palm tree or at the top of a utility pole. The birds feed on fruit and berries, frequenting gumbo-limbo trees as well as palms, and sometimes eating the flowers of orchids and other fragrant blooms. • Chances are you will hear palmchats chattering before you see them, their repertoire of squeaks, cheeps, buzzes, and whistles easy to recognize among the birds of the region, especially in towns and gardens. Their colony habitats often erupt in sound with many birds singing at once, giving away the location of their community. Sometimes they even imitate hawks that may see them as prey, a way to confuse a territorial bird as it approaches.

Ectopistes migratorius

Passenger Pigeon

Wild Pigeon

● **EXTINCT**

⚜ **COLLECTIVE NAMES**

Flight of pigeons | Kit of pigeons | Loft of pigeons | Passel of pigeons

✺ **SYMBOLIC MEANING**

Extinction through human activity.

✳ **POSSIBLE POWER**

Never to be discovered.

☾ **FOLKLORE AND FACTS**

Whatever Passenger Pigeons meant in the span of their lifetimes, that meaning has been lost in the tragic erasure of their species, the very last one (a bird named Martha, living at the Cincinnati Zoo) passing away in 1914. Once the most prolific and widespread bird in North America, with an estimated 3 to 5 billion individuals, the Passenger Pigeon became a cheap food source in the 1800s, leading to massive hunting operations and the wholesale slaughter of millions of them per day. • The birds' downfall came in part from their communal behavior, traveling in huge flocks of tens of thousands of birds. Despite a 62-mile (100-km)-per-hour flight speed, these flocks made it easy for marksmen to hit something with every shot. Over time, fewer birds were left to gather in communities, so fewer birds were born to restore their numbers. Between 1870 and 1890, the flocks vanished.• The ornithological community believed that the last Passenger Pigeon in the wild met its fate from the BB gun of Press Clay Southworth, a boy who did not realize what he had done. His parents recognized the species, however, and sent the bird to a taxidermist, finally passing it on to the Ohio Historical Society in 1915.

Emberiza citrinella

Yellowhammer

Ammer | Scribble Jack | Scribble Lark | Yelamber | Yellow Bunting | Yeorling | Yorlin | Yowley

● **LEAST CONCERN**

⚜ **COLLECTIVE NAMES**

Charm of yellowhammers | Flock of yellowhammers

✺ **SYMBOLIC MEANING**

Link to the devil.

✳ **POSSIBLE POWERS**

Messenger to Satan; Poetic muse.

☾ **FOLKLORE AND FACTS**

A-little-bit-of-bread-and-no-cheeeeese, the tenacious little Yellowhammer pronounces from its perch atop a hummock or shrub in wide-open country. The bright yellow male bird with its red-streaked breast and flanks makes itself fairly easy to spot, singing continuously in breeding season. The female shares the yellow face, but as a ground-nester, she camouflages herself in mottled, streaky brown over a yellowish chest. • Well-known by a wide variety of nicknames throughout its European, Middle Eastern, and west Asian range, the Yellowhammer has served as a muse for poets, composers, and prose writers. Scottish bard Robert Burns used the bird's nickname as a euphemism for a young maiden's private parts in his poem "The Yellow Yellow Yorlin," which is too risqué to repeat here. Samuel Taylor Coleridge wrote more literally about the bird and his disdain for its song: "The spruce and timber yellowhammer / In the dawn of spring, and sultry summer / In hedge or tree the hours beguiling / With notes as of one who brass is filing."
 • The Yellowhammer picked up the nickname Scribble Lark because its eggs have a pattern of delicate lines and spots, but these random patterns were believed to communicate messages that only Satan and his minions could read. The bird's link to the underworld remains in some minds, so not everyone is overjoyed to hear its song as it returns to European fields in spring.

No. 138

Emberiza hortulana

Ortolan

Ortolan Bunting

● **LEAST CONCERN**

🐾 **COLLECTIVE NAME**

Decoration of buntings

☀ **SYMBOLIC MEANINGS**

Gluttony; Nature's bounty; Sin.

🌀 **POSSIBLE POWER**

Deliciousness.

🐞 **FOLKLORE AND FACTS**

Fans of the television shows *Billions* and *Succession* may recognize the name of this bird, referenced as a French delicacy available only to the very rich—especially since 1999, when some countries passed laws prohibiting its preparation. • The culinary process involves fattening up this little yellow bird by placing it in a cage in the dark with unlimited millet for eighteen to twenty-four days, then drowning the bird in Armagnac brandy. The chef then cooks it, serving it whole to be swallowed in one bite (except for the bill). Diners usually drape a napkin over their faces so their consumption of the bird is not visible to the people around them—perhaps out of shame for the bird's life of torment, but more likely to hide the messy process from viewers until the consumer produces the beak. • Needless to say, this practice caused decades of outcries from many bird conservation groups around the world. They succeeded in banning the preparation and consumption of Ortolan in the United States and the European Union—but not only because of the way the birds were treated. Demand for the Ortolan in fancy restaurants nearly depleted this bird's numbers in Europe, as poachers received a tidy sum for each bird they could catch. Despite all the laws, a black market on the Ortolan continues today, so the birds are not entirely safe. Their numbers have been restored enough, however, that they are now listed as "Least Concern" by the IUCN.

No. 139

Eolophus roseicapilla

Galah

Pink and Grey Cockatoo | Rose-Breasted Cockatoo

● **LEAST CONCERN**

🐾 **COLLECTIVE NAMES**

Flock of galahs | Mob of galahs | Pack of galahs

☀ **SYMBOLIC MEANINGS**

Freedom; Silliness.

🌀 **POSSIBLE POWER**

Transforming pain into joy.

🐞 **FOLKLORE AND FACTS**

Fans of the *Angry Birds* video game may recognize the pink face and feathered crest of the Galah, the Australian cockatoo that gave its likeness to Stella, one of the game's most popular characters. The Galah is equally popular in real life, a particularly attractive cockatoo found all over the Australian continent and very common in cities, where it can be seen searching for food on the ground in parks with trees and mowed lawns. If one Galah is in sight, chances are there are many more nearby, making it easy and fascinating to watch these birds interact with one another. • It's common in Australia to hear that someone is "acting the Galah," or being silly or foolish in a public way. A particularly acrobatic bird, especially when gathered in flocks and clinging to the same branch together, Galahs interacting with each other often descend into antics that make observers laugh out loud. In Aboriginal myth, however, the Galah gets its pink chest from blood others have lost in battle, taking on their wounds to make them part of something beautiful.

No. 140

Eremophila alpestris

Horned Lark

Dusky Horned Lark (and 39 more subspecies) | Pallid Horned Lark | Shore Lark | Streaked Horned Lark

● **LEAST CONCERN**

🐾 **COLLECTIVE NAMES**

Ascension of larks | Chattering of larks | Exaltation of larks | Happiness of larks

☀ **SYMBOLIC MEANINGS**

Happy event; Hope; New beginning.

🌀 **POSSIBLE POWER**

Feminine energy drawn from the moon.

With two tiny tufts of dark feathers raised over their heads, male Horned Larks have a fierce expression that belies their small size. There's nothing malicious or threatening about these little birds, however—in fact, larks of all kinds have long been associated with glad tidings. Horned Larks do what they need to do to survive, taking possession of dry, brown spaces, recently mowed areas, and plowed fields with a dusting of snow to search for seeds left by last year's harvest, and insects just below the surface. • In excavating a nest on the ground, female Horned Larks often collect small items and build what looks like a walkway to the nest—except that the birds don't treat this as an entrance, so its use is not clear. It may be that these bits of stuff (pebbles, moss, dung, and more) help to hold the tailings in place, keeping the dirt from blowing back into the hole until the bird finishes digging out the nest cavity.

• Native American imagery suggests that the black crescent on the chest of Horned Larks is a link to the moon, drawing the power of feminine energy from the celestial body.

No. 141

Eudocimus albus

White Ibis

American White Ibis | Spanish Curlew | White Curlew

● **LEAST CONCERN**

✿ **COLLECTIVE NAMES**

Colony of ibises | Stand of ibises | Wedge of ibises | Whiteness of ibises

✳ **SYMBOLIC MEANINGS**

Danger; Hope.

🌀 **POSSIBLE POWERS**

Herald of clear weather after a storm; Predictor of severe storms.

☾ **FOLKLORE AND FACTS**

Every driver in Florida and along the coast of the Gulf of Mexico recognizes the tall white bird with the bright pink, downward-sloping bill. White Ibises and their patchy-looking brown-and-white young reveal themselves in wet fields, on the edges of ponds, in the middle of wetlands, and even on beaches throughout their range: The southeastern United States, on both coasts of Mexico, and in northern South America. • Seminole folklore tells us that White Ibis is the last bird to look for shelter when a tropical storm or hurricane approaches, making it an important predictor of

severe storms. Eager to resume its life and start scavenging again once the storm has passed, the ibises are the first to emerge from their hiding places, so they signal the "all clear" for believers from Florida to Texas. • Perhaps this tale encouraged the University of Miami Hurricanes football team to adopt the White Ibis as its mascot all the way back in 1926, and why the university named its yearbook *The Ibis*. (The team eventually named the ibis mascot Sebastian.) The bird's tendency to embrace potential danger and to arise, hopeful, from whatever depths it chose as its sanctuary seems to jibe nicely with the ups and downs of college football.

No. 142

Eudocimus ruber

Scarlet Ibis

Guará

● **LEAST CONCERN**

✿ **COLLECTIVE NAMES**

Colony of Ibises | Stand of ibises | Wedge of ibises | Whiteness of ibises

✳ **SYMBOLIC MEANINGS**

Achievement; Beauty; Pride.

🌀 **POSSIBLE POWERS**

Danger; Harbinger of storms.

☾ **FOLKLORE AND FACTS**

What does it take to become one of the two national birds of Trinidad and Tobago? Head-to-toe bright red feathers, for one. The spectacular Scarlet Ibis of northern South America includes Trinidad in its range (but not Tobago), where the island's 490-acre (198-ha) Caroni Swamp wetland reserve provides the easiest place in the world to see these birds. Here it roosts in trees by the hundreds, a favorite sight among birders and non-birders alike. Like its white and white-faced cousins, the Scarlet Ibis lives in colonies, usually with more than thirty birds and often with hundreds or even thousands.

No. 143

Eudyptes pachyrhynchus

Fiordland Penguin

Fiordland Crested Penguin | Tawaki

● **NEAR THREATENED**

🐾 **COLLECTIVE NAMES**

Colony of penguins | Creche of penguins | Formality of penguins | Huddle of penguins | Parade of penguins | Parcel of penguins | Rookery of penguins | Waddle of penguins

✹ **SYMBOLIC MEANINGS**

Lightning; Rain.

🌀 **POSSIBLE POWER**

Bringer of rain.

🌙 **FOLKLORE AND FACTS**

The Māori people of New Zealand believe in a god named Tawaki, who walked the Earth in human form. The humans around him had no idea that he was a deity until one day, when he climbed a high hill, tossed aside his clothing, and "clothed himself in lightning." So why do they call the Fiordland Penguin by the name Tawaki? If we look at this bird and squint a bit, the tufts on either side of the Fiordland Penguin's head definitely look like lightning bolts. • The name also may come from the god Tawaki's ability to bring rain—in fact, he "caused the flood when he created the crystal floor of heaven," according to legend, and caused all the water in the sky to fall on Fiordland. It may be that Fiordland Penguins that live in this area, which receives some of the most torrential rain in New Zealand, have been credited with actually making this rain fall. • Myths like these gain even more credence because Fiordland Penguins tend to be secretive creatures, nesting in caves and in vegetation so thick that the birds become virtually invisible. Their ability to mask their whereabouts makes them especially mysterious, so why not assume they have supernatural powers? • Unfortunately, this penguin's numbers have been dwindling in recent years. Just 3,000 pairs are still on the New Zealand coast, making their survival a precarious proposition.

No. 144

Eudyptula minor

Little Penguin

Blue Penguin | Djinan Yawa-dji Goyeep | Fairy Penguin | Kororā | Little Blue Penguin

● **LEAST CONCERN**

🐾 **COLLECTIVE NAMES**

Colony of penguins | Creche of penguins | Formality of penguins | Huddle of penguins | Parade of penguins | Parcel of penguins | Rookery of penguins | Waddle of penguins

✹ **SYMBOLIC MEANINGS**

Conscious community; Unity.

🌀 **POSSIBLE POWERS**

Problem solving.

🌙 **FOLKLORE AND FACTS**

The world's smallest penguin lives on the coast of New Zealand and southern Australia, where it stays at sea all day to avoid encounters with land-based predators, returning under cover of dusk. It further protects its offspring by nesting underground, digging burrows, or, in some areas, taking advantage of nest boxes offered by humans to help them sustain their numbers. These two facts tell us a lot about the adaptability and strong sense of survival of Little Penguins, birds that have had to change their way of life as Māori and European settlers arrived with mammals they used for hunting—some of which find Little Penguins to be tasty prey. • When a Little Penguin found its way to a sushi shop in Wellington, New Zealand, in 2019, and tried to make a home for itself under the store, the story became national news—and when the penguin returned to the sushi shop with a friend to share the experience, the incident became a legend. Today a children's book by Linda Jane Keegan, *Kororā and the Sushi Shop*, provides a poetic retelling of the Little Penguin's story, aided with illustrations by Jenny Cooper.

No. 145

Eumomota superciliosa

Turquoise-Browed Motmot

Clock Bird | Guardabarranco | Torogoz

● **LEAST CONCERN**

✥ **COLLECTIVE NAME**
Flock of motmots

✳ **SYMBOLIC MEANINGS**
Freedom; Liberty; Natural beauty.

🌀 **POSSIBLE POWER**
Morning alarm for the gods.

🌙 **FOLKLORE AND FACTS**
With so many South American birds to choose from, how did Nicaragua and El Salvador both select the Turquoise-Browed Motmot as their national bird? This gorgeous little creature provides most of the answer itself: Gray-green-backed with an orange patch and an orange underside, the motmot's light-turquoise eyebrows give it its name—but the colorful features only begin here. The bird's wings each have a wide turquoise stripe and black tips, and the bird's ultra-long tail begins and ends in turquoise and black as well, with two plumes gracing the very ends of two long, bare shafts.
• A Mayan story explains that in old times, the Turquoise-Browed Motmot had an assignment from the gods: It would wake before all the other birds and animals and sing its croaking song, rousing everyone else so they could start their day. One morning, however, the motmot overslept and did not wake the other animals. What chaos ensued is not specified, but the gods punished the little bird by stripping away all of its tail feathers except two. To this day, the motmot sways its tail feathers back and forth like the pendulum of a grandfather clock, earning it the nickname "Clock Bird."

No. 146

Eupsittula pertinax

Brown-Throated Parakeet

Brown-Throated Conure | Prikichi | St. Thomas Conure

● **LEAST CONCERN**

✥ **COLLECTIVE NAMES**
Chatter of parakeets | Company of parakeets | Pandemonium of parakeets

✳ **SYMBOLIC MEANINGS**
Expansion; Resourcefulness; Simple beauty.

🌀 **POSSIBLE POWERS**
Adaptability; Survival.

🌙 **FOLKLORE AND FACTS**
Bright green with a brown throat (and a yellow face in some subspecies), this bright parakeet makes its home in Costa Rica, Panama, islands off the South American coast, and on the continent's northern mainland. An 1860 subspecies introduction of the bird to the island of St. Thomas failed, so the birds now making this same island their home are assumed to be descendants of escaped pets.
• Of the parakeet's many subspecies, one stands out as endemic to the island of Aruba, so a movement began in the 2010s to have *Eupsittula pertinax arubensis,* also known locally as the Aruban Parakeet or Prikichi, declared the national bird of Aruba. This effort came to fruition in February 2017, so this little yellow-faced subspecies is now protected by national law, giving it a fighting chance against poachers. • Illegal hunters are not the bird's only enemy: Boa constrictors, introduced in 1999 by pet owners, enjoy a Prikichi snack fairly regularly. By 2005, boas had become a significant part of the island's wildlife, devouring many of Aruba's national animals—including an endemic Burrowing Owl known locally as Shoco—and reducing the population of both birds. Efforts to curb this infestation have proved unsuccessful, as one boa can produce fifty young every year.

No. 147
Falco cherrug

Saker Falcon

Altai Falcon (hybrid) | Hur

● **ENDANGERED**

✤ **COLLECTIVE NAMES**

Battalion of falcons | Cast of falcons | Tower of falcons

✹ **SYMBOLIC MEANINGS**

Power; Swiftness.

✺ **POSSIBLE POWERS**

Kingmaker; Speed.

✤ **FOLKLORE AND FACTS**

For thousands of years, the Saker Falcon has been the favorite bird of prey of falconers throughout its European, African, and Asian range, largely because it is the third-fastest animal in the world (after the Peregrine Falcon and the Golden Eagle). The Saker Falcon can achieve speeds of 93 miles (150 km) per hour in level flight, and as much as 200 miles (322 km) per hour in a swooping dive as it grabs prey from the ground. • A Hungarian legend tells us of the Turul, a bird most likely based on the Saker Falcon, which plays a role in the story of Emese, the ancestress of one of the Hungarian royal houses. Around the year 860, Emese has a dream that changes her life's path. In the dream, Turul visits Emese in her bed and impregnates her, telling her that from her womb, a mighty river would emerge and flow from her to all of the lands around them. Emese awakens and immediately consults her dream interpreters. They tell her that she will give birth to a son, and that he will lead their people away from this land. They also predict that her offspring will grow up to be kings in their own right. Sure enough, Emese bears a son she names Almos, and he eventually rises to power.

No. 148
Falco columbarius

Merlin

Pigeon Hawk

● **LEAST CONCERN**

✤ **COLLECTIVE NAMES**

Cast of merlins | Leash of merlins

✹ **SYMBOLIC MEANINGS**

Chaos; Honor; Nobility; Panic.

✺ **POSSIBLE POWERS**

Messenger to and from the gods; Warrior.

✤ **FOLKLORE AND FACTS**

North America, Europe, and most of Asia have their shares of the global Merlin population. This widespread bird represents one of the great success stories in bird conservation: From the 1950s through the 1970s, pervasive use of DDT as a pesticide nearly wiped out Merlins by upsetting the way birds process calcium—so the birds stopped laying viable eggs. In just a few years, these birds faced the very real possibility of extinction. Thanks in part to the book *Silent Spring* by author Rachel Carson, the dangers of DDT came to the attention of many governments, which eventually banned the substance and saved the birds. • The Native American Mississippian culture used falcon imagery in their stories and ceremonies, depicting the falcon as a deity from the Upperworld, living with the sun, moon, and stars. Falcons moved easily between the Upperworld and the Earth, so the birds were seen as messengers to the gods— but also as warriors. Falcon symbols in dances often included a dancer brandishing a mace and carrying a severed head, celebrating the prowess of a warrior in preparation for battle.

No. 149
Falco peregrinus

Peregrine Falcon

Bullet Hawk | Duck Hawk | Great-Footed Hawk | Ledge Hawk | Rock Hawk | Stone Hawk | Wandering Falcon

● **LEAST CONCERN**

✤ **COLLECTIVE NAMES**

Battalion of falcons | Cast of falcons | Tower of falcons

✹ **SYMBOLIC MEANINGS**

Freedom; Invincibility; Pride.

✺ **POSSIBLE POWERS**

Cleverness; Hunting prowess; Speed.

F

Since nomads crisscrossed central Asia three millennia ago, the Peregrine Falcon has served as a hunter for human falconers, nimbly catching prey for them after putting on a spectacular show. The falcon circles high in the air, dives down at top speed, and stops at the last second to grab its quarry before returning to its master. • Like many other birds of prey, Peregrine Falcons were nearly wiped out when the pesticide DDT caused their eggshells to weaken, becoming unviable for developing young. Aggressive recovery efforts have brought up Peregrine Falcon numbers so successfully that IUCN now considers them a species of Least Concern. • In ancient Egypt, artwork portrayed Ra, god of the sun, with the head of a Peregrine Falcon. • Native American Mississippian culture used many images of the Peregrine in their ceremonies, attributing the bird's characteristics to people of great power, and even costuming their dead leaders as falcons for burial. • Today, the Peregrine Falcon is the national animal of the United Arab Emirates, and Chicago, Illinois, made it the city's official bird because of its ability to nest on buildings.

No. 150

Falco punctatus

Mauritius Kestrel

🔴 ENDANGERED

🐾 COLLECTIVE NAME

Hover of kestrels

☀ SYMBOLIC MEANINGS

Swiftness; Vigilance.

🌀 POSSIBLE POWERS

Speed; Tenacity.

🌙 FOLKLORE AND FACTS

Mauritius Kestrels have not had an easy time at their only home on the island of Mauritius in the Indian Ocean. Human settlement in the 1700s depleted the island's forests, cyclones denuded its landscapes, invasive species actively killed the birds and destroyed their eggs … and then DDT arrived in the 1950s, making their eggshells too thin to sustain incubating young. By 1974, just four Mauritius Kestrels existed in the entire world. • In 1979, wildlife biologist Carl Jones created a sanctuary on a tiny island off the coast of Mauritius and raised hatchlings in incubators. After five years, fifty birds lived in the wild, and by the early 1990s, the population became able to sustain its own numbers. Today, about 400 Mauritius Kestrels live on their namesake island, their population still unsteady despite careful supervision.

• The Republic of Mauritius values this endemic species enough to honor it as the island's national bird on the republic's thirtieth anniversary in 2022. The little kestrel now adorns a variety of postage stamps.

No. 151

Falco rusticolus

Gyrfalcon

Gyr

🔴 LEAST CONCERN

🐾 COLLECTIVE NAMES

Bazaar of falcons | Eyrie of falcons | Ringing up of falcons | Tower of falcons

☀ SYMBOLIC MEANINGS

Courage; Strength; Swiftness.

🌀 POSSIBLE POWERS

Accuracy; Determination; Grief; Speed.

🌙 FOLKLORE AND FACTS

Only a king could hunt with a Gyrfalcon, according to medieval law, and there's logic in this: The world's largest falcon must be meant only for the highest-ranking individual. The great white (or gray, or nearly black) falcon lives and breeds in the harsh tundra and taiga of arctic and subarctic North America, Europe, and Asia, as well as in Greenland and Iceland—so this uncommonly tolerant and determined raptor commands respect. • An Icelandic legend tells us that the ptarmigan and the Gyrfalcon were close friends, playing and hunting together every day. One day, however, the much larger Gyrfalcon roughhoused too violently with the smaller bird, and she killed her ptarmigan friend. When the Gyr realized what she had done, she was overcome with grief and let out a cry of anguish that shook the island. This cry still echoes throughout Iceland, the long, high wail of a guilty, lonely sister lamenting her fate.

No. 152

Falco tinnunculus

Common Kestrel

Eurasian Kestrel | European Kestrel |
Old World Kestrel | Windhover

● **LEAST CONCERN**

✳ **COLLECTIVE NAME**
Hover of kestrels

✴ **SYMBOLIC MEANINGS**
Power; Vitality.

🌀 **POSSIBLE POWERS**
Hovering; Seeing in ultraviolet spectrum.

☾ **FOLKLORE AND FACTS**
The classic medieval text *The Book of Saint Albans* tells us that in the Middle Ages, a man of low class (a knave) who chose to indulge in falconry could keep only one kind of bird: a Common Kestrel. This small raptor may not have the majesty of a Gyrfalcon or the speed of a Peregrine Falcon, but it has one special talent of its own: It can hover in place for several seconds while it eyes the ground for prey. • This small falcon's extraordinary ability to see near ultraviolet light gives it an additional advantage over its prey: It can see urine trails shining in the sunlight, helping it follow voles and mice to their burrows. • Common Kestrels were no match for ancient Egyptians trying to curry favor with Ra, the sun god. The god's insatiable desire for animal sacrifices led his worshippers to breed kestrels just to kill and mummify the birds, demonstrating their over-the-top devotion to the god.

No. 153

Fratercula arctica

Atlantic Puffin

Clown of the Sea | Common Puffin | Lundi |
Sea Parrot

● **VULNERABLE**

✳ **COLLECTIVE NAMES**
Burrow of puffins | Circus of puffins |
Colony of puffins | Gathering of puffins

✴ **SYMBOLIC MEANINGS**
Companionship; Family;
Self-care.

🌀 **POSSIBLE POWERS**
Defense; Distraction;
Reincarnated monks.

☾ **FOLKLORE AND FACTS**
Wrapped in their black coats with their bright white shirtfronts, Atlantic Puffins reminded fishermen in northern ocean communities of monks in an abbey—which is how they got a Latin name that means "little brother." In Celtic folklore, puffins actually embody the reincarnated souls of these monks, giving the friars the opportunity to be as cute as a button in the afterlife. • These birds may be the most adorable of the northern seabirds, their orange, yellow, and dark blue bills glowing in the sun as they stand on a rocky island outcropping. They use these bills to gather lots of sandeel—small, skinny, silver fish—that they then bring to their young in burrow colonies dug in sand. Here they raise their pufflings, and guard them from marauding large seabirds. • Many generations of sea fishing experts tell us that when puffins have had enough of parenting, they stop feeding their fledglings until the young finally leave the nest to find food. Scientists, however, have found that the pufflings actually abandon their parents: The youngsters disappear into the ocean waves while their parents are out gathering sandeel, leaving them to stare blankly into the empty burrow.

No. 154

Fratercula cirrhata

Tufted Puffin

Crested Puffin | Toporok

● **LEAST CONCERN**

✳ **COLLECTIVE NAMES**
Burrow of puffins | Circus of puffins | Colony of puffins | Gathering of puffins

✴ **SYMBOLIC MEANINGS**
Companionship; Family; Self-care.

🌀 **POSSIBLE POWER**
Weather and storm control.

☾ **FOLKLORE AND FACTS**
The Pacific Ocean member of the *Fratercula* family wears darker plumage overall than its cousin on the Atlantic Ocean, but it sports a bright orange bill and yellow plumes on each side of its head. • At one time, Tufted Puffins were a major food source for cultures that subsisted on the animals and plants they found close to home. The birds' skins became coats, worn with the outer feathers on the inside and the waterproof skin outside; the skins and crests also became part of ceremonial regalia. • In the northernmost part of the birds' range along the coast of Alaska, the Inuit believed that the birds could control storms, though more recently, with large numbers of puffins falling prey to major storms, this belief has not withstood the test of time.

F

No. 155

Fregata magnificens

Magnificent Frigatebird

Man-o-War Bird | Pirate Bird

● **LEAST CONCERN**

✿ **COLLECTIVE NAMES**

Fleet of frigatebirds | Flotilla of frigatebirds

✺ **SYMBOLIC MEANINGS**

Endurance; Good fishing; Good luck; Strength.

✾ **POSSIBLE POWERS**

Dominance; Stealth.

☾ **FOLKLORE AND FACTS**

When a male Magnificent Frigatebird flies overhead, its red pouch inflated to attract mates, birders stop and stand stock still to watch. This grand bird's ability to float motionless above our heads, its deeply forked tail streaming behind it, makes it one of the most arresting avian sights in the western hemisphere. • Frigatebirds are known to attack other seabirds and force them to regurgitate whatever they just ate, then eat this pre-digested food themselves, earning them the nickname "Pirate Bird." • Explorers as far back as Christopher Columbus assumed this was the only way the frigatebird could eat. They were wrong: Frigatebirds glide just above the water to watch for prey, and then dip down just far enough to scoop the fish or crustacean out of the sea, devouring it on the wing. • On some Pacific islands, the Birdman cult of the 1500s selected its leadership based on which members won a seabird egg-collecting competition. Competitors swam to an islet where Magnificent Frigatebirds nested, and then tried to be the first to steal an egg from a bird's nest and swim all the way back to their home island—all without breaking the egg. This competition continued well into the nineteenth century.

No. 156

Fulica americana

American Coot

Coot | Mud Hen | Poule d'Eau

● **LEAST CONCERN**

✿ **COLLECTIVE NAMES**

Commotion of coots | Cooperation of coots | Cover of coots | Covert of coots | Fleet of coots

✺ **SYMBOLIC MEANINGS**

Community; New beginnings; Perseverance.

✾ **POSSIBLE POWERS**

Courage; Loyalty.

☾ **FOLKLORE AND FACTS**

An Ojibwa legend tells us that long ago, the Creator sent a great flood to purify the world and drown everything evil. One man, Waynaboozhoo, worked quickly and built himself a raft, and managed to keep himself and a few animals afloat for an entire month as they waited for the water to recede. The water did not go down, though, so he summoned several different birds to dive to the bottom and retrieve some dirt from the Old World to start a new one. The Loon tried and failed, as did the Dove. But a lone Coot named Aajigade took on the challenge. Time passed before the others noticed he was gone, but then they found the unconscious Coot floating behind the raft. Sure enough, his bill clung to a little bit of mud from the bottom. Aajigade had restarted the Earth!

F

Fulmarus glacialis

Northern Fulmar

Arctic Fulmar | Fulmar | Mallie | Mallimack

● **LEAST CONCERN**

✢ **COLLECTIVE NAME**

Colony of fulmars

✴ **SYMBOLIC MEANINGS**

Resourcefulness; Survival.

🌀 **POSSIBLE POWERS**

Deception; Ingenuity.

☾ **FOLKLORE AND FACTS**

Millions of years ago, the Northern Fulmar enjoyed summer's round-the-clock daylight and all of its benefits: The growth of krill and other tiny organisms which fed small fish, which in turn fed the larger fish that Northern Fulmar ate. The winter darkness, however, brought surprise attacks from unseen predators. So the resourceful bird evolved a way of protecting itself: Fulmars produce and spit a foul-smelling oil that makes any predator recoil from the stench. This is how the bird got its name: Fulmar is Old Norse for "foul gull." • In an Inuit myth, a Fulmar courts Sedna, a girl of the northern ocean, and promises to take her to a beautiful land across the sea. She consents, but when they arrive, it's nothing but cold, wet, and full of rocks. Her father finally arrives in his boat, kills the Fulmar, and he and Sedna flee. Soon, however, the other Fulmars catch up with the boat, and they cause a storm that threatens to capsize the vessel. Sedna's father panics and throws her overboard, but she grabs the edge of the craft and holds on with all her strength. To her horror, her father produces a knife and begins cutting off her fingers! She finally clambers back into the boat, but they both end up at the bottom of the sea, where Sedna rules the ocean to this day.

Furnarius rufus

Rufous Hornero

Red Ovenbird

● **LEAST CONCERN**

✢ **COLLECTIVE NAME**

Flock of horneros

✴ **SYMBOLIC MEANINGS**

Freedom; Strength; Unity.

🌀 **POSSIBLE POWERS**

Common sense; Diligence.

☾ **FOLKLORE AND FACTS**

The Rufous Hornero holds a special place in the minds and hearts of the people of Argentina, serving as both the country's national bird and its national animal. With more than 1,000 birds in the region, it won these honors by being a very common bird in Argentina, Brazil, Bolivia, and Paraguay, and readily adapting to the growth of urban areas. • Hornero is Spanish for "baker," which makes direct reference to the unusual way it builds a nest. While most common lawn birds use twigs and other found materials to build a cup nest, the Rufous Hornero creates a mud hut around itself with a large opening in front—much like a clay oven. The mud allows the nest to heat up in the sun, keeping eggs warm enough for proper incubation. • The bird's willingness to work hard at nest-building and raising its young has made it a symbol of diligence and the rewards of toil. Even more poignant to the Argentines, the Rufous Hornero renovates its nest after each use, keeping it in good repair in much the same way that we do with our own homes. Pride in ownership and good common sense are qualities that resonate with people where wastefulness is unpatriotic and frugality is a virtue.

No. 159

Galerida cristata

Crested Lark

● LEAST CONCERN

✿ **COLLECTIVE NAMES**
Ascension of larks | Exaltation of larks | Happiness of larks

✹ **SYMBOLIC MEANINGS**
Happiness; Self-discovery; Spirituality.

✺ **POSSIBLE POWERS**
Modesty; Self-sufficiency.

☾ **FOLKLORE AND FACTS**
Ancient legend tells us that the Crested Lark came into being even before the Earth itself, and Aesop used this belief to explain how the little brown bird with the stick-straight crest came to have such an impressively erect headdress. • When the lark's father died suddenly, the bird found herself with no way to pay her last respects to the body. Earth had not yet been created, so there was nowhere to bury him—and burial may not even have existed as a concept. On the sixth day after his death, the Crested Lark buried him in her own head. The resulting crest forever reminds the little bird of the father she lost. Aesop's moral is simple: All youths should honor their parents. • Beyond the crest, the Crested Lark wears an unassuming mantle. Once its liquid, burbling song pours out of this bird, however, its special quality leaves no room for argument: This bird lives up to the lark's reputation for musicality. • Saint Francis of Assisi made note of the ways that the bird could be a metaphor for the lives of friars at the time—choosing dull plumage the way the friars chose their dun-colored robes and hoods, its contentment with singing, and the way "it goes willingly along the wayside and finds grain of corn for itself," expecting no one to provide it with a living.

No. 160

Gallinago delicata

Wilson's Snipe

Common Snipe

● LEAST CONCERN

✿ **COLLECTIVE NAMES**
Volley of snipe | Wisp of snipe

✹ **SYMBOLIC MEANINGS**
Love of home; Search for answers.

✺ **POSSIBLE POWER**
Finding what's concealed.

☾ **FOLKLORE AND FACTS**
Yes, there is actually a bird called a snipe—several, in fact— but that doesn't stop camp counselors and scout leaders from sending children out into the woods on a "snipe hunt." These practical jokers tell the poor innocents that they must do something ridiculous to attract snipe into their net or trap: Whistle a certain tune, bang on a trash can lid, dance a silly jig, brandish a stick, carry salt to pour on the bird's tail. Naturally, none of these things will attract snipe, and usually the woods where these children must search for them contain no Wilson's Snipe at all. • The real Wilson's Snipe is a round, mottled-plumaged ground bird with an unusually long bill, which it uses to probe the earth for worms, grubs, and the like. The tip of its amazing bill is covered with sensitive filaments, allowing the bird to find food deep in the ground; this process can be quite fascinating to watch, as it searches with a motion like a sewing machine needle.

No. 161

Gallirallus owstoni

Guam Rail

Ko'ko'

● **CRITICALLY ENDANGERED**

🐾 **COLLECTIVE NAMES**

Covey of rails | Meekness of rails | Rush of rails

✹ **SYMBOLIC MEANING**

Guam national pride.

🌀 **POSSIBLE POWERS**

Resurrection; Survival against predators.

☾ **FOLKLORE AND FACTS**

One of only two bird species in the entire world to be reclassified from Extinct to Endangered (the other is No. 172: California Condor), the Guam Rail's factual story has all the twists and turns of an ancient folk tale. • Not long ago, tens of thousands of these ground birds wandered the island nation of Guam. After World War II, however, the brown tree snake of Papua New Guinea accidentally stowed away on military cargo ships and found its way onto Guam, and it began to multiply aggressively. Brown tree snakes eat birds at an alarming rate: Today, nine of the eleven species of Guam's native birds are now extinct. The last Guam Rail seen in the wild was spotted in 1987. After that, only a few remained in captive breeding programs. • The Guam Rail had a champion, however, in zoologist Bob Beck, who captured the last Guam Rails in 1982 and spent twenty years establishing programs to restore the population. He created a release site on Rota in the Mariana Islands, and worked with the Bronx Zoo, Philadelphia Zoo, and the National Zoo in Washington, DC, to encourage the birds to breed. Soon his network grew to seventeen zoos, and he had enough birds to reintroduce them in the wild in areas with snake barriers. Today more than 200 Guam Rails live in protected areas on Guam, Cocos Island, and Rota.

No. 162

Gallirex porphyreolophus

Purple-Crested Turaco

Plaintain-Eater | Purple-Crested Loerie | Touraco

● **LEAST CONCERN**

🐾 **COLLECTIVE NAME**

Flock of turacos

✹ **SYMBOLIC MEANING**

National bird of Eswatini (Swaziland).

🌀 **POSSIBLE POWER**

Bestowing of honor.

☾ **FOLKLORE AND FACTS**

Of the twenty-two species of turacos in Africa, the Purple-Crested Turaco shines with the widest range of colors, its purple crest topping a green head with a bright red-ringed eye, which in turn tops a pinkish breast and back that blend into bright blue wings, a green underside, and a long, luxurious blue tail. In flight, red patches on the wings flash into view, and the bird's overall plumage shimmers with iridescence. It's not very surprising, then, that the Swazi and Zulu royal families choose this bird's scarlet flight feathers to adorn their ceremonial clothes. • Committed fruit-eaters, turacos live primarily in dense woodlands where trees and shrubs bear plenty of fruits. Residents often find these birds plundering their backyard gardens, though locals advise that the birds be watched through windows, as they are shy and don't care for human interaction. • Nonetheless, poachers do pursue these stunning creatures outright, both to capture them for the pet trade and to harvest their feathers. The bird's numbers are dropping, especially in Tanzania, where hunting is particularly aggressive.

No. 163

Gallus gallus domesticus

Domestic Chicken

Biddy | Capon | Chook | Cock | Cockerel Gallic Rooster | Hen | Poultry | Pullet | Rooster | Yardbird

● **LEAST CONCERN**

🐾 **COLLECTIVE NAMES**

Brood of chickens | Flock of chickens | Mews of capons | Peep of chickens | Run of poultry

✹ **SYMBOLIC MEANINGS**

Abundance; Braggadocio; Cowardice; Fertility; Pride.

Fortune-telling; Predictors of good and evil; Production of golden eggs.

FOLKLORE AND FACTS

Here's a fun fact: At any given time, there are more than 26 billion domestic chickens on the planet—that's more than three times more chickens in the world than there are human beings. This makes 1928 presidential candidate Herbert Hoover's promise of "a chicken in every pot" much more plausible than it seemed at the time. • Before chickens became little more than commodities in a global market, they served as sacrifices to all manner of gods, prognosticators of good and evil, and the subjects of many a moralistic fable. Roosters, usually called cocks or cockerels in these stories, often represented puffery and pride in stories by Aesop. In the tale of the two cocks and the eagle, for example, two cockerels battled over dominance of the hens in a barnyard. One finally chased off the other, but instead of indulging immediately in his conquest, he flew up to the top of the barnyard fence and crowed loudly. Seconds into this exercise, an eagle swooped down, grabbed the cockerel, and broke its neck. The other cock, now the only male in the barnyard, reaped his reward with the hens. The moral: God's grace goes to the humble, not the proud. • Another of Aesop's fables uses one of folklore's favorite motifs: The hen that lays golden eggs. A man who receives eggs made of gold from his hen decides that she must have a big bar of gold in her belly. He kills her and cuts her open, but finds nothing unusual inside—and he no longer has the hen that brought him riches every day. The moral: Be content with what you have rather than destroying your current wealth or happiness to grasp for something more. • Chickens did yeoman's service to the Roman Empire, acting as soothsayers to the mighty government's leadership. Their *pullarius*, or chicken-keeper, watched carefully as the chickens scratched away at whatever grain they had. If the chickens ate the grain voraciously, the leaders took it as a good omen. If they refused the grain or turned away from it, this foretold a bad outcome, so the plan did not go forward. • While we can't imagine that a chicken understood its fate, they certainly did run from those trying to catch them—a first clue to the enduring slang that showing fear makes us "chicken." • Writer William Kemp used the term to mean "coward" in 1600, in his volume *Nine Days' Wonder*: "It did him good to have ill words of a hoddy doddy! A hebber de hoy! A chicken! A squib." More literary references followed over several hundred years, also giving rise to the terms "hen-pecked" husbands of nagging wives, and "chicken-livered" men who are cowardly to the core. • While we deride hens with all of these negative associations, roosters have long been revered by many cultures. The crowing cockerel awakened farmers to the start of a new day, tying the bird so closely to the sun that he became one of the sun god Apollo's familiars. Valorous for its willingness to pick a fight, the rooster is also associated with Hermes, the messenger god, and even Ares, god of war. • Indeed, in France, the Gallic Rooster has come to represent the French nation. It started out as a play on words: The Romans found Gaul, the early name for France, to be very funny, because *gallus* in Latin also means "rooster." The emblem of the rooster stuck with the French, and they had the good sense to embrace it. • The Gallic Rooster rose in popularity throughout the country during the Renaissance, and by the time the French people faced revolution in 1789, their bird stood front and center with them, representing Fraternity— the third of the trio of allegorical figures that symbolized France, alongside Liberty and Equality. • Napoleon I, emperor of France after the revolution, tossed out the Gallic Rooster and replaced it with the eagle, a bird he believed better represented his nation's strength and dominance. After his death and a regime change, however, the rooster returned for the French Revolution of 1830. • With the onset of World War I, as France resisted German aggression, the rooster came to represent the courage of a nation that began as people of the land—now proud, brave, and full of its own national identity. The connection continues today, especially in sports, where many French teams wear the Gallic Rooster on their uniforms.

No. 164

Garrulus glandarius

Eurasian Jay

Jay | Screachag Choille

● **LEAST CONCERN**

🦊 **COLLECTIVE NAMES**

Band of jays | Party of jays

✳ **SYMBOLIC MEANINGS**

Ancestral wisdom; The power of intelligence.

🌀 **POSSIBLE POWERS**

Caring for others; Mimicry.

🌙 **FOLKLORE AND FACTS**

The wide-ranging Eurasian Jay can be found throughout Europe and Asia. Easily recognizable to locals across the range, it glows with a muted, warm brown edged with black, white, and tightly striped patches on its outer wings and tail, and the white face and black moustache that give it a dapper but pensive expression. While its plumage is fairly unremarkable overall, its ability to mimic all kinds of calls—including human alarms and phones—draws attention to it in the mixed woodlands it calls home; even when it uses its own voice, the harsh, rasping, unmusical screech really can't be mistaken for any other bird. • The Eurasian Jay takes other birds' needs into consideration, planning to be sure it has plenty of food stashed away to feed itself and its mate in leaner seasons. While courting a potential mate, the male jay makes note of the female's food preferences and brings her the thing she craves most, a wondrous trait that certainly impresses her. The Eurasian Jay also keeps this information in mind while defending from thieves its carefully assembled cache of winter food, paying the most attention to predators' interest in the foods its mate likes best.

No. 165

Gavia immer

Common Loon

Ember Goose | Great Northern Diver | Hell Diver | Ring-Necked Loon | Walloon

● **LEAST CONCERN**

🦊 **COLLECTIVE NAMES**

Asylum of loons | Cry of loons | Raft of loons | Water dance of loons

✳ **SYMBOLIC MEANINGS**

Reawakening of old dreams; Serenity; Tranquility.

🌀 **POSSIBLE POWERS**

Messenger of the spirits; Omen of death.

🌙 **FOLKLORE AND FACTS**

An Abenaki legend tells of Glooskap, a revered figure, and the special relationship he established with Kwe-moo, the Common Loon. One day a chief of the loons flew in and landed near Glooskap. "What do you want?" asked Glooskap of the bird. "To be your friend and servant," the loon replied. So Glooskap taught him a long, haunting cry that loons should sing whenever they were in need of him. The loon accepted the song and went on his way. Years later, when Glooskap visited Newfoundland, he came to a town where all of the people had been loons. These men and women were delighted to see him, and thanked him for blessing them when they were birds. Glooskap made them his hunters and messengers, and from then on, any tale of Glooskap included the presence of Kwe-moo, his faithful companion. • Loons' legs are set back too far on their bodies to support their weight for crossing land, but this makes them some of the fastest and smoothest swimmers on any lake. The Mi'kmaq people believe that there was a time that a Loon ran about on land and made a nuisance of itself, until the people had had enough and caught him. "We've had all we can stand of you! We will throw you in the water," their leader said. Loon thought quickly and said, "Oh no, not the water! Please throw me in the fire." Just to annoy the Loon, the leader threw the bird in the lake . . . and the Loon, only too happy to be in water, swam off in great haste. And that is how the Loon became a water bird.

G

Geococcyx californianus

Greater Roadrunner

Chaparral Cock | Ground Cuckoo | Snake Killer

● **LEAST CONCERN**

✢ **COLLECTIVE NAMES**

Marathon of roadrunners | Race of roadrunners

✳ **SYMBOLIC MEANINGS**

Energy; Good luck; Magic; Speed.

✺ **POSSIBLE POWERS**

Deliverer of newborn babies;
Protector against evil spirits.

☾ **FOLKLORE AND FACTS**

Chances are good that everything you know about the Greater Roadrunner comes from the animated series *The Road Runner Show* created by Chuck Jones and Michael Maltese for Warner Brothers in 1948, an enduring classic of just forty-nine episodes—and one that remains foremost in our roadrunner consciousness more than seventy years later. The simple premise involves Wile E. Coyote setting trap after trap for the extraordinarily fast and undyingly cheerful Roadrunner, never succeeding in catching him for long, and always going away hungry. • The Greater Roadrunner does not actually say "Beep, beep," but it does run along the roadside as its name suggests, and it is the dominant member of the cuckoo family in the North American southwest. Its top speed is about 20 miles (32 km) per hour . . . which makes it easy prey for the much faster coyote. • The Hopi of the southwest see the Greater Roadrunner as a protector against the spirits of evil, so the bird is a welcome sight whenever it approaches. • Mexican families tell children that roadrunners bring newborn babies to their families, just as storks do in American and European cultures.

Geronticus eremita

Northern Bald Ibis

Hermit Ibis | Waldrapp

● **ENDANGERED**

✢ **COLLECTIVE NAMES**

Colony of ibises | Stand of ibises |
Wedge of ibises

✳ **SYMBOLIC MEANINGS**

Brilliance; Resplendence.

✺ **POSSIBLE POWERS**

Fertility; Intelligence.

☾ **FOLKLORE AND FACTS**

Don't look along lakeshores to find this ibis: the Northern Bald Ibis is not a wading bird, preferring desert-like habitat with high rock ledges where the birds gather to nest. At one time, this ibis had a widespread range throughout the Middle East, southern Europe, and northern Africa, but just about 700 birds remain in the wild today, nearly all of them in Souss-Massa National Park in Morocco. • This quirky ibis has a featherless red head, and its glossy black plumage does not have the iridescence of the Glossy Ibises of North and Central America. It does share the downward-curved red bill, however, making it unmistakably an ibis. • In the Birecik area of Turkey, people believe that Noah released a Northern Bald Ibis from the ark as a fertility symbol to guide the repopulation of the Earth. In Egypt, the gods' secretary, known as Thoth (see No. M011), wears the head of an ibis to indicate his high intelligence. Ibises represent the wonders of Egypt, and a bald ibis even appears in hieroglyphs as the symbol *akh*, meaning "to shine."

Goura victoria

Victoria Crowned Pigeon

● **NEAR THREATENED**

🦃 **COLLECTIVE NAMES**

Flight of pigeons | Kit of pigeons | Loft of pigeons | Passel of pigeons

☀ **SYMBOLIC MEANINGS**

Luxury; Royalty.

🌀 **POSSIBLE POWER**

Messenger to the gods.

☾ **FOLKLORE AND FACTS**

Four very similar but distinct bird species of Papua New Guinea are all crowned pigeons, each with an extravagant crest of lacy feathers and bright-colored blue or grayish plumage. Of these, the Victoria Crowned Pigeon attracts considerable attention for its showy brilliance, the regal bearing that earned it the name of a British monarch, and the precarious nature of its existence. • Other than the basics of body shape, this bird bears little resemblance to the Rock Pigeon of Europe or any of the New World pigeons. Nearly the size of a Wild Turkey, its bold blue coloration makes it distinctly different. The real departure, however, is in its tail: crowned pigeon tails have sixteen feathers, instead of the twelve feathers that make up Western pigeons' tails. This provides a luxurious look and additional stability.
• With dwindling numbers in the wild, this pigeon is more easily found in zoos around the world, its good-natured adaptability a key to its survival. While the wild population is under constant threat from hunters and trappers for illegal trade, birds in zoos and sanctuaries have the chance to raise young free from the challenges the birds find in their normal habitat.

Grus grus

Common Crane

Eurasian Crane | Peata Corr

● **LEAST CONCERN**

🦃 **COLLECTIVE NAMES**

Flock of cranes | Herd of cranes | Sedge of cranes | Siege of cranes

☀ **SYMBOLIC MEANINGS**

Bridge to the otherworld; Strength in battle.

🌀 **POSSIBLE POWERS**

Magic; Travel between realms.

☾ **FOLKLORE AND FACTS**

More than 300 years ago, Common Cranes vanished from Ireland, their habitat ruined by the draining of wetlands, and their numbers ravaged by the lack of food. Between 1600 and 1700, the birds died out, and a key symbol of the bridge between this world and the spirit world no longer graced the Irish countryside. • This may be changing in the 2020s, as the Peatlands Climate Action Scheme provides funding to organizations to restore targeted wetlands across the country. Common Cranes have been seen migrating over Ireland on their way to other areas of the United Kingdom, and one pair has actively nested in an Irish bog. • Why are Common Cranes so important to the Irish? Hundreds of years ago, cranes were the favored pets in affluent households, where they were kept near the dining table—and some stories say the birds could be taught to bow their heads as prayers were said. Cranes played a role in Druid rituals, and towns across Ireland have names that begin with Cor, the Celtic word for crane. • A story about Lugh, a mighty Irish warrior who may also have been a god, gives us a glimpse of the importance of cranes in Ireland. Before Lugh led his army into battle with the Fomorians, he performed the Crane Dance, hopping on one foot much like a crane standing in the water on one leg. This posture places the dancer with his foot in the world of the living and his raised leg on its way to the Otherworld. Lugh hopped in a circle to bless his warriors, giving them power to fight on water, land, and air. The Common Crane represented shifting between these realms, with enough magic to pass from one to the next.

Grus japonensis

Red-Crowned Crane

Fairy Crane | Japanese Crane | Manchurian Crane

● **VULNERABLE**

🐦 **COLLECTIVE NAMES**
Flock of cranes | Herd of cranes |
Sedge of cranes | Siege of cranes

✳ **SYMBOLIC MEANINGS**
Immortality; Morality.

🌀 **POSSIBLE POWERS**
Good luck; Loyalty.

🌙 **FOLKLORE AND FACTS**
This iconic, snow-white crane of the Pacific Rim is so much a part of Asian art and tradition that it has become a familiar sight to westerners. • In the Dao tradition of China, when a Chinese mythological figure achieves immortality, artwork often shows them riding on a Red-Crowned Crane. High officials of ancient China had the Red-Crowned Crane embroidered on their clothing, an honor denoting their rank. • A well-known story tells of a man who saves a crane that hunters shot out of the sky. That night, a woman visits the man and tells him that she is now his wife. "I am not wealthy enough to support you," he protests, but she tells him to have no fear: She brings with her a bag of rice that will keep them both fed. He doubts her, but over time they eat quite a bit of rice, and the amount in the bag never goes down. Meanwhile, she goes into a room and asks not to be disturbed—and after seven days, she emerges with a beautiful piece of clothing she has made. He takes it to market and sells it for a very high price, so they are now wealthy. Once again, she goes into a room and asks not to be disturbed, but now he can't help himself, and he knows exactly what he will see; sure enough, she is the crane he saved some time ago. Now that she has been found out, however, she can no longer stay, and she flies off, never to return.

Gygis alba

White Tern

Angel Tern | Common White Tern | Fairy Tern | Manu-o-Kū | White Noddy |

● **LEAST CONCERN**

🐦 **COLLECTIVE NAMES**
Colony of terns | Committee of terns | Ternery of terns

✳ **SYMBOLIC MEANINGS**
Peace; Purity; Renewal.

🌀 **POSSIBLE POWERS**
Connection to fairies; Navigation; Resiliency.

🌙 **FOLKLORE AND FACTS**
The official bird of Honolulu, Hawai'i may be a tern or a noddy, according to scientists who conduct molecular studies of birds, but for the time being, this delicate-looking, sea-hardened bird roams the Pacific Ocean. Watching this pure white bird with large black eyes float above the water absolutely brings angels to mind, giving this bird its highly appropriate nickname "angel tern." • This tern departs from its black-and-white cousins in another significant way: Instead of laying its eggs on the ground, the White Tern lays an egg on a bare branch, skipping over the tedious process of building a nest. The heavily speckled egg blends in with many tree branches—but any stiff breeze can knock this little egg right out of the tree to smash on the ground. Have no fear, however; when this happens, the White Tern just lays another one. The chick, meanwhile, has evolved feet that can cling to the branch until it learns to fly. • In Hawai'i, the "fairy tern" is also known as Manu-o-Kū, designating it as the bird of Ku, the god of war. Hawaiian sailors used the terns as navigation aids, watching which way they flew as the day came to an end to help guide their ships back to land.

G

Gymnogyps californianus

California Condor

California Vulture | Condor

● **CRITICALLY ENDANGERED**

✴ **COLLECTIVE NAMES**

Condo of condors | Scarcity of condors

✴ **SYMBOLIC MEANINGS**

Death; Grieving; Rebirth; Renewal.

◉ **POSSIBLE POWERS**

Path to the upper and lower worlds; Resurrection.

◔ **FOLKLORE AND FACTS**

It's no surprise that North America's largest bird has a place in the legends of many different Native American cultures—the surprise comes from the many roles it plays, and how they differ. While most animals named in myths maintain a distinctive personality even as they cross cultural lines, the California Condor's role changes with the tribe. • The Wiyot tribe, for example, gives the condor a central role in humanity's resurrection after the Great Flood, while the Mono tribe casts the condor in the role of singlehandedly wiping out all the people. In the Mono story, Condor gathers up people as they sleep and swoops off with them, carrying them to a "Skyland" from which they never return. • The California Condor's modern story of rescue from the brink of extinction has become a legend in itself, the first story of its kind in the world: No wild individuals remained when the project began, but they were raised in captivity and now live in Grand Canyon and Zion National Parks, still under careful supervision by humans.

Gymnorhina tibicen

Australian Magpie

Long-Billed Magpie | Piping Shrike | Top End Magpie | White-Backed Magpie

● **LEAST CONCERN**

✴ **COLLECTIVE NAMES**

Charm of magpies | Congregation of magpies | Gulp of magpies | Murder of magpies | Tiding of magpies | Tittering of magpies | Tribe of magpies

✴ **SYMBOLIC MEANINGS**

Boldness; Cheekiness.

◉ **POSSIBLE POWER**

Messenger from the higher powers.

◔ **FOLKLORE AND FACTS**

Australia's native magpie is everywhere in cities Down Under, making them a familiar symbol of Australian pride. • More than a dozen sports teams in Australia and New Zealand claim the magpie as their mascot, and the Government of South Australia named one of the subspecies, the White-Backed Magpie (locally known as the Piping Shrike) as its official emblem in 1901. The bird has appeared on South Australia's flag since 1904. • In 2017, the Australian Magpie became the first Australian Bird of the Year based on popular vote. Most recently, its melodic whistle won an ABC Science poll in 2023 as Australia's favorite animal sound. • So there's no question that Australia loves its cheeky magpie, even going so far as to say that its bold, devil-may-care attitude represents the Australian people to a T. In fact, a larger-than-life sculpture of the magpie in downtown central Canberra glorifies the bird right where it lives, in the heart of the city.

No. 174

Gypaetus barbatus

Bearded Vulture

Homa | Lammergeier | Ossifrage | Peres

● **NEAR THREATENED**

🦅 **COLLECTIVE NAMES**

Colony of vultures | Committee of vultures | Kettle of vultures | Wake of vultures

✷ **SYMBOLIC MEANINGS**

Happiness; Recognition of leadership; Wisdom.

🌀 **POSSIBLE POWERS**

Foretelling the future; Good luck.

🦉 **FOLKLORE AND FACTS**

The only vulture with a feathered head and neck, the Bearded Vulture has a storied past in mythology and in real life throughout its central Asian and North African range. • The creature called Huma in Iranian mythology is clearly based on a Bearded Vulture, and may even have been one, casting massive shadows with its nine-foot wingspan to foretell a person's rise to leadership and social status. • Ancient Romans and Greeks used Bearded Vultures to predict the potential success or failure of an upcoming battle, giving rise to the profession of ornithomancers, or people who could use birds to tell the future. • Historians guess that when a large bird dropped a tortoise on the head of Greek playwright Aeschylus, thinking the man's bald head was a rock that would split open the tortoise shell on impact, the bird was most likely a Bearded Vulture. (Whatever the bird was, it killed poor Aeschylus.) • Perhaps the oddest story about this bird took place in 1944, when Shimon Perski and David Ben-Gurion, two leaders of the people of Israel, found a Bearded Vulture nest in the Negev desert. Perski found the birds and their Hebrew name *peres* so compelling that he discarded Perski and changed his name to Peres. Ben-Gurion became the first prime minister of Israel, and Peres became its eighth prime minister and eventually its president.

No. 175

Gyps fulvus

Eurasian Griffon Vulture

Griffon Vulture

● **LEAST CONCERN**

🦅 **COLLECTIVE NAMES**

Colony of vultures | Committee of vultures | Kettle of vultures | Wake of vultures

✷ **SYMBOLIC MEANING**

Protector of the mother.

🌀 **POSSIBLE POWERS**

Fierce defender; Reproduction without male birds.

🦉 **FOLKLORE AND FACTS**

In ancient times, Egyptians celebrated the Eurasian Griffon Vulture as the protector of Mut, the Great Mother Goddess. Egyptians observed that griffon vultures are very protective of their nestlings, warding off predators by spreading their enormous wings and presenting a fierce defense. Egyptians took this a step further, believing that the female vultures produced their own fertile embryos without the need for male birds. This inaccurate idea sprang from the assumption that there were no male griffon vultures, as they could not tell the males and females apart. • Depictions of Mut in Egyptian art very often incorporate a vulture into her regalia: Sometimes she has a vulture's head and a woman's body, and sometimes she has a woman's head and a vulture's body with wings. Human queens of Egypt, including Nefertiti, wore a vulture symbol on their own crowns to display their connection with the goddess. • Today Eurasian griffon vultures have one major threat to their survival: eating carcasses of "nuisance" animals that have been fed poisoned bait. Wolves, jackals, foxes, and bears are often targeted by livestock owners who lure these animals onto their land to kill them, then leave their poisoned bodies out for vultures to consume. This practice has reduced vulture numbers dramatically.

G

No. 176

Haematopus bachmani

Black Oystercatcher

Pied Oystercatcher

● **LEAST CONCERN**

⚜ **COLLECTIVE NAMES**

Parcel of oystercatchers | Stew of oystercatchers

✹ **SYMBOLIC MEANINGS**

Concealment; Shelter.

🌀 **POSSIBLE POWERS**

Descendant of the South Wind; Ally to shamans.

🌎 **FOLKLORE AND FACTS**

Seeing an oystercatcher jam its bill into a slightly open oyster or mussel shell, slice through the muscle holding the contents in place, and then swallow the creature whole can be an early morning treat for beach walkers along North America's Pacific seashore. Beyond their pleasing appearance and fascinating skills, the Black Oystercatcher plays a role in ancient Tlingit culture along the southern coast of Alaska.
• Tlingit shamans saw oystercatchers as allies, capturing their image in carved rattles that they use in healing and divination rites. Shamans believed that rattling sounds pleased the spirits. • The Haida people of British Columbia tell us how the Black Oystercatcher came to be: Long ago, North Wind (Xaw's son) brought Southeaster, daughter of Xyuu, the South Wind, to live at his father's house. When they arrived, the house was covered in icicles, and she broke some without realizing that these were her father-in-law's fingers. This made Xaw very angry, so when she was out searching the shoreline for food, he trapped Southeaster in ice and snow. She could not move, but after quite a long time, she began calling to her father for help. Finally the South Wind blew and melted the ice that trapped her, but Xyuu wasn't finished yet: He brought rainstorms and washed away Xaw's icicles. Today the Black Oystercatcher represents Southeaster, skittering along looking for limpets, and still bent over from the ordeal of being frozen on the coastline. The oystercatcher's long, red nose is further evidence of the toll the snow and ice took on the girl, and her thin legs can never go far along the shoreline.

No. 177

Haematopus ostralegus

Eurasian Oystercatcher

Common Pied Oystercatcher | Oystercatcher

● **NEAR THREATENED**

⚜ **COLLECTIVE NAMES**

Parcel of oystercatchers | Stew of oystercatchers

✹ **SYMBOLIC MEANING**

Concealment.

🌀 **POSSIBLE POWER**

Saving Jesus from his enemies.

🌎 **FOLKLORE AND FACTS**

This black and white bird of European seashores dazzles onlookers with its bright orange eye ring, orange bill, and pink legs, making it a favorite sight on rocky North Atlantic shores. Wintering on the coasts of northern and central Africa, the Middle East, and India, these oystercatchers head inland in spring and summer to breed in eastern Europe and western Asia. • In the United Kingdom's West Highlands, the tale is told that Jesus Christ came to the Hebrides Islands with enemy pursuers close behind him. At low tide he came upon two oystercatchers, who immediately saw his plight and took him into their protection. They covered Jesus with seaweed and watched over his location until his enemies moved on. In gratitude for this, Jesus awarded the black birds a white plumage across their chest and wings, so when the wings are extended, the white takes the shape of a cross. Later, the oystercatcher was selected to be the servant of St. Bridget, Christ's foster-mother, in further recognition of the birds' good deed.

H

No. 178

Haemorhous purpureus

Purple Finch

Mountain Canary | Red Cap | Vermont Minister

● **LEAST CONCERN**

✤ **COLLECTIVE NAMES**

Charm of finches | Trembling of finches | Trimming of finches

✹ **SYMBOLIC MEANINGS**

Charm; Communication; Purity.

✺ **POSSIBLE POWER**

Yet to be discovered.

☾ **FOLKLORE AND FACTS**

"Like a bird dipped in raspberry juice," say most North American birders in describing the Purple Finch, an apt simile for this brown and white bird delicately washed in magenta from head to tail. New birders find it difficult to tell the very similar House Finch from a Purple Finch until they see their first purple one, and then the difference becomes simple and obvious. Even the female, though completely lacking in pink, has a bolder and more defined streaking on its chest and underside than a female House Finch, and a bold white eyebrow that helps define the species. • In 1957, the New Hampshire state legislature nominated the Purple Finch to be its official state bird. This well-supported and, to be honest, fairly innocuous proposal met with angry opposition from some, especially those who wanted the New Hampshire hen, a domestic species, to receive the designation. Nonetheless, the finch gained both legislative and public support, and the bill to claim the Purple Finch as New Hampshire's own quickly passed.

No. 179

Haliaeetus albicilla

White-Tailed Eagle

Ern | Erne | Eurasian Sea Eagle | Gray Sea Eagle | Sea Eagle | White-Tailed Sea-Eagle

● **LEAST CONCERN**

✤ **COLLECTIVE NAMES**

Aerie of eagles | Brood of eagles | Congregation of eagles | Exaltation of eagles

✹ **SYMBOLIC MEANINGS**

High rank; Majesty.

✺ **POSSIBLE POWERS**

Attracting fish to the surface; Totem of the Druids.

☾ **FOLKLORE AND FACTS**

Scattered across the eastern hemisphere from Europe to Japan, the White-Tailed Eagle makes its home near large bodies of water, so ocean coastlines and freshwater lakes are excellent places to watch for them. The eagle's reappearance in recent years after significant declines speaks to the diligent work by conservationists around the world to battle against pesticides like DDT, and fight for laws that protect native bird species in their natural habitats. • Ancient Druids seemed to have a special connection to the White-Tailed Eagle, though we don't know exactly what the eagles signified in their culture. In the Orkney Islands in Scotland, archaeologists discovered the remains of thirty-five eagles alongside hundreds of human skeletons in a 3000-year-old tomb now called the Tomb of Eagles. While this probably means that the Druids saw the eagle as a totem animal, we cannot say for certain—but more eagle remains turned up in caves in Gower and Carmarthenshire as well. • Shetland fishermen found a mundane use for the eagles, believing that the "Erne" (Anglo Saxon for "The Soarer") caused fish to rise to the surface, belly-up, when the birds passed over the water. So vivid was this superstition that the fishermen smeared their hooks with eagle fat in an attempt to turn the fish into a submissive catch.

No. 180

Haliaeetus leucocephalus

Bald Eagle

Eagle

● **LEAST CONCERN**

✤ **COLLECTIVE NAMES**

Aerie of eagles | Brood of eagles | Congregation of eagles | Exaltation of eagles

✹ **SYMBOLIC MEANING**

United States pride and power.

✺ **POSSIBLE POWERS**

Honoring of leaders; Protection for the sick; Spiritual messenger.

☾ **FOLKLORE AND FACTS**

If you live in the United States, you know the role that Bald Eagle plays as part of the American national image: Posed majestically against a blue-sky backdrop on countless stamps, flags, coats of arms, official seals, posters, mastheads, storefronts, and more. Seeing the eagle in its position as

H

the US national bird can be enough to bring a lump to an American's throat, especially in combination with the US flag. • Uniformly brown with a bright white head, yellow bill, and white tail, the Bald Eagle is one of the largest birds of prey in North America, building the largest stick nest of any bird in the world to raise one or two young annually. • In many Native American cultures, the Bald Eagle is a sacred symbol, its feathers and claws used in ceremonial dances and rituals, and in headdresses and cloaks worn by leaders. Navajo medicine men use the feathers as protectors of the sick, while Lakota leaders present an eagle feather to someone who has achieved an important milestone. • A popular story from the late 1700s suggests that Congressional representative Benjamin Franklin objected to the choice of the Bald Eagle as the national bird, promoting the Wild Turkey instead. The Franklin Institute in Philadelphia says that this story is a myth, born of Franklin's written comment to his daughter that the original design for the nation's Great Seal looked more like a turkey than an eagle. He did praise the turkey over the eagle in the letter, but he did not advocate for the turkey as the national bird.

No. 181
Haliaeetus pelagicus

Steller's Sea Eagle

Pacific Sea Eagle | Steller's Fish Eagle | White-Shouldered Eagle

● **VULNERABLE**

✿ **COLLECTIVE NAMES**

Aerie of eagles | Brood of eagles | Congregation of eagles | Exaltation of eagles

✴ **SYMBOLIC MEANINGS**

Power; Travel for curiosity.

✺ **POSSIBLE POWER**

Strength.

✾ **FOLKLORE AND FACTS**

The Steller's Sea Eagle may be the largest eagle in the world by weight, although this depends on the individual weighed—the Harpy Eagle and Philippine Eagle sometimes vie for this title successfully. By any standard, however, the Steller's Sea Eagle is a very large bird, its numbers living along the coast of northeastern Asia with a high concentration of birds in Kamchatka, at the far eastern end of Russia. It is unmistakable in the field, its all-black body

and head, large white wing patches, and bright yellow bill and legs making its identity obvious even at a great distance. • On August 30, 2020, a lone Steller's Sea Eagle put in an appearance at Denali National Park in Alaska, and since then this same individual—identified by its unique wing markings—has drifted around North America, crossing the continent and coming to rest for a time in Victoria, Texas, then in Quebec, Nova Scotia, Massachusetts, on the Maine coast, and in Newfoundland as recently as May 2023. Normally these birds overwinter in Japan, where they are classified as a national treasure and are therefore protected in many areas. • The travels of this specific eagle have raised scientific speculation that this bird may be wandering the unfamiliar continent strictly out of curiosity, much as human travelers do—and whether you consider this unnecessary anthropomorphism or an interesting theory, it does challenge what we believe we know about vagrant birds and how and why they visit unfamiliar territory.

No. 182
Haliastur indus

Brahminy Kite

Elang Bondol | Garuda Red-Backed | Sea Eagle

● **LEAST CONCERN**

✿ **COLLECTIVE NAMES**

Husk of kites | Kettle of kites | Roost of kites | Soar of kites | Wake of kites

✴ **SYMBOLIC MEANINGS**

King of the birds; Power; Superior abilities.

✺ **POSSIBLE POWERS**

Good luck to armies; Sacred bird of Vishnu.

✾ **FOLKLORE AND FACTS**

The large bird of prey with the glowing reddish back and wings has taken on deep meaning to people in its native India, especially to those of the Hindu faith. Seeing this bird fly over an army on its way to battle promises good luck and victory to the soldiers, who called it the "lucky-faced" bird. How it came to be seen as sacred, however, is a more complex story. • One version says that Parvati, wife of the Hindu god Shiva, became suspicious that Shiva enjoyed the company of other women when she was not with him, so she turned herself into a Brahminy Kite to see what he was up to. She flew to Shiva's meeting-place with these women, and sure enough, he was not alone. Parvati and the kite flew

H

at them and drove off these rivals. Because of this, Hindu people honor the bird when they see it above, greeting it and saying a prayer for its good health. Many call the bird Garuda, the Hindu king of the birds. • Bougainville Island off the coast of Papua New Guinea has its own folklore about the origins of the Brahminy Kite. A mother, out gardening on her property, placed her baby under a banana leaf for protection from the sun. The baby, left to its own devices, began to cry—and suddenly floated up into the sky and turned into Kaa'nang, the Brahminy Kite. The baby wore a copper-colored necklace that turned into the bird's reddish wings, giving them their glowing sheen.

No. 183

Harpia harpyja

Harpy Eagle

American Harpy Eagle

● **VULNERABLE**

☙ **COLLECTIVE NAMES**

Aerie of eagles | Brood of eagles | Congregation of eagles | Exaltation of eagles

✳ **SYMBOLIC MEANINGS**

Eagerness; Prowess.

🌀 **POSSIBLE POWERS**

Agility; Bone-crushing strength.

☾ **FOLKLORE AND FACTS**

The Harpy Eagle gets its name from the half-human, half-bird creature that caused the great winds of major storms, according to both Greek and Roman mythology. • Originally drawn as young women with the wings of an eagle, their hands distorted into claws, the depictions of harpies by various artists became less and less attractive over time until they became the ugly personifications of everything that was wrong with the world. Aeschylus described them as "altogether disgusting; they snore with repulsive breaths, they drip from their eyes hateful drops; their attire is not fit to bring either before the

statues of the gods or into the homes of men." • It must be the head, chest, and wings of the Harpy Eagle that invited this comparison in the eyes of Carl Linneaus, as he created the taxonomic system and named thousands of bird species. Beyond this, the bird certainly doesn't deserve to be compared to monstrous harpies; it presents an arresting sight as the largest bird in South America, an apex predator with the biggest talons of any extant eagle. Harpy Eagles can carry half of their own body weight in prey, and they have the speed and maneuverability to take a sloth or monkey right off a tree branch and fly off with it, even in dense forest.

No. 184

Hirundo rustica

Barn Swallow

Swallow

● **LEAST CONCERN**

☙ **COLLECTIVE NAMES**

Flight of swallows | Gulp of swallows | Kettle of swallows

✳ **SYMBOLIC MEANINGS**

Arrival of spring; Long-distance travel.

🌀 **POSSIBLE POWER**

Lucky charm.

☾ **FOLKLORE AND FACTS**

As early as 29 BCE, Virgil wrote of swallows building nests in the rafters of a building, making us wonder how the birds managed to reproduce before humans built barns, attics, and bridges. • The swallows' taste for mosquitoes makes them welcome housemates, so people all over the world tolerate the busy birds as they raise their young in their structures. • Barn Swallows appear on six continents, living anywhere where they find open land, water features that attract bugs, and buildings for their mud-and-grass nests.

H

Hydrobates

Northern Storm Petrel

Ainley's Storm Petrel | Ashy Storm Petrel | Band-Rumped Storm Petrel | Black Storm Petrel | Cape Verde Storm Petrel | European Storm Petrel | Fork-Tailed Storm Petrel | Guadalupe Storm Petrel | Leach's Storm Petrel | Least Storm Petrel | Markham's Storm Petrel | Matsudaira's Storm Petrel | Monteiro's Storm Petrel | Ringed Storm Petrel | Swinhoe's Storm Petrel | Townsend's Storm Petrel | Tristram's Storm Petrel | Wedge-Rumped Storm Petrel

● ● **LEAST CONCERN TO VULNERABLE**

✿ **COLLECTIVE NAME**

Gallon of petrels

✳ **SYMBOLIC MEANING**

Oncoming storms.

🌀 **POSSIBLE POWERS**

Bringer of storms; Good luck for sailors; Harbinger of storms.

☙ **FOLKLORE AND FACTS**

Storm petrels are pelagic birds, meaning that they do not come ashore to the mainland, instead spending their time gliding over the ocean looking for small fish on the water's surface. These birds nest in colonies on islands far offshore, so only the most intrepid ornithologists make their way to these breeding grounds. • Storm petrels received their name in honor of Saint Peter, one of the apostles who witnessed Jesus Christ's walk on water, because petrels often appear to walk on water as they hover just long enough to pick up a food item. • The "storm" part of this bird family's name comes from their habit of taking refuge from an oncoming gale by following closely behind a ship, letting the large structure block the worst of the weather. Sailors took this behavior as a dependable warning that a storm was on its way—but some thought that the birds actually brought the stormy weather with them, making a flock of storm petrels at a ship's stern a worrisome sight. • Some seafarers went so far as to call it good luck if a storm petrel happened to defecate on them as it passed over them. • Killing a storm petrel (even in retaliation for the defecation) was and is still considered bad luck, as if the shooter wishes to invite bad weather for a very long stay.

Hylocichla mustelina

Wood Thrush

Tawny Thrush

● **LEAST CONCERN**

✿ **COLLECTIVE NAMES**

Hermitage of thrushes | Mutation of thrushes | Skein of thrushes

✳ **SYMBOLIC MEANINGS**

Arrival of spring; Harmony; Self-improvement; Truthfulness.

🌀 **POSSIBLE POWERS**

Honesty; Tranquility.

☙ **FOLKLORE AND FACTS**

The flutelike, multidimensional voice of the Wood Thrush fills forests throughout the eastern United States every spring, making this time of year one of the great blessings of American birding. • Actually laying eyes on this bird can be nearly impossible, however, making it legendary for its skulking behavior and secretive nature. Wood Thrushes creep along the forest floor as they search for grubs and larvae among the leaves, so the most likely way to spot one is to listen for the rustling of last year's leaves, and watch for moving leaves in that direction. • The Wood Thrush has the ability to sing two notes simultaneously, harmonizing with itself to create a unique sound that only a few birds—all thrushes—can produce. Not surprisingly, hearing this sound reminds those who seek spiritual meaning in nature to live in harmony with one another, listening to our own inner voices to find our truth. Honesty, self-improvement, and tranquility are all traits that are attributed to the little reddish bird with the streaked breast and the miraculous voice.

H

No. 187

Icterus cucullatus

Hooded Oriole

● LEAST CONCERN

✿ **COLLECTIVE NAMES**
Array of orioles | Flamboyance of orioles | Plague of orioles | Trill of orioles

✹ **SYMBOLIC MEANINGS**
Brighter days ahead; Joy; Sun's energy.

✺ **POSSIBLE POWERS**
Acrobatics; Mimicry.

✦ **FOLKLORE AND FACTS**
With its bright orange head and black face, the Hooded Oriole stands out from other birds in fruit trees and at feeders offering grape jelly. These birds of South Texas and Mexico are particularly partial to nesting in palm trees, but a Native American folk tale tells us about orioles' relationship with the pecan trees, and why they may choose them for their sock-like hanging nests to this day. • A pair of orioles tended their nest of five hatchlings that had not yet grown all their flight feathers, when they noticed that the sky had begun to fill with clouds. They grew frightened for their little ones, but the pecan tree said, "Go into the hole under this branch. You can all fit, and the wind will not hurt you." The birds quickly moved into the hole, and the wind howled around the tree, but they were safe until the storm passed. The birds resumed their nesting and raised their young, and then went to Mexico to spend the winter. The winter was particularly warm at home, so the pecan tree began setting its buds for spring … but one day, the oriole felt a chill and knew that winter had one last pass to make over Texas. He flew north to warn the pecan tree, "Don't set your buds just yet. There's a cold spell on the way." The pecan tree believed him, and sure enough, the next day the cold came. If the pecan tree had set its buds, an entire year's harvest would have been lost. The other pecan trees heard about the good deed the oriole had done, and orioles have been welcome in pecan trees ever since.

No. 188

Icterus galbula

Baltimore Oriole
Northern Oriole

● LEAST CONCERN

✿ **COLLECTIVE NAMES**
Array of orioles | Flamboyance of orioles | Plague of orioles | Trill of orioles

✹ **SYMBOLIC MEANINGS**
Good tidings; Spring; Sun.

✺ **POSSIBLE POWER**
Lifting the spirits.

✦ **FOLKLORE AND FACTS**
The bright orange bird with the black head and wings and the clear, syrupy voice has long been a favorite of backyard birders, coming readily to feeders offering orange halves and grape jelly. Breeding primarily in the eastern United States but as far west as Montana, these beautiful birds prefer dark fruits like Concord grapes and cherries, actively ignoring green grapes even if they are ripe. • Which came first, the Major League Baseball team or the bird's name? The bird, of course; it took its name in 1808 from Sir George Calvert, 1st Lord of Baltimore, who founded the territory of Maryland, and for whom the city of Baltimore is named as well. Lord Baltimore's family coat of arms happens to be orange and black, so it made sense to grace the bird with this prestigious name. This common name certainly adds more panache to the bird's heritage than its Latin genus name, *Icterus*, which translates to "jaundice," a fairly unflattering reference to orioles' bright color. • The bird's honors continued in the twentieth century, when it was named the state bird of Maryland. • Science changed its name for a short time to Northern Oriole when the American Ornithologists' Union lumped it with the Bullock's oriole, another bright orange bird, because it appeared that the two species could interbreed. This observation was later disproved, however, so the Baltimore Oriole returned to its independent status, to Maryland's great relief.

Icterus oberi

Montserrat Oriole

● **VULNERABLE**

🦋 **COLLECTIVE NAMES**
Array of orioles | Flamboyance of orioles | Plague of orioles | Trill of orioles

✳ **SYMBOLIC MEANING**
National pride of Montserrat.

🌀 **POSSIBLE POWER**
Resilience.

🦉 **FOLKLORE AND FACTS**
Just a few hundred Montserrat Orioles remain on the island that gives them their name, making the Lesser Antilles in the West Indies the only place in the world where this species is found. • Hurricane Hugo in 1989 destroyed a substantial part of the forest where this oriole makes its home, and the Soufrière Hills volcanic eruptions on Montserrat in 1995 and 1997 laid waste to the southern half of the island, reducing the bird's population by 50 percent. Even where habitat remains, invasive mammals introduced to the island destroy the bird's nests and take their young. • The national bird of Montserrat has faced rough times and will most likely continue to do so, with the threat of continued volcanic activity and more violent storms likely in its future. So rare have they become that while their likeness appears on advertising and as a symbol all over the island, most Montserrat residents have never actually seen the little orange and black bird.

Icthyophaga vocifer

African Fish Eagle
African Sea Eagle | Nkwazi | Vis Arend

● **LEAST CONCERN**

🦋 **COLLECTIVE NAMES**
Aerie of eagles | Brood of eagles | Congregation of eagles | Exaltation of eagles

✳ **SYMBOLIC MEANINGS**
Independence; Zimbabwe national pride.

🌀 **POSSIBLE POWER**
Totem of the Shona.

🦉 **FOLKLORE AND FACTS**
Zimbabwean historians believe that the Zimbabwe Bird, a stone carving that now serves as the national emblem of Zimbabwe, is a stylized representation of the African Fish Eagle. The eagle is the national bird of Zimbabwe as well as of Malawi, Namibia, and Zambia, but its likeness showed up in Zimbabwe architecture as far back as the eleventh century, carved in soapstone among the ruins of the medieval city of Great Zimbabwe. • Historians have theorized that the fish eagle may have been one of the totems of the Shona, the people who built the capital city of Zimbabwe. The Shona used different totems to identify the many clans within their culture, a tradition that continues today throughout Shona society in Zimbabwe and Mozambique. • After centuries of decay in Great Zimbabwe, the Zimbabwe Bird came to light once again in 1889 when European hunter Willi Posselt visited the site against the wishes of the Indigenous Peoples. He found the sculptures, dug one out of the ruins and took it with him, despite being surrounded by angry native tribesmen, and the sculpture was sold, resold, and otherwise appropriated by British colonialists until Zimbabwe achieved its independence in 1981. South Africa then returned the original bird sculptures, where they remain in a museum at the Great Zimbabwe site. • Some suggest that the sculpted bird is actually the Bateleur (see No. 359), but without millennium-old written records, the exact specifications will likely never be known.

No. 191

Iduna rama

Sykes's Warbler

Sykes's Wagtail

● **LEAST CONCERN**

✥ **COLLECTIVE NAMES**

Bouquet of warblers | Confusion of warblers | Fall of warblers | Wrench of warblers

✷ **SYMBOLIC MEANINGS**

Spring; Youth.

🌀 **POSSIBLE POWERS**

Adaptability; Creativity.

☾ **FOLKLORE AND FACTS**

A tiny brown bird with few distinguishing characteristics may seem like an unlikely bringer of spiritual meaning, but the Sykes's Warbler, a warbler of west-central Asia with wintering grounds in India, gets its symbolism on the fringes of other cultures. • For reasons that have never been explained, this little bird's Latin name *Iduna* comes from the Norse goddess of spring and youth, perhaps because Loki, the Norse god of fire, once changed Iduna into a sparrow to rescue her from Thjassi, who had kidnapped her and kept her in the land of the giants. The Sykes's Warbler is not a sparrow, of course, but it's difficult to imagine another reason the bird would be named for this goddess from another culture. • The Sykes's Warbler's common name provides a much more logical story: It honors English naturalist William Henry Sykes, who served as an ornithologist in India in the late 1800s and discovered a total of fifty-six bird species there that were previously unknown to Western science. Sykes published many papers on birds of the Deccan region of India, and developed a list of 236 bird species he observed in his time on the subcontinent.

No. 192

Indicatoridae

Honeyguide

Brown-Backed Honeybird | Cassin's Honeybird | Dwarf Honeyguide | Greater Honeyguide | Green-Backed Honeybird | Least Honeyguide | Lesser Honeyguide | Lyre-Tailed Honeyguide | Malaysian Honeyguide | Pallid Honeyguide | Scaly-Throated Honeyguide | Spotted Honeyguide | Willcock's Honeyguide | Yellow-Footed Honeyguide | Yellow-Rumped Honeyguide | Zenker's Honeyguide

● **LEAST CONCERN** (13 SPECIES)
● **NEAR THREATENED** (3 SPECIES)

✥ **COLLECTIVE NAME**

Probe of Honeyguides

✷ **SYMBOLIC MEANINGS**

Cooperation; Reciprocity.

🌀 **POSSIBLE POWER**

Leading humans to hives and honey.

☾ **FOLKLORE AND FACTS**

Honeyguides and humans have an extraordinary relationship, one that stands as an example of cooperation between species

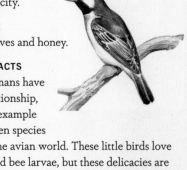

that has no equal in the avian world. These little birds love to devour beeswax and bee larvae, but these delicacies are carefully hidden by the bees under honey, a treat for which the birds have no taste … but they know that humans do. So honeyguides actively approach human beings in the wild to guide them to beehives, where humans can extract the honey and leave the beeswax and grubs for the birds to enjoy. • Ornithologists believe that this relationship between honeyguides and humans may have been crafted more than two million years ago. In some African cultures, honey makes up as much as 10 percent of people's diet, so partnering with the hungry birds to find and harvest honey is simply part of everyday life. These honey hunters have developed a system of calling out to honeyguides with a number of different summoning songs that the birds have been taught to recognize and associate with a meal. (Even young birds that have never heard the songs before seem to recognize them, suggesting that they have been internalized by the birds and are now part of their collective unconscious.) The birds arrive and lead the people to the nearest source of honey, and the people break into the tree trunk that holds the hive and harvest the honey. The wax and larvae go to the birds to thank them for their service.

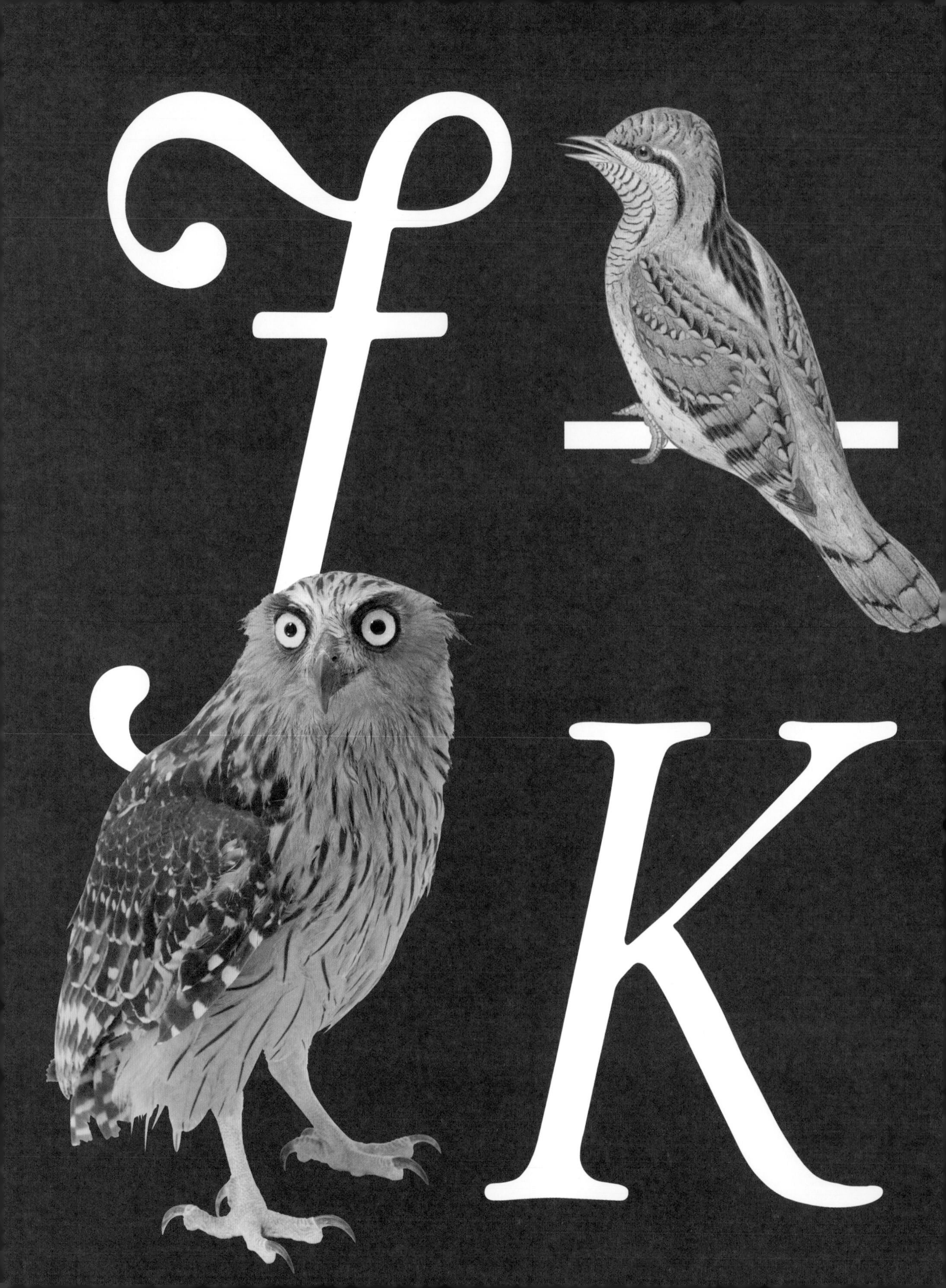
K

No. 193
Jynx torquilla

Eurasian Wryneck

Northern Wryneck | Snakebird

● **LEAST CONCERN**

✿ **COLLECTIVE NAMES**

Descent of wrynecks | Gatling of wrynecks

✹ **SYMBOLIC MEANINGS**

Eroticism; Fertility.

✦ **POSSIBLE POWERS**

Aid in conception; Dark magic; Desire; Fertility.

☾ **FOLKLORE AND FACTS**

How did a little brown bird become a tool in fertility rites in ancient Greece and Rome? We can only guess that the way this particular bird moves its head and neck suggested a tendency to the erotic: Wryneck gets its common name from its ability to extend its neck and loll its head around like a snake, twisting and even hanging its head as if its neck were broken. The technique works to ward off predators, who see this behavior and think the bird must be dead. Apparently it awakened the human imagination as well, but in a decidedly different direction. • The Greeks and Romans developed what they called a *iynx*, a wheel-shaped charm on which they spread a wryneck crosswise and secured it in place, then spun it to release its power. This device was intended to attract the affections of a desired partner, increase the chances of conceiving a child, or to bring back an absent lover. Stories are told of Aphrodite, goddess of love and beauty, using a *iynx* to help Jason win over Medea, and employed it again to make Zeus fall in love with the moon goddess Io. • Over the centuries, *iynx* turned into *Jynx*, which became the bird's Latin name—and the word morphed further into jinx, meaning bad luck or a curse placed upon someone for their hubris or bad intentions. This most likely came from the bird's use in what could be seen as dark magic.

No. 194
Ketupa blakistoni

Blakiston's Fish Owl

Blakiston's Eagle-Owl

● **ENDANGERED**

✿ **COLLECTIVE NAMES**

Group of owls | Hoot of owls | Parliament of owls

✹ **SYMBOLIC MEANING**

Protection.

✦ **POSSIBLE POWER**

Guardian of villages.

☾ **FOLKLORE AND FACTS**

The world's largest owl hunts the riparian areas of China, Japan, and far eastern Russia. Its 28-inch (72 cm) height makes it a little shorter than a Great Gray Owl, but its weight—especially the females at up to 10 pounds (5 kg)—exceeds any of the western hemisphere owls. Feeding on fish it catches in streams and rivers that never freeze over, this owl can catch prey that are two to three times its own weight, switching to abundant amphibians in spring. It's large enough to hold its own when competing for fish with the Steller's Sea Eagle and the White-Tailed Eagle in northeastern Russia. • To the Ainu peoples of Hokkaido, Japan, Blakiston's Fish Owl represents "God that Protects the Village," making this bird a revered part of their community. This is not the case farther north, where the Evens people of Siberia and the Udege people of Russia actually eat the owls; the Udege dried their extremities to use as fans to keep insects off of themselves while hunting, but this is no longer an accepted practice. • Neither of these communities is large enough to deplete the owl's numbers, however. Their dwindling population has much more to do with dam-building that eliminates the rivers and streams where these owls hunt. A dammed river swells too much to permit owls to sit on the riverbank and watch for prey.

No. 195

Lagopus lagopus

Willow Ptarmigan

Moorcock | Moorfowl | Red Grouse | Willow Grouse

● **LEAST CONCERN**

🐾 **COLLECTIVE NAME**
Covey of ptarmigans

✹ **SYMBOLIC MEANING**
Concealment.

🌀 **POSSIBLE POWERS**
Camouflage; Resistance to cold.

☾ **FOLKLORE AND FACTS**
There's a splendid
story about a
town called
Chicken,
Alaska, where in 1902
the town founders
decided to name
the town "Ptarmigan."
Unfortunately, the town
council could not agree on
how ptarmigan should be
spelled. After considerable
disagreement, they dropped the idea and went with Chicken,
a name that any grammar school student could spell. The
state of Alaska fared a little better in 1955, making Willow
Ptarmigan the state's official bird without stumbling over the
spelling. • A nearly spherical reddish-brown ball in breeding
season, turning snow-white in late fall for the perfect winter
camouflage, the Willow Ptarmigan roams the entire world's
subarctic region. In many countries, entire cultures have
flourished around the hunting of these birds, both for food
and for sport; the wholesale slaughter of millions of birds
in a single season ended in the twentieth century, but these
ptarmigans still appear regularly on dinner tables. • Native
Americans took careful note of the ptarmigan's feathered
feet, which allow them to walk easily even in deep snow.
With this as a clue, they designed snowshoes that mimicked
this attribute.

No. 196

Lagopus muta

Rock Ptarmigan

Aqiggiq | Ptarmigan | White Grouse

● **LEAST CONCERN**

🐾 **COLLECTIVE NAME**
Covey of ptarmigans

✹ **SYMBOLIC MEANINGS**
Defiance; Survival.

🌀 **POSSIBLE POWER**
Camouflage.

☾ **FOLKLORE AND FACTS**
While its Latin name *muta* means mute, the Rock Ptarmigan
actually does make a croaking sound. That's why ptarmigans
got their name from the Scottish word *tàrmachan,* or
"croaker." Scottish physicians added the silent *p* in 1684,
from *ptéryga,* a Greek word for wing. • Rock Ptarmigan
inhabits most of the world's subarctic regions, as well as parts
of central Asia. It remains a popular game bird because its
young reach breeding age when they are six months old,
allowing them to replace whatever population is lost in
fairly short order. For this reason, the Rock Ptarmigan reigns
comfortably as the official game bird of Newfoundland and
Labrador. It's also the official territorial bird of Nunavut in
northern Canada. • According to Icelandic legend, Rock
Ptarmigan was the *Rjúpa* invited by the Virgin Mary to
wade into a pit of fire along with representatives of every
bird species in the world. While all the other birds walked
through the fire, making their legs bare and featherless, *Rjúpa*
refused to perform this stunt. The bird retained its feathery
legs, a key to its survival in its subarctic territory, but Mary
took out her revenge by condemning the ptarmigan to be
the most harmless and essentially defenseless bird in the
region, forever hunted by the falcon that, until this moment,
had been the Rock Ptarmigan's trusted friend. Seeing that
this fate could wipe ptarmigans off the face of the Earth in
short order, she relented at the last moment and granted the
bird its white camouflage in winter and reddish brown in
summer, giving it a fighting chance for survival.

L

No. 197

Lanius borealis

Northern Shrike

Butcherbird | Choking Angel

● **LEAST CONCERN**

☘ **COLLECTIVE NAMES**

Abattoir of shrikes | Watch of shrikes

✳ **SYMBOLIC MEANINGS**

Death; Practicality; Storage; Transformation.

✺ **POSSIBLE POWER**

Strategic planning.

✤ **FOLKLORE AND FACTS**

The Northern Shrike's Latin name *Lanius* means "butcher," and for good reason. Male Northern Shrikes often kill more food than they can eat right away, so they store their prey by impaling it on thorns. • Don't worry, they kill it first (usually), breaking its neck or spine by shaking it with their strong, hooked bill while the prey is still pinned to the ground. All in all, it's a practical and effective solution: Not only does this keep the food close by until it's needed, but the cache also attracts females to the best provider of the available potential mates. Among humans who find this behavior a bit over the top, however, Northern Shrikes have earned the nickname "butcherbird." • Shrikes became the unlikely villain in a story that we now know suffered from an overabundance of caution. When English Sparrows—what we call House Sparrows in the US—first arrived in the United States in the 1850s, Northern Shrikes recognized them as a food source and began gathering around parks where the sparrows congregated. In Boston, protecting English Sparrows became a high priority, as the sparrows helped keep the exploding caterpillar population in check. The city hired sharpshooters to patrol Boston Commons and kill Northern Shrikes to keep them from devouring the sparrows. Shrike numbers declined in this and other cities, but sparrow numbers multiplied exponentially until 50 million of them populated the US. Today priorities have shifted back, so the Northern Shrike is a protected species, while the House Sparrow is not.

No. 198

Lanius collurio

Red-Backed Shrike

Butcherbird | Wereangel

● **LEAST CONCERN**

☘ **COLLECTIVE NAMES**

Abattoir of shrikes | Watch of shrikes

✳ **SYMBOLIC MEANINGS**

Death; Practicality; Storage; Transformation.

✺ **POSSIBLE POWER**

Strategic planning.

✤ **FOLKLORE AND FACTS**

Wearing the black bandit mask that all shrikes have in common, and sharing the name derived from the Old English word for "shriek," this bird of Eurasia winters in eastern Africa. Its breeding territory once extended into Great Britain, but the Red-Backed Shrike nearly disappeared from the UK in the twentieth century, with just two breeding pairs reported in recent years. • Shrikes get their "butcherbird" nickname from their grisly practice of impaling their prey on the long thorns of a hawthorn or blackthorn shrubs, storing it there while they go hunting for more. These stores of mice, bumblebees, and the occasional songbird are difficult to view for humans, but they mean ample food for shrike chicks. • BirdLife Switzerland voted this carnivorous songbird its Bird of the Year in 2020, in a bid to bring attention to its declining numbers throughout the region. Shrikes need open fields for hunting and the occasional nearby tree or shrub for nesting, both of which are vanishing throughout Europe as agriculture takes over the remaining land. Farming also uses pesticides to control weeds and insects, depleting the shrike's food supply and available nesting material. In Switzerland, shrikes have moved out of the lowlands and closer to the Alps, finding what natural areas they can to sustain their families.

L

Lanius excubitor

Great Gray Shrike

Choking Angel | Greater Butcherbird

● **LEAST CONCERN**

🌿 **COLLECTIVE NAMES**

Abattoir of shrikes | Watch of shrikes

☀ **SYMBOLIC MEANINGS**

Death; Practicality; Storage; Transformation.

🌀 **POSSIBLE POWER**

Strategic planning.

🌙 **FOLKLORE AND FACTS**

The Great Gray
Shrike's Latin
name translates
to "sentinel
butcher," no doubt
because of the long
periods it spends
watching for
prey from a high
perch, usually a
fencepost or tree branch.
Much of this larger
shrike's food supply comes
from rodents, so it waits patiently for the slightest
movement in the grasses and swoops in, ready to go for the
kill with its heavy, hooked bill and fly off with its conquest.
Then—like all shrikes—it gathers multiple prey in one
place, impaling them on the long blades of a hawthorn or
blackthorn tree for later consumption. • This shrike built a
portion of its reputation as a strategic and courageous hunter
from its propensity for pursuing magpies, birds at least as
large as the Great Gray Shrike. "Bird-catchers even report
that it from time to time slays certain woodland Pies, and
can put Crows to flight," wrote naturalist William Turner
in the mid-1500s. • Even before Turner, records from the
fifteenth century provide remarkably accurate drawings of
this bird, labeled *werkangel* or *waryangle*—which translate
from Old English as "little villain." Geoffrey Chaucer even
made passing reference to the bird in his *Friar's Tale*: "As full
of venym been thise waryangles," or in modern English, "as
shrikes are full of venom."

Larus argentatus

Herring Gull

American Herring Gull | Seagull | Sky Rat | Smithsonian Gull

● **LEAST CONCERN**

🌿 **COLLECTIVE NAMES**

Colony of gulls | Leash of gulls | Pack of gulls | Screech of gulls

☀ **SYMBOLIC MEANINGS**

Adaptability; Concern for the environment.

🌀 **POSSIBLE POWERS**

Persistance; Tenacity; Verbal abuse.

🌙 **FOLKLORE AND FACTS**

Birders are quick to tell us that there is no bird called a
"seagull." Indeed, each gull species has its own official name,
and many gulls have distinguishing physical characteristics,
but no gull is more closely associated with the seagull
moniker than the Herring Gull. Its dominance across North
America, Europe, and eastern Asia makes adult Herring
Gulls quickly recognizable, with their gray wings, black
wingtips, white body, yellow eye, and yellow bill with a
prominent red spot. • Native American stories are filled
with gull references. The Cree tell us of a flock of gulls on an
island in a bay, where they screamed and insulted visitors if
people came too close. Meanwhile, a family of Canada Jays
lived close to the Cree, and the people and birds treated one
another with courtesy and respect. When the people started
fishing with nets, the gulls came around to their camp and
scolded them at length, crying out that the fish belonged
to the birds, not the people. Sometimes the people would
toss a gull a piece of fish just to get them to be quiet, but
then the gulls would fight over the fish, which repulsed the
people—so they stopped giving the birds any fish, because
they now knew
what the birds
were like and
wanted nothing
to do with them.
Instead, they
fed fresh seeds
and berries to
the Canada
Jays, who were
always pleasant
and grateful.

L

Larus californicus

California Gull

Seagull

● **LEAST CONCERN**

🐾 **COLLECTIVE NAMES**
Colony of gulls | Leash of gulls | Pack of gulls | Screech of gulls

✳ **SYMBOLIC MEANINGS**
Adaptability; Concern for the environment.

🌀 **POSSIBLE POWERS**
Persistance; Tenacity; Verbal abuse; Voracious appetite.

🌙 **FOLKLORE AND FACTS**
The dominant gull of the western United States and Canada has darker gray wings than the very similar Herring Gull, as well as a black ring around the red spot on the lower part of its bill. The California Gull is also a little smaller than a Herring Gull, and it has a black eye instead of the Herring's yellow one. • How did a gull become the state bird of Utah? The Seagull Monument in front of Salt Lake Assembly Hall helps tell the story: In the second growing season after Mormons arrived in Utah, the settlers planted their crops and hoped for a good harvest, but in late May, huge swarms of insects arrived in the valley. Katydids ate everything in their path, threatening to wipe out the harvest and leave the Mormons destitute by fall. • In what came to be known as the Miracle of the Gulls, on June 9, 1848, flocks of California Gulls arrived and began devouring the katydids. For two weeks they ate these insects until there were none remaining. The gulls saved the Mormons' crops, and to this day, Mormons believe that these gulls came in direct response to their prayers. Historical records and scientific analysis suggest that other factors also helped rescue the crops and that the gulls' contribution was minor, but the Miracle of the Gulls remains a legend in Utah, and the gulls receive respect and gratitude for their role.

Larus hyperboreus

Glaucous Gull

Burgomaster Seagull | White-Winged Gull

● **LEAST CONCERN**

🐾 **COLLECTIVE NAMES**
Colony of gulls | Leash of gulls | Pack of gulls | Screech of gulls

✳ **SYMBOLIC MEANINGS**
Adaptability; Concern for the environment.

🌀 **POSSIBLE POWERS**
Endurance; Tenacity.

🌙 **FOLKLORE AND FACTS**
The second-largest gull in the world often gives the Great Black-Backed Gull a worthy challenge, as an individual Glaucous Gull can weigh more than its black-backed rival, but its height and wingspan may be just slightly smaller. • Immature Glaucous Gulls can appear completely white, giving them the misnomer "white-winged gull" in their first or second winter. Once they mature, Glaucous Gulls wear a light gray mantle, but their wing tips remain white, making them easier than you might think to pick out of a large mixed flock of gulls on a beach or on an iced-over bay. • Very much an Arctic species, Glaucous Gulls occasionally wander down as far as the Great Lakes, but they rarely come inland and normally don't appear any further south than winter beaches in the Canadian Maritimes or along the UK's rocky coasts. • The Inupiat people of Alaska hunted Glaucous Gulls in fall as the birds arrived on their way to slightly warmer waters. The hunters used a stick of wood, sharpened it at both ends, wrapped it in meat and blubber, and tied a strip of deer sinew to it. They placed it on the beach and waited for a gull to try to swallow the bait—and when the gull grabbed it, the hunter yanked it back, jamming the sharpened stick in the bird's throat. The gulls provided a reasonable meal, and the easy availability of cold storage in an Alaskan fall and winter made a gull harvest a plausible way to subsist until spring.

Larus marinus

Great Black-Backed Gull

Great Black and White Gull | Greater Black-Backed Gull | Minister of the Sea | Seagull

● **LEAST CONCERN**

✢ **COLLECTIVE NAMES**

Colony of gulls | Leash of gulls | Pack of gulls | Screech of gulls

✴ **SYMBOLIC MEANINGS**

Adaptability; Tyranny (of prey).

🌀 **POSSIBLE POWERS**

Endurance; Resourcefulness.

☾ **FOLKLORE AND FACTS**

Even on a beach with thousands of other gulls, the Great Black-Backed Gull is hard to miss. Its larger size and black back and wings stand out from the crowd, differentiating it easily from the more prevalent Herring Gull (gray back) and Ring-Billed Gull (gray back, much smaller, with a black ring around its yellow bill). • The world's largest gull, the Great Black-Backed Gull generally stays on the northeastern North American and European coasts, as well as along Greenland's and Iceland's coastlines, though a few wander inland to the Great Lakes and Hudson Bay. • John James Audubon called the Great Black-Backed Gull a "tyrant bird" and a "remorseless spoiler," coming at prey with mouth open and shrieks shattering the peaceful seashore, and killing whatever it wanted. Fish are just a sample of the bird's diet: Rodents, small mammals, other birds, bird eggs, and game birds all could be part of the menu. • Seafarers of old believed that gulls of all kinds hosted the souls of sailors who died at sea. Some went so far as to believe that gulls somehow owned daylight itself—so, naturally, killing a gull would make the killer go blind. • Gulls usually travel in groups, but if a solitary trio of gulls passed directly over a sailor's head, it almost certainly meant an impending death—not necessarily for the sailor, but possibly for someone close to him.

Leptotila wellsi

Grenada Dove

Pea Dove | Well's Dove

● **CRITICALLY ENDANGERED**

✢ **COLLECTIVE NAMES**

Bevy of doves | Covey of doves | Dole of doves | Paddling of doves | Piteousness of doves | Pretense of doves

✴ **SYMBOLIC MEANING**

National animal of Grenada.

🌀 **POSSIBLE POWER**

Concealment.

☾ **FOLKLORE AND FACTS**

Fewer than 120 Grenada Doves remain in the world, making this elegant dove a treasured but rare creature on the island of Grenada, the only place on Earth where it appears at all. This dove prefers to walk on the ground rather than fly, and with its pink forehead, white throat, and delicately beige plumage, it blends into its surroundings quite completely, visible only when it's moving. • Grenada Doves live in dry forest ecosystems, a very rare form of habitat that existed more broadly before people populated this Caribbean island. In a dry forest, trees shed their foliage during dry seasons, which then opens the understory to sunlight and allows thick underbrush to grow—the habitat the Grenada Dove needs to survive. In 1996, the government preserved 155 acres (63 ha) of remaining dry forest as Mount Hartman National Park, specifically to protect the Grenada Dove, but when a UK-based development company decided in 2006 to build a resort on this land, their plan neglected to provide for continued protection of the doves. Conservation activists have worked continually to stop it, and as of this writing, the project and the land have been purchased by a Chinese developer. The future for Grenada's national bird looks very bleak.

L

No. 205

Leucogeranus leucogeranus

Siberian Crane

Siberian White Crane | Snow Crane

● **CRITICALLY ENDANGERED**

✦ **COLLECTIVE NAMES**

Flock of cranes | Herd of cranes | Sedge of cranes | Siege of cranes

✹ **SYMBOLIC MEANINGS**

Kind spirits; Spring; Sun.

✿ **POSSIBLE POWER**

Transformation.

✦ **FOLKLORE AND FACTS**

Just two breeding populations of the Siberian Crane remain in their native spring and summer habitat, the Arctic tundra of western and eastern Russia. In winter the eastern flock heads to the Poyang Lake basin in China; the western flock spends the winter in Iran. Both migrations require the longest migration of any cranes in the world. • These snow-white birds with red faces have black feathers on their wings that are only visible in flight, so they make many people think of angels as the birds stand and feed in shallow wetlands. Perhaps this is why Yakut and Yukaghir natives of Siberia believe the Siberian Crane is sacred, a representative of the sun. • In one of the stories of the Olonkho, a series of Yakut epic stories, shamans actually turn into white cranes, and many orgiastic descriptions of beautiful people compare them to white cranes. • Today, the people of the Republic of Sakha (Yakutia) in Siberia open their annual Yhyakh festival, a celebration of spring, with the Dance of the Cranes, using music that incorporates the crane's actual call. The all-female dance troupe performs a ballet that uses white cloth to represent the birds' wings, and steps that mimic the bird's flight and mating dance.

No. 206

Limosa lapponica

Bar-Tailed Godwit

Chiuchiuchiak (Inuit) | Kūaka (Maori) | Tevatevaaq (Yup'ik)

● **NEAR THREATENED**

✦ **COLLECTIVE NAMES**

Congregation of godwits | Omniscience of godwits | Prayer of godwits

✹ **SYMBOLIC MEANING**

Perseverance.

✿ **POSSIBLE POWERS**

Endurance; Speed.

✦ **FOLKLORE AND FACTS**

What can this 16-inch (41 cm)-high shorebird do that no other bird on Earth can do? Every fall after its breeding season, it migrates more than 8,000 miles (12,875 km) from Alaska to New Zealand, an eight-day trip—without stopping once, and without eating a single bite. Then in spring, it repeats this miraculous feat to return to Alaska to breed. No other migratory animal can go this long without eating, making the Bar-Tailed Godwit one of the most amazing animals in the world, and the subject of considerable study and monitoring. • While all Bar-Tailed Godwits breed near the Arctic Circle, not all of them congregate in Alaska. Five subspecies each head off on a different route, choosing the Siberian Kola peninsula and migrating to Australia, or breeding in northern Scandinavia and heading to central Africa for the winter. Once they finally land, they devour large numbers of bristle-worms, bivalves, and tiny crustaceans, so they must come to rest at places where these foods are plentiful. • In October 2022, a particularly energetic four-month-old Bar-Tailed Godwit set a world record for nonstop migration, completing an 11-day trip of 8,425 miles (13,559 km) from Kuskokwim Delta on the Seward Peninsula in Alaska, to Tasmania in Australia. Scientists clocked the bird using a tiny solar-powered transmitter and satellite telemetry, the first time juvenile godwits had ever been tracked on their initial southbound migration.

No. 207

Limosa limosa

Black-Tailed Godwit

Blackwit | Jadreka Snipe | Shrieker | Yarwhelp

● **NEAR THREATENED**

COLLECTIVE NAMES

Congregation of godwits | Omniscience of godwits | Prayer of godwits

✳ **SYMBOLIC MEANING**

National bird of the Netherlands.

POSSIBLE POWERS

Endurance; Perseverance.

FOLKLORE AND FACTS

"My footman shall eat pheasants, / calvered salmons, Knots, godwits, lampreys …" waxed playwright Ben Jonson in 1610 in his now-classic play *The Alchemist*. Bird lovers of the twenty-first century probably can't imagine devouring a shorebird like Black-Tailed Godwit, but that's exactly what English people of means enjoyed at their tables for hundreds of years. Sir Thomas Browne, a contemporary of Jonson, called the Black-Tailed Godwit "the daintiest dish in England, and I think, for the bigness, the biggest price," indulging his fascination with the natural world by devouring this little 10-ounce (283 g) treasure. In his defense, godwits were more plentiful in the seventeenth century, probably numbering in the tens of millions; today about 800,000 are estimated to exist across their breeding range in Europe, western Asia, and eastern Russia. • Not quite the long-distance migrants of their bar-tailed cousins, Black-Tailed Godwits that breed in Iceland winter in the United Kingdom, France (where they are still hunted for food under strict limits), Spain, and Portugal. Birds that breed in eastern Europe and Asia migrate to central Africa, while the far eastern Russian birds migrate to Australia and the Pacific Rim.

No. 208

Lophophorus impejanus

Himalayan Monal

Danphe | Impeyan Monal | Impeyan Pheasant

● **LEAST CONCERN**

COLLECTIVE NAME

Bevy of monals

✳ **SYMBOLIC MEANINGS**

Authority; Community; Diversity; National bird of Nepal; State bird of Uttarakhand, India.

POSSIBLE POWER

Bestower of status.

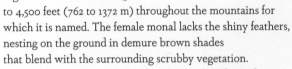

FOLKLORE AND FACTS

Covered in iridescent feathers that shimmer in shades of purple, turquoise, and green, and a sizable 28 inches (71 cm) long, the male Himalayan Monal is unmistakable in its native region—at elevations of 2,500 to 4,500 feet (762 to 1372 m) throughout the mountains for which it is named. The female monal lacks the shiny feathers, nesting on the ground in demure brown shades that blend with the surrounding scrubby vegetation. • In winter, the monal descends to lower altitudes and makes rhododendron forests its home, where it can hide from heavy snowfalls and dig for tubers with its powerful bill. • Choosing the Himalayan Monal as the national bird of Nepal made perfect sense to the country's population, as the bird's multicolored plumage reminds them of the diversity within their own region. Even the bird's preference for life in a covey speaks to the people's fondness for their own communities, and its dance-like moves have become part of the people's celebratory dances. • The Himalayan Monal is not endangered worldwide, but its status locally in Nepal is Near Threatened, according to the IUCN. Poachers pursue the gorgeous male relentlessly to steal the crest of individual plumes right off of its head—a prize they can only obtain by killing the bird. Their customers believe that this trophy brings status to the person who wears it, as only those in authority have the opportunity to acquire such a thing.

L

Lophura diardi

Siamese Fireback

Diard's Fireback | Lord Lo's Pheasant

● **LEAST CONCERN**

🐾 **COLLECTIVE NAMES**
Bevy of firebacks | Covey of firebacks

✹ **SYMBOLIC MEANING**
National bird of Thailand.

🌀 **POSSIBLE POWER**
Guidance.

🌙 **FOLKLORE AND FACTS**
Thailand's epic poem *Lilit Phra Lo,* written around the fifteenth century, tells the story of Phra Lo, king of the city of Suang, who falls in love with two princesses, Phuean and Phaeng, from a great distance away. The princesses hear of his great beauty and conspire to draw him to them using magic. While Lo has a queen and a family, he sets out to find these two princesses—a long journey, filled with adventures and obstacles. As the princesses become impatient with all the delays, they summon a wise man with skills as a magician to help Lo hasten his journey. The magician bewitches a large, beautiful pheasant to lead Lo to a pavilion in a park, where they wait to meet him face to face for the first time.
• Scholars believe that this pheasant is none other than the Siamese Fireback, a darkly flamboyant bird with a bright red face, black decorative crest plumes, a bright yellow spot mid-back, and a long, opulent, iridescently blue tail. Thailand agrees, making the Siamese Fireback its national bird and calling it Lord Lo's Pheasant in commemoration of this story. This bird's range is not limited to Thailand, though: You might see them in Cambodia, Laos, Vietnam, China, and Australia, as well as in zoos in the United States.

Loxia

Crossbill

Cassia Crossbill | Hispaniolan Crossbill | Parrot Crossbill | Red Crossbill | Scottish Crossbill | Two-Barred Crossbill (White-Winged Crossbill)

● **LEAST CONCERN** (4 SPECIES)
● **ENDANGERED** (HISPANIOLAN CROSSBILL)
● **CRITICALLY ENDANGERED** (CASSIA CROSSBILL)

🐾 **COLLECTIVE NAMES**
Crookedness of crossbills | Warp of crossbills

✹ **SYMBOLIC MEANING**
Devotion to Jesus Christ.

🌀 **POSSIBLE POWER**
Resourcefulness.

🌙 **FOLKLORE AND FACTS**
Six species of crossbills live in the upper reaches of the northern hemisphere, where they use their specially shaped bill to pry open seed-bearing cones on conifers and extract their seeds. The crossed mandible tips on these birds differ from any other bird of their size, giving them the leverage and maneuverability they need to obtain seeds from cones.
• While crossbills generally confine themselves to the far northern forests, a failed summer cone crop can drive these birds southward in a phenomenon known as an irruption (or a "finch winter"), causing great excitement among birders. Mixed flocks of Parrot, Scottish, Cassia, and Hispaniolan crossbills in northern Europe can be very

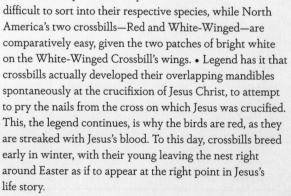

difficult to sort into their respective species, while North America's two crossbills—Red and White-Winged—are comparatively easy, given the two patches of bright white on the White-Winged Crossbill's wings. • Legend has it that crossbills actually developed their overlapping mandibles spontaneously at the crucifixion of Jesus Christ, to attempt to pry the nails from the cross on which Jesus was crucified. This, the legend continues, is why the birds are red, as they are streaked with Jesus's blood. To this day, crossbills breed early in winter, with their young leaving the nest right around Easter as if to appear at the right point in Jesus's life story.

No. 211

Luscinia megarhynchos

Common Nightingale

Caucasian Nightingale | Eastern Nightingale | Rufous Nightingale | Western Nightingale

● **LEAST CONCERN**

✿ **COLLECTIVE NAMES**

Match of nightingales | Pray of nightingales | Warren of nightingales | Watch of nightingales

✴ **SYMBOLIC MEANINGS**

Creative inspiration;
Muse; Spirit of a poet.

🌀 **POSSIBLE POWERS**

Guidance to lovers;
Inspiration.

☾ **FOLKLORE AND FACTS**

Poet John Keats called it "light-winged Dryad of the trees" in his "Ode to a Nightingale;" John Milton compared the nightingale's gentle guidance of lovers to the cuckoo's scolding of the unfaithful; while Samuel Taylor Coleridge rhapsodized over the Common Nightingale's song: "We may not thus profane / Nature's sweet voices, always full of love / And joyance! 'Tis the merry Nightingale ..." Even Shakespeare's Juliet does her best to keep Romeo close by, convincing him that the birdsong they hear in the dark is "the nightingale, and not the lark, that pierced the fearful hollow of thine ear." How this nondescript little brown bird captures the psyches of so many poets may be a mystery to those of us unfamiliar with its song, but the Common Nightingale's series of liquid trills, whistles, buzzes, and round notes has been the writer's muse for centuries. • Even in 600 BCE or so, Aesop made one of the first mentions of the nightingale in a fable. Back then, nightingales were supper for many Greek families, so when a swallow urged a nightingale to build its nest under the roof of a human's home, the nightingale declined. "No thank you," the bird said, "I have no desire to revive the memories of all my past misfortunes." The moral: When you have had a run of bad luck, there's no good in returning to the place where it happened.

L

No. 212
Mareca penelope

Eurasian Wigeon

European Wigeon | Widgeon

● **LEAST CONCERN**

🐾 **COLLECTIVE NAMES**

Bouquet of wigeon | Congregation of wigeon | Fall of wigeon | Flight of wigeon

✳ **SYMBOLIC MEANINGS**

Commitment; Fidelity; Loyalty.

🌀 **POSSIBLE POWERS**

Empathy; Rescue.

☾ **FOLKLORE AND FACTS**

The creamy white streak down the middle of a male Eurasian Wigeon's chestnut head makes it fairly easy to pick out in a flock, especially when its contrasting gray and white back and wings are visible. This particularly striking duck keeps close company with its far less showy, mottled brown mate, bonding as a pair in fall and remaining together through the breeding season, and making wigeons one of the avian world's many symbols of fidelity. • The Eurasian Wigeon gets its name from its brief role in the story of Penelope, Odysseus's wife. The lovely and faithful Penelope was the daughter of Spartan prince Icarius, a man so callous that when his daughter was born, he threw her into the sea to drown her because he only wanted sons. The infant almost certainly would have died among the waves had it not been for some ducks—later identified as Eurasian Wigeons, though no one seems certain why—who surrounded her and carefully held her out of the water as they escorted her back to shore. Icarius took this miraculous moment as a sign from Mount Olympus to embrace his daughter and raise her according to her birthright—as a princess. He named her Penelope, Greek for "duck."

No. 213
Megaceryle alcyon

Belted Kingfisher

● **LEAST CONCERN**

🐾 **COLLECTIVE NAMES**

A clique of kingfishers | A concentration of kingfishers | A crown of kingfishers

✳ **SYMBOLIC MEANINGS**

Peace; Tranquility.

🌀 **POSSIBLE POWERS**

Calming presence; Fertility.

☾ **FOLKLORE AND FACTS**

Much of the lore about the Belted Kingfisher actually comes from tales familiar to early European settlers in America. First, the bird's common name comes from Old English: Kyngges Fisscher, or King of the Fishers, because its richly colored plumage and flashy crest make it regal indeed. • Its Latin name *alcyon* arrived through Greek mythology, shared with the bird's European brethren: The goddess Alcyone, wife of Ceyx, managed to incur the wrath of Zeus—either by protecting sailors during the storms he whipped up, or by affectionately calling her beloved husband "Zeus" in jest. In anger, he wrecked Ceyx's ship, sending Ceyx to a watery grave—and then forbade anyone to tell Alcyone what he had done. When Zeus's wife Hera allowed Ceyx's body to wash up on the beach, Alcyone threw herself into the sea. Other gods turned both Alcyone and Ceyx into halcyon birds, the species that would become known as kingfishers. Every year, when Alcyone lays her eggs, her father, Aeolus, god of wind, calms the sea to ensure that her chicks will reach maturity. This is why "halcyon days" are times of peace and calm.

M

No. 214

Megadyptes antipodes

Yellow-Eyed Penguin

Hoiho | Tarakaka

● ENDANGERED

✤ **COLLECTIVE NAMES**

Colony of penguins | Creche of penguins | Formality of penguins | Huddle of penguins | Parade of penguins | Parcel of penguins | Rookery of penguins | Waddle of penguins

✴ **SYMBOLIC MEANING**

Conservation.

◉ **POSSIBLE POWERS**

Concealment; Privacy.

◖ **FOLKLORE AND FACTS**

The world's oldest and rarest penguin lives only on New Zealand, where it has developed considerable value to the local economy. Nature-based tourism to watch this bird from blinds positioned at its breeding grounds brings in $100 million NZD annually, making the preservation of this bird's dwindling numbers an economically sound decision. • Not that the penguins are not fascinating and precious in their own right: These shy creatures do not even want to nest in view of one another. Named *Mega* (large) and *dyptes* (diver), these penguins are the fifth-heaviest penguin in the world. • While the bird does not have traditionally symbolic significance to the people of New Zealand, it has come to represent the need for pristine shorelines and clean water. It serves as the mascot for the recycling and solid waste management program in Dunedin, and it appears on the back of New Zealand's five-dollar bill. In 2019, New Zealanders chose it as the country's Bird of the Year, the first time a seabird had won the popularity contest.

No. 215

Melanerpes erythrocephalus

Red-Headed Woodpecker

● LEAST CONCERN

✤ **COLLECTIVE NAMES**

Descent of woodpeckers | Gatling of woodpeckers | Whirlagust of woodpeckers

✴ **SYMBOLIC MEANINGS**

New opportunities; Shame.

◉ **POSSIBLE POWER**

Spiritual messenger.

◖ **FOLKLORE AND FACTS**

The traditional origin story of the Red-Headed Woodpecker has many similarities to the one told in Norway about the Black-Backed Woodpecker. A poor man with a tall walking stick ran out of supplies as he traversed a forest, so when he came upon a cabin in the woods, he knocked on the door. An old woman answered, and he said, "I have walked a long way and I am hungry. Might I ask you for a meal?" The old woman begrudgingly took a small amount of dough and put it in her oven, where it baked into a cake that would feed both of them easily. Appalled that she would part with so much food for a stranger, she tried again with an even smaller amount of dough, but this, too, baked into an enormous cake. She hid the second cake and pulled an old, stale crust of bread from the back of her larder, and gave him that to eat. The man said, "I am the spirit of the forest. You should be ashamed of yourself. You're a selfish woman!" He hit her over the head with his staff, and as blood ran from her wound, she turned into a bird. The red blood turned her head crimson. The solid red head, black back, and white chest and underside of this gorgeous bird makes every sighting a treat, though legend says the bird still hides on the other side of the tree from its onlookers, ashamed of its treatment of the spirit.

No. 216

Melanerpes formicivorus

Acorn Woodpecker

● LEAST CONCERN

✤ **COLLECTIVE NAMES**

Descent of woodpeckers | Gatling of woodpeckers | Whirlagust of woodpeckers

✴ **SYMBOLIC MEANINGS**

Opportunity; Preparation.

◉ **POSSIBLE POWERS**

Defense; Planning.

◖ **FOLKLORE AND FACTS**

Don't be fooled by the clownish face of this very visible woodpecker of the western United States and Mexico. The Acorn Woodpecker spends virtually all of its time on very serious business, providing for its family by collecting and storing acorns for consumption through months when natural food is scarce. These birds drill hundreds of holes in trees with softer wood and place an acorn in each hole, and then guard and defend their stores from other woodpeckers, squirrels, and other birds and animals that try to plunder this pantry. • Acorn Woodpeckers live in colonies of up to fifteen birds or more, nesting cooperatively and depending on one another to help incubate the eggs and feed the nestlings. In colonies with more than one breeding female, the females will all lay their eggs in one tree cavity, a level of cooperation seen in only a few species around the world. • While cartoonist Walter Lantz took inspiration for his Woody Woodpecker character from Pileated Woodpeckers, the character's iconic song comes from the Acorn Woodpecker's *waka-waka-waka* call. Woody's take is a bit more musical, but the Acorn Woodpecker definitely provided the rising and falling pattern and the authentic woodland spirit.

No. 217
Melanocorypha calandra

Calandra Lark

European Calandra Lark

● **LEAST CONCERN**

🐦 **COLLECTIVE NAMES**

Ascension of larks | Chattering of larks | Exaltation of larks | Happiness of larks

✷ **SYMBOLIC MEANINGS**

Exploration of the inner self; New beginnings.

🌀 **POSSIBLE POWERS**

Alertness; Concealment; Warning.

🌙 **FOLKLORE AND FACTS**

The Calandra Lark occupies open fields and grasslands from the Mediterranean Sea to southern Russia, its melodious and varied song filling the air from dawn to dusk. Songs and poems tell us of the importance of this lark singing early every morning, giving prisoners their only indication that a new day has begun (as in the Spanish song "Romance del prisionero") or warning Romeo and Juliet of dawn's arrival in Shakespeare's play. Shakespeare also supplied a lark in *A Midsummer Night's Dream* to awaken fairy king Oberon after his night in the enchanted woods, just in time to remove the spell that made his queen Titania fall in love with a man with a donkey's head. • Listeners might think that a bird with such a voice must be very beautiful indeed, but this lark's concern is with blending into its surroundings while it raises its young. Patterned in black and brown with a lighter underside and a black neckband, the ground-nesting Calandra Lark vanishes into fields as it raises its nestlings.

No. 218
Meleagris gallopavo

Wild Turkey

Tazhii (Navajo)

● **LEAST CONCERN**

🐦 **COLLECTIVE NAMES**

Gaggle of turkeys | Rafter of turkeys

✷ **SYMBOLIC MEANINGS**

Abundance; Nourishment.

🌀 **POSSIBLE POWERS**

Adaptation; Superior eyesight; Sustenance.

🌙 **FOLKLORE AND FACTS**

Long before European settlers arrived in the New World, Wild Turkey played a pivotal role in the lives of many Native American cultures. Not only was the bird a dependable food source, but its feathers became part of headdresses and cloaks used in ceremonies and to differentiate people in leadership. Navajo people revere the turkey as the animal that brought seeds of melon, squash, corn, and beans into the current world, giving them the crops they needed to feed their communities. • The Caddo people's traditional turkey dance is said to have originated in ancient times, when a Caddo hunter came upon a group of turkey hens dancing around a single tom turkey. He watched the dance and memorized it, so he could bring the concept home to his people—and they turned it into one of the most sacred dances of their culture. • When Europeans arrived, however, they hunted the abundant turkeys nearly to

M

extinction. By the early twentieth century, the population of millions of turkeys had dwindled to about 30,000 across the entire continent—and in the 1940s, turkeys were no longer found in Canada at all. After the release of hand-bred turkeys into the wild failed miserably, a wide-scale effort began to trap young Wild Turkeys and transfer them to places where turkeys were no longer found. This operation succeeded, and today we can find Wild Turkeys all over North America, with numbers back up in the millions thanks to well-regulated hunting limits.

No. 219

Mellisuga helenae

Bee Hummingbird

Helena Hummingbird | Zunzuncito

- **NEAR THREATENED**

- **COLLECTIVE NAMES**
Charm of hummingbirds | Chattering of hummingbirds | Hover of hummingbirds | Shimmer of hummingbirds

- **SYMBOLIC MEANINGS**
Beginnings; Joy; Rebirth.

- **POSSIBLE POWERS**
Fascination; Inhabited by spirits of the dead.

- **FOLKLORE AND FACTS**
Joyas voladoras, the Spanish term for hummingbirds, translates to "flying jewels," and this gives us a clear idea of how these tiny birds are regarded in Mexico, Cuba, and other Spanish-speaking countries in the western hemisphere. All hummingbirds are found only in this hemisphere, and the Bee Hummingbird—the world's smallest bird at just 2¼ inches (6 cm) long—lives only in Cuba, making it one of the rarest of the rare. • People in the Caribbean islands believe that hummingbirds embody the spirits of lost loved ones. The tiny Bee Hummingbird seems to feel no urgency to get in touch: It lives exclusively in parts of the Cuban archipelago, in the island's mogote (isolated hill) region, with a small population in the Zapata Swamp. It chooses just ten species of flowers for its sustenance, making it a very fussy bird, and very unlikely to leave its chosen habitat to expand its range. • Should you go seeking this little wonder, the adult male's glistening red gorget, contrasting mightily with its bright blue back, is a sight that serves as a fitting reward for the effort.

No. 220

Melopsittacus undulatus

Budgerigar

Budgie | Common Parakeet | Shell Parakeet

- **LEAST CONCERN**

- **COLLECTIVE NAMES**
Company of parakeets | Chatter/chattering of parakeets | Pandemonium of parakeets | Prattle of parakeets

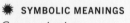

- **SYMBOLIC MEANINGS**
Communication; Domesticity.

- **POSSIBLE POWERS**
Affection; Mimicry of human speech.

- **FOLKLORE AND FACTS**
It may surprise budgie owners that these birds are actually found in the wild anywhere in the world, but they are native to Australia, and healthy populations still roam the open woodlands and grasslands there. Given the opportunity, these birds come together in flocks of tens of thousands and form impressive murmurations, a sight worth traveling to see. • Only the green individuals of this favorite pet species are the bird's natural color; the blue, white, yellow, and gray birds we see in pet stores have all been created by breeders. Budgerigars have adapted well to life as pets and breed readily in captivity, so the need to trap them has long since passed—any bird in a home today has been bred for life as a house bird. • The Guinness-certified world record for the bird with the largest vocabulary was Puck, a budgie in Petaluma, California, that knew 1,728 words. Puck passed away in 1994, but the bird's record stands as of this writing.

No. 221

Melospiza melodia

Song Sparrow

- **LEAST CONCERN**

- **COLLECTIVE NAME**
Host of sparrows

- **SYMBOLIC MEANINGS**
Determination; Industriousness.

- **POSSIBLE POWERS**
Courage; Ingenuity.

FOLKLORE AND FACTS

Male Song Sparrows attract mates through their extensive song repertoire, actually cycling through a "playlist" as much as half an hour long—and then starting over and repeating the series precisely. These sparrows can actually tell each other apart by their song vocabulary. • Widespread across North America, Song Sparrows are most likely the birds in an Indigenous folk tale about pride, wind, and rain. A young woman of great beauty shunned all of the suitors from her village, telling each that they were stupid or vain. The men came together and asked Whirlwind and Rain to punish the girl. Whirlwind went to her home and blew so hard that he knocked her over, angering her father, a great warrior, who then banished Whirlwind and Rain from the village. After many days without wind and rain, however, crops began to die and the village saw real hardship, so the villagers sent Bear and Fox to find Whirlwind and Rain. Soon they returned and said they could not locate them. • Sparrow said he'd give it a try. He took one of his feathers and tied it to a stick, then watched until he could see which way the wind blew. He followed the wind and found Whirlwind and Rain in a cave and convinced them to return to the village. Soon the village had rain and wind once again.

No. 222

Menura novaehollandiae

Superb Lyrebird

Bulln-bulln | Weringerong | Woorail

● **LEAST CONCERN**

✿ **COLLECTIVE NAME**
Corroboree of lyrebirds

✴ **SYMBOLIC MEANING**
Sacred harmony.

✺ **POSSIBLE POWER**
Speaker of all languages.

FOLKLORE AND FACTS
The world's largest songbird, the ground-dwelling Superb Lyrebird is

a creature of many facets and talents. Its ability to mimic a wide range of sounds results in a diverse repertoire, making each bird's song unique; meanwhile, its spectacularly long tail, closely resembling a lyre in its markings and curvature, makes it easily recognizable in the wild no matter what song it sings. • The Superb Lyrebird is one of the oldest continually living birds on the planet, with fossils dating back 15 million years. Restricted to southeastern Australia, the bird's numbers remain healthy and now include an introduced population in Tasmania as well as its native Queensland and Victoria. • This bird serves as part of the logo of the New South Wales National Parks and Wildlife Service, and it has been featured on the Australian ten-cent coin, the 100-dollar bill, and as the logo of the Australian Film Commission. • Arts organizations including the Victorian State Theatre and the Queensland Conservatorium of Music also used stylized images of Superb Lyrebird in their identity materials.

No. 223

Mergus merganser

Common Merganser

Goosander | Sawbill

● **LEAST CONCERN**

✿ **COLLECTIVE NAMES**
Creche of mergansers | Flock of mergansers

✴ **SYMBOLIC MEANINGS**
Courage; Perseverance.

✺ **POSSIBLE POWERS**
Bravery; Physical strength.

FOLKLORE AND FACTS
Many Native American creation myths involve a Great Flood, and a directive from a human leader to the waterbirds to restart the solid world after the rain stops. The only way to recreate land, however, is to bring up a bit of mud from the very bottom of the sea. A variety of waterbirds line up to show how brave they are, certain that they can keep going all the way to the bottom. • When the Algonquians tell this story, the loon attempts the dive and fails, as do most of the

M

ducks, the coot, and so on. When the Merganser makes the terrible dive, he pushes himself with both feet at once all the way to the bottom, grabs a morsel of earth in his bill, and rises to the top once again. He loses consciousness, and all the other birds work to revive him—and that's how they find the bit of dirt in his jaws. The Merganser is forever known as Earthdiver from that day forward. • In Europe, the Common Merganser is known as the goosander, and fishing interests see these fish-eating ducks as nuisances. The ducks prefer smaller fish than the professionals catch, but anglers say that the birds eat too many of the youngest fish, so there are fewer adults of regulation sizes to catch. For many years, this resulted in a bounty on the birds' heads. Despite this practice and illegal gathering of ducklings and eggs, the goosander holds its own in the United Kingdom, remaining a species of Least Concern.

No. 224

Meropidae

Bee-Eater

30 species in genus *Meropidae*

● **LEAST CONCERN**

✤ **COLLECTIVE NAME**

Bunch of bee-eaters

✹ **SYMBOLIC MEANING**

Endurance.

🌀 **POSSIBLE POWER**

Resistance against unkind words and deeds.

🜨 **FOLKLORE AND FACTS**

Yes, all thirty species of Bee-Eaters across Africa, Asia, the Pacific Rim, and Australia actually eat bees and wasps. These colony-nesters dig tunnels into banks along sandy rivers or flat, open ground, and lay their eggs at the far end of the tunnel, where the adult birds can protect their young from raptors, rats, snakes, and other predators. They hunt their bees on the wing over an open field rather than plundering an entire hive. • Greek mythology tells us the story of Botres, son of Eumelus, a devoted follower of the sun god Apollo. One day, Eumelus and Botres killed a ram as a sacrifice to Apollo, and Botres, thinking no one was looking, took a quick taste of the ram's brain before they had finished the ritual. Eumelus flew into a rage and struck Botres hard with a brand, inflicting a fatal wound. Eumelus and his wife were horrified and cried out to Apollo for forgiveness. While Apollo did not choose to save Botres, he did turn the boy into Aeropus, the Bee-Eater. Botres lived as a beautiful bird for the rest of his days.

No. 225

Milvus migrans

Black Kite

Fork-Tailed Kite | Tobi | Tombi (Japan)

● **LEAST CONCERN**

✤ **COLLECTIVE NAMES**

Husk of kites | Kettle of kites | Roost of kites | Soar of kites | Wake of kites

✹ **SYMBOLIC MEANINGS**

Commoner; Lesser being; Scavenger.

🌀 **POSSIBLE POWERS**

Adaptability; Sacred trust; Valor.

🜨 **FOLKLORE AND FACTS**

The Black Kite had the good sense to find ways to adapt to all the people in its natural habitat, turning from hunting live prey to scavenging dead animals, especially roadkill. For this apparent sin of adaptability, the Black Kite is much maligned by the people of Japan, who have many expressions in their vernacular that emphasize their disdain for the dark bird. "A kite breeds a hawk" means that a common family managed to raise an exceptional child; "Even a kite looks like a hawk when seated" means that a lowly person can put on airs and appear to be better than his class. • *The Chronicles of Japan* tells a story about a Black Kite that helped Emperor Jimmu achieve victory in battle: The kite glowed golden in the sunlight, so it perched on Jimmu's arrow and blinded the enemy by shining mightily in the sun. At that time, the Black Kite represented sacred trust and valor, but when it found ways to adapt to the expansion of mankind, it fell out of favor. • Not every country loathes the Black Kite—across most of its range in the eastern hemisphere, the Black Kite is just another common hawk, though its habit of perching on electrical wires leads to many birds' electrocution, and it falls prey to poisoning when eating rodents tainted with pesticides.

No. 226
Milvus milvus

Red Kite

European Red Kite

● **LEAST CONCERN**

🐾 **COLLECTIVE NAMES**

Husk of kites | Kettle of kites | Roost of kites | Soar of kites | Wake of kites

✳ **SYMBOLIC MEANINGS**

Resilience; Transformation.

🌀 **POSSIBLE POWER**

Adaptability.

🌙 **FOLKLORE AND FACTS**

Not so long ago, it was perfectly acceptable to hunt Red Kites across the United Kingdom, especially by gamekeepers and farmers who thought the birds would harm their livestock. While the birds had once been a revered species in London—even protected for their value as street cleaners in medieval times, eating whatever scraps people threw into the street—by the 1980s, these birds had nearly disappeared from the UK altogether. In 1989, just 52 kite nests remained in Wales. • Today, thanks to heroes like Welsh farmer Christopher Powell, whose Gigrin Farm became a feeding station for Red Kites in 1992, the birds' numbers have grown to the point where the IUCN has listed them as a species of Least Concern—an enormous victory. Feeding stations like this have been part of one of the world's great bird recovery success stories, with as many as 2,500 Red Kites feeding weekly at Gigrin Farm alone.

No. 227
Mimus polyglottos

Northern Mockingbird

● **LEAST CONCERN**

🐾 **COLLECTIVE NAMES**

Echo of mockingbirds | Exactness of mockingbirds | Plagiary of mockingbirds | Ridicule of mockingbirds

✳ **SYMBOLIC MEANING**

Self-expression.

🌀 **POSSIBLE POWERS**

Connection to the spirits/elders; Mimicry; Origin of language.

🌙 **FOLKLORE AND FACTS**

Five states claim the Northern Mockingbird as their state bird: Arkansas, Florida, Mississippi, Tennessee, and Texas. The bird's ability to mimic dozens of other birds and many human sounds—like car alarms and sirens—have made it an object of fascination for thousands of years. • Native Americans of the southwest believed that the Northern Mockingbird actually brought language to many different cultures throughout their region, and the Zuni people of New Mexico collected mockingbird feathers and adorned their prayer-sticks with them. • In Florida and Georgia, Indigenous Peoples believed that the mockingbird's ability to mimic could be passed through their eggs, feeding them to children who were slow to speak. • One of the most famous books in American literature, *To Kill a Mockingbird,* tells the story of a man wrongfully accused of a crime and expected to take the fall for another man's terrible acts. Author Harper Lee draws a parallel between this wrong and killing a bird that simply shares its vast song repertoire with anyone who cares to listen.

M

No. 228
Molothrus ater

Brown-Headed Cowbird
Buffalo Bird

● **LEAST CONCERN**

⚘ **COLLECTIVE NAMES**
Corral of cowbirds | Herd of cowbirds

✴ **SYMBOLIC MEANINGS**
Parasitism; Unrest; Villainy.

✺ **POSSIBLE POWERS**
Irresponsibility; Symbiosis with cattle.

☾ **FOLKLORE AND FACTS**
Well-known across North America for their unusual reproductive strategy, Brown-Headed Cowbirds have become the object of widespread scorn and dislike among birders and their allies. These birds lay their eggs in the nests of other birds and abandon them to their usually smaller foster parents, a practice that often becomes detrimental to the birds trying to raise their own young. As the hatched cowbird chick starts to grow, it quickly becomes larger than its stepparents and may crowd the smaller chicks out of the nest. Some finches and others now recognize a cowbird egg and chick and push it out of the nest before or shortly after it hatches, but many try to raise the chick, often losing their own young in the process. • Cowbirds get their name from their ancient relationship with cattle. In Native American cultures, cowbirds were known as "buffalo birds," and were admired for their partnership with cattle: Cowbirds hung around with buffalo because the large mammals kicked up bugs as they roamed the plains. The birds devoured the bugs, keeping them from irritating the buffalo, a symbiotic relationship that worked until buffalo disappeared from the American plains.

No. 229
Monticola solitarius

Blue Rock Thrush
Merill

● **LEAST CONCERN**

⚘ **COLLECTIVE NAME**
Mutation of thrushes

✴ **SYMBOLIC MEANINGS**
Healthy relationships; Long-term commitment.

✺ **POSSIBLE POWERS**
Concealment; Keeping of secrets.

☾ **FOLKLORE AND FACTS**
A uniformly bright blue bird with an orange belly in some regions, the Blue Rock Thrush is an abundant species across its long but narrow range in southernmost Europe, North Africa, southern  Asia, and the Pacific Rim. Flocks of males are usually accompanied by their subdued, brown-striped females, a fact that gives them credibility as symbols of healthy relationships and lasting commitments. • Malta selected the Blue Rock Thrush as its national bird, chiefly because this thrush lives on the rocky cliffs that typify the country, especially on its western coasts. Here it keeps to itself, showing no interest in nearby human activities and nesting in cracks between the rocks, and it is so secretive that most Maltese people have never seen one. It gained its protected status in 1971 to deter poachers and nest thieves from capturing it and selling it into the pet trade, a process that had nearly eliminated the birds from Malta in the 1960s.

No. 230
Morus bassanus

Northern Gannet
Solan Goose

● **LEAST CONCERN**

⚘ **COLLECTIVE NAMES**
Company of gannets | Gannetry of gannets | Plunging of gannets

✴ **SYMBOLIC MEANINGS**
Answered prayers; Devotion; Divinity; Gluttony.

M

🌀 POSSIBLE POWERS
Connection to Jesus; Fidelity; Long marriage.

🌙 FOLKLORE AND FACTS
When a Northern Gannet flies, its slender body and outstretched wings form the shape of a cross—so some Christians have embraced it as a symbol of divine power and a sign that their prayers will be answered. The sheer quantity of gannets along the Atlantic coasts dilute this meaning, however, allowing the birds to become a symbol of something far less angelic. • In England, the slang term "gannet" refers to someone who habitually overeats, as these birds are observed doing regularly. Gannets fly along the horizon, turn nearly vertical and plunge headfirst into the sea to catch their prey. If they encounter a large quantity of fish, gannets all dive in at once, creating a "feeding frenzy" of catching and devouring them.

No. 231
Motacilla alba

White Wagtail

Baltā Cielava | Willie Wagtail

● LEAST CONCERN

🌿 COLLECTIVE NAMES
Flight of wagtails | Roost of wagtails | Volery of wagtails

☀ SYMBOLIC MEANINGS
Diligence; Toil.

🌀 POSSIBLE POWER
Protection.

🌙 FOLKLORE AND FACTS
A bird of Europe, North Africa, and Asia, the White Wagtail won its position as the national bird of Latvia by being part of the country's folk music history (the song "The Wagtail Was Soaring" remains a traditional tune). It's a common bird throughout its range, living in open areas with water features and cohabitating nicely with humans. • All wagtails get their name from the tail-bobbing behavior, but scientists have no firm explanation for the wagging, speculating that it may help them flush prey out of hiding, or that it may show other wagtails that they have nothing to fear from it. A recent study suggested that it may be a warning to predators that the bird knows they are close by, and that it will not permit them to plunder its nest or young. • To date, eighteen countries in the White Wagtail's range have honored the bird with its portrait on a postage stamp. This has helped to raise awareness of the threats against the bird, from poachers who take the birds as food to those who trap them for the illegal pet trade.

No. 232
Motmotidae

Motmot

Clock Bird; 14 species in genus *Motmotidae*

● LEAST CONCERN (13 SPECIES)
● VULNERABLE
(KEEL-BILLED MOTMOT)

🌿 COLLECTIVE NAME
Flock of motmots

☀ SYMBOLIC MEANINGS
Change; Evolution; Inevitable destiny.

🌀 POSSIBLE POWERS
Beauty used for status; Social climbing.

🌙 FOLKLORE AND FACTS
The birds that wag their pendulum-shaped tails back and forth can't help but take their nickname from the ticking of a grandfather clock, though their song—similar across all fourteen species in this genus—provides their common name. All birds in this Central and South American family have brightly colored plumage in greens, turquoise, red, or gold, and all have the unusual tail with bare vanes that end in feathery paddles. • Mayans told the story of a Motmot that they called Toh, who was so beautiful that animal royalty revered him. This glory went right to Toh's head, so he shirked from any work assigned to him, saying it would ruin his beautiful feathers and tail. One day, Mottled Owl warned them all that a storm was coming, so they needed to build shelter immediately. All the birds went to work except Toh, but when others refused to build a shelter for him, he started helping. He tired quickly and hid in a cave, but the cave was too small and his tail remained exposed to the storm. When the storm ended, he came out—but all the other birds pointed and laughed. His tail had been stripped clean of feathers except for two small disks at the end. The moral: Be humble and do your share, and that will be its own reward.

M

No. 233

Neophron percnopterus

Egyptian Vulture

Gier-Eagle | Pharaoh's Chicken | White Scavenger Vulture

● **ENDANGERED**

✷ **COLLECTIVE NAMES**

Colony of vultures | Committee of vultures | Kettle of vultures | Wake of vultures

✸ **SYMBOLIC MEANINGS**

Death and rebirth; Motherhood; Purity.

✺ **POSSIBLE POWER**

Representative of pharaoh and the gods.

☾ **FOLKLORE AND FACTS**

In Leviticus 11:18 in the Old Testament, God places the Gier-Eagle on the list of animals that "shall be an abomination unto you," and that should not be consumed. Scholars have translated Gier-Eagle to mean the Egyptian Vulture, and there's a good reason why we shouldn't eat this bird: It eats all the things that other animals leave behind, as well as things it finds in human garbage dumps. Like all vultures, the Egyptian Vulture serves an important purpose in the world, cleaning up the rotting meat and other offal that would otherwise turn the planet into a stinking mess.
• Egyptian Vultures appear in ancient hieroglyphs as the symbol for the letter A, and back then the bird enjoyed special protections as "Pharaoh's Chicken," with a death sentence to anyone who harmed a vulture. Egyptians even believed erroneously that all of these vultures were female, and that they reproduced without the need for males to fertilize their eggs. This may be why the goddess Nekhbet, protector of Upper Egypt and the Pharaoh, revered these birds and wore a headdress shaped like an Egyptian vulture, as well as a robe made from the bird's feathers. • The bird's connection to the gods extended into Greek mythology as well, when Zeus broke up a conflict between Neophron and Aegypius by turning them both into vultures. Neophron gave his name to the vulture, cementing their relationship in the annals of science as well as in the mythic realm.

No. 234

Nestor notabilis

Kea

Clown of the Mountains

● **ENDANGERED**

✷ **COLLECTIVE NAMES**

Circus of keas | Curiosity of keas

✸ **SYMBOLIC MEANING**

Mischief.

✺ **POSSIBLE POWER**

Use of tools.

☾ **FOLKLORE AND FACTS**

New Zealand's endemic parrot can be a bit of a jerk, if you're driving through the mountainous South Island and happen to stop your car. Keas are known to attack side mirrors and windshield wipers, and they have the ability to do some significant damage. With their long, curved upper bill and considerable strength, this large parrot can not only dismantle rubber features on your vehicle, but it can also solve complex problems and even use tools (rocks or sticks) to achieve whatever goal the bird decides is important. In particular, these birds love ski resorts and often fly off with brightly colored articles of skiers' clothing. (If you play the video game *Dwarf Fortress*, you know what these birds can do.) • Keas are not showy parrots, but their olive-green bodies hide the flashy orange undersides of their wings, making them easy to recognize in flight. This identifying mark has helped sheep farmers determine which parrots were attacking their herds, a controversy that began in the mid-1800s and continues to this day. • Keas can use their curved bill to tear into a sheep's back and eat the fat they find there, without killing the sheep—although most sheep injured in this manner die of infection before long. Up until the 1970s, New Zealand put a bounty on Kea, paying for each bird beak that hunters brought in to prove they had killed the bird. Hunters killed more than 150,000 birds before the practice ended in the 1970s. As the birds are now a protected species and their numbers have dwindled to between 3,000 and 7,000 in recent years, sheep farmers now coexist with them and protect their sheep without injuring the birds.

N

No. 235

Ninox novaeseelandiae

Morepork

Boobook | Mopoke | Ruru

● LEAST CONCERN

🦎 **COLLECTIVE NAME**

Haunting of moreporks

☀ **SYMBOLIC MEANINGS**

Guardian; Intuition;
Wisdom.

🌀 **POSSIBLE POWERS**

Guide through trouble;
Knowledge; Predictor of death.

🌙 **FOLKLORE AND FACTS**

Just three birds of prey remain in New
Zealand, and none has adapted more readily
to sharing its habitat with humans than the Morepork,
more popularly known as the Ruru. This owl feeds on the
invasive rats and mice that now populate the islands, so it
has maintained its numbers more easily than other, more
choosy raptors. • Like owls around the world, the wide-
eyed appearance of the Morepork in the night gives the
impression of wisdom and intelligence, and while science
has not always backed this belief, the Ruru continues to
be a symbol of knowledge and intuition, especially for the
Māori people. Māori artists emulated this facial expression in
carvings throughout their meeting houses, and the practice
of *pukana*, or widening the eyes for emphasis and to add
excitement to a *haka* (dance performance), may be inspired
by the Ruru's glowing yellow eyes. Widening the eyes allows
the opposition to see your true intentions, so the Māori carry
this motif into their totem carvings as well as their personal
practice. • Not all tidings brought by a visiting Morepork
are positive. Māori culture says that if a Morepork sits by
your house for an extended period of time, there will soon
be a death in your family. Taranaki Māori actually killed
and ate Morepork when this happened, believing that this
would extend the family's lives. In some traditions, a family's
ancestral spirit could take the form of a *Hine-ruru*, or "owl
woman," to guide the family through trouble and serve as
an advisor.

No. 236

Nisaetus bartelsi

Javan Hawk-Eagle

Garuda

● ENDANGERED

🦎 **COLLECTIVE NAMES**

Cast of hawk-eagles | Kettle of hawk-eagles

☀ **SYMBOLIC MEANINGS**

Strength; Vigilance.

🌀 **POSSIBLE POWER**

Connection to Hindu god of birds.

🌙 **FOLKLORE AND FACTS**

A medium-sized eagle
with a pronounced crest
when perched, the Javan
Hawk-Eagle has been an
endangered species for some
time, its habitat on the island of
Java disappearing with the spread
of agriculture and residential areas.
Fewer than 1,000 individuals remain, and even these may
fall to predatory poaching and capture for the exotic bird
trade. • Indonesia made the Javan Hawk-Eagle its national
rare/precious animal to extend additional protection to
it, but this has not stopped the taking of these birds to sell
as pets. The Indonesian government reports that thirty to
forty of these birds appear in the pet trade annually—and
these are just the ones that are reported to authorities; many
more may be traded under the radar. In an effort to curtail
poachers and discourage young people from joining this
illegal business, conservation awareness activities include
school visits and nest protection programs. The real need,
however, is the enforcement of current laws, with officers in
the field catching and arresting poachers. • Javans call the
bird Garuda after the Hindu god of the birds, often depicted
as a human figure with wings, or as an actual bird. Indonesia
includes Garuda in its coat of arms, making the god even
more of a symbol for the country as Javan Hawk-Eagle.
While Garuda does not share the Javan Hawk-Eagle's crest,
the god's grand wings could represent any of the region's
many magnificent eagles.

No. 237

Numenius arquata

Eurasian Curlew

Common Curlew | Curlew | Guilbhron | Whaup

● **NEAR THREATENED**

✿ **COLLECTIVE NAMES**

Herd of curlews | Curfew of curlews

✴ **SYMBOLIC MEANINGS**

Darkness; Sorrow; Storms.

🌀 **POSSIBLE POWER**

Predictor of disaster.

☾ **FOLKLORE AND FACTS**

The Eurasian Curlew's long, curved bill sets it apart from many other shorebirds of the western hemisphere, especially along the coasts of the United Kingdom and Ireland. Its numbers are dwindling rapidly in these areas as their accustomed grassland habitat disappears, but Scandinavian efforts to remove successional forests and restore grassland have attracted the curlews to spend the breeding season there. • Before Oulunsalo, Finland, merged with the city of Oulu, the Eurasian Curlew had a place of honor on the municipality's coat of arms. Over time, curlews have appeared in a number of emblems and coats of arms across the UK, including Cumberland County, UK; the Lord Brittan of Spennithorne; Baron Phillips of Worth Matravers; and several others. • Curlews' connection with death becomes particularly vivid in what is known in British and Irish folklore as the legend of the seven whistlers. In 1862, miners at some of the collieries in Bedworth, North Warwickshire, refused as a unit to go into the coal pits one morning because of sounds they had heard overnight. They called these sounds "the seven whistlers," and they believed them to be curlews warning them of a disaster that would happen the following day. Superstition overwhelmed logic, and the men determined that they would not go into the mines. Eerily, those who did go down into the pit that day lost their lives. The largest pit disaster in the area's history happened that day, with a collapse that killed 204 miners.

No. 238

Numenius phaeopus

Whimbrel

Common Whimbrel | Eurasian Whimbrel | European Whimbrel | Hudsonian Whimbrel | White-Rumped Whimbrel

● **LEAST CONCERN**

✿ **COLLECTIVE NAMES**

Bind of whimbrels | Fling of whimbrels

✴ **SYMBOLIC MEANING**

Harbinger of death.

🌀 **POSSIBLE POWERS**

Endurance; Long-distance migration.

☾ **FOLKLORE AND FACTS**

Not quite as large as a Long-Billed Curlew with a gracefully downward-curved bill (but also not as long as a curlew's), the Whimbrel wears stripes on its head, making it fairly simple to tell it apart from a curlew on the beach. Like the curlews, its genus name *Numenius* refers to the crescent moon shape of its bill—"new moon" in English. • Whimbrels make a long-distance migration from their breeding grounds in the northern hemisphere down to the southern, often as far as 2,500 miles (4,023 km) without stopping. They go where they can find fiddler crabs at any time of year, reaching into their burrows with their long bill and washing the shellfish in water before breaking off its limbs and swallowing the rest. • While some cultures attribute dark predictions to the appearance of a Whimbrel out of place in a parking lot or mall lawn, scientists tracking one individual's migration route named the bird Hope, fitted it with a satellite transmitter, and watched as the bird flew more than 50,000 miles (80,467 km) in three years. Hope became the subject of a children's book, and the story of Hope's annual return to Great Pond in Saint Croix, U.S. Virgin Islands, became a catalyst for preserving the pond in its natural state and preventing development there.

Numida meleagris

Helmeted Guineafowl

● **LEAST CONCERN**

🐾 **COLLECTIVE NAME**
Confusion of guineafowl

✷ **SYMBOLIC MEANINGS**
Comfort; Healing.

🌀 **POSSIBLE POWERS**
Healing; Relief from grieving.

🌙 **FOLKLORE AND FACTS**
The so-called helmet on the head of the Helmeted Guineafowl does not cover the head, but actually forms it: The head's featherless skin is bright blue and red, with a yellowish protrusion from the crown that looks very much like a protective helmet. Males have a bigger bony knob than females, giving humans one way—though not a terribly obvious one—to tell male and female guineafowl apart. As these African birds now populate zoos, game farms, and estates all over the world, it's handy to know how to be sure which gender is which. • These birds take their Latin name from a Greek myth. Meleager leads the hunt to kill a wild boar that Artemis, goddess of the hunt, sent to ruin the Calydon countryside when its king, Oeneus (Meleager's father) neglected to provide his daily sacrifice to her. Meleager kills the boar, but those who band with him for the hunt then begin quarreling over who should get the spoils, and their squabble leads to war. On the battlefield, Meleager kills his own uncle, and his horrified mother, Althaea, has in her possession a log that is believed to match Meleager's life span—so she burns the log, and Meleager dies. His two sisters are so stricken with grief that Artemis takes pity on them and turns them into Helmeted Guineafowl. The teardrop-shaped dots on each of the birds' wings come from the tears shed by the two sisters.

Nycticorax nycticorax

Black-Crowned Night-Heron

Auku'u (Hawaiian) | Black-Capped Night-Heron | Night Heron | Qua-Bird | Quark

● **LEAST CONCERN**

🐾 **COLLECTIVE NAMES**
Battery of night-herons | Hedge of night-herons | Pose of night-herons | Rookery of night-herons | Scattering of night-herons

✷ **SYMBOLIC MEANING**
Foreboding without harm.

🌀 **POSSIBLE POWER**
Transformation into magical beings.

🌙 **FOLKLORE AND FACTS**
Widespread in wetlands around the world, the stealthy Black-Crowned Night-Heron hunts from dusk to dawn for fish, bugs, amphibians, and other birds' chicks, a schedule that allows it to feed without competition from day-feeding large wading birds. This behavior has led many cultures to see the heron as secretive and even sneaky, which in turn has brought it something of a bad reputation in legends and myths. Its Latin name *nycticorax* comes from the writings of Aristotle and means "bird of ill omen," and Swiss naturalist Conrad Gessner applied it to this specific bird in 1555, sealing its fate in subsequent texts. • Even with its ominous taxonomic name, Black-Crowned Night-Heron appears only briefly in folklore: In Japanese artist Toriyama Sekien's illustration *Aosaginohi* ("blue heron fire" in English). In the accompanying story, *Aosagibi*, elderly Black-Crowned Night-Herons turn into yōkai, or magical beings, in a flash of iridescent blue light. Once the transformation has occurred, the yōkai regularly breathe out a golden powder that coalesces and forms a fiery light. "Their powdery brak [breath] ignites into bright blue fireballs, which they blow across the water or high in the trees," the story says. The metamorphosis doesn't actually change much about the night-heron: It continues to live in the wetlands and feed, and shies away from people, just as it would as a bird. Now, however, its shiny blue scales evanesce in the moonlight, making it more difficult to hide from view completely.

Nymphicus hollandicus

Cockatiel

Quarrion | Weero | Weiro

● **LEAST CONCERN**

❃ **COLLECTIVE NAME**
Flock of cockatiels

✸ **SYMBOLIC MEANINGS**
Positive news; Social
connection.

✿ **POSSIBLE POWERS**
Arrival of good news; Service to the
local goddess.

☾ **FOLKLORE AND FACTS**
This Australian native holds second place as the
most popular pet bird in the world, adapting long
ago to life in captivity and breeding easily to stock
the legal pet trade. Living as pets seems to agree
with the birds: In the wild, their average life span is
twelve to fifteen years, but a pet bird may live as long as
twenty-five years (and the record is thirty-six years).
• The first Europeans to see these birds in their native
habitat back in 1832 found them so beautiful—and cute, to
boot—that they named them Nymphicus, after the mythical
maidens who live in all outdoor places and serve the goddess
(Nature, or whomever the local deity may be). The moniker
remains in their Latin name; the *Hollandicus* part comes
from New Holland, one of the original names Europeans
gave Australia in the nineteenth century. • Export of
Cockatiels began in the 1830s as European naturalists
brought them home to England, and by 1864, the birds had
already become a favorite pet. Their popularity spread
throughout Europe and soon crossed the ocean to the United
States. • If Cockatiels have a symbolic purpose, it must be
to promote friendships and social connection, as they are
among the most social and friendly birds that humans ever
encounter. Some Australians believe that the appearance of
a flock of Cockatiels can also signal the arrival of positive
news, as well as the simpler joys of freedom and spiritual
renewal.

No. 242

Oenanthe oenanthe

Northern Wheatear

Wheatear

● **LEAST CONCERN**

✿ **COLLECTIVE NAME**

Flock of wheatears

✴ **SYMBOLIC MEANINGS**

Endurance; Persistence.

🌀 **POSSIBLE POWER**

Long-distance migration.

🐦 **FOLKLORE AND FACTS**

Found only in Alaska and
the Canadian Maritimes
on the North American
continent, but plentiful in much of Europe
and Asia in spring and summer, the Northern
Wheatear makes a mighty migratory journey every autumn
to sub-Saharan Africa, no matter where its breeding grounds
may be. Some of these birds travel as much as 18,640 miles
(30,000 km) every year—roughly 9,000 miles (14,484 km)
each way, the longest migration for a songbird. • Imagine,
then, a little bird that puts in all of that work to get to and
from its near-Arctic breeding grounds, only to be scooped
up by shepherds in Sussex, England, and brought to hotels
and fancy restaurants by the thousands to be devoured as
a delicacy. Wheatears of the 1600s through the 1800s often
found this to be their fate, as they were considered "the
English Ortolan," a dainty dish for the wealthy and refined.
This practice came to an end in the twentieth century. • The
name "wheatear" does not refer to its ears at all, but actually
comes from *hwit*, the Old English world for white, and *aers*
for rump. Time has made the moniker more polite than its
originators intended.

No. 243

Onychoprion fuscatus

Sooty Tern

'Ewa 'Ewa (Hawaiian) | Kaveka (Marquesas Islands) | Manutara | Wideawake Tern

● **LEAST CONCERN**

✿ **COLLECTIVE NAMES**

Colony of terns | Committee of terns | Ternery of terns

✴ **SYMBOLIC MEANING**

Good luck.

🌀 **POSSIBLE POWER**

Connection to island spirits.

🐦 **FOLKLORE AND FACTS**

A visit to a colony of Sooty Terns is enough to wake the
dead, as any Hawaiian neighbor to one of the state's massive
colonies can tell us. In Hawai'i, the bird's nickname says it all:
'Ewa 'Ewa, which is a pretty good assessment of its persistent
call. The best legend about this bird comes from a different
island—Rapa Nui (Easter Island), where ancient inhabitants
worshipped the bird they called manutara. • At first, no one
lived on Rapa Nui except a spirit called Hitu. Hitu kept a
skull as treasure, storing it in a rock cavity. One day, a great
wave came and carried away the skull, and Hitu swam all
day and night until she saw the rocks of Motu Motiro Hiva
ahead. As soon as the skull touched the shore, it turned into
the Creator, Make Make, who took some of the seabirds
there and traveled to Easter Island, where he freed them.
• A year later, Make Make returned to discover that the
island's inhabitants had eaten all the eggs. He gathered the
birds and took them to another island, and then another, but
the same thing happened on each of them. Finally, he took
the birds to Rapa Nui, and villagers inadvertently left one egg
in a nest there. The egg produced the first manutara on the
island. Make Make taught the people to collect only a certain
number of
eggs, and the
birds became
a vast
colony of
Sooty Terns.

No. 244

Opisthocomus hoazin

Hoatzin

Canje Pheasant | Hoactzin | Reptile Bird | Stinkbird

● **LEAST CONCERN**

✿ **COLLECTIVE NAME**

Dongle of hoatzin

✴ **SYMBOLIC MEANINGS**

Ancient and forgotten things; Contradictions.

🌀 **POSSIBLE POWER**

Warning that things are not what they seem.

🐦 **FOLKLORE AND FACTS**

Our hats are off to the South American nation of Guyana for
choosing the bizarre Hoatzin as its national bird. This bird
of Amazon forests and swamps looks as if it were assembled
with random leftover pieces: A featherless blue face, red

eyes, a punk-style gold and red crest, a pheasant-like body with large, rufous wings, and a long, dark brown tail with bands of greenish gold and white. • Hoatzin chicks are born ready to move, and they have something only a few other birds have: Two claws on the ends of each wing, allowing them to climb trees and move along branches within hours of birth. This draws comparisons to the first prehistoric bird fossil, *Archaeopteryx*, considered by paleontologists to be the link between dinosaur and bird. *Archaeopteryx* also had claws on the ends of its wings, but the two birds share no other major traits, and today ornithologists believe that the Hoatzin evolved its claws independently. • South Americans believe that a Hoatzin sighting can be a warning that things are not what they seem in your life. The bird is such a mass of contradictions that seeing one can indicate the same sorts of conflicts between assumption and fact.

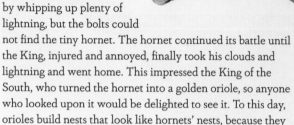

as a stinging hornet, and that it attacked and overpowered the evil King of the North to stop the King from sending destructive storms to the planet. The King responded by whipping up plenty of lightning, but the bolts could not find the tiny hornet. The hornet continued its battle until the King, injured and annoyed, finally took his clouds and lightning and went home. This impressed the King of the South, who turned the hornet into a golden oriole, so anyone who looked upon it would be delighted to see it. To this day, orioles build nests that look like hornets' nests, because they learned to do this before they were birds.

No. 245

Oriolus oriolus

Eurasian Golden Oriole

European Golden Oriole | Western Eurasian Golden Oriole | Woodweele

● **LEAST CONCERN**

✷ **COLLECTIVE NAMES**
Array of orioles | Flamboyance of orioles | Plague of orioles | Trill of orioles

✳ **SYMBOLIC MEANINGS**
Goals bearing fruit; Springtime.

🌀 **POSSIBLE POWER**
Fertility.

🜲 **FOLKLORE AND FACTS**
High in the treetops, behind hundreds of green leaves, a flash of yellow signals the arrival of a male Eurasian Golden Oriole. The springtime return of these birds to Europe and western and central Asia heralds good weather and the coming of ripe fruit. • The Victorian passion for collecting bird eggs from a wide variety of woodland species essentially wiped out Eurasian Golden Orioles in the United Kingdom, with the last of them failing to reproduce in 1910. Happily, the end of the egg-collecting hobby shortly thereafter allowed the birds to return to the British Isles in the 1960s. • Folklore tells us that the golden oriole started its existence

---

No. 246

Ortalis ruficauda

Rufous-Vented Chachalaca

Cocrico (Trinidad and Tobago) | Goacharaca (Venezuela)

● **LEAST CONCERN**

✷ **COLLECTIVE NAME**
Collaboration of chachalacas

✳ **SYMBOLIC MEANINGS**
Chatter; Family.

🌀 **POSSIBLE POWERS**
Friendliness; Voracious appetite.

🜲 **FOLKLORE AND FACTS**
Chachalacas are big, friendly birds almost always seen in pairs or family groups, and the Rufous-Vented variety (with a patch of chestnut at the back of the rump below the tail) is every bit as gregarious and noisy as its plain counterpart to the north. This fruit-eating bird of several South American countries hops easily from one branch to another despite its size and long, thick tail, navigating through trees and shrubs to devour the available fruit. • The name chachalaca is Nahuatl for "chatter," so the entire genus's name specifies exactly what makes these large, chicken-like birds impossible to ignore. • Also difficult to tolerate is the chachalaca's taste for tomatoes, melons, beans, and radishes, and their ability to plunder an entire garden in one visit. If a dozen chachalacas arrive in a backyard in the morning, they can clean out all of the expected harvest in just a few hours.

No. 247

Ortalis vetula

Plain Chachalaca

Chacharaka | Jayketzo' (Q'eqchi' Mayan)

● **LEAST CONCERN**

✵ **COLLECTIVE NAME**
Collaboration of chachalacas

✴ **SYMBOLIC MEANINGS**
Balance; Family; Natural harmony.

🌀 **POSSIBLE POWER**
Lamenting for world balance and harmony.

☾ **FOLKLORE AND FACTS**
From south Texas to southern Mexico, the Plain Chachalaca is a familiar bird around backyard feeders, as well as a willing consumer of cultivated fruits and vegetables—especially tomatoes, radishes, beans, and melons. • This bird nearly always shows up in pairs or family groups, and its morning and evening songs create a cacophony that some find amusing, while others can't wait for it to stop. • The Q'eqchi' Maya people of Guatemala's central highlands knew Plain Chachalacas as Jayketzo', an onomatopoetic variation of its incessant *hai-KE-tso* call, beginning about half an hour before sunrise. Q'eqchi' Maya hear something different from the rest of us in the chachalaca's call: They believe the birds call out in distress for the world's hungry, and that they cry for sun when it rains, and rain when it's sunny. Essentially, they call for balance between mountains and sky, with enough moisture, sunlight, and nutrients to achieve a healthy harvest for all species.

No. 248

Oxyura jamaicensis

Ruddy Duck

● **LEAST CONCERN**

✵ **COLLECTIVE NAMES**
Badelynge of ducks | Plump of ducks | Raft of ducks (when on water)

✴ **SYMBOLIC MEANINGS**
New opportunities; Swiftness.

🌀 **POSSIBLE POWER**
Rapid propagation.

☾ **FOLKLORE AND FACTS**
A cute, little blue-billed duck, whose Latin name *oxyura* means "stiff tail," caused a row of epic proportions in England starting back in the 1950s when Sir Peter Scott, son of the Antarctic explorer Robert Falcon Scott, became very involved in creating a major bird sanctuary at Slimbridge Wetland Centre in Gloucestershire, England. Scott imported three pairs of Ruddy Ducks from the United States and set about breeding them—but when the ducklings hatched, they took off from Slimbridge. Soon they bred and inhabited lakes, ponds, and reservoirs throughout the area, and they spread further out into UK waters. Before long, Ruddy Ducks were all over Europe. • Over the next forty years, Ruddy Ducks made their way into Spain and discovered a close relative, the White-Headed Duck, which was genetically similar enough for interbreeding. Would Ruddy Ducks absorb and essentially wipe out the struggling White-Headed Duck? • A program began to eradicate Ruddy Ducks from European waters, supported by the Royal Society for the Protection of Birds. By 2012, some 6,500 Ruddy Ducks had been exterminated in England, and just two years later, estimates suggested that fewer than 100 Ruddy Ducks remained in the country.

O

No. 249

Pagophila eburnea

Ivory Gull

● **NEAR THREATENED**

✤ **COLLECTIVE NAMES**

Badelynge of ducks | Plump of ducks | Raft of ducks (when on water)

✺ **SYMBOLIC MEANINGS**

Clean environment; New opportunities.

🌀 **POSSIBLE POWER**

Endurance of Arctic conditions.

☾ **FOLKLORE AND FACTS**

Among gulls, no bird is more pristinely white than the Ivory Gull, a small gull that lives and breeds above the Arctic Circle and finds Newfoundland, northern Norway, and Alaska to be temperate enough for it to winter in these harsh environments. No gull lives and breeds farther north, either: The Ivory Gull chooses areas covered in sea ice, taking tiny polar cod and small shellfish for its sustenance, and following along as polar bears and arctic foxes catch and kill their own prey, so the little gulls can feed on what they leave behind. It's a peculiar irony that the most purely white gull in the world is perfectly happy to devour some of the most distasteful stuff in the Arctic: The placentae of newly whelped seals, for example, or even walrus excrement. • As waters warm above the Arctic Circle, sea ice melts—which means that the Ivory Gull faces the same potentially disastrous consequences of climate change that polar bears do. The lack of ice could leave this gull with nowhere to nest, which could result in a rapid decline for this bird in very short order. In the interim, Ivory Gulls are showing up more frequently in the northern reaches of the United Kingdom, mainland Canada, and even as far south as the Great Lakes in the United States, with the occasional bird on the northern New England coast.

No. 250

Pandion haliaetus

Osprey

Fish Hawk | River Hawk | Sea Hawk

● **LEAST CONCERN**

✤ **COLLECTIVE NAME**

Colony of ospreys

✺ **SYMBOLIC MEANINGS**

Absolute confidence in one's own greatness; Mastery over air and sea.

🌀 **POSSIBLE POWER**

Frightening fish into surrender.

☾ **FOLKLORE AND FACTS**

One of the world's most widespread and recognizable birds of prey, the Osprey brings the benefit of having a high tolerance for sharing its world with humans, so we have the opportunity to observe it at length as it nests on purpose-built platforms at the tops of utility poles, or fishes openly on rivers and in open wetlands. Large and grand with a wingspan as wide as 71 inches (180 cm), an Osprey can be seen carrying whole fish in its talons to feed its nesting young, or gliding through the air as it watches for prey just below the water's surface. • The Osprey's Latin genus, *Pandion*, honors a storied king of Athens in Greek mythology, though the Osprey has no connection to Pandion's story. The majestic bird does find its way into ancient texts, however: Pliny the Elder theorized that Ospreys test their young's mettle by making them fly all the way to the sun; any birds that didn't make it there and back were executed by their own parents. • Much more recently, the poet William Butler Yeats used an Osprey as a figure of sadness in his 1889 poem "The Wanderings of Oisin," referring to it as "the grey wandering osprey Sorrow." • In medieval times, fishermen believed that fish were so terrified by Ospreys that they simply turned belly-up and waited to die when the raptor appeared. The belief even found a place in Shakespeare's *Coriolanus*, Act IV: 5: "I think he'll be to Rome / As is the osprey to the fish, who takes it / By sovereignty of nature." • Cities and provinces have chosen the Osprey as their animal representative, including Nova Scotia, where it is the provincial bird; and Södermanland, Sweden, where it is the official bird. Countries around the world have placed an Osprey on more than fifty postage stamps. The bird even caused a bit of a row in the Oregon state legislature in a conflict known as the Battle of the Birds. The Western Meadowlark had long been the state bird of Oregon, but Senator Fred Girod wanted to replace it with the Osprey—much to the consternation of birding groups. The legislature finally compromised by designating the Meadowlark as the state songbird, and the Osprey as the state raptor.

Paradisaea raggiana

Raggiana Bird-of-Paradise

Cenderawasih | Kumul

● **LEAST CONCERN**

❄ **COLLECTIVE NAMES**

Brace of birds-of-paradise | Flight of birds-of-paradise

✹ **SYMBOLIC MEANING**

National bird of Papua
New Guinea.

🌀 **POSSIBLE POWER**

Yet to be discovered.

🜨 **FOLKLORE AND FACTS**

When Italian naturalist and
explorer Luigi Maria D'Albertis
traveled to Papua New Guinea in 1875 and charted the
Fly River, he named some of the plant, animal, and bird
species he saw in his travels. He chose to name one of the
bird specimens he collected Raggiana, after the Marquis
Francesco Raggi of Genoa, though the historical record
does not say why. • Thanks to this magnanimous gesture,
today we continue to call this bird the Raggiana Bird-of-
Paradise—and it has risen to become the national bird of
Papua New Guinea, a high honor from an island nation that
has such a wealth of bird species from which to choose.
• The emerald-green-faced, yellow-crowned male of
this species is otherwise a deep reddish-brown, with a
particularly exotic-looking tail, adorned with two long, black
tail "wires." Long orange-to-red plumes extend from the
bird's flanks, making its overall plumage particularly lush.
The female lacks the long tail wires and is a drabber color
overall. • This Bird-of-Paradise appears in bright yellow
silhouette on Papua New Guinea's national flag, and the
country's national rugby team is the Kumuls, the
bird's name in native Tok Pisin.

Paradisaeidae

Bird-of-Paradise

43 species in genus *Paradisaeidae*

● **LEAST CONCERN (35 SPECIES)**

● **NEAR THREATENED (6 SPECIES)**

● **VULNERABLE (2 SPECIES)**

❄ **COLLECTIVE NAMES**

Brace of birds-of-paradise | Flight of birds-of-paradise

✹ **SYMBOLIC MEANINGS**

Bravery; Gift from God; Lofty position; Power.

🌀 **POSSIBLE POWER**

Otherworldly beauty.

🜨 **FOLKLORE AND FACTS**

Any trip to eastern Indonesia, Papua New Guinea, or
northeastern Australia simply must include a birding
expedition to see some of the forty-five species in the family
Paradisaeidae, or Bird-of-Paradise. These generously
feathered birds in their flamboyant colors represent all
that is exotic in the avian world, and the stories and myths
that surround them are equally colorful, granting them
even more mystique than they come by naturally. • While
these birds furnished plumes for rituals and adornment
to the Indigenous Peoples of these lands for centuries,
the first Europeans to see the birds came with Ferdinand
Magellan as he circumnavigated the world in the early
1500s. They brought a Bird-of-Paradise skin back to Spain,
but to best showcase the beauty of the bird's plumage,
indigenous hunters had prepared the skin by removing
the wings and feet. This led Europeans to surmise that the
birds had no feet and never landed on the ground, instead
floating on air currents until their eventual death. • Other
speculators decided that Birds-of-Paradise were actually
the Phoenix described in Greek mythology (see No. M007
in this book), though this belief did not last long. The
concept that established the strongest hold on European
imaginations was that these birds had come from paradise
on Earth, a place that God had blessed with otherworldly
splendor and unimaginable treasures. • With all the myths
eventually debunked, Birds-of-Paradise drew the attention
of the fashion trade, and in the eighteenth and nineteenth
centuries, hunting the birds to adorn ladies' hats and dresses
became a boon to industry. • This drove many species
nearly to extinction, until feathers
finally went out of fashion in the early
1900s. Birds-of-Paradise now draw
thousands of birding tourists annually
to their native lands to see them in their
natural habitats, giving even the most
endangered species a fighting
chance of survival.

No. 253

Parus major

Great Tit

Saw-Sharpener (archaic)

● **LEAST CONCERN**

✢ **COLLECTIVE NAME**

Murmuration of tits

✺ **SYMBOLIC MEANINGS**

Happiness; High energy.

◉ **POSSIBLE POWERS**

Control of their own weight; Prediction of rain.

☾ **FOLKLORE AND FACTS**

Widespread throughout Europe, Asia, and northern Africa, the Great Tit is one of the most easily recognized birds in the eastern hemisphere—and also one of the most studied. Great Tits love nest boxes provided by humans, making it very easy to observe them carefully and document their behavior. Research facilities throughout Europe have made use of this propensity for manmade housing, learning a great deal about the bird's lifecycle and adaptability to its surroundings. • It doesn't take a science degree to note some specifics about this bird, especially in terms of its song: Its many variations have led birders throughout its range to comment, "If you hear a song in the woods and you don't know what it is, it's a Great Tit." The standard double-note song sounds like "see-saw" or "teach-er," a call that some believe signals rain in the forecast. • Birders can tell visitors all about the plumage variations that make one bird dominant over another, and about how the birds control their own weight gain to make themselves less attractive to predatory hawks. Not many birds pay attention to their own physical fitness, but these birds know that a fit bird is less likely to look tasty than a fat bird. • For all their boldness in fraternizing with humans and their resourcefulness in looking out for their own welfare, Great Tits are not prominent in mythology or folklore. Regardless, they do carry special significance for entire cultures that consider them bringers of happy tidings and positive energy.

No. 254

Passer domesticus

House Sparrow

English Sparrow

● **LEAST CONCERN**

✢ **COLLECTIVE NAME**

Host of sparrows

✺ **SYMBOLIC MEANINGS**

Bad luck; Domesticity; Familiarity; Good luck.

◉ **POSSIBLE POWERS**

Adaptability; Opportunism.

☾ **FOLKLORE AND FACTS**

In 1852, pharmaceutical magnate Eugene Schieffelin of New York City made a decision that would affect the entire country for many generations to come: He imported House Sparrows from Europe so the birds would eat the larvae of the linden moth that had infested trees throughout the city. The birds multiplied so rapidly that New York soon lost control of the population. Within fifty years, tens of millions of House Sparrows lived everywhere in North America . . . and today, more than 540 million House Sparrows live on six continents, making them the most invasive bird species in history. • Why are House Sparrows so successful at adapting to any environment? Research published in 2018 found that the birds' ability to digest starchy grains, including processed foods like pizza crust, French fries, and bread, has made them particularly suited to urban environments. An enzyme in their digestive system allows them to break down carbohydrates that other birds can't eat. • In the *Infancy Gospel of Thomas*, an apocryphal book that surfaced in the second century, seven-year-old Jesus and a group of children make birds and animals out of clay. Jesus fashions some sparrows, and then he commands the clay birds to come to life and walk. The figures do so, he commands them to fly, and they do. The boys around him go home and tell their parents what they witnessed, and the children's fathers order them never to play with young Jesus again. The author doesn't designate a species for the clay sparrows, but it's likely that Jesus and his friends had some familiarity with House Sparrows, which are native to the Middle East and North Africa.

P

No. 255

Passer italiae

Italian Sparrow

Cisalpine Sparrow

● **VULNERABLE**

⁂ **COLLECTIVE NAME**
Host of sparrows

✳ **SYMBOLIC MEANINGS**
Resourcefulness; Simplicity.

🌀 **POSSIBLE POWER**
Adaptability.

🌑 **FOLKLORE AND FACTS**
Mottled brown sparrows with a reddish-brown cap, dark
mask and bib, and spotted chest, Italian Sparrows are very
like House Sparrows except for additional black areas on
the face. The Italian Sparrow is a common sight in Italy,
so much so that it serves as the country's national bird.
It also maintains limited populations in Corsica, France,
Switzerland, Austria, and Slovenia. • Like its close relatives,
the Italian Sparrow is a highly adaptable bird, living in
quantity across rural and urban settings and consuming all
kinds of agricultural grains and seeds. It is said to reflect
the spirit of all Italians, people who have had to deal
with change for many centuries while preserving their
unique culture and traditions. • Sparrows have all sorts of
connotations in folklore, much of it contradictory from one
culture to the next. Some believe that a sparrow entering
the house is good luck, but some Europeans see sparrows as
lower class, and therefore not worth much consideration.
Some superstitions say that if a sparrow flies into a closed
window and dies, it might mean that someone you know will
die soon; if it just hits the window but survives, it may mean
that something in the household will come to an end—a
job, relationship, or friendship. • Sailors of old got tattoos of
sparrows in hopes that if
they died at sea, the
sparrows would
find their soul and
carry them into the
next world.

No. 256

Passer montanus

Eurasian Tree Sparrow

German Sparrow | Mayang Simbahan (Philippines) | Tree Sparrow

● **LEAST CONCERN**

⁂ **COLLECTIVE NAME**
Host of sparrows

✳ **SYMBOLIC MEANINGS**
Resourcefulness; Simplicity.

🌀 **POSSIBLE POWER**
Adaptability.

🌑 **FOLKLORE AND FACTS**
Related to the House Sparrow, but with a redder cap and
a sporty black patch against its bright white cheek, the
Eurasian Tree Sparrow inhabits a neighborhood area in St.
Louis, Missouri, as its only domain in the United States. • In
Europe and Asia, however, the Tree Sparrow enjoys wide
distribution from the British Isles to the Pacific Rim. The
bird has the same food preferences as its close cousin, but
when it crosses paths with the House Sparrow, it leaves the
urban areas to the more aggressive sparrow and feasts on
cereals, rice, and fruit in farmlands instead. • The sparrow
in the Japanese fable "The Tongue-Cut Sparrow" is most
likely a Eurasian Tree Sparrow. In one version of the story,
an old woman and her husband feed an ailing Tree Sparrow.
Afterward, the sparrow visits the couple every morning,
singing to express his gratitude. A neighbor, angered at being
woken up by the sparrow's song, seizes the sparrow and cuts
his tongue out. The saddened couple visit the Tree Sparrow,
who offers them a choice of two baskets, one small and one
large. The couple choose the smaller basket, which turns out
to contain piles of silk and gold. The neighbor, catching sight
of this, visits the Tree Sparrow. He also offers her the choice
of two baskets. The greedy neighbor chooses the larger
basket. But when she finally opens it, the basket turns out to
be full of demons, and
she is never seen
again.

No. 257

Passerina ciris

Painted Bunting

Mexican Canary | Nonpareil | Painted Finch | Pope

● LEAST CONCERN

COLLECTIVE NAMES

Decoration of buntings | Mural of buntings | Sacrifice of buntings

SYMBOLIC MEANINGS

Intelligence; Knowledge; Nature's bounty.

POSSIBLE POWER

Embodiment of God's covenant.

FOLKLORE AND FACTS

A legend shared by Indigenous Peoples of the Great Plains tells us how the Painted Bunting became one of the most beautiful birds in North America. The Great Spirit himself brought all of the birds together while they were still dressed in drab, gray feathers. One by one, he chose colors for them and painted them himself: Bright red for the Northern Cardinal, many shades of blue for the Blue Jay, dabs of red and yellow for the American Redstart, and so on. • When he thought he had finished, just one gray bird stood before him, its eyes cast downward as it watched the Great Spirit gather his brushes. The Great Spirit saw the bird's sadness, but he looked at his remaining drops of paint and wondered how he would give the bird a bright color. • The solution came to him: He painted the bird with all of his remaining paint, giving it a bright blue head, red chest and underside, and green back and wings. To this day, the Painted Bunting is the envy of songbirds throughout the continent. • Some American Christians associate this rainbow-colored bird with the Old Testament story of Noah and the Great Flood. As the rain stopped, God sent Noah a rainbow to demonstrate his promise that he would never send another flood to destroy the Earth. In Genesis 9:9, God says, "I have placed my rainbow in the clouds. It is the sign of my covenant with you and with all the Earth." Painted Bunting, then, is the living embodiment of this rainbow, reminding people of this covenant and God's protection of the natural world.

No. 258

Patagona gigas

Giant Hummingbird

● LEAST CONCERN

COLLECTIVE NAMES

Charm of hummingbirds | Chattering of hummingbirds | Hover of hummingbirds | Shimmer of hummingbirds

SYMBOLIC MEANINGS

Perseverance; Toil.

POSSIBLE POWER

Good luck.

FOLKLORE AND FACTS

Ten times larger than the world's smallest bird, the Bee Hummingbird, the Giant Hummingbird is nearly the size of a Northern Cardinal at a staggering 0.85 ounces (24 g). Being so much larger than most of the birds in its family, the Giant Hummingbird attracted the imagination of folklorists throughout South America. • The Quechua people tell a parable of a massive fire that broke out in a woodland, consuming all of the animals' homes. Everyone raced out of the forest ahead of the flames and stood along the riverbank, watching as their trees, nests, burrows, and more succumbed to the flames. That is, everyone watched except for the Hummingbird. Instead of observing in horror, the tiny bird dove to the water's surface, picked up a few drops, and flew back to the fire to drip water on the flames. It kept doing this as the animals watched, feeling helpless. Some of the animals actively tried to discourage the tiny bird, saying, "What you are doing doesn't help, and your wings may burn. Why don't you stop?" Hummingbird replied, "I am doing what I can." The Quechuan moral: Small efforts can make a difference.

Pavo cristatus

Indian Peafowl

Blue Peafowl | Common Peafowl | Peacock (male) | Peahen (female)

● **LEAST CONCERN**

✿ **COLLECTIVE NAMES**

Bevy of peafowl | Muster of peafowl | Ostentation of peafowl | Party of peafowl | Pride of peafowl | Pulchritude of peafowl

✸ **SYMBOLIC MEANINGS**

Courage; Courtship; Healing; Vanity; Wisdom.

✾ **POSSIBLE POWERS**

Confidence; Second sight.

✿ **FOLKLORE AND FACTS**

From the NBC network logo to its use in heraldry and fashion, the Indian Peafowl is among the most iconic birds in the world. The male's instantly recognizable fan of blue, gold, and green feathers, each decorated with an enormous "eye" near the outer tip, serves as a symbol for male vanity and bravado in cultures throughout Europe and North America. • In India, where the Indian Peafowl is the national bird, the Shiva god of war, Kartikeya, rides an Indian Peacock into battle, and Indra, the Hindu king of all the gods, gets relief from being cursed with a thousand ulcers when Vishnu transforms him into a peacock with a thousand eyes. Peacock feathers and iconography can be found all over Indian temples and other buildings, as well as in art, on coins, and as an inspiration for fashion. • Peacocks appeared in Europe and Africa thousands of years ago, playing a role in Greek mythology as the bird that sprung from the blood of Argus Panoptes, the hundred-eyed giant. Some versions of this myth include Hera, Zeus's wife, actually turning Argos into a peacock, while in others, Hera places Argos's many eyes into the peacock's tail. • Even Aesop provides fables about the birds: In one, a jay attempts to disguise himself as a peacock by picking up discarded plumes and tying them to its own tail, then strutting around the courtyard with the other birds. The peacocks soon discover the deception and drum the bird out of the corps. His fellow jays chide him: "It's not the fine feathers that make a fine bird."

Pelicanus conspicillatus

Australian Pelican

● **LEAST CONCERN**

✿ **COLLECTIVE NAMES**

Pod of pelicans | Scoop of pelicans

✸ **SYMBOLIC MEANINGS**

Cooperation; Going with the flow; Self-forgiveness.

✾ **POSSIBLE POWER**

Bravery.

✿ **FOLKLORE AND FACTS**

An Aboriginal Dreaming story tells us about Moola the Australian Pelican, back in the days when pelicans were all black (according to the story) instead of white with black wingtips, as they are today. • Moola was very vain, spending hours of every day preening his feathers, and riding around in a canoe. He felt very important in his bark canoe, and never gave rides to other pelicans. One day, a huge rainstorm stranded some people on a high spot, and Moola in his canoe was the only one who could save them. He saw three older people and one beautiful young girl, so he hatched a plan to save the older folks first and then take the girl to be his wife. As he transported the older people to higher ground one at a time, however, the young girl caught on to his plan. She wrapped her coat around a log and slipped into the water, swimming away before he could return for her. Moola found the log and soon realized he had been fooled, so he went to his own camp and covered himself with splotches of white war paint, ready to go off in search of the clever young girl. Other pelicans saw him, however, and made fun of his white paint, and when he got angry, they all attacked him. Moola fought bravely, so much so that the rest of the pelicans decided they should wear white paint like him. They got the paint and covered themselves with it, and they have stayed white ever since in deference to Moola. • Australian Pelicans can soar continuously for twenty-four hours, riding thermals to gain altitude without flapping. While they eat mostly fish, their large bills can trap turtles, crustaceans, and even birds, which they hold underwater to drown before swallowing them whole, head-first. The pelican's pouch is not used for storage, but for collection of food and to help position it for easy swallowing.

No. 261

Pelicanus occidentalis

Brown Pelican

● LEAST CONCERN

⚶ **COLLECTIVE NAMES**
Pod of pelicans | Scoop of pelicans

✹ **SYMBOLIC MEANING**
Survival against all odds.

🌀 **POSSIBLE POWER**
Creation of the world.

☙ **FOLKLORE AND FACTS**
The national bird of Saint Martin, Barbados, St. Kitts and Nevis, and the Turks and Caicos Islands, as well as the state bird of Louisiana, the Brown Pelican stands for all things Caribbean: Sun, sand, surf, and seafood. While the actual birds may not be as vivacious as Nigel, the pelican in the animated movie *Finding Nemo*, they do delight onlookers on beaches from New Jersey to the Amazon River on the Atlantic coast, and from British Columbia to Peru on the Pacific coast. • Brown Pelicans are large and charismatic, pursuing prey by executing a nosedive that looks as if they've fallen out of the sky. Piercing the water with a mighty splash, they seize their prey and carry it off, a show of strength that would be awesome were it not so darned funny.
• On the island of Tiburón in the Gulf of California, part of the Mexican state of Sonora, the Seri tribe believed that a Brown Pelican actually created their world, beginning by raising its own island out of the sea. • More recently and in real life, Brown Pelicans became the symbol for the Deepwater Horizon oil spill's effect on birds in the Gulf of Mexico in 2010. The Center for Biological Diversity estimates that more than 9,300 Brown Pelicans were among the 82,000 birds harmed by the spill.

No. 262

Pelicanus onocrotalus

Great White Pelican
Eastern White Pelican | Rosy Pelican | White Pelican

● LEAST CONCERN

⚶ **COLLECTIVE NAMES**
Pod of pelicans | Scoop of pelicans

✹ **SYMBOLIC MEANINGS**
Generosity; Humility.

🌀 **POSSIBLE POWER**
Maternal sacrifice.

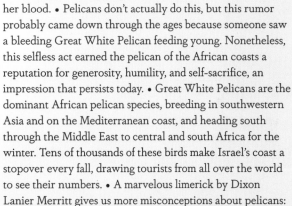

☙ **FOLKLORE AND FACTS**
In ancient times, a belief surfaced that must have been based on misinterpreted evidence: A pelican that couldn't find its usual fish catch was so desperate to feed her young that she pricked her own breast until it bled, giving the chicks her blood. • Pelicans don't actually do this, but this rumor probably came down through the ages because someone saw a bleeding Great White Pelican feeding young. Nonetheless, this selfless act earned the pelican of the African coasts a reputation for generosity, humility, and self-sacrifice, an impression that persists today. • Great White Pelicans are the dominant African pelican species, breeding in southwestern Asia and on the Mediterranean coast, and heading south through the Middle East to central and south Africa for the winter. Tens of thousands of these birds make Israel's coast a stopover every fall, drawing tourists from all over the world to see their numbers. • A marvelous limerick by Dixon Lanier Merritt gives us more misconceptions about pelicans:

> A wonderful bird is the pelican.
> His bill can hold more than his belican.
> He can hold in his beak
> Enough food for a week,
> But I'm damned if I see how the helican.

Pelicans do not actually store food in the pouch under their bill, but the three-gallon (11-L) pouch certainly is roomy, and the birds can gather quite a volume of food as they catch it. • They also gather water, allowing it to drain away just before they eat the fish. When they have tilted the head back and let the water drain out of the pouch, they snap the head back and toss the fish into their throat, swallowing it headfirst.

P

Perisoreus canadensis

Canada Jay

Camp Jay | Gray Jay | Whisky Jack

● **LEAST CONCERN**

✿ **COLLECTIVE NAMES**

Band of jays | Party of jays

✺ **SYMBOLIC MEANINGS**

Commitments to one another; Resilience.

✿ **POSSIBLE POWER**

Charming humans into feeding them.

☾ **FOLKLORE AND FACTS**

Algonquin, Cree, and Menominee cultures tell stories of a combined Creator and benevolent trickster, Wisakedjak (or one of dozens of other spellings), who caused the Great Flood that wiped out life on the North American continent. Wisakedjak also re-started the world after the flood waters receded, sometimes on his own, and sometimes with the help of birds, depending on who's telling the story. • Exactly how Wisakedjak's name came to be associated with Canada Jays is not particularly clear, but the playful bird, decked out in its muted shades of gray and white, often gets the name Whisky Jack as a shortened way to refer to the Native American Creator. • Canada Jays live in the boreal forests of the northern contiguous United States, Canada, and Alaska, hanging together in small flocks and often coming to a human hand offering sunflower seed or peanuts. Once a Canada Jay has learned to take food from a person's hand, the bird never forgets this—so even in places not visited often by humans, the bird will fly close to whatever people it sees and will keep pestering them for food. • *Canadian Geographic* magazine conducted a poll in 2015 and 2016 that ended in the nomination of Canada Jay for Canada's national bird. This has yet to lead to an official designation by the Canadian government, but the bird's popularity keeps the contest in the public eye, with the hope that one day, the Canada Jay will have its day.

Phalacrocorax carbo

Great Cormorant

Black Cormorant | Black Shag | Great Black Cormorant | Kawau (Māori) | Large Cormorant | White-Breasted Cormorant

● **LEAST CONCERN**

✿ **COLLECTIVE NAMES**

Flight of cormorants | Gulp of cormorants

✺ **SYMBOLIC MEANINGS**

Good luck; Nuisance to fishermen.

✿ **POSSIBLE POWER**

Carrying the spirit of someone lost at sea.

☾ **FOLKLORE AND FACTS**

While its actual size varies widely throughout their northern Atlantic and Asian range, the Great Cormorant usually presents itself as bigger than its close cousin, the Double-Crested Cormorant, and may grow to weigh nearly 12 pounds (5 kg). It spends much of its time fishing on lakes, rivers, and open ocean, where it plunders the same fish that commercial fishermen pursue, putting the bird at odds with the fishing industry. • In the nineteenth century, fishing interests hunted Great Cormorant nearly to extinction. Thanks to aggressive conservation efforts, the bird has recovered its numbers and millions now roam the seas. • In China and Japan, a practice known as "cormorant fishing" involves tying a line around the bird's throat just tight enough to prevent the bird from swallowing, and then setting the bird off to hunt from the deck of a small fishing boat. The bird returns with a fish in its bill, but it can't swallow it, so the fishermen pry the bird's bill open and take the fish from it. • Norwegians see the Great Cormorant as a tasty delicacy, shooting as many as ten thousand birds each year to serve at dining room tables. This seems to contradict the belief that a Great Cormorant may carry the soul of a loved one lost at sea. Some Norwegians believe that the soul-carrying birds gather on the island of Utrøst, and only visit the homes of their human families on rare and special occasions.

No. 265

Pharomachrus mocinno

Resplendent Quetzal

Guatemalan Quetzal

● **NEAR THREATENED**

✿ **COLLECTIVE NAME**

Parliament of quetzals

✺ **SYMBOLIC MEANINGS**

Freedom; Wealth.

🌀 **POSSIBLE POWER**

Association with Quetzalcoatl (Snake God).

☾ **FOLKLORE AND FACTS**

Birders never forget their first sighting of a male Resplendent Quetzal, an iridescently bright green bird with a gleaming crimson chest and a 30-inch (76 cm) tail. This startlingly glorious Central American bird is the largest member of the trogon family, and its size, colors, and elusive nature in the continent's cloud forests helped solidify its place in Guatemalan culture thousands of years ago.
• Mesoamerican cultures, including both Aztec and Mayan peoples, associate the quetzal with the snake god that bears its name, Quetzalcoatl. This deity wore quetzal feathers in his regalia, carefully clipped from living birds that were released back into the wild. The Resplendent Quetzal flew overhead to guard the troops when Mayan prince and warrior Tecún Umán fought Pedro de Alvarado, the Spanish conquistador, in the mid-1500s. Mayans also believed that Resplendent Quetzals once sang a melodious song, but when the conquistadors took their land, the bird stopped singing and will not resume until the land is freed once again.
• Guatemala chose the Resplendent Quetzal as the nation's national bird, and even named the country's currency after it. This honor extended protection of the bird, keeping it out of the pet trade—a wise move, as it is said that the Resplendent Quetzal would rather starve itself to death than live in captivity. These birds also make themselves particularly difficult to find, much less catch: Their iridescent feathers turn the same color as the cloud forest's wet leaves after the daily rain, blending with their surroundings so completely that attempts to find them would be futile.

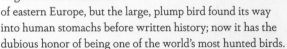

No. 266

Phasianus colchicus

Ring-Necked Pheasant

Common Pheasant | Phezzen

● **LEAST CONCERN**

✿ **COLLECTIVE NAMES**

Bevy of pheasants | Bouquet of pheasants | Creche of pheasants | Head of pheasants | Nide of pheasants | Warren of pheasants

✺ **SYMBOLIC MEANING**

Creativity.

🌀 **POSSIBLE POWER**

Good luck.

☾ **FOLKLORE AND FACTS**

Introduced in the United States in 1773, Ring-Necked Pheasants had long been bred almost exclusively for hunting in Europe, and this purpose has remained the bird's destiny wherever it lives. This pheasant originated in the Balkans

of eastern Europe, but the large, plump bird found its way into human stomachs before written history; now it has the dubious honor of being one of the world's most hunted birds.
• Pheasants have a storied history full of captive breeding and release into the wild, with stories of their naturalization in the United Kingdom dating back to the eleventh century.
• Ancient Greeks regularly dined on pheasant, though a story that says the Greeks brought the birds to the Balkans when they marched into that region has been proven false—instead, the Greeks may have brought pheasants home from that campaign. • South Dakota made the Ring-Necked Pheasant its official state bird, the only state in the country to choose an introduced bird rather than a native one. • Known as the Pheasant Capital in the Midwest, the state enjoys a population of roughly 12 million pheasants, largely because the birds consume winter wheat, a major cash crop for the state's farmers. South Dakota's wetlands feature many prairie potholes, areas that produce insects that pheasants feed to their young, making this a great place to raise lots of these game birds.

P

No. 267

Phasianus versicolor

Green Pheasant

Japanese Green Pheasant

● **LEAST CONCERN**

☘ **COLLECTIVE NAMES**

Bevy of pheasants | Bouquet of pheasants | Creche of pheasants | Head of pheasants |
Nide of pheasants | Warren of pheasants

✴ **SYMBOLIC MEANING**

Harmony.

🌀 **POSSIBLE POWER**

Domestic bliss.

☾ **FOLKLORE AND FACTS**

Japan honors its endemic pheasant as the country's national
bird, making this possible subspecies of the Ring-Necked
Pheasant a protected species throughout the archipelago.
The Green Pheasant is green from the base of its neck to its
flanks, sporting a blue head with a red mask, light brown
wings and tail, and long tail feathers with the barring that
typifies most pheasant species. The female's plumage is much
less showy, allowing her to blend into her surroundings with
cryptic, mottled brown and white feathers. Females are often
seen strolling through parks and neighborhoods with their
chicks scurrying behind them, a vision of domestic bliss that
has given the birds their symbolic meaning: Harmony and
domesticity. • Common wisdom in Japan says that Green
Pheasants are so frightened by earthquakes that they cry
through them, screaming every time a tremor takes place.
An actual research paper published in the *Japanese Journal
of Ornithology* in 1971 examined this phenomenon and
determined that the bird only cries out during an earthquake
if it happens to be breeding season, when he may be more
prone to crow to females in proximity already, and if rattling
windows and other loud noises startle the bird. This piece
of credible research has not deterred the popular notion,
however, so
people in Japan
still listen for
the birds when
a quake shakes
their homes.

No. 268

Philesturnes

Saddleback

North Island Saddleback | South Island Saddleback | Tīeke (Māori) | Wattlebird

● **LEAST CONCERN**

☘ **COLLECTIVE NAMES**

Colony of saddlebacks | Murmuration of saddlebacks | Rookery of saddlebacks

✴ **SYMBOLIC MEANINGS**

Bad luck; Good luck.

🌀 **POSSIBLE POWERS**

Defense against larger birds; Defiance.

☾ **FOLKLORE AND FACTS**

New Zealand's two Saddlebacks get their common name
from the brown saddle-like patch on their otherwise
black backs. These feisty little birds are a bit larger than
a blackbird, and they have a wattle of red skin hanging
on each side of their black bill—a strange feature for a
songbird. • Saddlebacks are colony birds that defend their
nests fiercely against predators, something they need to do
fairly regularly. They nest quite close to the ground, either
in a tree cavity or in a plant that grows on another plant
(an epiphyte). The fledglings climb out of the nest and
hop around on the ground as they gain enough strength
to fly, making them particularly vulnerable to predators.
• A Māori legend tells us how Saddlebacks acquired their
rufous patch. Maui, a trickster and lesser deity in Māori
stories, felt that the sun traveled across the sky too quickly,
leaving almost no time for meals and tending to crops. He
took it upon himself to slow down the sun's progression,
and he and his brothers set out to find the sun god,
Tama-nui-te-rā. They built a noose with ropes and
encircled the sun god's pit, where he slept during the night;
when Tama-nui-te-rā arose in the morning, they caught
him and beat him until he agreed to slow down his daily
trip across the sky. When Maui returned to his home after
this exhausting battle, he asked Tīeke to bring him water
to drink … but the cheeky little bird ignored him, and the
trickster became enraged. Maui grabbed the bird with his
still-scorching hand, and left an imprint on the bird's back
that remains to this day.

P

No. 269

Phoebastria albatrus

Short-Tailed Albatross

Ahodori (Japanese) | Steller's Albatross

● **VULNERABLE**

✿ COLLECTIVE NAMES

Flight of albatross | Rookery of albatross | Weight of albatross

✹ SYMBOLIC MEANINGS

Bad luck (if you kill one); Burden.

❀ POSSIBLE POWER

Causing shipwrecks and death.

✾ FOLKLORE AND FACTS

For centuries, having "an albatross around your neck" has been synonymous with carrying a weighty burden, one we can't wait to dispose of as soon as the crisis is over. This expression comes from Samuel Taylor Coleridge's poem *The Rime of the Ancient Mariner*, in which we learn that killing an

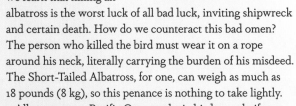

albatross is the worst luck of all bad luck, inviting shipwreck and certain death. How do we counteract this bad omen? The person who killed the bird must wear it on a rope around his neck, literally carrying the burden of his misdeed. The Short-Tailed Albatross, for one, can weigh as much as 18 pounds (8 kg), so this penance is nothing to take lightly. • Albatrosses are Pacific Ocean pelagic birds, rarely if ever coming ashore on the mainland. The Short-Tailed Albatross nests on islands off the coast of Japan, and spends its non-breeding time far to the north in Alaska's Bering Sea, as well as over the waters near eastern Russia. Here they ran into trouble in the nineteenth century as targets of the millinery trade, their numbers dropping so dramatically that estimates suggest that more than 10 million birds fell prey to feather hunters. • Efforts in Japan have worked to repopulate their preferred islands, moving chicks hatched on one island to another nested historically by the birds. So far, this effort is making impressive progress. Today there are 3,540 Short-Tails on Torishima National Wildlife Protection Area, up from 25 individuals in 1954.

No. 270

Phoebastria immutabilis

Laysan Albatross

Mōlī (Hawai'i)

● **NEAR THREATENED**

✿ COLLECTIVE NAMES

Flight of albatross | Rookery of albatross | Weight of albatross

✹ SYMBOLIC MEANINGS

Bad luck (if you kill one); Good luck; Protection.

❀ POSSIBLE POWERS

Immortality of the soul; Predictor of storms at sea.

✾ FOLKLORE AND FACTS

All but a tiny fraction of the world's Laysan Albatrosses nest at the northwestern end of the Hawaiian Islands, with 70 percent of them on Midway Atoll, a US Navy base during World War II. When the Navy built the base, they painted all of its buildings with lead paint—and more than sixty years later, paint flakes strewed large areas of the island, and albatross chicks ate the paint chips and developed a condition called droop wing, preventing them from flying and eventually killing them. A massive lawsuit forced the U.S. Fish and Wildlife Service to begin a $22-million cleanup project on the island, and today the paint chips are gone, and Laysan Albatross numbers are rebounding. • As of this writing, the oldest known wild bird in the world is a Laysan Albatross named Wisdom, a female estimated to be more than 70 years old—and still laying eggs and raising chicks. Wisdom was first banded in 1956, just before she reared her first chick. As albatrosses cannot breed for the first five years of their lives, banders guessed that she was five at that time. • Albatross lore on the high seas can govern the lives of sailors, with considerable speculation of whether an albatross following a ship is a good omen with a promise of the bird's celestial protection, or a bad omen of an oncoming storm, with the bird hiding behind the ship to avoid the worst of it. Whichever it turns out to be, the albatross most likely carries the soul of a sailor lost at sea, so its protection or its warning are all meant with the best of intentions.

No. 271

Phoeniconaias minor

Lesser Flamingo

● **NEAR THREATENED**

🐾 **COLLECTIVE NAMES**

Colony of flamingoes | Flamboyance of flamingoes | Flurry of flamingoes | Regiment of flamingoes | Stand of flamingoes

✳ **SYMBOLIC MEANINGS**

Community; Elegance; Grace; Resilience.

🌀 **POSSIBLE POWER**

Withstanding toxic environments.

🌙 **FOLKLORE AND FACTS**

A dark bill, red legs, and glowing red eyes set the Lesser Flamingo apart from its larger family members. This pink bird of southern Africa, Kenya, Madagascar, and India is the world's smallest flamingo as well as the most populous, with more than 1 million birds in some flocks. • Lesser Flamingoes seek out caustic lagoons and alkaline lakes to feast on the blue-green algae they produce, which react with light to give the birds their pink and red attributes. Most Lesser Flamingoes breed on Lake Natron in Tanzania, where they find this algae . . . but as of this writing, threats to this and other preferred breeding grounds include a proposal to build a soda ash plant, heavy metal poisoning from commercial operations, and expanding development in South Africa. One of these proposals involves bringing in an exotic brine shrimp to consume the algae, making the water usable for industrial interests, but effectively annihilating the flamingoes' food supply. • In addition to their value as a food source, the harsh environments Lesser Flamingoes choose also limit the number of predators that seek out the birds. Only a handful of animal species can tolerate the alkaline content and salt, and even these cannot drink this caustic water. These clever evolutionary choices allow Lesser Flamingoes to maintain large flocks in what seem like very unlikely places.

No. 272

Phoenicoparrus andinus

Andean Flamingo

● **VULNERABLE**

🐾 **COLLECTIVE NAMES**

Colony of flamingoes | Flamboyance of flamingoes | Flurry of flamingoes | Regiment of flamingoes | Stand of flamingoes

✳ **SYMBOLIC MEANINGS**

Balance; Fun; Truth.

🌀 **POSSIBLE POWER**

Long-distance flight.

🌙 **FOLKLORE AND FACTS**

Second only to the Greater Flamingo in size, the Andean Flamingo shares the same pink color as the world's other five flamingoes, but its deeper lower jaw and the triangle of black feathers at the ends of its wings help differentiate it from the rest. • As its name implies, the Andean Flamingo lives in the Andes mountains in South America, centered on the area where Peru, Bolivia, Argentina, and Chile meet in the central-western continent. Foraging in shallow water in wetlands among the mountains, these birds feed on fish, invertebrates, and lots of small particles called diatoms—the oxygen-producing algae deep in the waterlogged soil. • Three flamingo species congregate in this region—Chilean and James' Flamingoes are the other two. Visitors often assume that these birds cannot fly because they rarely see them do so, but they are perfectly capable of flying; they just don't do much of it in daylight. Andean Flamingoes have the ability to fly up to 700 miles (1,126 km) in a single night, so the large flock of birds in the mirrorlike Laguna Colorada in Chile at sunset may simply disappear *en masse* overnight.

No. 273
Phoenicopterus chilensis

Chilean Flamingo

● **NEAR THREATENED**

✿ **COLLECTIVE NAMES**
Colony of flamingoes | Flamboyance of flamingoes | Flurry of flamingoes |
Regiment of flamingoes | Stand of flamingoes

✹ **SYMBOLIC MEANINGS**
Balance; Fun; Truth.

❀ **POSSIBLE POWER**
Long-distance flight.

☾ **FOLKLORE AND FACTS**
A little brighter pink overall than the neighboring Andean
Flamingo, with salmon-colored feathers at the tips of the
wings, the Chilean Flamingo's territory reaches down
the length of Chile and Argentina, and then up along the
Peruvian coast. Its gray legs also differentiate it from
other flamingoes, as do its bright pink feet and knees.
• These flamingoes seek out salt lagoons and soda lakes,
looking for algae and plankton that prefer these harsher
environments. They use these food sources and others in
their diet to produce a fluid with which to feed their chicks,
creating this nursing liquid in the crop under their bill.
Remarkably, this fluid is bright red, though feeding it to
chicks does not make the birds turn from their gray birth
feathers to pink any faster. It takes young birds at least two
years to begin to molt into their pink plumage. • Flamingo
fans may recall Pink Floyd, a Chilean Flamingo that escaped
from the Tracy Aviary in Salt Lake City, Utah, in 1988
and made its own way in the western United States for an
astonishing seventeen years. Pink Floyd spent its winters
eating brine shrimp in Utah's Great Salt Lake, and relocated
to Montana or Idaho in spring and summer. In spring
2005, he flew north to Idaho, put in an appearance in that
state, and then vanished. The bird's last whereabouts were
never determined.

No. 274
Phoenicopterus roseus

Greater Flamingo

● **NEAR THREATENED**

✿ **COLLECTIVE NAMES**
Colony of flamingoes | Flamboyance of flamingoes |
Flurry of flamingoes | Regiment of flamingoes |
Stand of flamingoes

✹ **SYMBOLIC MEANINGS**
Balance; Fun; Luxury; Truth.

❀ **POSSIBLE POWER**
Use in sacrifices to predict the future.

☾ **FOLKLORE AND FACTS**
Here's the big, pale pink bird with the pink and black bill
that inspired a whole industry of lawn ornaments around
the world, and an accompanying, good-natured controversy
about whether the plastic birds are the ultimate in kitschy
fun or the worst of the worst in tacky suburban design. The
Greater Flamingo lends its image to all kinds of items, from
loud flowered shirts to the front of a Las Vegas casino. Even
the classic children's book *Alice's Adventures in Wonderland*,
by Lewis Carroll, incorporated this familiar flamingo as the
mallet for a royal game of croquet. • A derivation of the
Greek word for flame, "flamingo" became the bird's name
even in the ethnocentric Roman empire, and its likeness
seems always associated with exotic luxuries. Architects
and designers incorporated it into buildings like the floor
of the basilica of Sabratha in Libya, the synagogue of Gaza
Maiumas in Israel, and other Middle Eastern antiquities.
• Greek, Roman, and Egyptian polytheists sacrificed
flamingoes to their gods and goddesses. Of the many
predictions and portents that preceded the death of the
tyrant emperor Caligula, spilling the blood of a flamingo
on the ruler's toga had particular potency. • Not only have
the birds been important symbolically, but some have even
provided practical uses. A reference to the construction of
a Sardinian wind instrument called the launeddas calls for
the use of hollow flamingo bones. • Later, in the fifteenth
century, flamingoes inevitably made it onto the tables of
aristocrats. Lorenzo de' Medici, ruler of the Florentine
Republic, ordered the import of live flamingoes from Sicily
to serve for dinner, and the bird's tongue was served as a
delicacy right into the eighteenth century.

P

Phoenicopterus ruber

American Flamingo

Caribbean Flamingo

● LEAST CONCERN

✿ **COLLECTIVE NAMES**

Colony of flamingoes | Flamboyance of flamingoes | Flurry of flamingoes | Regiment of flamingoes | Stand of flamingoes

✹ **SYMBOLIC MEANINGS**

Community; Elegance; Grace; Resilience.

✺ **POSSIBLE POWERS**

Romance; Strengthening family relationships.

✧ **FOLKLORE AND FACTS**

Don't miss the irony of how closely the American Flamingo is tied to the identity of the state of Florida. Flamingoes have not lived in the wilds of Florida since 1900, when the state looked the other way while poachers frequented southern Florida habitats and summarily executed every flamingo in the state, toting them up north by the dozen to sell them into the fashion trade. This continued until two women in Boston learned of the wholesale slaughter of flamingoes, egrets, herons, and other birds down south, and held tea parties at which they convinced their friends to stop buying these fashion items. We can thank the work of Harriet Hemenway and Minna B. Hall for the fact that we can see any large wading birds in Florida at all. • No American Flamingoes live wild in Florida now; today they all live in the West Indies, northern South America, and the Yucatan Peninsula. The state now draws its connection to flamingoes from the decision to name a Miami Beach hotel after them in the 1920s, simply to make the area sound more attractive and tropical to snowbound northerners. Parks and attractions like Disney World, Busch Gardens, Cypress Gardens, Hialeah Park, and others kept (and some still keep) captive flamingoes to maintain that connection between tropical paradise and the state's offerings. Today visitors to Florida can purchase just about any souvenir item with a flamingo painted on it, the last reminder of a bird that has not made the effort to return, even though its status is now protected.

Pica hudsonia

Black-Billed Magpie

American Magpie

● LEAST CONCERN

✿ **COLLECTIVE NAMES**

Charm of magpies | Congregation of magpies | Gulp of magpies | Murder of magpies | Tiding of magpies | Tribe of magpies

✹ **SYMBOLIC MEANINGS**

Communication; Time for a new path.

✺ **POSSIBLE POWERS**

Determining destiny (depending on how many you see).

✧ **FOLKLORE AND FACTS**

Black and white with iridescent blue patches, the Black-Billed Magpie already presents itself as a striking, dynamic bird, even before it flashes its extra-long tail. The magpie is one of only four birds in North America with a tail longer than its body (the others are the Scissor-Tailed and Fork-Tailed Flycatchers and the Yellow-Billed Magpie, a bird of limited range in California). • Magpies provide good or bad luck according to a traditional rhyme that has its origins in something called ornithomancy, or superstitions connected with birds. How many magpies do you see? Find the number and know your destiny:

One for sorrow,
Two for joy,
Three for a girl,
Four for a boy.
Five for silver,
Six for gold,
Seven for a secret never to be told.
Eight for a wish,
Nine for a kiss,
Ten a surprise that you won't want to miss.
Eleven for health,
Twelve for wealth,
Thirteen beware, it's the devil himself.
Fourteen for love,
Fifteen for a dove,
Sixteen for the chime of a bell.
Seventeen for the angels' protection,
Eighteen to be safe from hell,
Nineteen to be safe from a crime,
Twenty and an end to this rhyme.

English tradition suggests that if you encounter a magpie, it's prudent to address it directly and politely, asking after its family and general health. This heads off bad luck before it can come calling on you.

No. 277

Pica serica

Oriental Magpie

Asian Magpie | Chinese Magpie

✥ COLLECTIVE NAMES

Charm of magpies | Congregation of magpies | Gulp of magpies | Murder of magpies | Tiding of magpies | Tribe of magpies

✳ SYMBOLIC MEANINGS

Development; Prosperity.

✺ POSSIBLE POWERS

Bringing new teeth to children; Good fortune; Wealth.

✦ FOLKLORE AND FACTS

The Oriental Magpie just became a separate species from the Eurasian Magpie in 2018, according to DNA research completed by the International Ornithologists' Union (IOU). The world's largest magpie, it serves as the national bird of both South and North Korea, while its range also extends south through eastern China and into Japan and Myanmar. • Koreans love their magpies and believe that the bird brings them good luck and prosperity, as well as opportunities for people to broaden their personal development. • Korean children believe that when they lose a tooth, they should throw it up onto the roof of their own home while singing a song that will alert the local magpies that it's there. The magpies bring the children a new tooth. • According to Korean legend, a young man walking to Seoul hears a magpie calling, and finds two magpies about to be eaten by a snake. He shoots the snake with his bow and arrow, saving the birds, and then continues on his way. That evening he stops at a cabin in the woods and asks the women there for a place to sleep. As he is sleeping, he suddenly awakens to find a snake wrapped around his body. The snake says, "I am the mate of the snake you killed today. If you want to live, you must ring a bell three times, right now." The man has no bell, but out of nowhere, he and the snake hear a bell ring three times outside. The snake releases him and departs. The man gets up and finds the two magpies he had rescued earlier, lying on the ground beneath a bell tower. The birds gave their lives to save him. He honors them by dedicating his life to making this a place of prayer and thanksgiving, then he founds the temple of Sangwonsa.

No. 278

Picus viridis

Eurasian Green Woodpecker

Jack Eikle | Laughing Betsey | Yaffingale Yaffle

● LEAST CONCERN

✥ COLLECTIVE NAMES

Descent of woodpeckers | Gatling of woodpeckers | Whirlagust of woodpeckers

✳ SYMBOLIC MEANING

Wisdom.

✺ POSSIBLE POWER

Sage advice.

✦ FOLKLORE AND FACTS

You are much more likely to see the Eurasian Green Woodpecker on the ground searching for ants among the fallen leaves than clinging to a tree trunk, as it doesn't need to dig through bark to find its favorite meal. Indeed, chances are that you will hear this bird long before you see it, as its high-pitched, squeaky, repeated "yaffle" call pierces its forested habitat as the bird flies through the treetops. • Bright olive-green with a yellow rump, red cap, and a black mask over its otherwise gray face, the Eurasian Green Woodpecker lives up to its name. Most of its range is in Europe, but this has expanded into western Asia, where it finds plenty of older trees for nesting and raising young. • Even people who have never seen or sought a woodpecker may remember *Bagpuss*, the stop-motion animated children's television series that ran in Great Britain for thirteen episodes in 1974. The story of a stuffed cloth cat included a wooden bookend with a carved, talking woodpecker named Professor Yaffle, a character that its creators said was based on a Eurasian Green Woodpecker. The short-run series still enchants adults who were children when it ran half a century ago, even topping a 1999 BBC poll of all-time favorite children's shows.

P

No. 279

Pipilo erythrophthalmus

Eastern Towhee

Ground Robin | Red-Eyed Towhee | Rufous-Sided Towhee

● **LEAST CONCERN**

🐾 **COLLECTIVE NAMES**

Tangle of towhees | Teapot of towhees

✹ **SYMBOLIC MEANINGS**

Good luck coming soon; Slowing down to enjoy life.

🌀 **POSSIBLE POWER**

Good fortune.

🐦 **FOLKLORE AND FACTS**

"Drink-your-tea-tea-tea-tea-tea!" says the Eastern Towhee, a song that leads directly to its collective noun, a "teapot" of towhees. Chances are that you will hear a towhee singing away in a hedgerow long before laying eyes on one, as these birds are willing to sit in one place for an extended period, especially when singing on territory (during breeding season). • The towhee's black head, rusty orange flanks, and bright white chest make it a very striking spring bird, with the female just slightly less boldly marked, her head and wings a warm chocolate brown instead of black. It seems as if such a brightly colored bird should be easy to see, but towhees love to skulk on the ground just under thick shrubs or along the edges of gardens, so it's important to keep an eye out for movement in the understory. • The Eastern Towhee actually speaks its message to us: Its "Drink your tea!" song reminds us to slow down, savor the moment, and see what may be ahead. Its sung message and careful scavenging behavior are always positive signs, suggesting that something good may be just around the corner or under the next leaf.

No. 280

Pipilo maculatus

Spotted Towhee

Oregon Towhee | Rufous-Sided Towhee | Socorro Towhee

● **LEAST CONCERN**

🐾 **COLLECTIVE NAMES**

Tangle of towhees | Teapot of towhees

✹ **SYMBOLIC MEANINGS**

Confidence; Persistence; Uncovering hidden things.

🌀 **POSSIBLE POWER**

Revealing secrets.

🐦 **FOLKLORE AND FACTS**

If you have a secret to keep, the Spotted Towhee may not be the bird you want to encounter while doing it. Plying its industry on the floor of a forest or garden, this bird—a recent split from the Rufous-Sided Towhee, creating the two distinct species Eastern and Spotted Towhee—spends its time flipping leaves over by hopping forward and immediately back, making it easier to see what lies beneath the woodland detritus. In this way, the striking black, white, and orange bird, decked out with a shower of white spots across its back, makes the most of whatever it finds. This behavior sends a message to those who watch: Guard your secrets well, because something as basic as a couple of missteps may expose them to the world . . . and this may be your undoing. • The Spotted Towhee can spend whole days hopping about on the ground, engaged in its ritual of overturning leaves, pecking at what it finds, and moving on. This persistence rewards the bird with a good meal, conceivably providing hundreds or even thousands of yummy bugs over the course of a morning. The bird tells us to be patient and carry on with our endeavors, so that they may soon bring us the results we seek.

Pitangus sulphuratus

Great Kiskadee

Bem-te-vi (Brazil) | Benteveo (Argentina) | Cristofué (Venezuela) | Derby |
Pitogue (Paraguay) Flycatcher

● **LEAST CONCERN**

✿ **COLLECTIVE NAME**
Shower of kiskadees

✸ **SYMBOLIC MEANINGS**
Courage; Self-preservation; Truth.

✿ **POSSIBLE POWER**
Valiance against enemies.

☾ **FOLKLORE AND FACTS**
A large flycatcher of Central and South America with a
population in Texas's Lower Rio Grande Valley, the Great
Kiskadee gets its Latin name from its bright yellow breast
and belly. This, combined with its black-and-white striped
face, makes it an easy bird to identify at feeders, in trees, or in
open grasslands. Its name, according to folklore, came from
French explorers who heard the bird and asked one another,
"*Qu'est-ce qu'il dit*?" or in English, "What is he saying?"
• This omnivorous bird prefers to catch insects on the wing
like any other flycatcher, but it also enjoys food at backyard
feeders, and even the occasional frog or lizard. • A South
American Arawak story tells us that during a great war of
the birds at the summit of Mount Ayanganna, the Great
Kiskadee wanted no part of the battle, because he was a
coward. He stayed home and tied a bandage around his head,
saying that he was ill. When the other birds returned home,
the hawks quickly removed the bandage from his head and
proved that he was not ill at all. His punishment for lying
was to continue to wear the white line around the
top of its head forever, a mark that continues to this day.
Because of this, the Great Kiskadee attacks and harasses
raptors that may be foolish enough to approach it in hopes
of catching it for dinner. The kiskadee calls harshly to
summon reinforcements to help it mob any hawk that comes
too close.

Pithecophaga jefferyi

Philippine Eagle

Great Philippine Eagle | Monkey-Eating Eagle

● **CRITICALLY ENDANGERED**

✿ **COLLECTIVE NAMES**
Aerie of eagles | Brood of eagles | Congregation of
eagles | Exaltation of eagles

✸ **SYMBOLIC MEANING**
National bird of the
Philippines.

✿ **POSSIBLE POWER**
Resiliency.

☾ **FOLKLORE AND FACTS**
By the time the Philippine
Eagle was declared the national bird of the Philippines
in 1995, its numbers had already declined to fewer than
500 individuals throughout the country. The honor of
representing the nation came with another designation from
the Zoological Society of London, calling it the Philippines'
most "evolutionarily distinct and globally endangered"
species—more a warning than an honor. • Why are these
eagles disappearing? Forests throughout the Philippines have
vanished as logging companies and developers clear-cut
thousands of acres of old-growth trees, the very habitat these
eagles need. Long before it became the national bird, the
Philippine Eagle had attracted global attention, however:
Pioneering aviator Charles Lindbergh found this bird
fascinating, and he traveled to the Philippines several times
in the late 1960s as a representative of the World Wildlife
Fund to try to determine how to save it. Decades of attempts
to raise it in captivity finally came to fruition in 1999, but
each time an eagle grew to adulthood and was released into
the wild, it would encounter some mishap (like a hunter's
bullet) and die within a year—even though killing one of
these eagles gets the hunter a twelve-year prison sentence.
• Meanwhile, the nation tries to raise awareness of the eagle's
plight by placing its image on postage stamps and currency.
In a wildlife loan agreement between the Philippines and
Singapore, two Philippine Eagles traveled to Jurong Bird
Park in Singapore in 2019—each with its own authentic
Philippine passport. The Philippine Eagle Foundation has
had more success in recent years with its captive-breeding
program, and now has thirty-six eagles at its center in
Davao City.

P

No. 283

Platalea ajaja

Roseate Spoonbill

Flame Bird | Rose-Colored Curlew

● **LEAST CONCERN**

🐾 **COLLECTIVE NAME**
Colony of spoonbills

✳ **SYMBOLIC MEANINGS**
Adaptability; Rebirth.

🌀 **POSSIBLE POWERS**
Fertility; Hunting by touch.

🌙 **FOLKLORE AND FACTS**
If you've been following along in this book about the near loss of long-legged wading birds in Florida, then you can guess the story of the Roseate Spoonbill. Gorgeously attired in bright pink feathers—the result of a diet rich in canthaxanthin, a carotenoid pigment that provides their brilliant pink color—these birds became a direct target of the plumage trade of the late 1800s. Hunters came in great numbers, finding the birds' rookeries filled with hundreds of nests (often in communal areas with egrets, ibises, and herons), and blasted every bird they saw. This reduced spoonbill numbers to just fifteen pairs in Florida by 1900. It took quite some time for the fashion trade to notice that Roseate Spoonbill feathers fade quickly, because the bird's diet is what maintains the color. Dead birds can't eat, so the pink feathers turned white. • The feather boycott of the early 1900s finally brought this carnage to a halt, and today, Roseate Spoonbills are a protected species with tens of thousands of birds stretching from southern South Carolina down into South America. • Ornithologist Robert Porter Allen nicknamed these birds Flame Birds while he studied them in Florida's Bottlepoint Key in 1935, because he thought they looked like walking flames when they built their nests in trees. Their bill, shaped like an extra-long salad spoon, allows them to sweep the water back and forth as they gather tiny crustaceans.

No. 284

Platalea leucorodia

Eurasian Spoonbill

Common Spoonbill | Shovelard

● **LEAST CONCERN**

🐾 **COLLECTIVE NAME**
Colony of spoonbills

✳ **SYMBOLIC MEANINGS**
Abundance; Harmony.

🌀 **POSSIBLE POWER**
Hunting by touch.

🌙 **FOLKLORE AND FACTS**
Way back when cave paintings were the dominant way to record history, a scribe in a cave in southern Spain drew more than 200 birds on the wall of Tajo de las Figuras. Two of these birds were spoonbills, most likely the local variety: Eurasian Spoonbill, also known as the Common Spoonbill. Like so many birds on this cave wall, we can bet that this bird's bill drew enough attention to make the painter wonder what it was about. Drawings of spoonbills also show up in Egyptian tombs, which tells us that ancient Egyptians placed considerable value on these peculiar birds. • Why does a spoonbill have a spoon bill? Spoonbills hunt for prey by touch rather than sight or smell, sweeping their hypersensitive bill back and forth in shallow water until it finds tiny crustaceans and small fish. As soon as they come into contact with food, they snap their bill shut so quickly that the animal barely knows it's happening. • In contrast to the roseate variety, Eurasian Spoonbills are quite white, with black wing tips that are only visible in flight. Find these birds on a European coast or on bodies of water throughout central Asia, even all the way to Japan.

Plectrophenax nivalis

Snow Bunting

Snowflake

● **LEAST CONCERN**

✲ **COLLECTIVE NAMES**

Decoration of buntings | Mural of buntings | Sacrifice of buntings

☀ **SYMBOLIC MEANING**

Guardian against harsh winters.

🌀 **POSSIBLE POWER**

Good luck.

🌜 **FOLKLORE AND FACTS**

Snow Buntings nest farther north than any other songbird, a feat made possible by their ability to withstand temperatures as low as -50°F (-45°C). They are uniquely adapted to live in the coldest conditions in the world, burrowing into the snow for warmth—as counterintuitive a decision as we can imagine—and migrating south just far enough to find open fields in winter, well above the frost line. In breeding season, their plumage turns bright white with a black back, allowing them to blend completely into the year-round snow above the Arctic Circle; in winter, the male takes on some browner hues to mask it in plowed fields, where large flocks of buntings (often with Horned Larks and various longspurs, depending on the region) congregate to feast on seeds and grains left behind after the harvest.

• The Inuit believe that Snow Buntings bring good luck to people who build nest boxes for them, so many Arctic-dwelling folks place wooden nest boxes among the rocks, repairing and maintaining them year after year to keep the little birds as neighbors. Wood is a very recent commodity for the Inuit, so before they had that available, they created nesting cavities by piling up rocks and gravel and leaving an opening for the birds to enter and exit.

Pluvialis apricaria

European Golden Plover

Eurasian Golden Plover | Golden Plover

● **LEAST CONCERN**

✲ **COLLECTIVE NAMES**

Band of plovers | Congregation of plovers | Stand of plovers | Wing of plovers

☀ **SYMBOLIC MEANING**

Arrival of spring.

🌀 **POSSIBLE POWER**

Speed.

🌜 **FOLKLORE AND FACTS**

Every culture has a migrating bird whose arrival signals the beginning of spring, but in Iceland, there's an official ambassador—and it even gets covered by the media. The European Golden Plover makes its entrance sometime in the second half of March, a day that gets catalogued and re-examined annually, scrutinized as closely as when Americans watch to see if a groundhog in Pennsylvania sees its shadow. • A European Golden Plover in Ireland turned out to be the catalyst for launching one of the world's most popular books. In 1951, Sir Hugh Beaver, managing director of Guinness Breweries, shot at a European Golden Plover on a hunting trip and missed it, and moments later found himself in a debate over which game bird was faster—this plover or the Red Grouse. Finding no ready resource to answer this definitively, he began to wonder how many other such world records were established but inaccessible to average people. This hatched into an idea for a book, and before long, the *Guinness World Records* book grew into an empire, with judges traveling all over the world to decide if people, animals, structures, stunts, and more actually have beaten a current record. (To answer the question: The Red Grouse is faster, often flying at more than 70 miles/113 km per hour.)

No. 287
Pluvianus aegyptius

Egyptian Plover

Crocodile Bird

● **LEAST CONCERN**

✽ **COLLECTIVE NAMES**

Band of plovers | Congregation of plovers | Stand of plovers | Wing of plovers

✴ **SYMBOLIC MEANING**

Crocodile hygienist.

❂ **POSSIBLE POWER**

Symbiotic relationship with crocodiles.

✾ **FOLKLORE AND FACTS**

Unmistakable on mud flats in sub-Saharan Africa, the Egyptian Plover's black-and-white-striped head, black necklace against its buffy chest, and gray back and wings with bright white flight feathers make it one of the most striking shorebirds in the region. Usually seen in pairs but sometimes in small congregations, this bird does not actually live in Egypt, though the area it inhabits today was once part of the Egyptian empire. • In an old story told by Herodotus, a Greek historian in the fifth century BCE, a bird species he called Trochilus flies into the open mouth of a resting Nile crocodile and picks leftover meat from the beast's most recent meal from between its teeth. • Observations today indicate that Trochilus must have been the Egyptian Plover, a bird that does indeed approach crocodiles as they cool themselves by basking on the shore with their mouths wide open. Small flocks of plovers enter the animal's mouth and remove meat and parasites from between their teeth, and the crocodiles allow them to do so. This behavior has led to the rumor that these plovers must be poisonous to crocodiles, so they leave the birds alone; there is no truth to this, however. Bird and reptile simply enjoy an improbable but mutually beneficial relationship.

No. 288
Podargidae

Frogmouth

Marbled Frogmouth | Papuan Frogmouth | Tawny Frogmouth

● **LEAST CONCERN**

✽ **COLLECTIVE NAME**

Parliament of frogmouths

✴ **SYMBOLIC MEANING**

Stealth.

❂ **POSSIBLE POWER**

Spiritual protection during dark times.

✾ **FOLKLORE AND FACTS**

Nocturnal birds like nightjars and swifts often have large, wide mouths, allowing these birds to scoop insects out of the air all night when the bugs are most active. This is what gives the three birds in the Frogmouth family their peculiar name: Their wide, flat bill opens broadly as they fly, so they can catch plenty of insects as they dart through the air. • As their feet are small and fairly weak, Tawny, Marbled, and Papuan frogmouths also pick up small animals like mice and frogs from the ground with their bills, landing to bash their prey to death before swallowing it whole. Their front-facing eyes allow them to hunt from overhead and spot animals moving on the ground, much as owls do—but while they resemble owls, they are not related to them. • It's not easy to see a Frogmouth, but those who have managed to spot them at rest and photographed them have received a pleasant surprise of late: A research group at a hospital in Germany discovered that photos of frogmouths on the largest bird photography accounts on Instagram received the most likes relative to their views. This makes the three Frogmouth species the "most Instagrammable," according to the study. The researchers called this "poetic justice, as this nocturnal bird with very distinct facial features was once designated 'the world's most unfortunate-looking bird'" by a writer for *Nature Australia*. • Aboriginal cultures believe that when they hear a Tawny Frogmouth after dark, it's a signal that someone will die soon. The bird's ability to blend in seamlessly with a background of tree bark led some cultures to believe that they could actually turn themselves into wood and communicate with the trees and other natural spirits.

No. 289

Podiceps cristatus australis

Pūteketeke

Australasian Crested Grebe | Great Crested Grebe

● **LEAST CONCERN**

✤ **COLLECTIVE NAME**

Water dance of grebes

✳ **SYMBOLIC MEANINGS**

Courage; Peace.

✺ **POSSIBLE POWER**

Deep water swimming.

☾ **FOLKLORE AND FACTS**

Fewer than 1,000
Australasian Crested Grebes
remain of the once-healthy
New Zealand population, where the bird is known
by its Māori name, Pūteketeke. This bird is common in
parts of Europe and much of Asia, however, so its IUCN
ranking of Least Concern is indeed appropriate—though in
New Zealand it is classified as Nationally Vulnerable.
• Pūteketeke performs an elaborate courtship display that
includes an upright posture, a dance on the water's surface,
and sharing a clump of grass between the mated pair. The
male birds add to the display by spreading their chestnut
neck ruff to surround their head like a crown. • The grebe's
dwindling numbers in the southern hemisphere earned it
a place in the competition for New Zealand's Bird of the
Century, where it became one of seventy birds on the ballot.
This brought the grebe to the attention of British-American
comedian John Oliver, host of the HBO program *Last
Week Tonight*, who declared himself the official campaign
manager for Pūteketeke and launched an advertising and
media relations blitz in support of the bird. Oliver went so
far as to have a full-body costume made, which he wore on
NBC's *The Tonight Show Starring Jimmy Fallon*, and to place
billboards in cities all over the world, dubbing the bird "Lord
of the Wings." With an unprecedented 290,374 votes in an
election that normally attracts about 56,000 total votes, the
Pūteketeke won in a landslide, with the North Island Brown
Kiwi coming in second with just 12,904 votes.

Podicipedidae

Grebe

20 species in the genus *Podicipedidae*

●● **LEAST CONCERN TO VULNERABLE**

✤ **COLLECTIVE NAME**

Water dance of grebes

✳ **SYMBOLIC MEANINGS**

Courage; Peace.

✺ **POSSIBLE POWER**

Cleverness.

☾ **FOLKLORE AND FACTS**

Grebes earn their reputation as some of the best divers in
the bird world. Their feet are double-webbed to make them
strong enough to propel the bird down through lakes, and
fast enough to catch the fish they pursue. This dominance
of the lake environment gives them their nickname, "Hell-
diver," but the adaptations for diving make them very clumsy
on land. Grebes rarely come ashore and struggle if they
do, walking only a few steps before they lose balance and
momentum. • In Chippewa and Ojibwa legend, Hell-Diver
the grebe outsmarts the Spirit of Winter when the grebe
decides not to migrate, but to stay in northern Wisconsin to
take care of a whooping crane and a mallard who are injured
and can't fly south. The Spirit of Winter dislikes Hell-Diver
and tries to freeze him under the lake when he dives for food,
but Hell-Diver makes his way through the reeds at the edge
of the lake and pulls himself out. The Spirit of Winter comes
to Hell-Diver's wigwam to make it too cold to live, but
Hell-Diver builds up his fire and makes it too hot for Winter
to come in. Finally, they try a truce, and Hell-Diver invites
Winter in for a wild rice dinner. As they eat, Hell-Diver
builds up his fire and the Spirit of Winter begins to melt—
and Hell-Diver's fire becomes so hot that he actually brings
on an early spring. Winter barely makes his way home to
the north as
spring arrives.

Nos. 291 and 292
Poecile atricapillus
Poecile carolinensis

Black-Capped Chickadee; Carolina Chickadee

● **LEAST CONCERN**

COLLECTIVE NAMES
Banditry of chickadees | Cluck of chickadees |
Dissimulation of chickadees |
Troubling of chickadees

SYMBOLIC MEANINGS
Charisma; Cheekiness.

POSSIBLE POWER
Defense against predators.

FOLKLORE AND FACTS
Two North American
chickadees are so closely
related that only a slight
variation in their songs makes them perceptibly different.
The Black-Capped Chickadee dominates the northern half
of the United States and most of Canada, while the Carolina
Chickadee inhabits the southeastern United States as far
west as east Texas and Oklahoma. • Birders often say that
chickadees bring their friends with them—allies including
titmice, warblers, nuthatches, and other small birds that
prefer to travel in numbers. Chickadees come together in
small flocks from mid-fall to early spring, inviting their
own kind and others of their relative size to forage with
them through the colder seasons. • These cheeky little birds
are often the first to sound the call to other birds to mob a
screech-owl, hawk, falcon, or crow that may be looking for
eggs or chicks to plunder. They can create such an annoying
racket that they actually drive off the much larger predator.
• Two Indigenous tribes, the Mi'kmaq of Nova Scotia and
the Iroquois on the St. Lawrence Seaway, see a chickadee
as one of the three stars in the handle of the Big Dipper
(Ursa Major, or the Big Bear). The chickadee is the second
star, the one carrying the pot to cook the Big Bear once the
hunters, Robin and Moose Bird, manage to bag it. • The
Black-Capped Chickadee has gained status throughout its
range, serving as the state bird of Maine and Massachusetts,
the provincial bird of New Brunswick, and the official bird
of Calgary, Alberta. In 2015, Vancouver, British Columbia,
chose it as the year's official bird.

No. 293
Polyplectron bicalcaratum

Grey Peacock-Pheasant
Burmese Peacock-Pheasant | Chinquis

● **LEAST CONCERN**

COLLECTIVE NAMES
Bevy of pheasants | Bouquet of pheasants | Creche of pheasants | Head of pheasants |
Nide of pheasants | Warren of pheasants

SYMBOLIC MEANINGS
Pride; Resistance.

POSSIBLE POWER
Concealment.

FOLKLORE AND FACTS
It takes some courage to be the national bird of Myanmar, a
Southeast Asian country that has been a center of civil war,
regime change, and military rule for decades. This
large ground bird's region also includes Bangladesh and
Northeast India, but its status is highest in the country
formerly known as Burma. • The Grey Peacock-Pheasant
gets its name from the bright blue spots at the end of
each feather on its back and wings, resembling the larger
"eyespots" of the Indian Peafowl. Males have a spiky crest
that sets them apart from females, although the female's
more muted plumage helps differentiate them as well. Both
birds can virtually vanish into the forest floor, helping them
surprise unsuspecting invertebrates, especially termites.
• The peacock's connection to the people of Myanmar began
with the Konbaung dynasty in the 1800s. These rulers wore
a Green Peafowl image on their robes and even named the
seat of power the Peacock Throne, reigning until the British
Empire arrived and took over the country. The Burmese
then embraced their peacock as their symbol of defiance.
Peacocks could be seen anywhere that resistance took
place—at rallies and protests, and even in people's offices. In
more recent times, the democracy movement chose the more
common Grey Peacock-Pheasant as its national bird.

No. 294
Priotelus temnurus

Cuban Trogon

Tocororo

● **LEAST CONCERN**

✤ **COLLECTIVE NAME**
Stillness of trogons

✳ **SYMBOLIC MEANINGS**
Cuban national pride; Freedom.

🌀 **POSSIBLE POWER**
Yet to be discovered.

🜨 **FOLKLORE AND FACTS**
If choosing a national bird because its red, white, and blue colors match your national flag seems a little on-the-nose, you probably have never seen a Cuban Trogon. This gorgeous bird with its bright blue head, back, and tail, white breast and belly, and bright red underside could not make a more perfect emblem for the island of Cuba. Even better, the bird is endemic to Cuba, meaning that it lives only on this island and nowhere else in the world. • Even if all of these factors were not enough to make this bird a national treasure, the Cuban Trogon must be wild to live. Every attempt to keep and raise this bird in captivity has failed, making it the ultimate representation of the Cuban people's national pride and passion for freedom. • The Cuban Trogon is common and widespread on the island, so seeing one is very likely if you visit: It prefers woodlands and thickets, living and nesting in areas of dense vegetation. Listen for its call, a low *toco-toco-tocoro,* continuing steadily for some time. This may help you locate its perch, as the bird loves to sit still for long periods, giving little hint of its position.

No. 295
Probosciger aterrimus

Palm Cockatoo

Goliath Aratoo (archaic) | Goliath Cockatoo | Great Black Cockatoo

● **LEAST CONCERN**

✤ **COLLECTIVE NAMES**
Chattering of cockatoos | Crackle of cockatoos

✳ **SYMBOLIC MEANINGS**
Endurance; Spirit; Strength.

🌀 **POSSIBLE POWERS**
Communication; Use of tools.

🜨 **FOLKLORE AND FACTS**
If its striking appearance is not enough to make the Palm Cockatoo an instant hit, here's a fun fact about this bird of the Queensland, Australia, rainforests: It corresponds with other birds of its species by drumming on a dead tree branch with a stick—a use of tools that sets it apart from most of the avian world. Exactly why it does this is a mystery, though educated guesses suggest that it drums to mark its territory, telling other palm cockatoos to find their own area to breed. The loud drumming may also impress potential mates.

• The Palm Cockatoo's shaggy crest, huge bill, and bright red facial patches make it distinctive in the field; these attributes have also made the bird popular in the pet trade. The birds are hunted in some areas, especially in New Guinea, even though laws prohibit their export without a permit. Wild birds do not adapt well to captivity.

No. 296
Procnias nudicollis

Bare-Throated Bellbird

Mbororó | Smoking Bird

● **NEAR THREATENED**

✤ **COLLECTIVE NAMES**
Chiming of bellbirds | Colony of bellbirds | Pealing of bellbirds

✳ **SYMBOLIC MEANINGS**
Paraguayan pride; Plight of the South American rainforest.

🌀 **POSSIBLE POWER**
"Call of the Forest."

🜨 **FOLKLORE AND FACTS**
The bare, vividly blue-green skin on this South American bird gives it the first part of its name, and its call, eerily like a single clang of a high-pitched bell, supplies the rest. Many consider its voice to be the call of the forest, a stirring reminder that an unspoiled landscape has value far beyond the development proposed to replace it. • Paraguay chose this pure white male bird and its greenish female as its national bird, a symbol of the country's pristine wilderness. The Bare-Throated Bellbird also plays an important role in eating mistletoe berries and dispersing the seeds throughout the forests, ensuring a continuous food supply for it and many other fruit-eating birds. • In October 2022, a video of a Bare-Throated Bellbird singing went viral on social

media—not because of its remarkable song, but because the bird appeared to exhale a puff of smoke at the end of a phrase. The moniker "smoking bird" soon became the bird's new nickname. The smoke is most likely water vapor, not an uncommon occurrence in places with very high humidity, but the lucky shot by Ananth Rupanagudi became an internet sensation.

No. 297

Progne subis

Purple Martin

Gourd Martin | Hose Martin | Western Martin

● **LEAST CONCERN**

✿ **COLLECTIVE NAME**

Richness of martins

✹ **SYMBOLIC MEANINGS**

Community; Cooperation.

🌀 **POSSIBLE POWERS**

Speed; Symbiotic relationship with humans.

☾ **FOLKLORE AND FACTS**

Purple Martins have many attributes, from their flight speed to their ability to maneuver in the air to catch lots of insects, but they are most lauded for their choice of communal living. Hundreds of years ago, European settlers in the eastern United States observed Cherokee, Chickasaw, and Choctaw peoples hanging clusters of gourds to create a nesting colony of martins, which in turn kept the local mosquito population in check. The new settlers joined in with this effort, and this began martins' symbiotic relationship with people, now demonstrated by the popularity of martin houses in coastal residential areas across the eastern half of the country.

• We see each of these Purple Martin colonies with dozens of birds, so it's easy to assume that there are plenty of martins to go around. The arrival of House Sparrows and European Starlings in the mid-1800s, however, created an entirely new and quite dire threat to martins' survival. Both of these invasive species will fight to the death for the right to move into a martin house, and they will evict the already-settled martins and throw out their eggs and nestlings. This war between native and invasive birds resulted in a major crash in martin populations in the mid-twentieth century. Many human owners of martin houses now monitor the arrival of House Sparrows and European Starlings and pull them out of martin houses before they can nest, becoming the martins' staunchest defenders in the battle for home and children.

No. 298

Protonotaria citrea

Prothonotary Warbler

Golden Swamp Warbler

● **LEAST CONCERN**

✿ **COLLECTIVE NAMES**

Bouquet of warblers | Confusion of warblers | Fall of warblers | Wrench of warblers

✹ **SYMBOLIC MEANINGS**

Music; Positive feelings.

🌀 **POSSIBLE POWER**

Good luck.

☾ **FOLKLORE AND FACTS**

What could be a happier occasion than spotting this bright yellow warbler at work on its tree cavity nest? Named for the bright yellow robes worn by prothonotaries, clerks in service to the Pope in the Roman Catholic Church, these gorgeous little birds bring light to wooded wetlands. Many wildlife refuges place nest boxes in favored Prothonotary Warbler habitats to assist the birds, a necessary step in recent years because of competition with House Wrens, which seek a cavity of about the same size. Nest boxes also help guard these birds against the Brown-Headed Cowbird, which will lay an egg in another bird's nest and leave the involuntary parent to raise the young. • The Prothonotary Warbler played a particularly dramatic role during hearings by the House Un-American Activities Committee in 1948. Intelligence agent Whittaker Chambers accused government official Alger Hiss of being a Communist spy, but Hiss testified that he didn't know Chambers and that his accusations were lies. Young Richard Nixon served on the committee, however, and he persuaded the committee to call Chambers to the stand again, so Chambers testified that Hiss bragged to him about seeing a Prothonotary Warbler while birding on the Potomac River. Sure enough, when the committee recalled Hiss, they steered the questioning in such a way that Hiss told them about seeing the warbler. The committee then charged Hiss with perjury, and Nixon became a hero for his strategic thinking.

No. 299
Prunella modularis

Dunnock
Hedge Accentor Hedge Spadger | Hedge Sparrow | Hedge Warbler | Titling

● **LEAST CONCERN**

✿ **COLLECTIVE NAME**
Jovial of dunnocks

✺ **SYMBOLIC MEANINGS**
Fertility; Polygamy.

✸ **POSSIBLE POWER**
Rapid and frequent copulation.

☾ **FOLKLORE AND FACTS**
What a cheery courtship and mating season Dunnocks have! Copulating with more than one mate only begins to describe what goes on between individuals of this species. The actual act of conception lasts less than a second, but the birds repeat it with the same or different partners hundreds of times a day for days on end. The result is a very successful breeding season, during which the females lay a clutch of bright blue eggs, and the males valiantly defend the nest from predators.
• Dunnock means "small brown bird" in Middle English, but the little birds have picked up many nicknames over the centuries. William Shakespeare used its colloquial name "hedge sparrow" in Act 1, Scene 4 of *King Lear*, as the king's Fool warns him that Lear's daughter, Goneril, may be about to ruin him. "The hedge sparrow fed the cuckoo so long / That it's had it head bit off by it young," the Fool notes. As cuckoos are brood parasites and lay their eggs in nests of other birds, including the Dunnock—and then the fledgling cuckoo may bite off its own foster parent's head—the Fool delivers a shrewd observation. (Lear, sadly, does not pay much attention.)

No. 300
Psaltriparus minimus

Bushtit
American Bushtit | American Long-Tailed Tit | Coast Bushtit | Long-Tailed Titmouse

● **LEAST CONCERN**

✿ **COLLECTIVE NAMES**
Cloud of bushtits | Flash mob of bushtits

✺ **SYMBOLIC MEANINGS**
Agility; Cooperation.

✸ **POSSIBLE POWERS**
Stealth; Teamwork.

☾ **FOLKLORE AND FACTS**
If you live in western North America, you may be surrounded by Bushtits and have no idea these tiny birds are there. Gray, fairly quiet except for some polite buzzing, and capable of professional-level stealth, a cloud of fifteen or more Bushtits may visit an oak tree in your yard and give you no indication of their attendance—unless you have a suet feeder, in which case they may mob it by the dozen.
• The Bushtit's trademark is its shaggy, 10-inch (25 cm)-long nest, a sock-like structure made of lichens, moss, spiderwebs, and grasses. It takes weeks for the birds to build this masterpiece, and some never finish because of wind, storms, or predators. When this happens, the birds with the failed nest find other bushtits who have been more successful, and they team up with them to finish the job and care for the nestlings once they hatch. This cooperative behavior makes the Bushtit a spiritual ambassador for collaboration and mutually shared success.

P

Psarocolius

Oropendola

6 species in the genus *Psarocolius*

● **LEAST CONCERN**

✴ **COLLECTIVE NAME**

Somersault of oropendolas

✴ **SYMBOLIC MEANINGS**

Community life; Cooperation.

✴ **POSSIBLE POWER**

Living together in harmony.

☾ **FOLKLORE AND FACTS**

Men are Oropendolas, women are Green Parrots. That's what the Airo-Pai people of the Peruvian Amazon believe that their dead relatives think, and they've stuck to this for centuries, according to researcher Luisa Elvira Belaunde in a 1994 scholarly paper. Oropendolas "weave beautiful nests for bringing up their offspring," making them strong, capable providers; Green Parrots passively move into nesting holes already created by other birds (specifically woodpeckers), making them receivers. Beyond this, the two bird families are quite similar to one another: talkative, gregarious, and showy.
• The six species of Oropendola all share dark brown to black bodies, very large, light-colored bills; and some areas of bright yellow in their tail feathers. Male oropendolas earn this bird family its name (literally "gold pendulum") through their unusual mating ritual: They hold onto a tree branch and swing under it and back up in a circular motion, like an Olympic gymnast on parallel bars. This continues for months until the males attract willing females. The males then come together in a single tree to build a colony of hanging nests, an example of cooperation that many Amazonians took to heart. The longhouses built by some of these tribespeople have a connection to these communal nesting sites, where female birds raise their young and help one another to feed and fledge them.

Pseudibis gigantea

Giant Ibis

Tror Yorng (Cambodian)

● **CRITICALLY ENDANGERED**

✴ **COLLECTIVE NAMES**

Colony of Ibises | Stand of ibises | Wedge of ibises | Whiteness of ibises

✴ **SYMBOLIC MEANINGS**

Natural beauty; Peace.

✴ **POSSIBLE POWERS**

Connection to the afterlife; Helping to treat malaria.

☾ **FOLKLORE AND FACTS**

Only about 200 Giant Ibises remain in the wild in northern Cambodia, with some individuals sighted recently in southern Laos. Nearly 4 feet (122 cm) tall and uniformly grayish brown with red legs, this ibis's numbers have dwindled as their habitat disappears with wetland drainage throughout Cambodia, a necessity for growing food to support this impoverished country. • It's hard to imagine how a country can allow its national bird to dwindle away, especially when the bird's blood has been used in a traditional treatment for malaria—but it is not until recently that the nation extended protections to the Giant Ibis in hopes of maintaining its population. • The bird the Cambodian people call Tror Yorng is celebrated in folk songs and Khmer tales that describe the lives of Cambodian farmers, making it an important part of their national heritage. Around the world, ibis species serve as a symbol for the human soul, a connection to the afterlife, and a transition between the worlds of the dead and the living; in Cambodia, people believe that if the Giant Ibis encounters hunters in their habitat, the birds will leave that area and never return.

No. 303

Psittacus erithacus

Grey Parrot

African Grey Parrot | Congo African Grey Parrot | Congo Grey Parrot

● **ENDANGERED**

✵ **COLLECTIVE NAMES**

Company of parrots | Pandemonium of parrots | Prattle of parrots | Psittacosis of parrots

☀ **SYMBOLIC MEANINGS**

Communication; Sharing.

🌀 **POSSIBLE POWERS**

Creating their own words; Intelligence; Mimicry.

☙ **FOLKLORE AND FACTS**

From Kenya to the Ivory Coast, the Grey Parrot struggles to populate the forests of equatorial Africa, with numbers in some areas declining by 99 percent just since 1992. In a ten-year span from 1994 to 2003, more than 359,000 Grey Parrots appeared for trading on the international pet market. Since 2021, it is illegal in Kenya to own a Grey Parrot without a permit, a move that may slow traffic of this beleaguered bird. • Since around 2000 BCE, Greek and Roman households have had these parrots as pets, and Egyptian hieroglyphics portray Grey Parrots in cages. What is the attraction? Grey Parrots are one of the most intelligent parrot species, learning number sequences and even creating their own words for things. • A nineteen-year-old Grey Parrot in Michigan actually became a witness in a murder trial, after his owner, Martin Duram, was shot and killed in 2015. When the parrot went to live with Duram's ex-wife, Christina Keller, he kept repeating "Don't […] shoot" in a fair imitation of Duram's voice until Keller finally brought the bird to the attention of the prosecuting attorney. The bird repeated the last conversation Duram had with his wife, Glenna, imitating both voices and always ending with Duram's last words. The bird's "testimony," along with other evidence, led to Glenna Duram's conviction.

No. 304

Psophia crepitans

Grey-Winged Trumpeter

● **LEAST CONCERN**

✵ **COLLECTIVE NAME**

Fanfare of trumpeters

☀ **SYMBOLIC MEANINGS**

Sentinel; Warning.

🌀 **POSSIBLE POWER**

Scrappiness.

☙ **FOLKLORE AND FACTS**

Arawak people of British Guiana tell us how the Grey-Winged Trumpeter got its gray wings and bare legs. Long ago, during the Great Flood that covered the world, the god Sigu commanded all the animals to either climb trees or go into a cave that he sealed tight with wax. Trumpeter went into the cave with the others, but he became impatient as the waters receded, so he left the cave too early. He walked on the ground looking for food, and entire colonies of ants, starving for food themselves, swarmed up his legs and left nothing but the bare shanks. Sigu rescued the bird, but his legs remained naked forever. • Sometime later, a Grey-Tailed Trumpeter and a kingfisher came to blows over which of them should get the loot after a war. They knocked one another to the ground and rolled into the ashes left from the previous night's fire. The birds remain gray with ashes to this day. • One more traditional story tells us why the Grey-Tailed Trumpeter has a short tail. The Maquritari people at the headwaters of the Orinoco River tell us that a trumpeter and a curassow decided to marry, but things did not go well after their wedding. They took their case to the gods, who told them to fight it out—and in the ensuing battle, the curassow pushed the trumpeter into a fire, which singed off his tail. The trumpeter pushed the curassow into the fire and burnt off her crest. The gods decided that they should remain that way for eternity, so the curassow has no crest to this day, and the trumpeter has a short tail.

No. 305

Pterodroma cahow

Bermuda Petrel

Cahow

- ENDANGERED

☣ COLLECTIVE NAMES

Gallon of petrels | Tank of petrels

✸ SYMBOLIC MEANING

National bird of Bermuda.

🌀 POSSIBLE POWER

Lazarus Bird (returned from presumed extinction).

☾ FOLKLORE AND FACTS

Scientists call a bird that has come back from presumed extinction a Lazarus Bird, and only a few birds worldwide have achieved this distinction. Bermuda Petrel is a Lazarus Bird, one of the two rarest seabirds in the world, and thought to be extinct as far back as the 1620s. The bird had fallen prey to Spanish sailors who landed in Bermuda in the 1500s and killed thousands of the birds for food, then brought hogs there to vary their diet, allowing the hogs to destroy petrel nesting areas. In the early 1600s, English colonization brought rats, dogs, and cats to the island, and by 1621, no petrels remained in Bermuda. • Then in 1935, a bird flew into a lighthouse in Bermuda and died in the collision, and when no one could identify it, they sent it to the American Museum of Natural History in New York. Ornithologist Robert Cushman Murphy determined that it had to be a Bermuda Petrel. In 1941, a live petrel was discovered in Bermuda, and the search began for a breeding colony. Ten years later, Murphy, naturalist Louis Mowbray, and 15-year-old David Wingate found eighteen breeding pairs of Bermuda Petrel on an islet in Castle Harbour. The find changed Wingate's life, and he devoted his career to saving the bird. Today about 130 breeding pairs live on islands off the Bermuda coast.

No. 306

Ptilinopus pelewensis

Palau Fruit Dove

- LEAST CONCERN

☣ COLLECTIVE NAMES

Bevy of doves | Covey of doves | Dole of doves | Paddling of doves | Pretense of doves

✸ SYMBOLIC MEANING

National bird of Palau.

🌀 POSSIBLE POWER

Flying through a rainbow.

☾ FOLKLORE AND FACTS

A colorful dove with a bright magenta crown, white face and breast, green wings and tail, and a bright orange belly, the Palau Fruit Dove deserves a long look—and as it's common in Palau (and found nowhere else), you'll have many opportunities to admire it. • Local folklore tells us that fruit doves get their colors by starting out as white doves and flying through a rainbow. Their steady diet of fruit helps maintain all of these brilliant shades, and they can be seen drifting from one part of the island to another as fruits ripen in specific areas. These fruit doves are particularly partial to figs, and they play an important role in dispersing the seeds of this fruit, dropping them all over the island to ensure the continuation of their own food supply. • As the national bird of this South Pacific island, the Palau Fruit Dove appears on several postage stamps, on signs, and in promotional materials for the tiny island nation.

No. 307

Ptilinopus roseicapilla

Mariana Fruit Dove

Mwee'mwe | Paluman Totot | Totot

- NEAR THREATENED

☣ COLLECTIVE NAMES

Bevy of doves | Covey of doves | Dole of doves | Paddling of doves | Pretense of doves

✸ SYMBOLIC MEANING

Official bird of the North Mariana Islands

🌀 POSSIBLE POWER

Flying through a rainbow.

☾ FOLKLORE AND FACTS

Meet the official mascot of the 2006 Micronesian Games—and the official bird of the North Mariana Islands, an unincorporated US territory. This vividly colored, purple-capped dove with green, orange, and white plumage is endemic to Guam as well as the Marianas. Local lore suggests that this dove started its existence as a white bird, but it flew through a rainbow and changed itself forever. • Gorgeous color doesn't necessarily lead to long life, however. After World War II, the brown tree snake came over from Australia, most likely on cargo ships or by entwining itself in aircraft landing gear. Unnoticed at first, it slipped into forests and reproduced like crazy, finding a seemingly unlimited supply of birds and rodents to satisfy its hunger. Today the islands work to eradicate this species, but the snakes have done considerable damage to the endemic birds, reducing their numbers into the endangered realm.

No. 308

Ptilonorhynchidae

Bowerbird

27 species in the genus *Ptilonorhynchidae*

● ● **LEAST CONCERN TO NEAR THREATENED**

✿ **COLLECTIVE NAME**

Bower of Bowerbirds

✸ **SYMBOLIC MEANINGS**

Creativity; Homemaking, Redecoration.

✺ **POSSIBLE POWERS**

Decorating its nesting area.

☾ **FOLKLORE AND FACTS**

Birds with a flair for architecture and interior decoration, the twenty-seven species of male Bowerbird build elaborate, complex structures to attract a mate. The armature begins with lots of sticks and twigs, constructed into "bowers" and festooned with whatever colorful, shiny objects the bird can find in the vicinity. Some structures have been found that measure up to 9 feet (3 m) high and 6 feet (2 m) wide, enough to attract even the most social-climbing female.

• Each bower contains a domed central entrance just big enough for a female Bowerbird to enter and exit, and an entryway paved with large, flat leaves and rocks. Objects discovered in these bowers include flower petals, colored stones, shiny insect skeletons, seeds, shells, berries, ferns, bones, leaves, shards of glass, aluminum foil, bright-colored plastic, and vegetable juices used as paint. The male bird may work on this bower for weeks or even months, and he may return to the same bower year after year to remodel it.

• Even after he has mated with a female, the male bird continues to fuss with his creation, adding other objects he comes across and protecting it from predators. The female goes off to create her own nest for laying eggs, and the male waits for the next female to arrive, so he can mate again.

• Observing a Bowerbird at work can be an explicit reminder that we all have control over our own environment, and if it does not please us, we can change it. Some Bowerbirds are as choosy about the colors they bring into their bowers as humans are about furniture styles or painted walls. Making your own place a reflection of your taste and personality is the message we receive from these creative birds.

No. 309

Puffinus puffinus

Manx Shearwater

Manks Puffins (archaic)

● **LEAST CONCERN**

✿ **COLLECTIVE NAMES**

Colony of shearwaters | Improbability of shearwaters | Raft of shearwaters (when on water)

✸ **SYMBOLIC MEANING**

Supernatural connections.

✺ **POSSIBLE POWER**

Long-term flight.

☾ **FOLKLORE AND FACTS**

When Norse people landed on Scotland's Isle of Rum in the eleventh century, they may have been the first people to visit the rain-soaked, mosquito-infested place. As they explored the rocky, mountainous, and generally unpleasant island, these otherwise courageous Vikings heard strange, hoarse cackles coming from between the rocks. Their conclusion: This Scottish island had its own population of trolls. They even named a mountain Trollval, so others would take heed and stay clear of the area. • What they did not see were the colonies of Manx Shearwaters covering the coastline. These plump pelagic birds nest by the thousands on this and other islands off the UK's northern coast, often flying hundreds of miles daily in search of food to bring back to a single chick in a concealed burrow. • Despite their preference for colony nesting, Manx Shearwaters are solitary birds, so their time in the air is generally spent alone. In fact, once the fledgling leaves the island, it may soar over the ocean continuously for as long as three years before deciding to mate, migrating to South America in the meantime.

P

No. 310

Pycnonotus barbatus

Common Bulbul

Black-Eyed Bulbul | Brown Bulbul | Brown-Capped Geelgat | Common Garden Bulbul | White-Vented Bulbul

● **LEAST CONCERN**

🐾 **COLLECTIVE NAME**

Leaflove of bulbuls

✳ **SYMBOLIC MEANINGS**

Beauty; Love; Song.

🌀 **POSSIBLE POWER**

Relationship with spirits of the dead.

🌙 **FOLKLORE AND FACTS**

People of northern and central Africa know the song of the Common Bulbul well, though they often confuse the plain brown bird with the Common Nightingale—even though the nightingale has a far more melodious song. Portrayed in local poetry and children's songs as singing its heart out as if deeply in love, the Common Bulbul has come to mean love and beauty throughout its region. • Coming across a singing Common Bulbul in the wild may mean that you are about to receive a message that may be unpleasant. The bird's harsh voice warns listeners to keep an open mind and to hear what needs to be said. • A fairly gruesome Persian tale tells us about a young boy and his father collecting wood together. The boy's stepmother suggests a contest: Whichever of the two collects the most wood must behead the other one. To the boy's horror, his father accepts this preposterous challenge, and they labor all day, with the boy collecting the most wood until he pauses to drink from a stream. With his back turned, his father switches the bundles. The father wins the contest and moves all too quickly to cut off his son's head. Later his sister discovers the terrible wrong and consults a priest, who tells her to bury her brother's remains respectfully. She does this, and a bulbul appears at the grave and tells her through song that he is actually her brother. The bird then steals a needle from a seamstress, and drops it down the stepmother's throat, killing her and taking his revenge.

No. 311

Pycnonotus jocosus

Red-Whiskered Bulbul

Crested Bulbul

● **LEAST CONCERN**

🐾 **COLLECTIVE NAME**

Leaflove of bulbuls

✳ **SYMBOLIC MEANINGS**

Privilege; Prosperity.

🌀 **POSSIBLE POWER**

Luck.

🌙 **FOLKLORE AND FACTS**

A Buddhist practice involves releasing a caged bird into the wild, thus giving it back its normal life, in exchange for which the person receives a gift of good luck from the grateful bird. Red-Whiskered Bulbuls are prime candidates for this release program, as they are very popular in the pet trade for their striking appearance, their high black crest and red cheeks creating an attractive contrast against their muted plumage; in fact, in some communities in India and Thailand, owning a bulbul is a testament to the prosperity and privilege of the household. Buying the bird from a market only to release it may be a costly proposition, but it is an acknowledged gesture of goodwill, and it earns some bird sellers a reasonable living. • Until fairly recently, the sport of Red-Whiskered and Red-Vented Bulbul fights was popular in India, withholding food from the birds until they were placed in the "arena" and watching them pull on their opponent's red cheeks. Bulbul fights were banned in 2016, replaced in some places by singing contests—placing two birds in separate cages next to one another so they would sing to establish their individual territories.

No. 312

Pycnonotus leucotis

White-Eared Bulbul

Arabian White-Cheeked Bulbul

● **LEAST CONCERN**

✿ **COLLECTIVE NAME**
Leaflove of bulbuls

☀ **SYMBOLIC MEANING**
Freedom.

✹ **POSSIBLE POWERS**
Good luck; Love.

☾ **FOLKLORE AND FACTS**
The bulbul of southwest Asia and the Middle East has an all-black head with a bright white cheek patch, as well as a yellow vent under its light-brown back and tail. Bulbuls lend their name to the Bulbul Collective, a storytelling group of Arab, Middle Eastern, Muslim, and South Asian people working toward a common identity in the United States; and to the channel Bulbul Stories on Wattpad, a social storytelling platform. The *bulbul tarang*, a well-known Indian musical instrument resembling a banjo, is also named for this bird. • In one traditional Middle Eastern story, a Raja went hunting in a forest, but as night came, he became lost and decided to sleep under a tree. Bulbuls nested above him, and they sang so beautifully in the morning that when the Raja returned to his palace, he sent his courtiers out to capture one of the birds to live at the palace. The courtiers brought back the bird and the Raja placed it in a golden cage and gave it food, but the bird would neither sing nor eat. Finally, seeing no other choice, the Raja had the bird returned to the wild, and as soon as it was out of its cage, it began to sing. No moral is offered, but we can glean that all souls thrive best in their own environment, no matter how pleasant the situation they are offered as captives.

No. 313

Pyrrhocorax pyrrhocorax

Red-Billed Chough

Beckit | Chough | Cornish Chough

● **LEAST CONCERN**

✿ **COLLECTIVE NAME**
Chatter of choughs

☀ **SYMBOLIC MEANINGS**
Sacred to Greek gods; Soul of King Arthur.

✹ **POSSIBLE POWER**
Fire-starting.

☾ **FOLKLORE AND FACTS**
A black bird with a red bill and red legs, the Red-Billed Chough has drawn a great deal of attention over the centuries. Ancient Greeks believed the bird to be sacred to Cronus, father of Zeus, and that it lived with the great god on the island of Ogygia. Homer's *Odyssey* mentions the bird as one of three that make their home on Calypso's island: "The chough, the sea-mew, the loquacious crow." • Aesop provides a fable involving a Chough: Ravens were believed to predict the future, so a Chough became envious of them and tried to raise himself to the Raven's level. He perched in a tree and waited for some people to come by, and when he saw them, he called loudly with his clanging voice. The travelers stopped and looked at him, and one said, "Oh, it's only a Chough. His cries are not an omen." The moral: Competing with stronger rivals is a losing proposition. • Cornwall has long honored the Chough as part of its coat of arms, as did followers of Saint Thomas Becket, Archbishop of Canterbury. Cornish knights believed that in his last battle, King Arthur's soul transferred into a Red-Billed Chough, and that the king's blood stains its bill and legs. • In more pedestrian terms, the Chough appears on postage stamps for the Isle of Man, Gambia, Bhutan, Turkmenistan, and Yugoslavia, and it serves as the national animal of the island of La Palma.

P

Quiscalus mexicanus

Great-Tailed Grackle

Blackbird | Chanate | Zanate (Mexico)

● **LEAST CONCERN**

✤ **COLLECTIVE NAME**
Plague of grackles

✹ **SYMBOLIC MEANINGS**
Courage; Scavenger; Thief.

✺ **POSSIBLE POWERS**
Adaptability to human environments; Planning ability.

☾ **FOLKLORE AND FACTS**
From their original range in the South American tropics to their current dominance in south Texas, Great-Tailed Grackles gather by the tens of thousands at sunset to roost together on utility wires in city centers, or blanket the ground in agricultural fields and open meadows. Great-Taileds have established massive populations in the western United States from New Mexico to the Pacific coast. The secret of their success is their diverse diet: Bugs and larvae, small reptiles, other birds' nestlings, grains, fruit, invertebrates, tiny fish, and crustaceans. They also dominate other birds at feeders, making nuisances of themselves in backyards and parks. • Aztecs brought these grackles from their original home along the Gulf coast in Mexico to their new, permanent home at Tenochtitlan, using their iridescent feathers in ceremonies and ritual garments. • A native Mexican legend speaks of the Great-Tailed Grackle, which they call Zanate, having no voice when the world was created. Zanate rides on the back of the sea turtle and steals seven songs from him, as the wise turtle knows of the seven passions: Love, hate, fear, courage, joy, sadness, and anger. Each of these passions becomes part of Zanate's song. Today the grackle sings many different kinds of songs, from grunts and squeaks to a sound like a slamming screen door.

Quiscalus quiscula

Common Grackle

Florida Grackle | Purple Grackle

● **NEAR THREATENED**

✤ **COLLECTIVE NAME**
Plague of grackles

✹ **SYMBOLIC MEANINGS**
Boldness; Courage; Scavenger.

✺ **POSSIBLE POWER**
Amassing flocks to plunder together.

☾ **FOLKLORE AND FACTS**
Smaller to Great-Tailed or Boat-Tailed Grackles, Common Grackles are the dominant grackle of the eastern and central United States. This bird has spent its existence earning a reputation as a nuisance, especially to farmers of grains that grackles particularly love to harvest. • Native American myths and legends do not draw a distinction between grackles and other black birds, but people of the plains who led an agrarian life certainly faced Common Grackles in defending their cornfields from avian marauders. While crows have long been associated with corn—hence the scarecrows that have little effect on crows—Common Grackles are the true corn bandits, devouring all they can and returning after the harvest to pick up every last kernel on the ground. • Sioux culture tells us that if black birds plundered their corn, the Sioux were being punished by divine forces for neglecting to honor the corn to their satisfaction. The Hopi people believed that black birds were associated directly with the Underworld, serving as guardians of that realm. The Arapaho used black bird medicine in their Sun Dance rituals, and they named one of their youth societies the Blackbirds.

No. 316
Ramphastidae toco
Toco Toucan

Tucán Grande (Spanish) | Tucano-Boi (Brazil) | Yubibi (Bolivia)

● **LEAST CONCERN**

⚘ **COLLECTIVE NAME**
Durante of toucans

✳ **SYMBOLIC MEANINGS**
Communication; Creativity;
Showmanship.

🌀 **POSSIBLE POWERS**
Flamboyance; Majesty.

☾ **FOLKLORE AND FACTS**
While the Rainbow-Billed
Toucan may be most
recognizable in the Americas,
the Toco Toucan is a celebrity in the United
Kingdom, where it became the central figure in a
Guinness Stout ad campaign. • This toucan's huge, bright
yellow bill is the stuff of Brazilian legend: While Toco
Toucan stood inside a hole so that other birds could see him
only by looking in, they admired the size of the bill and made
him their king. Once he stepped out of the hole, however,
he became an instant object of ridicule for being "all nose."
• With a body the same size as its bill, the Toco Toucan
became a favorite meal in many South American countries,
and its habit of forming large flocks at the end of the
breeding season for winter foraging makes it an easy target.
On top of this, the Toco Toucan is the second most popular
bird in the exotic pet trade, as well as the most expensive,
with a single individual commanding as much as $15,000 USD
in 2022.

No. 317
Ramphastos sulfuratus
Keel-Billed Toucan

Keel Toucan | Rainbow-Billed Toucan | Sulfur-Breasted Toucan

● **NEAR THREATENED**

⚘ **COLLECTIVE NAME**
Durante of toucans

✳ **SYMBOLIC MEANINGS**
Communication; Creativity; Showmanship.

🌀 **POSSIBLE POWERS**
Blessings for theater people; Flamboyance.

☾ **FOLKLORE AND FACTS**
Perhaps one of the most iconic of all
birds to Americans, the toucan
with the rainbow bill is instantly
recognizable even for people
who pay no attention to birds
(but who do pay attention to Kellogg's Fruit
Loops cereal boxes). Toucans use this bill
with great dexterity, picking and peeling
ripe fruit, catching lizards, and tucking
it under a wing so that its heat keeps the
bird warm white asleep. • How did this toucan get
such a bill? One South American legend tells us
that the bird had a much shorter and more modest
bill, but the other birds made fun of it, so he went into the
forest and asked the spirits for a showier bill. The spirits took
pity on the dowdy bird and gave him a bill more colorful
and exciting than any of the other birds. • Another, quite
opposite tale from Brazil says that the toucan always had a
beautiful bill, but the bird spent so much time looking at its
own reflection in water that the sun god touched it, making
it grow so large that the toucan could no longer see around it
to admire its reflection.

No. 318
Raphus cucullatus
Dodo

Dodo Bird

● **EXTINCT**

⚘ **COLLECTIVE NAMES**
Dearth of dodos | Extinction of dodos

✳ **SYMBOLIC MEANINGS**
Exotic lands; Gluttony;
Stupidity.

🌀 **POSSIBLE POWER**
Never to be discovered.

☾ **FOLKLORE AND FACTS**
The record of the Dodo's brief history with humans begins
in 1601, when the Second Dutch Expedition to Indonesia
encountered the bird on the island of Mauritius. Thanks to
reports written on this voyage, we have a description and
illustration, as well as commentary on how palatable the sailors
found the bird to be—the flightless creatures with no fear of
humans turned out to be very easy to hunt. This led inevitably
to its rapid extinction before the century ended. • A 1662
report of catching the birds noted that when one of the sailors
on the Dutch ship *Arnhem* grabbed a Dodo by the leg, "the

others all on a sudden came running as fast as they could to its assistance, and by which they were caught and made prisoners also." This was the last report of live Dodos in the wild. • Since then, and perhaps unfairly, the Dodo has become a symbol of stupidity and failure, with any waning experiment, trend, or product said to be "going the way of the Dodo." Foolish people are often called Dodos, even though the birds themselves were not stupid. The most useful connection with Dodos today comes from environmental organizations that use the Dodo as a symbol for squandering resources, with the Center for Biological Diversity actually giving a "Rubber Dodo Award" to organizations or individuals who have "done the most to destroy wild places, species, and biological diversity."

No. 319
Regulus regulus
Goldcrest

Gold-Crested Wren | Herring Spink | King of the Birds | Tot O'er Seas | Woodcock Pilot

● **LEAST CONCERN**

❈ **COLLECTIVE NAME**
Dynasty of goldcrests

✳ **SYMBOLIC MEANING**
Early arrival of spring.

✺ **POSSIBLE POWERS**
Deception; Good luck for fishermen; Trickster.

☙ **FOLKLORE AND FACTS**
This member of the kinglet family happens to be Europe's smallest bird, so it plays a role in one of folklore's most common bird stories—one told around the world with each region's tiniest bird cast as the trickster. • Legend has it that the gods (or the Creator) invited the birds to participate in a contest to decide which of them would be King of the Birds. The title would go to the one who could fly the highest. The birds lined up and flew straight up, but soon the thrushes, swifts, jays, and so on dropped back to earth. The eagle looked likely to become the winner, but unbeknownst to the majestic bird, a tiny Goldcrest rode under the feathers on his back. Just as all the other birds had given up and the eagle was about to win, the Goldcrest leapt out and flew past the eagle. The Goldcrest won the title, and the gods gave him his bright golden crest to denote his rank. • The tiny bird has other distinctions, especially among the fishing community: Fishermen in the North Sea often found spunky little Goldcrests stopping to rest on their herring boats, so they nicknamed them Herring Spink or Tot O'er Seas.

No. 320
Regulus satrapa
Golden-Crowned Kinglet

● **LEAST CONCERN**

❈ **COLLECTIVE NAMES**
Castle of kinglets | Court of kinglets | Dynasty of kinglets | Princedom of kinglets

✳ **SYMBOLIC MEANINGS**
Energy; Joy; Potential.

✺ **POSSIBLE POWERS**
Speed; Trickery.

☙ **FOLKLORE AND FACTS**
Folklore truly sells Golden-Crowned Kinglets short, as it does their close relatives, Ruby-Crowned Kinglets. Tales of these tiny birds usually have them hitching rides on the backs of unsuspecting larger birds, either to cheat at the contest of which bird can fly the highest (see Goldcrest, No. 319), or to migrate without putting in any effort. In real life, kinglets are some of the feistiest and most active birds, seemingly never resting as they flit through trees or shrubs. • The Golden-Crowned Kinglet breeds in the lower half of Canada and the northeastern and far western United States. Its bright yellow crown bordered in black and its single wing bar set it apart from warblers and other small birds, though getting a good look at this bird can tax a birder's patience. The good news is that kinglets tend to move in small flocks, so we have many opportunities to get binoculars on them.

No. 321
Rhea americana
Greater Rhea

American Rhea | Common Rhea | Gray Rhea | South American Ostrich

● **NEAR THREATENED**

❈ **COLLECTIVE NAMES**
Flock of rheas | Mob of rheas

✳ **SYMBOLIC MEANING**
Earth mother.

✺ **POSSIBLE POWER**
Ability to live among humans.

At up to 60 pounds (27 kg) and 55 inches (140 cm) tall, the Greater Rhea is the largest bird on the American continents, making its home in Argentina, Bolivia, Brazil, Paraguay, and Uruguay. How this flightless, ostrich-like bird received the name of the Greek goddess of the earth is an odd story: Back in the mid-1700s, German zoologist Paul Möhring referred to the bird as Rhea because it always stayed on the ground, and the Greek word *rhea* translates as "ground" in English. The bird's association with Rhea goes no further than this. • The much more mundane side of the Greater Rhea's story includes its excellent adaptability to life as livestock, living on farms, giving up their feathers for feather dusters, and feeding much of South America with their meat. The people who manage these birds are known as *gauchos*, and they work with the birds on horseback, creating quite the picture as they lasso the birds with a device called a *boleadora*.

No. 322

Rhinoplax vigil

Helmeted Hornbill

Tajaku

● **CRITICALLY ENDANGERED**

✥ **COLLECTIVE NAME**

Party of hornbills

✴ **SYMBOLIC MEANINGS**

Guard and protector; Warbird.

🌀 **POSSIBLE POWER**

Guarding the river to the afterlife.

☾ **FOLKLORE AND FACTS**

If your job involved guarding the river between life and the afterlife, what protection would you want to have? The Helmeted Hornbill evolved a solid shield called a casque, rising from the bill and covering its entire forehead. The bird uses this in combat with other male hornbills for the ultimate prize: the privilege of mating. • Large and unlike any other

bird in Malay Peninsula, it would be easy to identify in the field if people could see them: Fewer than 100 of these birds remain in the wild, hunted nearly to extinction by poachers who collect the casque to be sold as "hornbill ivory," worth a high price on the black market. • In Borneo's Dayaknese culture, hornbills are the physical manifestation of the Bird Commander, a mountain-dwelling figure that stays hidden in its supernatural form in peacetime, but turns into a hornbill in times of war. The bird's long tail feathers appear in Dayak ceremonial garb, a sign of a tribe leader's prosperity. • The Punan Bah people of the region believe that a Helmeted Hornbill sits at the far end of the bridge on one side of the river of death, and screams to scare an approaching ghost into falling into the river, where the bird's partner, a giant fish, will swallow it. On the other side of the river waits Ungap, a woman with a cauldron and a spear; if the ghost brings her a gift, she will help the ghost escape from the terrifying bird and fish. The Punans place pebbles or beads in the nostrils of a dead person, so the ghost may present these gifts to Ungap.

No. 323

Rhipidura leucophrys

Willie Wagtail

Djiti-Djiti | Kuritoro | Willaring

● **LEAST CONCERN**

✥ **COLLECTIVE NAMES**

Flight of wagtails | Roost of wagtails | Volery of wagtails

✴ **SYMBOLIC MEANING**

Thief of secrets.

🌀 **POSSIBLE POWER**

Messenger to and from the afterlife.

☾ **FOLKLORE AND FACTS**

If a bird can be a vixen, then the Willie Wagtail certainly qualifies: According to the First Nations peoples of Australia, this black-and-white songbird hangs around campsites in the quiet of evening and steals secrets from gossiping women. This belief ends many a conversation around cooking fires when the wagtail hops into view or sings in the gathering dusk. What does it do with the information? Tattle to your dead relatives, according to the Kunwinjku in Arnhem Land, who also say the bird embellishes the stories with its own lies. • The Willie Wagtail gets credit for making off with fire in a Dreaming tale told by the Yindjibarndi people, and trying to put the fire out in the sea. When frightened, they said, the bird could conjure up a big gust of wind to blow away its enemies. Alternately, the Kalam of New Guinea saw the bird as a good omen, coming to approve of a newly planted garden or to round up and care for livestock. • The Willie Wagtail visits new widows to let them know that their husband's souls have been accepted in the afterlife, bringing comfort to the bereaved by singing near the funeral.

No. 324

Rhynchotus rufescens

Red-Winged Tinamou

Perdiz Grande | Rufous Tinamou | Ynambu

● **LEAST CONCERN**

✣ **COLLECTIVE NAME**

Flock of tinamous

✳ **SYMBOLIC MEANING**

Severed friendship.

✺ **POSSIBLE POWER**

Holding a grudge.

☾ **FOLKLORE AND FACTS**

According to Brazilian legend, Red-Winged Tinamou and Undulated Tinamou were the best of friends, but the two birds began to argue, and they flew off in opposite directions. Undulated Tinamou headed into the darkest part of the forest, while Red-Winged Tinamou hurried off into the plains. Then Undulated Tinamou began to miss his companion, so he came out to the edge of the forest and whistled a plaintive three-note song, "Let's make up?" Red-Winged Tinamou replied, "What? Not me, never!" To this day, the two birds call the same messages to one another, but they rarely show themselves outside of their own habitats.

No. 325

Rhynochetos jubatus

Kagu

Cagou

● **ENDANGERED**

✣ **COLLECTIVE NAME**

Flock of kagu

✳ **SYMBOLIC MEANING**

Survival.

✺ **POSSIBLE POWER**

Messenger to chiefs.

☾ **FOLKLORE AND FACTS**

Long legs, bluish plumage, and a shaggy, relaxed crest that raises with excitement, the Kagu is the only living species in its genus, and only a few of its kind remain on Grand Terre, east of Australia. Its genus name *rhynochetos* combines the Greek words for "nose" and "corn," a direct reference to the flaps over its nostrils that look like corn kernels—a feature unique to the Kagu. Ornithologists believe that these "nasal corns" evolved to keep dirt and dust out of the bird's nasal passages, a clever solution for a bird that spends its life on the ground. • The Kagu played a major role in the rituals and lives of the Kanak people of New Caledonia. The people harvested the bird's crest to build into its chiefs' headdresses, and warriors imitated its high-pitched, whooping call in their war dances. The Kanak believed that the call carried messages that only the chiefs could understand, so a great deal of ceremony went into their interpretation. • Today the Kagu serves as the national symbol for New Caledonia, and the island's television station plays its whooping call every night as it signs off the air.

No. 326
Riparia riparia
Bank Swallow

Collared Sand Martin | Common Sand Martin | Sand Martin

● **LEAST CONCERN**

❖ **COLLECTIVE NAMES**

Flight of swallows | Gulp of swallows | Kettle of swallows

✳ **SYMBOLIC MEANING**

Arrival of spring.

✺ **POSSIBLE POWER**

Good luck.

☾ **FOLKLORE AND FACTS**

Nesting in the sandy banks of rivers and creeks, the Bank Swallow (known as the Sand Martin throughout Europe and Asia) is dark above, white below, and wears a dark band around its neck. Dozens or hundreds of birds may come together in a colony, digging tunnels high up in a wall of sand. • Some cultures place more meaning on Bank Swallows' spring arrival than the return of sunlight and warmth. The ancient Greeks associated swallows with Aphrodite, goddess of love, and Greek legend suggests that the gods could take the form of swallows, so harming any swallow could bring down the wrath of the entire pantheon. • Sailors follow an entire culture of swallow lore: They believe that swallows always find their way home, so a swallow tattoo is a virtual guarantee of good luck and safe voyages. That being said, a sailor has to earn the right to a swallow tattoo by traveling more than 5,000 nautical miles, so only the most seasoned can participate. Seeing a swallow from the deck of a ship not only brings good luck, but it almost always means that the ship is approaching the shore, as swallows do not wander far out to sea.

No. 327
Rynchops niger
Black Skimmer

Cutwater | Flood Gull | Scissor-Bill | Seadog | Stormgull

● **LEAST CONCERN**

❖ **COLLECTIVE NAMES**

Conspiracy of skimmers | Embezzlement of skimmers | Scoop of skimmers

✳ **SYMBOLIC MEANING**

Precision.

✺ **POSSIBLE POWERS**

Dependability; Grace.

☾ **FOLKLORE AND FACTS**

Just three birds in the world have the Black Skimmer's specialized bill, with the extra-long lower mandible for flying just above the water's surface and skimming for fish, insects, and crustaceans. Black Skimmers are great fun to watch, a year-round treat on North America's Atlantic and Gulf of Mexico coasts from Virginia to Texas, as well as coastal and inland eastern South America. • In 1961, at a Dow Chemical plant in Freeport, Texas, on the Gulf coast, Black Skimmers discovered a parking lot made of crushed oyster shell and limestone, their preferred nesting surface, right on the edge of a marsh and beach. They settled in and nested on the lot, and a thoughtful Dow employee blocked off the area so the birds would not be disturbed. The following year, the skimmers returned and brought their friends, and within a few years Dow became the keeper of a significant skimmer colony. Now Gulf Coast Bird Observatory partners with Dow to monitor the colony of 1,220 birds and keep track of its success.

R

No. 328

Sagittarius serpentarius

Secretary Bird

● ENDANGERED

🐾 **COLLECTIVE NAME**
Flight of Secretary Birds

☀ **SYMBOLIC MEANING**
Ascent of South Africa.

🌀 **POSSIBLE POWER**
Protection from enemies.

🦉 **FOLKLORE AND FACTS**
The African bird, with the body of an eagle and the legs of a heron, appears to have been assembled at random—especially when it flies, extending its stork-like neck forward and its two longest tail feathers backward. The Secretary Bird hunts on the ground rather than soaring or gliding over land like other birds of prey, stalking large insects and small animals and the occasional snake. • How the Secretary Bird got its name has puzzled taxonomists, but the best guess is that the stiff feathers on the back of its head look like quills scribes often tucked behind an ear before the invention of the pen. Its Latin genus suggests a connection to the zodiac sign Sagittarius, the archer, but the only direct link seems to be that the bird walks and stands a bit like an archer might. ("Secretary" also may be a sloppy linguist's pronunciation of Sagittarius.) • South Africa has adopted the Secretary Bird as the central figure in its coat of arms, even though the bird does not live in South Africa. The bird stands atop the emblem with wings uplifted and outstretched, its quill-like crest extended, and its legs represented by a spear and a knobkerrie, two weapons used in African culture.

No. 329

Sarcoramphus papa

King Vulture

Cozcacuauhtli (Nahuatl) | White Crow

● LEAST CONCERN

🐾 **COLLECTIVE NAMES**
Colony of vultures | Committee of vultures | Kettle of vultures | Wake of vultures

☀ **SYMBOLIC MEANING**
Suffering.

🌀 **POSSIBLE POWERS**
Messenger between gods and humans; Protection from sickness.

🦉 **FOLKLORE AND FACTS**
The King Vulture presents an imposing image, its large size and rose-tinted white feathers are only the beginning of its striking features. The bare red, orange, and purple skin of its head and neck offsets the white iris and red eye ring, and a bright orange, folded mound of skin called a caruncle makes any drawing of the bird instantly recognizable.
• That's how anthropologists know that the King Vulture appears in the codices of ancient Mayan culture: Written in the bark-paper manuscripts are glyphs that clearly represent the King Vulture, its hooked bill and caruncle illustrated accurately. Mayans believed that this bird carried messages from humans to gods and back, and in some cases, the codices portray the birds as gods themselves.
• Even beyond the Mayans, some indigenous South Americans used King Vulture feathers and blood in rituals to attempt to ward off sickness. Some believed that if a vulture flew over them and cast a shadow on a person, suffering or death would come to them soon.

No. 330

Saxicola torquatus

Common Stonechat

Blacky-Top | Chickstone | Furze Chitter | Stanechacker | Stane Chipper | Stonesmith
Related species: African Stonechat | Amur Stonechat | European Stonechat |
Fuerteventura Chat | Madagascar Stonechat | Reunion Stonechat | Siberian Stonechat |
White-Tailed Stonechat

● LEAST CONCERN

🐾 **COLLECTIVE NAME**
Flock of stonechats

☀ **SYMBOLIC MEANING**
Connection to the devil.

🌀 **POSSIBLE POWER**
Constant communication with the devil.

🦉 **FOLKLORE AND FACTS**
The name "Common Stonechat" has recently been upgraded to a superspecies, a group of species that are separated by geography but that come from the same parent species.
• All birds in this superspecies share a black head, white collar, black wings, and at least some rufous coloring on their breast, often spreading to their underside. Some have more white on their flanks. All of these birds prefer open gorse, heath, grasslands, and dunes, with some gravitating to rockier areas. • Several cultures believe that the stonechat's

S

metallic chip note, endlessly repeated as the birds hunt insects, means that they are in constant communication with the Underworld. Their red breast is considered proof that the devil is protecting these birds. Legend says that if a stonechat leaves its nest, a toad will come and continue to incubate the eggs until they hatch. Another tale suggests that a stonechat carries a drop of Satan's blood, though it offers no information on how it came to have it.

No. 331

Scolopax minor

American Woodcock

Bogsucker | Hokumpoke | Timberdoodle

● **LEAST CONCERN**

✿ **COLLECTIVE NAMES**
Covey of woodcocks | Fall of woodcocks

✹ **SYMBOLIC MEANINGS**
Hope; Resilience.

🌀 **POSSIBLE POWER**
Spectacular courtship.

☾ **FOLKLORE AND FACTS**

It's the big event every spring: Waiting for the *peent, peent* call of the American Woodcock at dusk that signals the beginning of his mating dance. After giving us fair warning, the woodcock launches himself straight up into the air and executes a tumbling spiral in an arc over an open field, finally landing perfectly on his feet . . . and starting over with the *peent* call. • A member of the shorebird family, American Woodcock somehow found its way into the woods and developed plumage that masks it completely as it sleeps or nests in last year's leaves. It feeds on earthworms, extending its cleverly hinged bill and rough tongue into the ground to catch and devour its prey. Evolution saw fit to place the woodcock's nostril high up on its bill so it can breathe while probing the ground—and its ears are in front of its eyes, a position unique among all bird species. • One Native American legend tells us that when the gods finished creating all the other animals, they had some bits left over. They put these together and came up with the woodcock, making it the mismatched jackalope of the bird world.

No. 332

Scolopax rusticola

Eurasian Woodcock

Mickle Snippeck

● **LEAST CONCERN**

✿ **COLLECTIVE NAMES**
Covey of woodcocks | Fall of woodcocks

✹ **SYMBOLIC MEANINGS**
Easily duped; Foolishness.

🌀 **POSSIBLE POWER**
Flying to the moon.

☾ **FOLKLORE AND FACTS**

With an *orr, orr, orr, pist*, the male Eurasian Woodcock launches himself into the air to perform a mating ritual Europeans call "roding," designed to impress the females. Very similar in appearance and habits to the American Woodcock, the Eurasian Woodcock keeps a low profile outside of the breeding season, hunting for earthworms with a bill and rough tongue that have evolved for this specific purpose. • Most European countries consider the woodcock a game bird, though recent studies have shown that despite regulations already in place, hunting is reducing their numbers. Woodcock is a popular menu item from October to December in some countries, while others consider the bird "unwholesome," though their eggs have become a delicacy. • British lore suggests that outside of breeding and hunting seasons, woodcocks fly to the moon until spring—giving the November full moon the name "woodcock moon." When migrating woodcocks arrive in early autumn, a good harvest lay ahead; but calling a person a woodcock meant that they were foolish or easily bluffed. This even dates back to Shakespeare's *Hamlet*, when in Act 1, Scene 3, Polonius calls Hamlet's declarations of love for Ophelia nothing more than "springes to catch woodcock," meaning traps for fools.

No. 333

Scopus umbretta

Hamerkop

Anvil Head | Lightning Bird | Njaka (rain doctor) | Umberbird

● **LEAST CONCERN**

✢ **COLLECTIVE NAME**
Flock of hamerkops

✺ **SYMBOLIC MEANINGS**
A hostile god; In league with Khauna.

✺ **POSSIBLE POWERS**
Foreshadowing death or rain; Striking intruders with lightning.

☾ **FOLKLORE AND FACTS**
An all-brown wading bird with a hammer-shaped head, Hamerkop lives throughout sub-Saharan Africa wherever water is available, as it dines on fish, amphibians, and insects found in and around shallow water. • The Hamerkop gets the most attention for its enormous nests, however, especially because the nests have an internal chamber for egg-laying, a feature otherwise expected only of bowerbirds. • Kalahari bushmen once believed that if they tried to raid a Hamerkop's nest for its eggs or young, they would be struck by lightning—so they called the Hamerkop "Lightning Bird." They left these birds alone for the most part, believing that Khauna, a hostile god, didn't want anyone messing with hamerkops.
• Malagasy people of Madagascar took this belief even farther afield, calling the bird "evil" and avoiding Hamerkop nests because they were certain the nests gave people leprosy.

No. 334

Seiurus aurocapilla

Ovenbird

Accentor | Golden-Crowned Thrush

● **LEAST CONCERN**

✢ **COLLECTIVE NAME**
Stew of ovenbirds

✺ **SYMBOLIC MEANING**
Arrival of spring.

✺ **POSSIBLE POWERS**
Concealment;
Unique nest-building.

☾ **FOLKLORE AND FACTS**
For the Birds radio program host Laura Erickson calls the Ovenbird "the Linda Ronstadt of the Bird World, belting out a simple tune with all of Ronstadt's vigor, vibrancy, and volume." This dead-on description of the Ovenbird's piercing *teacher-teacher-teacher* call, splitting the spring forest air in a grand crescendo, brings home the sheer joy of this secretive bird's song. Officially a warbler, the Ovenbird sings with abandon as it establishes the territory in which it will build its clay, dome-shaped nest, a structure that looks so much like the clay ovens of old that it gave the bird its peculiar name.
• American poet Robert Frost lauded this bird in "The Oven Bird," his 1916 poem that begins, "There is a singer everyone has heard, / Loud, a mid-summer and a mid-wood bird, / Who makes the solid tree trunks sound again." Indeed, just about everyone who has taken a spring walk in the eastern states has heard an Ovenbird, and while the rest of Frost's poem credits this bird with recognizing the early departure of spring and summer, this bird certainly reminds us to enjoy the long days of May and June, when forests are filled with song.

No. 335

Serinus canaria domestica

Domestic Canary

Canary | Tweety Bird

● **DOMESTICATED**

✢ **COLLECTIVE NAME**
Breast of canaries

✺ **SYMBOLIC MEANINGS**
Informant; Sentinel species for poisoned air.

✺ **POSSIBLE POWER**
Enchanting humans with its song.

☾ **FOLKLORE AND FACTS**
The bright yellow canary that is so popular with households around the world has actually been bred in captivity to achieve its lemony color. Canaries in the wild (Atlantic Canary, *Serinus canaria*) hail from the Canary Islands, and are generally more yellow-green with brown-streaked backs.

S

• Spanish sailors brought canaries home to their families and to the pet trade, where breeding the birds became an immediate hit. Soon canaries were all the rage with British and Spanish royalty, and they caught on overseas in America as well. The birds we enjoy today have not seen their natural habitat in many generations, so they do not survive in the wild, even when released in climates like Florida and California. • Beyond their lives as pets, canaries have been repurposed for industry and research. Miners since the 1700s brought canaries in cages into mines as a first warning against carbon monoxide leaks; if the bird lost consciousness, miners bolted for the surface. This practice continued well into the twentieth century, until carbon monoxide detectors were invented. • Canaries have come to symbolize anyone who sings readily and easily, including criminals who inform on their comrades—i.e., "he sang like a canary." • Of course, the most popular and enduring image of a canary is Tweety Bird, the 1950s Warner Bros. cartoon character who repeatedly and dependably outsmarted Sylvester the Cat.

No. 336
Setophaga petechia
Yellow Warbler

● **LEAST CONCERN**

🐾 **COLLECTIVE NAMES**
Bouquet of warblers | Confusion of warblers | Fall of warblers | Wrench of warblers

✹ **SYMBOLIC MEANINGS**
Good cheer; Optimism; Pollen.

🌀 **POSSIBLE POWER**
Good luck to farmers.

🐾 **FOLKLORE AND FACTS**
Yellow Warblers are found all over the United States and southern Canada during spring and summer, and they return to Central and South America for the winter. These bright yellow birds have delicate red streaks on their breast, which become brighter in spring for the breeding season. Their sweet song is echoed in the first bars of Antonio Vivaldi's *The Four Seasons*, concerto No. 1, "Spring." • The Pueblo people used Yellow Warbler feathers in their spring rituals, because their feathers are the color of pollen and could help bring a good growing year. Some Native American folk tales see the Yellow Warbler as a messenger from the spirit world, specifically chosen by the spirits to relay good news to those on the surface. The Hopi believe that yellow birds bring fertility, while the Cherokee see yellow birds as signaling a time to be happy and prosper.

No. 337
Setophaga ruticilla
American Redstart

● **LEAST CONCERN**

🐾 **COLLECTIVE NAMES**
Bouquet of warblers | Confusion of warblers | Fall of warblers

✹ **SYMBOLIC MEANINGS**
Courage; New beginnings; Overcoming hardship; Passion.

🌀 **POSSIBLE POWER**
Boosting the spirits.

🐾 **FOLKLORE AND FACTS**
Black with orange patches on its wings and tail (and browner with yellow patches in the female), the American Redstart sometimes confuses birders with its repertoire of songs, ranging from a wispy, one-note *vee-vee-vee-vee-vee* to a more

chirrupy series of rising and falling syllables. This bird lives to communicate, singing throughout the spring and summer in forests all over the eastern United States and across most of Canada. • The Cherokee hold the American Redstart in particularly high esteem. The story goes that when a huge earthquake came to the land, the redstart was the only bird with the courage to fly to the tribal people and awaken them to the danger. The little bird saved many lives, and the Creator rewarded him with the bright orange feathers he wears today. Redstart stayed with the Cherokee to boost their spirits as they repaired their homes and recovered from the damage of the earthquake, becoming even more a part of their culture. • The American Redstart's arrival every spring means renewal and rebirth to several Indigenous tribes. When the redstart appeared, they knew it was time to begin planting and otherwise put away the trappings of winter. Lenape and Miwok tribes have Redstart clans, and they use likenesses of the little bird on their clothing and in headdresses and artwork.

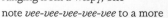

S

No. 338

Sialia currucoides

Mountain Bluebird

Twitter Bird

● LEAST CONCERN

COLLECTIVE NAMES

Breast of bluebirds | Plaza of bluebirds | Skein of bluebirds | Volery of bluebirds

SYMBOLIC MEANINGS

Happiness; Hope; Positivity.

POSSIBLE POWER

Messenger from deceased loved ones.

FOLKLORE AND FACTS

The bluest of the American bluebirds, the Mountain Bluebird inhabits the westernmost United States at higher elevations than the Western Bluebird, its closest cousin. This bluebird lends its profile to the former logo for X (formerly known as Twitter). • The Mountain Bluebird serves as the state bird of Idaho and Nevada, but for people throughout the western United States, it symbolizes hope, love, happiness, and new beginnings. It has long been a custom to believe that bluebirds carry salutations from deceased loved ones. • The Navajo sing the Bluebird Song every year at sunrise on the last day of the annual winter night-way ceremony; the lyrics open with, "Bluebird said to me: Get up, my grandchild, it is dawn." The Navajo also have a Bluebird Clan in their societal structure, as do the Hopi and Pueblo tribes. • A Native American story tells us how the bluebird got its color: The bird was gray until one night when the Dream Spirit told him to go far up into the mountains to a lake that has no inlet or outlet, so the water always stays a bright blue. "Bathe in the lake for five mornings," the Dream Spirit said, "and sing this song: 'The water is blue / I went in / And now I'm blue, too." The gray bird did as he was told, and on the fourth morning, all of his gray feathers fell out and floated away in the water. The bird didn't panic, though, and sure enough, on the fifth day, when he came out of the water, he had new, bright blue feathers.

No. 339

Sialis sialis

Eastern Bluebird

Blue Robin

● LEAST CONCERN

COLLECTIVE NAMES

Breast of bluebirds | Plaza of bluebirds | Skein of bluebirds | Volery of bluebirds

SYMBOLIC MEANINGS

Happiness; Hope; Joy.

POSSIBLE POWER

Good luck.

FOLKLORE AND FACTS

The state bird of New York and Missouri is one of the most welcome sights in the eastern United States, thanks to the nickname all bluebirds share: Bluebird of Happiness. • Bluebirds have figured in mythology for thousands of years, with the first known appearances coming from ancient China. The Indigenous Cochiti tribe tells the story of a young girl who doesn't want to marry, but does want children. The Sun impregnates her, and she has a child: A boy, whom she and the Sun name Bluebird (*Culutiwa*). Later, she has another son, whom she names Turquoise. The boys grow up and begin to ask a lot of questions about the father they have never met. Finally, she relents, and tells them about the Sun. They go to meet him, and learn that he is their father—and that this is why these bluebirds have a bright orange breast, a gift from the Sun. • Recent popular culture also reveres the cheery bluebird, from Robert Frost's poem "The Last Word of a Bluebird" to the bluebirds that fly beyond the rainbow in *The Wizard of Oz*. The common bird in all its forms delights people who believe with certainty that its appearance means good luck for all.

No. 340
Sitta

Nuthatch

5 species in the genus *Sitta*

● **LEAST CONCERN**

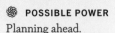 **COLLECTIVE NAME**

Booby of nuthatches

☀ **SYMBOLIC MEANINGS**

Fresh perspective; Looking at things from a different angle; Preparation.

🌀 **POSSIBLE POWER**

Planning ahead.

☾ **FOLKLORE AND FACTS**

Several species of Nuthatch appear across North America, Europe, and Asia, all with very similar appearance and habits. These birds gather nuts and seeds and store them up in the cracks in tree bark or in tree cavities, preparing for the inevitable coming of winter. • Their passion for preplanning and putting away food for another day makes Nuthatches a model of preparedness, demonstrating the power of forethought. Perhaps this is why the Navajo associate Nuthatches with old age: The birds behave responsibly with the intention of taking care of themselves. • You might think that birds that can travel quickly down a tree trunk head first would delight anyone who saw them, but the Pueblo associated anything that moved backwards or upside down with wartime, making these little birds very suspicious-looking in their eyes. • The Cherokee gave the bird the name *tsulie'na*, which means "deaf," apparently because Nuthatches have little fear of humans and allow people to get quite close to them without flying off, so they thought the birds must not hear people approach.

No. 341
Spindalis portoricensis

Puerto Rican Spindalis

Reina Mora | Stripe-Headed Tanager

● **LEAST CONCERN**

COLLECTIVE NAME

Flock of spindalis

☀ **SYMBOLIC MEANING**

Official bird of Puerto Rico.

🌀 **POSSIBLE POWER**

Standing up to boa constrictors.

☾ **FOLKLORE AND FACTS**

The eye-catching Puerto Rican Spindalis is found only on Puerto Rico, making it a prime candidate for the island's official bird. These birds have become legendary for their bravery against Puerto Rican boa constrictors, frequent attackers of the birds' nest and eggs. Unafraid to pounce on these snakes, the spindalis makes a huge racket while doing so, which invites other birds to fly in and mob the boa as well. As part of this defense scheme, Puerto Rican spindalises build their nests within a quick flight of one another, forming a line of scrimmage that presents a united front against this common enemy.

No. 342
Spinus tristis

American Goldfinch

Subspecies: Eastern | Northwestern | Pale | Willow Goldfinch

● **LEAST CONCERN**

COLLECTIVE NAMES

Charm of goldfinches | Drum of goldfinches | Pantheon of goldfinches | Troubling of goldfinches

☀ **SYMBOLIC MEANINGS**

Celebration; Forthrightness; Prosperity.

🌀 **POSSIBLE POWERS**

Camouflage; Resourcefulness.

☾ **FOLKLORE AND FACTS**

Iowa, New Jersey, and Washington all have chosen the American Goldfinch as their state bird, though Iowa and New Jersey call it Eastern Goldfinch, and Washington's subspecies is Willow Goldfinch. Widespread throughout the northern United States and Canada, the sprightly little

S

yellow bird and its more muted spouses come readily to bird feeders. • The Iroquois tell a story of how the goldfinch got its bright yellow color—a tale that other native cultures use to explain the hummingbirds' iridescence or other bright-plumaged birds. In this version, a fox chases a raccoon up a tree and waits at the bottom, but the raccoon does not come down, and eventually the fox dozes off. When he awakens, he finds that the raccoon is gone and his own eyes have been painted shut with tree resin, which has hardened and won't come off. The fox calls for help, and some drab little finches take pity on him and peck off the resin. The fox thanks them for this good deed by using some yellow flowers to color their plumage bright yellow, the color of sunshine.

No. 343

Steatornis caripensis

Oilbird

Diablotin | Guácharo

● **LEAST CONCERN**

✤ **COLLECTIVE NAME**

Echo of oilbirds

✳ **SYMBOLIC MEANINGS**

Distinction; Uniqueness.

◉ **POSSIBLE POWERS**

Carrier of souls of the deceased; Echolocation.

◐ **FOLKLORE AND FACTS**

The Oilbird recently landed at the very top of a list of the 100 most "evolutionarily distinct" birds in the world. This cave-nesting bird is the only nocturnal-flying, fruit-eating bird in the world; other nocturnal birds either eat insects or are flightless. Oilbirds also use echolocation to track one another's proximity, and to navigate in general. This combination of traits makes them more like bats than birds. • Oilbirds get their name from the layers of fat that insulate Oilbird chicks, their main source of protein until they reach adulthood. Indigenous peoples living near Oilbird caves in South America rendered the fat from these birds and used it in cooking or for fueling torches. • While ancient mythology

includes few tales of these birds, their raspy, screeching cries, usually heard only in the far reaches of dark caves, have probably figured in many a campfire horror story. Indigenous peoples believed that the strange cries were actually the souls of the deceased, passing through the cave on their way to the afterlife—and only the people who did wrong in their lives were forced through this ordeal.

No. 344

Stercorarius skua

Great Skua

Bonxie

● **LEAST CONCERN**

✤ **COLLECTIVE NAMES**

Robbery of skuas | Shishkebab of skuas

✳ **SYMBOLIC MEANINGS**

Murderer; Thief.

◉ **POSSIBLE POWERS**

Bullying; Overpowering smaller birds.

◐ **FOLKLORE AND FACTS**

The Great Skua is the only bird that breeds in both the Arctic and the Antarctic, nesting from the Orkney Islands to Iceland in the north, and from South America's southern end to within 150 miles (241 km) of the South Pole. No other living thing except daredevil humans goes closer to the South Pole than this skua does. • Fast, agile, and with no apparent conscience, the Great Skua gets many of its meals by forcing other birds to give up theirs. They nest near penguins, petrels, terns, and gulls and steal their eggs and young, or they attack gulls and other fishing birds in midair or just as they land with their catch still in their claws. While these birds do acquire some of their own meat—particularly lemmings in the north, and carrion when they miss someone else's fresh catch—their preferred feeding method is to be a jerk to everyone else. • Some have suggested that the namesake bird of the Seattle Seahawks football team may refer either to an Osprey or a skua. The Seahawks, however, are actually named for the thunderbird, a ceremonial bird of one of Seattle's local native communities, the Kwakwaka'wakw nation.

S

No. 345

Sterna paradisaea

Arctic Tern

Pickie-Terno | Sea Swallow | Tirrock

● **LEAST CONCERN**

🦅 **COLLECTIVE NAMES**
Colony of terns | Committee of terns | Ternery of terns

✹ **SYMBOLIC MEANINGS**
Endurance; Navigation; Safe return; Tenacity.

🌀 **POSSIBLE POWER**
Fierce defense.

🦊 **FOLKLORE AND FACTS**
Imagine traveling 20,000 miles
(32,187 km) in one direction,
from the waters just south of
the North Pole to the edges of
the Antarctic ice—and then
turning around and going
back six months later. This
is the great migration of
the Arctic Tern, the longest
migration of any waterbird on
Earth, with some individuals traveling as
far as 44,100 miles (70,972 km) in the global
round trip. • While widespread and numerous, the birds
can be quite difficult to see, requiring some willingness to
take a boat to a remote, rocky island off the coast of Maine
or a treacherous coastline in the Orkneys of Scotland, where
the birds congregate to avoid all the invasive mammal
species that inhabit previous nesting colony sites. Those
who make the trip soon discover that Arctic Terns defend
their nesting sites with fierce intensity—so bring a hard hat.
• Such an extraordinary bird hardly needs folklore, but one
legend tells us of an Arctic Fox approaching an Arctic Tern.
"Why do you fly so far away in winter?" the fox asks. The
tern considers this, and replies, "I just do. I never thought
about why." The fox challenges him further: "Why don't you
just stay here and see if you like it?" So the Arctic Tern resists
his own instincts and watches as all of his fellow terns depart
for the south. Soon the days grow shorter and darkness
comes, and the tern doesn't like this at all. He starts to make
ready to migrate, but finds that he is now frozen fast to the
rock. The Arctic Fox approaches the tern from behind, and
noiselessly jumps him. In moments, the tern becomes his
dinner. This is why Arctic Terns always migrate, and never
question their own motives.

No. 346

Streptopelia decaocto

Eurasian Collared Dove

Television Dove (Germany)

● **LEAST CONCERN**

🦅 **COLLECTIVE NAMES**
Bevy of doves | Covey of doves | Dole of doves | Paddling of doves | Piteousness of doves |
Pretense of doves

✹ **SYMBOLIC MEANING**
Peace.

🌀 **POSSIBLE POWER**
Communicating the woes of
the poor.

🦊 **FOLKLORE AND FACTS**
Only a handful of species
worldwide have expanded
their own range as rapidly as
the Eurasian Collared Dove.
Originally a continental European
bird, it can now be found in abundance in the
United Kingdom, most of the United States, the
Caribbean islands, Japan, southern Asia, and India. The
secret to its success is its ability to raise two or three broods
every summer, with some pairs even producing five broods.
• This dainty dove is now a fixture at bird feeders around
much of the world. The birds nest happily in backyard trees,
giving them close proximity to feeders. • Ancient Greek
mythology gives us one story of the origin of these gentle
birds: A poor maidservant toiled in a wealthy but stingy
home, where her lady paid her no more than eighteen coins
per year. She prayed to Zeus, asking that the gods tell the
world how poorly she was treated. The great god created a
dove that sang a mournful song, *deca-octo*—the Greek word
for eighteen. Eurasian Collared Dove sings to us of this
maid's woes to this very day.

S

No. 347
Streptopelia orientalis
Oriental Turtle Dove
Eastern/Western Oriental Turtle Dove | Rufous Turtle Dove

● **LEAST CONCERN**

❖ **COLLECTIVE NAMES**
Bevy of doves | Covey of doves | Paddling of doves | Piteousness of doves | Pretense of doves

❋ **SYMBOLIC MEANINGS**
Commitment; Love.

✺ **POSSIBLE POWER**
Connection between physical and spiritual world.

☾ **FOLKLORE AND FACTS**
A patch of silvery-tipped, black-and-white feathers on each side of its neck marks the Oriental Turtle Dove, making it distinctly different from other doves in its breeding range in China, and in its wintering areas in India, the Maldives, and Japan. These doves are very familiar to people who feed birds in their backyards, as sunflower seeds, the most popular backyard bird food, is a staple of their diet. • Doves were a method of communication in ancient China, with families sending them back and forth between widely separated homes to bring messages of love and commitment. Doves are mentioned in the *Book of Odes*, the oldest existing collection of Chinese poetry, and the Daoist fertility goddess Songzi Niangniang sometimes is drawn with doves on her headdress. Customs involving doves included giving an elderly person a jade scepter with a dove carved at the top, wishing them a long life. Doves are often displayed in meditation rooms, as an old Chinese saying notes that when a dove sings, the veil between the physical and spiritual worlds is lifted, and harmony and inner peace are possible.

No. 348
Streptopelia risoria
Barbary Dove
Java Dove | Ring Dove | Ringed Turtle Dove | Ringneck Dove | Sacred White Dove

● **DOMESTICATED**

❖ **COLLECTIVE NAMES**
Bevy of doves | Covey of doves | Paddling of doves | Piteousness of doves | Pretense of doves

❋ **SYMBOLIC MEANINGS**
Commitment; Love.

✺ **POSSIBLE POWER**
Yet to be discovered.

☾ **FOLKLORE AND FACTS**
For a dove kept domestically and used in magic acts on stages around the world, the Barbary Dove's history is missing a lot of specifics. Some say it's a domesticated subspecies of the Eurasian Collared Dove, while others say it came from the African Collared Dove. Some believe Barbary Doves have been around in captivity for thousands of years and that these are the doves mentioned in the Bible, while others note that the first actual record of them appeared in 1758, so their origin as domestic birds is much more recent. • Whatever the truth may be, these doves are often combined with pure white racing homing doves by people who rent doves for release at weddings and other ceremonies, a practice for which the homing doves have been trained to return to their dovecote. Barbary Doves are not homing doves, so they are often lost in the wild at these events. Left to their own devices, they do not survive. If you are considering such a release, be sure to ask the supplier about the dove species and how they will be returned to their owner.

No. 349

Streptopelia turtur

European Turtle Dove

Turtle Dove

● **VULNERABLE**

⚘ COLLECTIVE NAMES

Bevy of doves | Covey of doves |
Paddling of doves | Piteousness of doves |
Pretense of doves

☀ SYMBOLIC MEANINGS

Commitment; Love.

✺ POSSIBLE POWER

Sacred to Greek and Roman gods.

☾ FOLKLORE AND FACTS

"Four calling birds, three French hens, two turtle doves …" The second-day birds of "The Twelve Days of Christmas" actually exist, and if you have wondered about their peculiar name, it may surprise you to learn it has nothing to do with the reptile. "Turtle" is actually an English spelling of their onomatopoetic song, *tur-tur*. • A smaller dove than most, this Turtle Dove's range covers much of Europe and the Middle East, and it migrates into central Africa south of the Sahara Desert. • Turtle Doves have a long and storied history: Demeter, Greek goddess of the harvest, held the Turtle Dove sacred, as did Fides, the Roman goddess of trust. While Turtle Doves are not specifically mentioned in the Bible, the doves referenced throughout Leviticus, Numbers, and Song of Songs were most likely European Turtle Doves: Song of Songs (2:12) makes reference to the cooing of doves as a first sign of spring, and they are present in the Gospels of Matthew, Mark, and John, as products sold in the temple courts when Jesus enters and drives out the merchants.

No. 350

Strigops habroptilus

Kākāpō

Owl Parrot

● **CRITICALLY ENDANGERED**

⚘ COLLECTIVE NAMES

Booming of kākāpō | Island of kākāpō | Looming of kākāpō | Rumble of kākāpō |
Trek of kākāpō

☀ SYMBOLIC MEANING

Conservation.

✺ POSSIBLE POWERS

Climbing; Jogging; Walking long distances.

☾ FOLKLORE AND FACTS

The Kākāpō differs from all other parrots in the world in a number of important ways. It has the facial disc of an owl with forward-facing eyes, and the distinction of being the world's only flightless parrot, as well as the heaviest one— but it can climb trees like a monkey, and it can jog across the forest floor for several kilometers at a stretch. • The Kākāpō is nocturnal, and it is the only parrot that mates using a lek system: The birds walk from their usual range to a mating area that may be as much as 3 miles (5 km) away, where the males battle for the right to mate with one or more females. • Despite all of its skills and evolutionary adaptations to its environment, the Kākāpō found itself no match for the mammals imported to New Zealand when humans arrived. The bird could avoid the raptors that hunted it by day, but when night-hunting rats, stoats, ferrets, weasels, cats, and dogs entered Kākāpō territory, it simply could not compete. Today the Kākāpō is critically endangered, with zoos around the world participating in a recovery program to maintain the species in captivity, and New Zealand's Department of Conservation working to protect the bird's habitats from invasive mammals. • Sir David Attenborough's *The Life of Birds* BBC nature series devoted an episode to the Kākāpō. Stephen Fry and Mark Carwardine's reboot of *The Life of Birds* spent time annually on updates about the Kākāpō's recovery—most famously in 2009, when a Kākāpō attempted to mate with Carwardine's head and the clip went viral. This elevated the Kākāpō to worldwide fame, leading New Zealand to make it the national spokes-bird for conservation of wildlife throughout the country.

No. 351

Strix nebulosa

Great Gray Owl

Bearded Owl | | Cinereous Owl | Lapland Owl | Phantom of the Forest | Sooty Owl |
Spectral Owl | Spruce Owl

● **LEAST CONCERN**

✤ **COLLECTIVE NAMES**

Group of owls | Hoot of owls | Parliament of owls

✺ **SYMBOLIC MEANINGS**

Balance; Trust.

◉ **POSSIBLE POWERS**

Messenger from the Underworld; Silent hunting.

◔ **FOLKLORE AND FACTS**

No one forgets their first Great Gray Owl, its bright yellow eyes surrounded by the concentric circles of its flat, gray face The largest owl in its North American range and one of the largest in northern Europe and Asia, this owl flies through the forest so silently that it acquired the nickname Phantom of the Forest, and the secondary species name Spectral Owl. Even its Latin name, *nebulosa* ("foggy" in English), speaks to its stealthy movements. • Great Gray Owls are found in the northernmost forests around the world. Mixed conifer forests with swamp areas are its preferred habitat, where it can watch the ground for rodents and descend on the unsuspecting critter with a single pounce. It can even spot moles and other animals burrowing in foot-deep snow. • Most indigenous cultures around the world see their resident owl species as a messenger from the Underworld, calling in the night to announce the departure of a human soul and its arrival in the next realm. The Great Gray Owl embodies all of these beliefs, sitting in watchful stillness or gliding through the treetops in darkness, its low, repeated *hoo* an eerie lament in a silent forest.

No. 352

Struthio camelus

Common Ostrich

Ostrich

● **LEAST CONCERN**

✤ **COLLECTIVE NAMES**

Flock of ostrich | Herd of ostrich | Pride of ostrich | Troop of ostrich

✺ **SYMBOLIC MEANINGS**

Justice; Purity; Truth.

◉ **POSSIBLE POWERS**

Devotion; Fertility.

◔ **FOLKLORE AND FACTS**

Pliny the Elder, naturalist of ancient Rome, made observations about the Common Ostrich that set the tone for millennia of misunderstandings about the world's largest and heaviest bird. He believed that the Common Ostrich could eat iron and glass, and that the bird dug a hole in the sand and stuck its head into it to hide from whatever adversity might be plaguing it. Ostriches cannot and do not eat manmade materials, nor do they stick their heads in the sand to hide—in fact, they nest in the sand by digging a hole and laying their eggs in it, a behavior that Pliny must have mistaken for cowardice. • Now found almost exclusively on farms around the world, ostriches have become very useful to humans: their plumes are harvested for feather dusters (without harming the bird), their very lean meat substitutes nicely for beef, and their skin produces a particularly strong and desirable leather. • Ostriches have played a role in human lives for more than 5,000 years, with drawings of them appearing in Egyptian tombs and the shells of their enormous eggs serving as water carriers, perfume holders, and drinking cups. Greeks and Romans hung Ostrich eggs in their temples as offerings to their gods, and European Christians in medieval times believed that the eggs symbolized the Virgin Mary. • People were once convinced that ostriches did not sit on their eggs like other birds, but stared at them continuously for weeks on end to make them hatch. If the bird looked away even for a moment, the eggs would fail. In reality, both male and female ostriches alternate sitting on the eggs day and night, and then work together to raise their chicks.

S

No. 353

Sturnella magna

Eastern Meadowlark

● **NEAR THREATENED**

✻ **COLLECTIVE NAMES**
Field of meadowlarks | Flock of meadowlarks

✳ **SYMBOLIC MEANINGS**
Homemaking; Music; Poetry.

✺ **POSSIBLE POWER**
Generosity.

☾ **FOLKLORE AND FACTS**
Nearly identical except for their very different songs, Eastern and Western Meadowlarks divide North America between them, their territories overlapping in a narrow north-south band through the Great Plains. • Actually members of the blackbird family, these birds are songbirds of open grasslands and meadows, standing atop fenceposts and tall wildflowers and singing until they establish their breeding territories and go to ground to build nests and raise their young. • A Cherokee story tells us of the Bird with Big Feet: A meadowlark lives deep in the tall grasses because other birds and animals tease her mercilessly about her big feet. One day, a grasshopper comes to find the bird to ask for her help. A mother bird has laid her eggs in a field that is about to be harvested, and she knows that the harvesting activity will crush her eggs and kill her young. The grasshopper says to the meadowlark, "You are the right one to help, because of your big feet." Sure enough, the meadowlark comes to the aid of the distraught bird, picks up her eggs with her feet, and carries them to an open field. The mother bird is so grateful that she tells all of the other animals what a wonderful thing the meadowlark did for her. From then on, no one teased the meadowlark, and she could stand atop a fencepost and sing to her heart's content.

No. 354

Sturnella neglecta

Western Meadowlark

● **LEAST CONCERN**

✻ **COLLECTIVE NAMES**
Field of meadowlarks | Flock of meadowlarks

✳ **SYMBOLIC MEANING**
Truth-telling.

✺ **POSSIBLE POWERS**
Communication; Oracle.

☾ **FOLKLORE AND FACTS**
The Western Meadowlark serves as the state bird of six states: Kansas, Montana, Nebraska, North Dakota, Oregon, and Wyoming. Widespread and prevalent throughout the Great Plains, western deserts, chaparral, and other open spaces, this meadowlark's voice is part of the landscape of the western United States. • Indigenous Peoples thought the Western Meadowlark's song provided insights into the future, making its every syllable a soothsaying. Meadowlarks sang to hunters of where to find game, or they brought news of an upcoming wedding or an impending death. Pawnee, Omaha, and Dakota peoples attributed actual words to the song, differing with each situation (while the bird's song itself stayed the same): In particular, the Dakota people tell a story of a rough season with little game, when many people went hungry. The tribe camped along a stream when two spirits appeared before them, telling them where to find herds of antelope and buffalo. The hunters went to the places the spirits sent them and came home with plenty of meat for the entire tribe. The tribe wished to thank the two spirits, but when they returned to the stream, they found only two meadowlarks singing to them. They knew these birds were the spirits in disguise, and honored them for their help. • The Dakotas of Standing Rock Reservation interpreted a meadowlark's song as a prophecy that the United States would have a great victory overseas. On November 10, 1918, the day before the World War I armistice was called, the Dakotas reported that the meadowlark oracle had said, "The President has conquered and the boys are coming home." Sure enough, the war ended the next day, sealing the meadowlark's role in seeing the future.

S

No. 355
Sturnus vulgaris

European Starling

Common Starling

● **LEAST CONCERN**

🐾 **COLLECTIVE NAMES**

Chattering of starling | Cloud of starlings | Congregation of starlings | Murmuration of starlings

✳ **SYMBOLIC MEANINGS**

Communication; Freedom to love.

🌀 **POSSIBLE POWER**

Murmuration.

🌙 **FOLKLORE AND FACTS**

In 1890, Eugene Schieffelin, president of the American Acclimatization Society, released sixty European Starlings into New York's Central Park as part of the society's mission: Bring species from the native countries of many European immigrants into the areas where these people settled, to enrich the flora and fauna and to add species these people recognized from home. The birds thrived and multiplied, and today more than 150 million starlings crowd North America's streets, fields, backyards, bridges, and cities, huge flocks moving in spellbinding synchronization across the skies. Similar releases took place all over the world, making the starling one of the most widespread and numerous birds on the planet. • Starlings played a role in happy marriages in the United Kingdom in the mid-1700s, when a new marriage act in England required couples under a certain age to have their parents' permission to marry. Desperate to get out from under this law, many young people fled to Scotland, where they had been told to watch for a murmuration of starlings that flew constantly over Gretna Green. Here the biggest flock in the country drew lovers to the place where they could marry freely—and Gretna Green remains a romantic destination and the area's marriage capital.

No. 356
Sula nebouxii

Blue-Footed Booby

● **LEAST CONCERN**

🐾 **COLLECTIVE NAMES**

Congress of boobies | Hatch of boobies | Trap of boobies

✳ **SYMBOLIC MEANINGS**

Balance; Creativity; Fearlessness; Fun.

🌀 **POSSIBLE POWERS**

Agility; Cleverness.

🌙 **FOLKLORE AND FACTS**

No other name is required for the bird with the bright blue feet—Blue-Footed Booby describes everything unique about this large seabird. Like all members of its family, the Blue-Footed Booby lives most of its life at sea in the Pacific Ocean, making it much more dexterous on the wing than it is on its feet. Stumbling a bit as it makes its way over rocks, this bird can look silly enough to make you laugh out loud, but that's just part of its charm. Even more disarming is its lack of fear of humans, allowing people to approach with their cameras and exhibiting real curiosity about what we are. • "Booby" comes from the Spanish word *bobo*, which means "stupid" in English, but despite their peculiar gait on land and their clueless expression, boobies are clever birds at sea. They dive straight down into the waves to bring up a mouthful of sardines, as agile underwater as they are in the air. When they return to their nesting areas on islands including the Galapagos, they use their blue feet to attract a mate, dancing about and lifting their feet so their potential mate can get a closer look. Here they lose the clumsiness, knowing exactly what they are about.

No. 357

Tadorna ferruginea

Ruddy Shelduck

Brahminy Duck

● LEAST CONCERN

✿ COLLECTIVE NAMES

Badelynge of ducks | Plump of ducks | Raft of ducks (when on water)

✹ SYMBOLIC MEANING

Marital fidelity.

✺ POSSIBLE POWER

Sacred in Buddhism and Hinduism.

☾ FOLKLORE AND FACTS

The aptly named Ruddy Shelduck glows
orange against calm waters, its
strikingly paler head rising
above its bright back and
wings. This Asian
duck can be found all
across the continent
in spring and summer, until it
heads south to its wintering grounds
on the Indian subcontinent. A dabbling
duck with a preference for nocturnal hours, it escapes many
of the threats that ducks encounter in areas with daylight
hunting, so its population holds steady even as wetland
habitats are drained for other uses. • How exactly these
ducks have been selected by Buddhists and Hindus as sacred
is not really clear from outside of these circles, but some
believe that they received their local name, Brahminy Duck,
because these birds are the same color as the Brahmins' robes
of ancient India. • Beyond the ducks' religious significance,
an Indian folk legend tells the story of a pair of lovers who
made a fatal mistake: They interrupted sages during their
time of meditation. The angered sages cursed the pair and
turned them into Ruddy Shelducks. As part of the curse, the
pair had to separate every day from sundown to sunrise, and
were reduced to plaintive calls to each other throughout the
night. The ducks remain apart in the dark to this day.

No. 358

Tauraco erythrolophus

Red-Crested Turaco

Go-Away Bird

● LEAST CONCERN

✿ COLLECTIVE NAME

Flock of turacos

✹ SYMBOLIC MEANING

National bird of Angola.

✺ POSSIBLE POWER

Messenger from the dead.

☾ FOLKLORE AND FACTS

The tropical forests and lowlands of Angola are the only
place on Earth where the Red-Crested Turaco occurs in
the wild, but it's quite common and easy to see in this area.
These turacos stay together in colonies of up to thirty birds,
making them even easier to find, and their *go-away* call helps
narrow down their location. • Like other turacos in southern
Africa, the Red-Crested Turaco is believed to have the power
to bestow good luck on people, even to the point of gaining
wealth or improving fertility. Some believe it may be able to
hear messages from the dead, and somehow bring word of
the spirits of dead loved ones to their living relatives.
• The Red-Crested Turaco became famous for a short time
in 1998, when it appeared in
the movie remake of *The
Parent Trap*. The bird stood
on Meredith's chest as
she slept in her tent on a
camping trip in Northern
California—an impossible
place for this bird to appear in
the wild, setting the birding
world abuzz in high dudgeon
for a short but exciting time.

T

No. 359

Terathopius ecaudatus

Bateleur

Gawarakko | Kgwadira | Nkona | Petleke

● **ENDANGERED**

COLLECTIVE NAMES

Aerie of eagles | Brood of eagles | Congregation of eagles | Exaltation of eagles

☀ SYMBOLIC MEANINGS

Service with wisdom; Zimbabwean pride.

POSSIBLE POWER

Messenger from deceased ancestors.

FOLKLORE AND FACTS

As thrilling as an eagle sighting may be, spotting a Bateleur truly takes the viewer's breath away. Its jet-black head and chest, brown back, gray wings with white bands, and bright orange and red bill make it easy to distinguish from other large African birds, especially in flight or when landing at the top of a bare tree. • The

Bateleur is one of the eagles that may have inspired the Zimbabwe Bird, an emblem discovered in the ruins of the city of Great Zimbabwe, built in the eleventh century. The original perched eagle was carved from soapstone and stood atop columns on walls within the city. Anthropologists speculate that either the Bateleur or African Fish Eagle (see No. 190) was the model for this totem. The Bateleur may be the frontrunner because the Shona people who built the city believed that this bird brought messages from Mwari, their god, and from their deceased ancestors. • Other cultures throughout Africa believe that the Bateleur served as confidant and advisor to its masters throughout their mythology. Sultans often kept and traveled with a Bateleur, a representation of their wealth and power.

No. 360

Tetrao urogallus

Western Capercaillie

Cock-of-the-Woods | Eurasian Capercaillie Heather Cock | Western Grouse | Wood Grouse

● **LEAST CONCERN**

COLLECTIVE NAME

Tok of capercaillie

☀ SYMBOLIC MEANINGS

Helping others;
Hidden treasures.

POSSIBLE POWER

Bringer of riches.

FOLKLORE AND FACTS

Pine forests throughout Europe and Asia provide the preferred habitat of this large member of the grouse family, but its numbers have been threatened

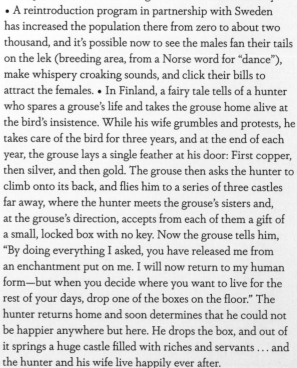

over the last two centuries by clear-cutting of forests, especially in the UK. In Scotland, for example, just 1 percent of the original pine woods remain, and with the forests went the capercaillie until not a single one lived in the country. • A reintroduction program in partnership with Sweden has increased the population there from zero to about two thousand, and it's possible now to see the males fan their tails on the lek (breeding area, from a Norse word for "dance"), make whispery croaking sounds, and click their bills to attract the females. • In Finland, a fairy tale tells of a hunter who spares a grouse's life and takes the grouse home alive at the bird's insistence. While his wife grumbles and protests, he takes care of the bird for three years, and at the end of each year, the grouse lays a single feather at his door: First copper, then silver, and then gold. The grouse then asks the hunter to climb onto its back, and flies him to a series of three castles far away, where the hunter meets the grouse's sisters and, at the grouse's direction, accepts from each of them a gift of a small, locked box with no key. Now the grouse tells him, "By doing everything I asked, you have released me from an enchantment put on me. I will now return to my human form—but when you decide where you want to live for the rest of your days, drop one of the boxes on the floor." The hunter returns home and soon determines that he could not be happier anywhere but here. He drops the box, and out of it springs a huge castle filled with riches and servants . . . and the hunter and his wife live happily ever after.

T

No. 361
Threskiornis aethiopicus
African Sacred Ibis

● **LEAST CONCERN**

🐾 **COLLECTIVE NAMES**
Colony of ibises | Stand of ibises |
Wedge of ibises | Whiteness of ibises

✹ **SYMBOLIC MEANING**
Living representation of Thoth.

🌀 **POSSIBLE POWER**
Sacrifice.

🌙 **FOLKLORE AND FACTS**
For as long as a thousand years, Ancient Egyptians believed that the African Sacred Ibis was the earthly form of Thoth, god of the moon and many other parts of human lives, and calculator of the formulae that led to the Earth's creation. To honor such a powerful and influential god, they killed millions of these ibises over the course of a millennium, embalmed them, and mummified them—wrapping the carcasses in linen and saturating them with resin, and then placing them in caverns beneath cities throughout Egypt. Thousands of years later, between 1798 and 1801, archaeologists on an expedition for Napoleon Bonaparte discovered this mass sacrifice of ibises. When more archaeologists studied the sites in more detail, they unearthed staggering numbers of mummified birds: Four million birds in the tombs at Tuna el-Gebel alone. • While the African Sacred Ibis is no longer found in Egypt, its numbers are stable farther south, with more than 200,000 of them throughout central and southern Africa.

No. 362
Thryothorus ludovicianus
Carolina Wren
Great Carolina Wren

● **LEAST CONCERN**

🐾 **COLLECTIVE NAMES**
Cabinet of wrens | Chime of wrens |
Flock of wrens

✹ **SYMBOLIC MEANING**
State bird of South Carolina.

🌀 **POSSIBLE POWER**
Yet to be discovered.

🌙 **FOLKLORE AND FACTS**
The shy bird with the loud voice and the *teakettle-teakettle-teakettle* song, the Carolina Wren graces the eastern half of the United States and extreme southern Canada with its nimble presence. It's the second-largest US wren, just slightly smaller than a Cactus Wren. • Fans of the Carolina Wren waged a long battle in South Carolina to name it the state's official bird. The South Carolina Federated Women's Club chose it as the unofficial state bird back in 1930, when many state legislatures across the country had started choosing official state symbols. South Carolina's legislature got on the symbol bandwagon in 1939, but they ignored the women's club's nomination and named the Northern Mockingbird as the state bird. This kicked the women's efforts into high gear, and they waged a campaign to convince the General Assembly to choose the bird that actually had Carolina in its name. In 1948, the state repealed its earlier choice, and Governor Strom Thurmond signed an act that made the Carolina Wren South Carolina's state bird.

No. 363
Tinamus major
Great Tinamou

● **LEAST CONCERN**

🐾 **COLLECTIVE NAME**
Flock of tinamous

✹ **SYMBOLIC MEANINGS**
Deception; Hiding in the dark.

🌀 **POSSIBLE POWER**
Concealment.

🌙 **FOLKLORE AND FACTS**
Of all the birds we can see in the tropical forests of South America, the dun-colored Great Tinamou is one of the most difficult to spot, both because of its dull plumage and its preference for shadowy forests with thick vegetation. Panamanian folklore has a theory about this: After the Great Flood covered the world in water, the sun returned and a rainbow appeared. The Great Tinamou saw the rainbow and became frightened of its intense colors, and flew away from Noah's ark and the other animals to hide in the murkiest part of the forest. It lives there to this day, shunning the colors it can see from a distance and remaining in the dark. • The Great Tinamou does not itself try to deceive people, but the Guahibo tribe of eastern Colombia tells the story of one of its young men rowing a canoe and hearing a tinamou in the distance. He paddled toward the bank, but as he got closer, he heard that the bird's call had a

harshness he'd never heard from a Great Tinamou before. Just as he decided to push away from the bank, a jaguar came running out of the vegetation. Ever since, forest tribes have believed that jaguars imitate the tinamou's call to lure the birds out of hiding, so they can catch and eat them.

No. 364

Todiramphus sanctus

Sacred Kingfisher

Green Kingfisher | New Zealand Kingfisher | Tree Kingfisher | Wood Kingfisher

● **LEAST CONCERN**

✿ **COLLECTIVE NAMES**

Clique of kingfishers | Concentration of kingfishers | Crown of kingfishers

✴ **SYMBOLIC MEANING**

Power over the ocean.

✦ **POSSIBLE POWER**

Carrying the souls of the dead.

☺ **FOLKLORE AND FACTS**

This medium-sized Australian kingfisher somehow convinced Polynesian Indigenous Peoples that it had power over the ocean and its waves; they treated this bright green bird with great respect to keep it from sending them storms. • The Indigenous Wurundjeri people of Australia believed that when the Sacred Kingfishers left their area at the end of the summer, they took with them the souls of the dead, an efficient cleanup operation for people and birds. This made it particularly disturbing when the kingfishers stopped coming to the Melbourne area for more than twenty years, in what became a clarion call to local environmentalists to determine why the birds were gone and what could be done to bring them back. • This movement in the late 1970s led to the 1982 establishment of CERES, an education center, community garden, and urban farm along the Merri and Darebin Creeks in Melbourne. As the project grew, people watched closely to see if the Sacred Kingfisher would return. It took ten years for the bird to put in an appearance, but in 1992, one showed up, and the birds have returned here during migration every year since. This community now holds an event every November with storytellers, dancers, singers, and schoolchildren to retell the story of the bird's return to Merri Creek.

No. 365

Torgos tracheliotos

Lappet-Faced Vulture

Nubian Vulture

● **ENDANGERED**

✿ **COLLECTIVE NAMES**

Colony of vultures | Committee of vultures | Kettle of vultures | Wake of vultures

✴ **SYMBOLIC MEANINGS**

Guardian; Maternal love.

✦ **POSSIBLE POWER**

Protection for Nekheb and kings.

☺ **FOLKLORE AND FACTS**

Ancient Egyptians revered their local vultures from the earliest days of their worship, back in 3200 BCE. The featherless red head, blue-tipped bill, and white chest of the Lappet-Faced Vulture became synonymous with Nekhbet, patron of the city of Nekheb, whom the Egyptians portrayed as a vulture in their iconography.

The vulture appeared next to a stiffly upright cobra in the classic "snake charmer" pose, as well as hovering over the land holding a shen symbol, which meant protection for the city that bore her name. • Before the advancement of science, people believed that all vultures were female, and that their eggs were fertilized by the east wind. This made every vulture a maternal figure, so frescos often bore paintings of vultures of several different species. The full commitment to this belief did not become fully apparent to archaeologists, however, until the opening of the tomb of Tutankhamun in 1922, when the boy king was found in his sarcophagus wearing a solid gold pendant with a spot-on depiction of a Lappet-Faced Vulture. Surely this last veneration of Egypt's largest vulture proved that this bird was sacred to these people, providing Tutankhamun protection as he passed from this world to the next.

T

No. 366

Toxostoma rufum

Brown Thrasher

Brown Thrush | Fox-Colored Thrush

● **LEAST CONCERN**

⚝ **COLLECTIVE NAME**
Flock of thrashers

☀ **SYMBOLIC MEANING**
State bird of Georgia.

🌀 **POSSIBLE POWER**
Mimicry.

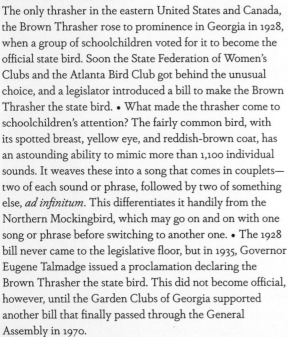

🜨 **FOLKLORE AND FACTS**
The only thrasher in the eastern United States and Canada, the Brown Thrasher rose to prominence in Georgia in 1928, when a group of schoolchildren voted for it to become the official state bird. Soon the State Federation of Women's Clubs and the Atlanta Bird Club got behind the unusual choice, and a legislator introduced a bill to make the Brown Thrasher the state bird. • What made the thrasher come to schoolchildren's attention? The fairly common bird, with its spotted breast, yellow eye, and reddish-brown coat, has an astounding ability to mimic more than 1,100 individual sounds. It weaves these into a song that comes in couplets—two of each sound or phrase, followed by two of something else, *ad infinitum*. This differentiates it handily from the Northern Mockingbird, which may go on and on with one song or phrase before switching to another one. • The 1928 bill never came to the legislative floor, but in 1935, Governor Eugene Talmadge issued a proclamation declaring the Brown Thrasher the state bird. This did not become official, however, until the Garden Clubs of Georgia supported another bill that finally passed through the General Assembly in 1970.

No. 367

Trochilidae

Hummingbird

Flying Jewels

● **LEAST CONCERN (312 SPECIES)**

● **VULNERABLE (13 SPECIES)**

● **NEAR THREATENED (20 SPECIES)**

● **ENDANGERED (13 SPECIES)**

● **CRITICALLY ENDANGERED (8 SPECIES)**

⚝ **COLLECTIVE NAMES**
Charm of hummingbirds | Chattering of hummingbirds | Hover of hummingbirds | Shimmer of hummingbirds

☀ **SYMBOLIC MEANINGS**
Magic; Sun in disguise.

🌀 **POSSIBLE POWERS**
Courtship of the moon; Emissaries of the sun.

🜨 **FOLKLORE AND FACTS**
Tiny jewels that move like no other being on earth, hummingbirds may have more myths and fairy stories told about them than any other bird family. Their ability to hover above a flower or feeder as they drink the nectar, their speed and grace in the air, their myriad colors and plumages, and their lack of fear of humans all make these little birds something special in every culture. • Mayans decided that hummingbirds were emissaries of the sun, come to Earth as messengers or to court the moon. One Mayan legend speculates that the Creator made the first two hummingbirds out of scraps left over from making all the other birds, and that he so delighted in his creation that he held a wedding for these two tiny birds, with butterflies and spiders as the attendants. When the sun reached the birds, they lit up like fairies. • In North America, a Navajo legend tells of a Hummingbird that was sent straight up into the sky to see what lay beyond it. The answer: Nothing at all; it just went black. • The Cherokee tell a story of a woman courted by a crane and a Hummingbird, who chooses the Hummingbird because he is so pretty. The crane objects, and he proposes a contest: Both birds should fly all the way around the world, and whichever of them returns first will marry the woman. She agrees, certain that the speedy little Hummingbird will win the contest, but she fails to take into account that the crane can fly all night, while the Hummingbird burns energy so quickly that he must rest overnight. The crane circles the globe and returns first, but the woman, repulsed by the crane's drab plumage and long neck, refuses to marry him anyway. • A Mexican legend tells of a Taroscan woman who makes sure a Hummingbird at her home has sugar water every day, even though the area is stricken with drought. The grateful Hummingbird teaches her to weave baskets in a special way that she finds beautiful and useful. To this day, baskets in these patterns are used in celebrations on the Day of the Dead.

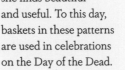

T

No. 368

Trochilus polytmus

Red-Billed Streamertail

Doctor Bird | God Bird | Scissors Tail

● **LEAST CONCERN**

🐾 **COLLECTIVE NAMES**

Charm of hummingbirds | Chattering of hummingbirds | Hover of hummingbirds | Shimmer of hummingbirds

✹ **SYMBOLIC MEANING**

National bird of Jamaica.

🌀 **POSSIBLE POWER**

Reincarnation of souls.

☾ **FOLKLORE AND FACTS**

"The most beautiful bird in Jamaica, and some say the most beautiful bird in the world, is the streamer-tail or doctor humming-bird," wrote Ian Fleming, the first line in his short story "For Your Eyes Only." It's hard to argue with that: the male Red-Billed Streamertail's dark crest and nape, glimmering green back and wings, bright red bill, and 5-inch (13 cm)-long tail streamers set it apart from all other hummingbirds on the island. The streamers and black cap remind many Jamaicans of an old-fashioned doctor in a tailcoat and top hat, so it enjoys the nickname "doctor bird" throughout the island. • Such a wondrous bird could not possibly exist just for the pleasure of doing so, so the native Arawaks, the first inhabitants of Jamaica, decided that each Red-Billed Streamertail must be a reincarnation of a dead loved one. The bird's ability to elude predators by flying off with great speed earned it the nickname "God Bird," imbued with magical powers that made it virtually impossible to catch, thus further protecting the soul within. • As the most abundant hummingbird in Jamaica, the Red-Billed Streamertail and its close relative, the Black-Billed Streamertail, were the logical choices to become the island's national bird. The two birds were lumped together just for this decision, as the red-billed bird is found everywhere on the island except for its far eastern tip, and the black-billed bird inhabits only that eastern end.

No. 369

Troglodytes troglodytes

Eurasian Wren

Northern Wren

● **LEAST CONCERN**

🐾 **COLLECTIVE NAMES**

Cabinet of wrens | Chime of wrens | Flock of wrens

✹ **SYMBOLIC MEANINGS**

Freshness; New insights.

🌀 **POSSIBLE POWERS**

Good luck; Inclusion in Celtic zodiac.

☾ **FOLKLORE AND FACTS**

The tiny Eurasian Wren became its own species according to the IOC in 2010, in a split that also acknowledged the Winter Wren and Pacific Wren in the United States as separate species. The only wren in Europe, this little bird could not help but come to the attention of ancient Celts living in the UK's forests, so they made it part of the Celtic Zodiac.
• If you are born between June 10 and July 7, your Celtic animal sign is the wren, making you a natural caregiver and a person of sweet disposition. The Wren sign gives you the ability to remain calm in a crisis, to work to get what you want, and to lead projects for your community.
• Wrens have figured prominently in European folklore for centuries: Sailors believe that carrying a wren feather with them was good luck—but the wren had to be slain on New Year's Day for it to become lucky. In a story told by Plutarch that may apply to either this wren or the Goldcrest (No. 319), in a contest to decide which bird would be king of all birds, the title would go to the bird that flew the highest. The wren stowed away on the eagle's back, staying in place until all other birds had tired and dropped back down to the ground. When the eagle's strength finally flagged, the wren jumped out and flew higher, proving that cleverness is more important than strength and endurance.

No. 370

Turdus grayi

Clay-Colored Thrush

Clarín Jilguero (Mexico) | Clay-Colored Robin | Yigüirro (Costa Rica)

● **LEAST CONCERN**

🐾 **COLLECTIVE NAMES**

Hermitage of thrushes | Mutation of thrushes | Skein of thrushes

SYMBOLIC MEANINGS
Fertility; Renewal.

POSSIBLE POWER
Indicator of healthy harvest.

FOLKLORE AND FACTS
Why would Costa Rica, a nation that has attracted more than 800 bird species to its yards, forests, and mountains— some of which are the most colorful birds in the world— choose a relatively drab-looking bird like the Clay-Colored Thrush as its national symbol? Familiarity breeds comfort in this case, as this tawny bird always begins singing just as the rainy, green season begins, a good omen for healthy harvests to come. • Costa Ricans have known the Clay-Colored Thrush since long before recorded history, making it an old, dependable friend and a frequent backyard visitor throughout the country. Numerous at feeders throughout the Lower Rio Grande Valley in Texas, this bird is also familiar in central and southern Mexico, with the southernmost part of its range in Colombia. • One folk tale from the Mayan culture tells of the relationship between a seed and Xkook, the Mayan name for the Clay-Colored Thrush. Writer Hai-Dang Phan tells this story in the *New England Review* (paraphrased here): When we plant a seed, the seed is afraid, because the Underworld is dark. But in the world of the sun, Xkook showers its song on the Earth, and the song filters down through the ground with the rain, and keeps the seed company in the darkness. Comforted, the seed germinates, and the crop grows.

No. 371
Turdus merula

Eurasian Blackbird
Blackbird | Blackie | Common Blackbird

● **LEAST CONCERN**

COLLECTIVE NAMES
Grind of blackbirds | Merl of blackbirds

SYMBOLIC MEANING
Sacred, but potentially sinister.

POSSIBLE POWER
Harbinger of death.

FOLKLORE AND FACTS
Few birds have had more songs and rhymes about them than the Eurasian Blackbird, the star of The Beatles' song "Blackbird" and the fourth-day bird in "The Twelve Days of Christmas," just for starters. Historians believe that "four calling birds" actually started out as "four colly birds," a Middle English word for "black as coal," making it clear that only the Common Blackbird could play this role.
• Of course, one of the weirdest and most cryptic songs about this familiar bird is in the nursery rhyme "Sing a Song of Sixpence": "Sing a song of sixpence / A pocket full of rye, / Four and twenty blackbirds baked in a pie. / When the pie is opened, the birds began to sing, / Oh, wasn't that a dainty dish to set before the king?" It turns out that in olden times, the royal kitchen invented a thing called a surprise pie: A pre-baked piecrust covering a crowd of live blackbirds. When the pie was opened, the birds sang if the pastry chef was lucky, and panicked and flew about the room if he was not. • These blackbirds are not associated directly with either good or bad luck, but a belief persists that if a blackbird pecks at your window, a death will soon occur. A less ominous superstition suggests that a woman can tell what career her future spouse will choose by the first bird she sees on Valentine's Day. A blackbird means that the spouse will be a clergyman, a sparrow indicates a poor man, and a goldfinch means she will marry a rich man.
• The Eurasian Blackbird serves as the national bird of Sweden, where it is known as Koltrast. The bird won a newspaper contest back in 1962 in which five thousand people voted, and despite calls for a new contest, the blackbird reigns supreme.

No. 372
Turdus migratorius

American Robin
Robin

● **LEAST CONCERN**

COLLECTIVE NAME
Worm of robins

SYMBOLIC MEANING
Arrival of spring.

POSSIBLE POWER
Good luck.

FOLKLORE AND FACTS
A Native American tale tells us how the American Robin got his red breast. Once the robin was completely brown, but one summer, he flew far north to where polar bears live.

T

One day a man and a little boy came that far north as well. Polar Bear told Robin that the man and boy would freeze up there, but Robin decided to see if the people had crumbs for him. Robin stayed near the man and boy as they built a fire and kept it going for days. One day, however, the man got sick, and he told the boy that he would have to tend the fire. The boy kept the fire going all day, but by evening he was exhausted. He went to sleep, leaving no one to tend the fire. But Robin flew off, came back with a twig, then found an ember that he fanned with his wings, and the fire flared up again. Robin kept feeding it more twigs, and he kept the man and boy warm all night. In the morning the man was better, so he took over tending the fire—but now Robin's breast was bright red from the fire, and all robins carry this mark of the good deed one did in the cold country. • So ubiquitous is the image of the first robin of spring in American culture that songs, poems, Sunday comics, and every other medium have celebrated it. Its happy arrival helped make the American Robin the state bird of three northern us states: Connecticut, Michigan, and Wisconsin.

No. 373
Turdus rufiventris
Rufous-Bellied Thrush
Red-Bellied Thrush | Sabiá-laranjeira (Brazil)

● **LEAST CONCERN**

✿ **COLLECTIVE NAME**
Mutation of thrushes

✳ **SYMBOLIC MEANINGS**
Beauty; Connection to the land; Simplicity.

✺ **POSSIBLE POWER**
Spirit of the Brazilian people.

☾ **FOLKLORE AND FACTS**
One of Brazil's most common birds, this beloved songster is present there year-round, but gathers by the thousands throughout the nation's urban and rural forests from August through November to sing all night in urban wooded areas. Its orange belly gives it its name, while its solid brown-gray mantle and pale-streaked breast indicate its genetic link to other thrushes in the Americas. • Much beloved by the people of Brazil, the Rufous-Bellied Thrush appears in many folk songs and in the poetry of Carlos Drummond de Andrade, drawing a connection between the bird, its song, and the souls of common Brazilian people. Gonçalves Dias, writing in Portugal in 1843, wrote in the poem "Song of Exile" about his longing for his homeland in Brazil: "My land has

palm trees where the thrush sings, the birds that chirp here don't chirp like they do there…" • Like so many birds in South America, the Rufous-Bellied Thrush faces threats of habitat loss as developers destroy forests to make way for their own enterprises. Conservation efforts are underway in Brazil to protect this bird, and the added protections it receives as the national bird help keep its population healthy and thriving.

No. 374
Turdus viscivorus
Mistle Thrush
Jeremy Joy | Missel Thrush | Mizzly Dick | Stormcock

● **LEAST CONCERN**

✿ **COLLECTIVE NAME**
Mutation of thrushes

✳ **SYMBOLIC MEANINGS**
Courage in a storm; Self-undoing.

✺ **POSSIBLE POWER**
Symbiotic relationship with mistletoe.

☾ **FOLKLORE AND FACTS**
The bird that will sing even in the face of wind and rain (hence the nickname "stormcock"), the Mistle Thrush has a long and storied past throughout Europe, western Asia, and northern Africa. Known for its love of mistletoe and holly berries, it lives in parks, woodlands, and farmland, as long as it can locate its favorite berries and a healthy number of invertebrates for protein. • Mistletoe is a parasitic plant, sprouting right on branches alongside the tree's natural growth. The Mistle Thrush eats the plant's berries and excretes them onto tree branches, thus enabling mistletoe to grow freely in forested areas. • This sounds like an excellent symbiotic relationship, but as far back as the early 1500s, proverb collector Desiderius Erasmus noted a Latin saying, *Turdus malum sibi ipse cacat*, or "The thrush himself excretes his own trouble." This makes reference to the use of mistletoe berries, which are quite sticky, in birdlime, a bird-trapping material that hunters smeared on branches so the birds would stick fast. (Use of birdlime was outlawed in the European Union as recently as 2021.) The proverb points to the Mistle Thrush's practice of literally sowing the seeds of its own destruction, making this bird's habit the origin of a universal metaphor. That being said, country folk believed that mistletoe seeds could not germinate until they passed through the digestive system of an obliging thrush. While mistletoe berries are toxic to humans, people once believed that eating the bird that ate them could cure epilepsy, making the Mistle Thrush's life quite precarious.

Tympanuchus cupido

Greater Prairie Chicken

Subspecies: Attwater's Prairie Chicken | Boomer | Pinnated Grouse

● **NEAR THREATENED**

COLLECTIVE NAMES

Little house of prairie chickens |
Pack of prairie chickens

SYMBOLIC MEANING

Prairie conservation.

POSSIBLE POWER

Yet to be discovered.

FOLKLORE AND FACTS

In the 1800s, millions of prairie chickens inhabited the
state of Illinois alone, but today, fewer than 200 individuals
remain there. This is the plight of this game bird in the
grouse family across its North American range; it no
longer lives in Canada at all, where it was once abundant,
and scattered packs of 500 or fewer birds remain in Iowa,
Missouri, and Wisconsin. Kansas, Nebraska, and South
Dakota still have substantial populations, however, keeping
them off the critically endangered list. • These birds are
best known for a mating ritual called booming, which
they perform on a lek, or mating ground: The males inflate
brightly colored air sacs on both sides of their neck while
making a low, three-syllable booming sound, and the females
choose which of these males are most impressive to them.
This process goes on for months, with just a few of the males
tallying up nearly all of the opportunities to mate. • Because
of their precipitous drop in population and the many
efforts in progress to try to increase their numbers, Greater
Prairie Chickens have become a national symbol of prairie
conservation, especially in Great Plains states. • A Blackfoot
(Siksika) legend tells of a young hunter who happened
across some Greater Prairie Chickens while he was in the
field. He killed one with his bow and arrow and brought it
home to his family for dinner. That night, the hunter had a
dream: The bird came to him and asked, "Why did you kill
me?" The hunter answered simply: "My family was hungry,
and I needed to feed them." The bird understood, but he
said, "I will show you a dance that you must teach to your
people. If you do this, I will leave you alone. But if you do
not teach them this dance, I will come back and kill you." So
the hunter learned the dance, and in the morning he taught
it to his people. It has been performed by Siksika and Plains
Cree people ever since, mimicking the booming dance of the
prairie chickens on the lek.

Tympanuchus phasianellus

Sharp-Tailed Grouse

Brush Chicken | Fire Bird | Sharptail

● **LEAST CONCERN**

COLLECTIVE NAMES

Brace of grouse (two birds) | Brood of grouse | Covey of grouse | Drumming of grouse

SYMBOLIC MEANING

Provincial bird of Saskatchewan.

POSSIBLE POWERS

Yet to be discovered.

FOLKLORE AND FACTS

A grouse of open prairies and brushy habitats,
the Sharp-Tailed Grouse obtained its Native
American nickname "fire bird" because of its
attraction to burned-
over prairie. The
bird populated
the Great Plains
aggressively until the
mid-1800s, when the
Homestead Act opened
up millions of acres of land
to would-be farmers for free
as long as they actively farmed it.
Homesteaders flocked to the Midwest
and staked their claims on the land, and before long the
prairies were gone and fields of corn, wheat, and other grains
and vegetables replaced them. The Sharp-Tailed Grouse's
habitat dwindled, even more so when cattle ranchers arrived
and the remaining prairies became pastures, and cattle
trampled the pastures underfoot. It took well into the 1950s
before early environmentalists began to understand what
kind of toll this activity took on native bird and animal
populations. • The Sharp-Tailed Grouse performs a spring
courtship display on a lek, or mating ground, inflating bright
purple air sacs on either side of its neck while stomping,
cooing, and rattling its tail feathers. It's a sight to behold,
and the females have the opportunity to select a mate
from these showy, dancing birds. • Meanwhile, in Canada,
the Sharp-Tailed Grouse has been the official provincial
bird of Saskatchewan since 1945. The grouse is "one of
Saskatchewan's most popular game birds," which implies that
there are plenty of them available there for hunting.

T

No. 377

Tyrannus forficatus

Scissor-Tailed Flycatcher

Swallow-Tailed Flycatcher | Texas Bird-of-Paradise

● **LEAST CONCERN**

✤ **COLLECTIVE NAMES**

Outfield of flycatchers | Swatting of flycatchers | Zipper of flycatchers

✳ **SYMBOLIC MEANING**

State bird of Oklahoma.

🌀 **POSSIBLE POWER**

Aid to farmers.

🌓 **FOLKLORE AND FACTS**

The North and Central American flycatcher with a tail longer than its body, the Scissor-Tailed Flycatcher is unmistakable in flight or perched on a utility wire or fencepost. The lengthy, forked tail is black above and white below, and may be as much as 12 inches (30 cm) long in males; females have shorter tails, but still longer than any other North American flycatcher. • Found primarily in Kansas, Oklahoma, and Texas in the United States, and from Mexico to Panama in winter, the Scissor-Tailed Flycatcher is the state bird of Oklahoma, where the bird is found in abundance. The state honored it further by featuring it on its commemorative quarter in the America's 50 States series. Oklahoma selected the bird in 1951, in part because it eats insects that would otherwise be harmful to crops, but also because more Scissor-Tails nest in Oklahoma than in any other state. The bird won a hard-fought campaign in which a contest among schoolchildren in 1932 first resulted in the Northern Bobwhite's selection for state bird, but the legislature had other things to worry about that year with the massive drought that began the Dust Bowl era of famine, so the state bird never came up for a vote. A coalition of garden clubs, wildlife groups, and the state's Audubon Society all kept pushing for the flycatcher, however, and in 1951, Oklahoma became the only state to choose this unique bird as its state emblem.

No. 378

Tyrannus tyrannus

Eastern Kingbird

● **LEAST CONCERN**

✤ **COLLECTIVE NAME**

Coronation of kingbirds

✳ **SYMBOLIC MEANINGS**

Courage; Protection.

🌀 **POSSIBLE POWER**

Chief of all birds.

🌓 **FOLKLORE AND FACTS**

Known across the United States and in northern South America for its monochrome head, back, and wings, white chest, and a strip of white at the end of its tail feathers, the Eastern Kingbird takes its role as king of the "lower birds"—birds that live close to the ground rather than soaring above it—quite seriously. This feisty flycatcher stands ready to attack anyone who comes too close to its nest or who challenges it for food. An insect-eater with a tyrannical personality (hence its Latin name), the Eastern Kingbird will even challenge humans, raising its wings straight up from its body to appear larger than it actually is. • The Bear Clan of the Oneida people in Wisconsin tell a kingbird's story: The village chief has two sons and a daughter. The elder brother disgraced himself somehow (it's not specified, but it doesn't really matter to the story), so his father has the son sewn into a bear skin and thrown into the Wisconsin River. There a water spirit rescues him and takes him into its lodge. Meanwhile, the chief determines it's time to move the village, so they pack up and leave, but the younger brother stays behind in the woods until everyone has gone. When he returns to the village site, a kingbird has turned itself into an old woman and starts building a lodge, so the younger brother helps her and they live together. One day, as he is out walking, he crosses a stream on a log and hears someone say, "Pull me out and you may be chief!" He runs home, where he and the old woman fashion a net, and the young man returns to the stream and pulls out what had called to him. It's his older brother, now half-man, half-fish. The younger brother and the old woman try to bring his brother home, but he needs to be near water, so he does not fare well. They revive him with steam when they reach the lodge, and sure enough, his younger brother becomes chief of all the spirits—and immediately transforms into a kingbird.

No. 379

Tyrannus verticalis

Western Kingbird

● LEAST CONCERN

⚒ **COLLECTIVE NAME**
Coronation of kingbirds

✳ **SYMBOLIC MEANINGS**
Courage; Protection.

🌀 **POSSIBLE POWERS**
Risk-taking; Self-confidence.

🐾 **FOLKLORE AND FACTS**
The dominant kingbird west of the Mississippi River and in Mexico and Central America, the Western Kingbird differs significantly in appearance from its eastern relative. Its gray head, throat, and back graduate into brown wings, all offset with a bright yellow chest and underside. This bird has flourished in the transformation of the Great Plains into more treed areas, enjoying hedgerows and additional foliage that has allowed it to gain footing across Kansas, Nebraska, Oklahoma, and Texas. • All kingbirds are known for their bravado in dealing with potential predators, especially when guarding their nests. They are quick to lash out at any threat, even those that are much larger and fiercer than they are. This supreme confidence startles many predators, who sulk away and leave the scrappy little bird to its own devices—making kingbirds the spiritual model for bravery, self-confidence, and risk-taking. • The Western Kingbird should not be confused with all the other lemon-bellied kingbirds of the western states: Cassin's, Couch's, Thick-Billed, and Tropical Kingbirds, each with enough of its own subtle characteristics that you will need a good field guide to sort them out. The Western Kingbird is the most common and prevalent, and is the only one of the western species in most of the Great Plains.

No. 380

Tyto alba

Barn Owl
Common Barn Owl | Death Owl | Demon Owl | Ghost Owl | Lich Owl

● LEAST CONCERN

⚒ **COLLECTIVE NAMES**
Group of owls | Hoot of owls | Parliament of owls

✳ **SYMBOLIC MEANINGS**
Ghost; Hindu symbol of wealth and fortune.

🌀 **POSSIBLE POWER**
Harbinger of death.

🐾 **FOLKLORE AND FACTS**
It flies silently in the dead of night, its white face, body, and wings gliding over like a fluttering shroud. It doesn't hoot, instead emitting a ghastly shriek that gives new meaning to phrases like "blood-curdling." It's no wonder that Barn Owls have frightened people around the world for thousands of years, emerging from manmade structures or hollow trees only after dark, and hunting so stealthily that we don't even know they are there until they pounce on their prey. • Before people understood all the benefits of owls, including their ability to eat up to three thousand rodents per year each, farmers killed Barn Owls indiscriminately to keep them away from their livestock. Barn Owls do not eat chickens or cats, however, or anything else that is bigger than they are. • One superstition about Barn Owls lingers to this day: The idea that if a Barn Owl lands on your house, someone in the house will die soon. For those who have Barn Owls nesting in their barns, this is a very somber thing to believe. • Hindus in India see Barn Owls from quite a different perspective. This bird is the symbol of Lakshmi, goddess of wealth, beauty, and fertility, who is one of the three deities of supreme divinity in Hinduism. The Barn Owl is Lakshmi's vehicle, there to symbolize wisdom in her decisions to provide prosperity to specific people and places. Unfortunately, during the festival of Diwali, some sects perform rituals to Lakshmi in which they actually sacrifice a Barn Owl or an Indian Eagle Owl, with the goal of keeping Lakshmi from leaving their homes and taking away their prosperity. A sophisticated rescue operation now monitors this situation and does its best to prevent owls from being sacrificed, arresting trappers and sellers, retrieving the owls, and releasing them into the wild when they are rehabilitated (if necessary).

No. 381

Upupa epops

Eurasian Hoopoe

Duchifat (Hebrew)

● **LEAST CONCERN**

🦋 **COLLECTIVE NAME**
Hoop of hoopoes

☀ **SYMBOLIC MEANINGS**
Leadership; Thievery; Virtue.

🌀 **POSSIBLE POWER**
Foretelling of war.

🌙 **FOLKLORE AND FACTS**
With its peach-colored head and extravagant crest, black-and-white-striped back and wings, and long bill, the Eurasian Hoopoe can't help but draw attention to itself. It's fairly common in Europe, Asia, and parts of Africa, where its *oop-oop-oop* call makes it clear where the bird got its name. • Perhaps its distinctive appearance has given rise to many points of view about the bird's meaning in society, from its inclusion on the walls of Egyptian tombs to being featured as a character in children's programs. The Arabs believed that the bird had medicinal value, while Persian poetry lavishes praise on the bird for its virtuous nature. • The Old Testament, however, calls out the hoopoe specifically as an unkosher bird. • The Qur'an tells of the bird being tardy in bringing important news to Solomon. • In Greece, Aristophanes featured the hoopoe as king of the birds in his ancient comedy *The Birds*, and in Ovid's *Metamorphoses*, some translators believe that after Philomela and Procne turn into a swallow and a nightingale to escape the torment of Tereus, Procne's husband, the gods turn Tereus into a hoopoe. • In Scandinavian tradition, hoopoes are seen as bringers of the news of war, while Germans believe the bird is phallic-looking, and therefore obscene. It seems that no one is neutral about this dynamic-looking bird. • In 2008, tens of thousands of Israeli citizens voted to make the Eurasian Hoopoe the nation's national bird on the occasion of Israel's sixtieth birthday. The hoopoe bested more than fifty other choices on the ballot, perhaps because of its ability to develop its own defensive strategies—coating its eggs with a bacteria-laden substance it produces itself to keep predators away—and its survival in the face of many challenges.

No. 382

Urocissa erythroryncha

Red-Billed Blue Magpie

Blue Magpie

● **LEAST CONCERN**

🦋 **COLLECTIVE NAMES**
Charm of magpies | Congregation of magpies | Tribe of magpies

☀ **SYMBOLIC MEANINGS**
Happiness; Wedded bliss.

🌀 **POSSIBLE POWER**
Revealing infidelity.

🌙 **FOLKLORE AND FACTS**
This large blue bird can be up to 27 inches (69 cm) in length, with a black head, red bill and feet, and an unusually long black, white, and blue tail. Its willingness to walk right up to people has made it a favorite with residents throughout their range in India, Nepal, Bangladesh, China, and Southeast Asia. • The Chinese words for "two magpies" is a homonym with "two happinesses," so pictures of two Red-Billed Blue Magpies together have become a metaphor for increased happiness and wedded bliss. • In Chinese mythology, if a husband and wife must be apart for a length of time, they should break a mirror in half and each should keep their half close at hand. If one of the spouses is unfaithful to the other, the unfaithful spouse's half of the mirror will turn into a magpie and fly back to the other spouse.

U

No. 383

Vanellus chilensis

Southern Lapwing

Cayenne Lapwing | Chilean Lapwing | Quero-Quero (Brazil) | Tero (Argentina) |
Tero-Tero (Paraguay) | Queltehue (Chile)

● **LEAST CONCERN**

✼ **COLLECTIVE NAME**

Deceit of lapwings

✻ **SYMBOLIC MEANINGS**

Adaptability; Resilience; Vigilance.

◉ **POSSIBLE POWERS**

Defense; Protection.

☾ **FOLKLORE AND FACTS**

The Southern Lapwing
serves as the national
animal of Uruguay
and as mascot of the
Uruguayan rugby team,
as it can become very
aggressive and territorial
if anyone threatens its nest
and young. The bird even has
a hard spur at the bend in each wing,
giving it a decisive advantage over many
of its foes. • Probably as a result of its
impressive appearance and bold nature,
the Southern Lapwing appears on
postage stamps throughout South
America and the Caribbean islands,
even though it doesn't actually live in some of these places.
More logically, Uruguay, Argentina, Brazil, Paraguay, and
the Falkland Islands have all honored the Southern Lapwing
with postage.

No. 384

Vanellus vanellus

Northern Lapwing

Green Plover | Peewit | Pilibin (Ireland) | Pyewipe | Tuit

● **NEAR THREATENED**

✼ **COLLECTIVE NAME**

Deceit of lapwings

✻ **SYMBOLIC MEANINGS**

Defiance; National bird of Ireland.

◉ **POSSIBLE POWERS**

Contrarian; Craftiness.

☾ **FOLKLORE AND FACTS**

A Swedish story tells us of a young woman serving as a
handmaiden to the Virgin Mary. The girl stole Mary's
scissors, and Mary punished her by turning her into a
Northern Lapwing with a tail that resembles a pair of
scissors, and a voice that can only say "Tyvit," Swedish for
"I stole." • Centuries later its eggs became a delicacy: Called
"plover's eggs" though lapwings are not related to plovers,
the eggs had to be found in the wild, making them a pricey
item indeed in markets. The practice has been banned by
the European Union, but in the Netherlands, finding the
first lapwing egg of the season is still a custom. The finder
now has to leave the egg where it was found, however.
• The Northern Lapwing is said to have been present at the
crucifixion of Jesus, according to a story about three birds
that came to his aid on the cross. First the stork came and
called "Strengthen him!"; then the swallow tried to remove
the thorns from his crown. Finally, the Northern Lapwing
came and circled the cross, crying, "Let him suffer!" Jesus
blessed the stork and the swallow, but he condemned the
lapwing for all time. • A creation story in Russia says that
when God made the world, he instructed the birds to carry
water to fill many indentations for seas, lakes, and rivers.
Everyone pitched in except the lapwing, who refused.
God punished the bird by
declaring that it
would always
have to get its
water from
puddles.

No. 385

Vultur gryphus

Andean Condor

- **VULNERABLE**

COLLECTIVE NAMES
Condo of condors | Scarcity of condors

SYMBOLIC MEANINGS
Health; Power.

POSSIBLE POWERS
Causing the sun to rise; Communication with the gods;
Improving eyesight; Preventing nightmares.

FOLKLORE AND FACTS
The Andean Condor is widely considered to be the world's
largest bird of prey, as well as one of the largest flying birds,
with its distinctive white ruff surrounding its featherless
gray head. • The countries of Bolivia, Chile, Colombia,
Ecuador, Peru, as well as the Andes states of Venezuela have
all selected this bird as their national symbol. • The condor
has been associated with the sun god of Andean culture for
millennia, and the Incas believed that it actually brought the
sun into the sky every morning, and that it communicated
directly with the gods. • Even in the twenty-first century,
some cultures believe that the Andean Condor can provide
miraculous cures for everything from cancer to bad eyesight.
Some think that eating the stomach of a condor will cure
breast cancer, or that collecting, roasting, and eating condor
eyes will improve their own sight. A condor feather placed
under a bed is thought to prevent nightmares.

No. 386

Zenaida aurita

Zenaida Dove

Turtle Dove

- **LEAST CONCERN**

COLLECTIVE NAMES
Bevy of doves | Covey of doves |
Dole of doves | Paddling of doves |
Piteousness of doves | Pretense of doves

SYMBOLIC MEANING
National bird of Anguilla.

POSSIBLE POWER
Peace.

FOLKLORE AND FACTS
Smaller than a Mourning Dove but otherwise very similar in
appearance, the Zenaida Dove shows a white trailing edge
on its wings, especially in flight, as well as a small, iridescent
purple patch on each side of its neck. This Caribbean-island
dove shares its range with the Mourning Dove, so knowing
these two field marks can help alleviate hours of confusion.
• As the national bird of Anguilla, a British territory in the
Lesser Antilles, the Zenaida Dove has free rein of open
habitat along the island's coastline. It's easy to find on
beaches and dunes with desert scrub, in vacant lots in towns,
and along town edges. Many residents report finding Zenaida
Dove nests in their shrubs or in potted plants on or near their
porches, where the doves lay just two eggs and guard them
judiciously; they may raise as many as four broods annually.
Unlike their Mourning Dove cousins, Zenaida Doves are
wary of human contact and unlikely to approach people.

V–Z

No. 387

Zenaida macroura

Mourning Dove

● **LEAST CONCERN**

⚘ **COLLECTIVE NAMES**
Bevy of doves | Covey of doves |
Dole of doves | Paddling of doves |
Piteousness of doves | Pretense of doves

✴ **SYMBOLIC MEANINGS**
Love; Monogamy.

🌀 **POSSIBLE POWERS**
Good or bad luck; Predictor of death; Protection for young
mothers.

🌙 **FOLKLORE AND FACTS**
The life of the Mourning Dove, North America's most
widespread dove, is filled with meaning, folklore, and
superstition. Some consider just seeing one a good omen,
though they are so prevalent across the country—they are the
only bird that nests in all fifty states—that this could happen
every few minutes. Some suggest that Mourning Doves bring
messages from people in the afterlife, but as they rarely wander
alone and usually show up in coveys, it may be tough to guess
which dove is your messenger. • Aztecs believed that doves
represented the goddess Xochiquetzal, who influenced fertility,
love, and beauty, and protected young mothers. The Pueblo
people believed that Mourning Doves were birds of rain,
cooing to bring showers and to tell one another where to get
water. • More recently, farmers in Georgia share the common
wisdom that if a Mourning Dove is calling somewhere above
your head, you will prosper; if it is calling from the ground or
even farther below your feet, it could foretell of a coming death.
It's inevitable that these birds would be considered predictors
of death to come, as their low, throaty call makes them
sound like they are already in mourning; it even gave them
their name. • These doves have represented monogamy for
centuries, as they take a long time to choose a mate and then
mate for life, always appearing with their mate at feeders or
wherever they go. During breeding season, both parents take
turns incubating eggs, and when squabs are born, both parents
raise them. This partnership is a model for young couples,
making these birds an important symbol for monogamy and
the marital partnership. • One of the most poignant roles of
the Mourning Dove is to appear to comfort us at funerals. If
you are fortunate enough to see a Mourning Dove as you lay
a loved one to rest in a cemetery, take heart: The person you
have lost is still with you in another form, letting you know that
they are all right, and that you are never really alone.

V–Z

FANCIFUL & MYTHICAL BIRDS

AROUND THE WORLD

Long before we began to understand birds in scientific terms, miraculous flying creatures became part of nearly every culture's mythology. As we have seen so far in this book, birds served as companions of Greek and Roman gods and goddesses; key players in the Creation among many Indigenous cultures across North, Central, and South America; sacred beings in Buddhism and Hindu mythology; and key figures in Chinese symbology. They play important roles in African and Caribbean religions as well, especially birds that can mimic human speech.

Despite the many remarkable and imaginative ways that birds became enmeshed in so many mythologies, however, sometimes the powers of actual living birds simply did not rise to the levels the gods and storytellers required. Birds needed to do something more: meld with the body of a god or goddess, for example, or become the lead character in a myth so vivid that it needs a supernatural species to tell it.

Some of the most flamboyant, color-saturated, and powerful birds in this book spring from mythology, so they are included here in a section of their own. The cultures that produced them credit these fictitious birds with the ability to heal the sick, determine if crops will thrive or wither, bestow happy marriages and fidelity on lucky couples, bring good luck and prosperity, or guide people to new lands on which to build their capital city. In ancient Egypt, a god takes on the mantle of a bird while he controls the passage of time and the change of seasons. On the flip side of this benevolence, one mythical bird provides an excuse for foolishness, shifting the blame for mistakes away from humans and onto a bird too silly to behave itself. A goddess in Ireland turns herself into a bird to predict death on the battlefield, while a mythical bird species spreads destruction and gathers riches for itself, appearing in myths of great heroes and warriors throughout the European continent. Creating birds that have supernatural powers makes them larger than life, allowing those who believe in them to attach all manner of deeds and stories to them. This makes these mythical birds the catalysts for just about any situation that requires an explanation beyond the ordinary, whether it's a Japanese gremlin that cuts up whenever it wishes, or a Greek and Roman myth that grants eternal life—with conditions—to a single bird that a god finds especially beautiful.

The eleven birds described in this section each play a critical role in the cultures in which they emerged. Some of them have been at it for thousands of years, their tales passed orally or in hieroglyphics from one generation to the next. Artists' depictions and iconography have refined their images since ancient times, so some have metamorphosed from their original bird (or birdlike) forms into something more human or superhuman. The spirit of their winged origins remains, however, and their legends continue to be told around the world.

Caladrius

Caladrius

✿ COLLECTIVE NAME
None—this bird is always solitary

✺ SYMBOLIC MEANINGS
Purity of Jesus Christ; Sickness and healing.

֍ POSSIBLE POWER
Prediction of life or death.

▥ CULTURE
Ancient Rome

☾ FOLKLORE AND FACTS
Roman mythology conjures up the Caladrius, a bird that has the ability to remove a human being's sickness and absorb it, and then fly off to the sun, where the sickness burns away. Tales were told of the all-white bird looking deep into the soul of a person with a dangerous illness. If the bird looked directly into the person's face, the person would live; if the bird turned away, death was imminent. • While more recent theories suggest that the Caladrius may have been based on an actual bird—a white dove, for example—no direct parallel to any specific bird has ever been drawn conclusively.
• This did not stop NBC's *Saturday Night Live* from including Caladrius in the 1978 sketch "Theodoric of York: Medieval Barber," in which Steve Martin as the twelfth-century barber/surgeon employed a series of barbaric rituals to treat patients, one of which was the use of a white dove he described as a Caladrius. Rather than perform its magic on the patient, however, the bird flew off into the audience.
• In medieval times, Christians embraced the Caladrius as a symbol of Jesus Christ, its pure white plumage a direct parallel to the purity of Christ's soul. They extended the Christian morality through this metaphor as well, with the bird's choice to turn away from some ill people a direct parallel to the medieval belief that Jesus turned away from the Jewish people who did not see him as the son of God; instead, he saved only the souls of the Christians who accepted him as their savoir.

Chickcharney

Chickcharney

Chickcharnee | Chickcharnie

✿ COLLECTIVE NAME
A family of chickcharnies

✺ SYMBOLIC MEANINGS
Mischief; Reminder to be kind.

֍ POSSIBLE POWER
Ability to kill humans who offend it.

▥ CULTURE
The Bahamas (Andros)

☾ FOLKLORE AND FACTS
On the Bahamian island of Andros, locals speak of an odd creature that lives among the trees, raising its young and generally minding its mythical business ... unless a human manages to offend it. The Chickcharney stands 3 feet (1 m) tall, the legend says, and has a barn owl's face, wings, tail, and long pink legs with three-toed feet; arms and hands with three fingers each, and a longer, monkey-like prehensile tail for swinging through the trees. • Whether it's a bird or a humanoid critter depends on who's telling the story, but one thing is clear across the board: If a visitor treats the Chickcharney with kindness, he will live to tell the tale. Woe be to the traveler who laughs derisively at the creature, because the Chickcharney will grab the person's head and twist it all the way around, ending his life. This is why Andros Islanders carry treats with them whenever they go into the wild: Lengths of bright cloth, pretty flowers, or other items they can use to honor the Chickcharney and come home with their necks straight and their lives intact.
• Apparently Neville Chamberlain, once prime minister of England, ran afoul of the Chickcharney when he moved to the island. Chamberlain inherited his father's Bahamas plantation, and he came to tend to it himself, clearing wide swaths of land for planting. Without realizing it, he tore up a great deal of land Chickcharnies called home. The beasts exacted their revenge, making sure that nothing grew well on the plantation, and eventually plunging Chamberlain into financial ruin. • The message is clear: Don't mess with an island's endemic species, mythical or mortal.

No. M003

Fenghuang

Fenghuang

Chinese Phoenix | Hōō | Phung Hoàng

✥ COLLECTIVE NAME
Pair of Fenghuang

✱ SYMBOLIC MEANINGS
Credibility; Duty; Grace;
Mercy; Propriety; Virtue.

⚜ POSSIBLE POWERS
Fidelity; Good fortune.

⛩ CULTURE
China

☙ FOLKLORE AND FACTS
A rooster's beak, a swallow's face, a chicken's forehead, a goose's chest, a tortoise's shell, a stag's back half, and a fish's tail … what could this strange conglomerate be? This is just one of many hodgepodge descriptions of the Fenghuang, or the Chinese Phoenix, a mythical creature created to pair with a dragon as one of China's Twelve Ornaments, ancient symbols that denoted the power and authority of the wearer. The ornaments date back at least to 2294 BCE and perhaps much earlier than that, embroidered on the clothing of high-ranking people in Chinese society. More recently, all twelve symbols were incorporated into a single national emblem in 1913 as the country's rulers changed, and appeared on flags and coats of arms until 1928. • The Fenghuang's history may go back even farther, with its first known form discovered at a site from 5000 BCE. The bird's many forms over the centuries all have a few elements in common: A crest or head ornament of some kind, a large frame, and a long, luxurious tail. More recent depictions provide a more cohesive look for the phoenix: A Golden Pheasant's head, a Mandarin Duck's body, a peacock's tail, a crane's legs, and a parrot's bill. • Wherever the Fenghuang appears, it implies the virtue and honesty of the people it adorns. Dragon and phoenix imagery often appears at weddings as a blessing of fidelity and harmony, and some households bring out their dragon and phoenix imagery to display it in good times, and hide it away when times turn tough.

No. M004

Huitzilopochtli

Totec | Uitzilopochtli | Xiuhpilli

✱ SYMBOLIC MEANINGS
Sun worship; War.

⚜ POSSIBLE POWERS
Guidance; Leadership; Warrior.

⛩ CULTURE
Aztec (modern-day Mexico)

☙ FOLKLORE AND FACTS
The Aztecs believed that their fallen warriors were reincarnated as hummingbirds, so they portrayed their sun god Huitzilopochtli as a hummingbird; conversely, Huitzilopochtli often disguised himself to walk the Earth, choosing the much larger and more forbidding eagle as his costume. This dichotomy plays out throughout Aztec myths, making Huitzilopochtli one of the most interesting characters in their pantheon. • Huitzilopochtli's mother, earth goddess Coatlicue, conceived her son after carrying a ball of hummingbird feathers—a fallen warrior—against her breasts for some time. Tales of the sun god include his role in guiding the Aztecs in their lengthy migration from Aztlan to the Valley of Mexico, his priests carrying an image of him in his hummingbird form, and commanding them to build their great city Tenochtitlán on an island in Lake Texcoco. When the priests arrived at the island, they found an eagle standing on a rock, devouring a snake—a certain sign from Huitzilopochtli that this was the place to build his temple. • The eagle imagery extends to the Aztecs' practice of daily human sacrifice to the sun god, the fulfillment of their certainty that Huitzilopochtli needed to be fed on a human heart and blood every morning. They offered a heart at sunup to the "eagle who rises," and then burned the heart in "the eagle's vase." Those who died in battle became "the eagle's people," joining Huitzilopochtli as the sun's rays for four years, then moving on to be reincarnated forever as hummingbirds.

Morrigan

Celtic Goddess of Death | Morrigu | Queen of the Triple Goddesses | The Phantom Queen

🦋 COLLECTIVE NAME
Triple Goddess (with sisters Badb and Macha)

✳ SYMBOLIC MEANING
Death in battle.

🌀 POSSIBLE POWERS
Ability to predict soldiers' death;
Predicting success or failure in battle;
Shape-shifting.

🏛 CULTURE
Ireland

🌐 FOLKLORE AND FACTS
Celtic mythology tells us of Morrigan,
an Irish war goddess who had the ability to predict the
deaths of warriors going into battle. She performed this
remarkable feat by turning herself into a crow and flying
over a raging battle. Seeing Morrigan above their heads
either frightened the fighters out of their wits—usually
leading to their deaths—or inspired them to fight even
harder. The latter often led the men to victory. • Morrigan
met and fell instantly in love with Cú Chulainn, a mighty
warrior defending Ulster from Queen Maeve's army. He was
unmoved by her fiery beauty, however—and, as you might
imagine, this did not go well for him. Morrigan transformed
into an eel and tripped Cú Chulainn in the midst of battle;
when he attempted to kill the eel, she turned herself into
a wolf and stampeded a herd of cattle at the warrior. He
blinded the wolf with a slingshot shot, but Morrigan shape-
shifted once again, becoming a cow and redirecting the herd.
Cú Chulainn was quick, however, and aimed a rock at the
cow, this time breaking its leg. • As he made his way home,
Cú Chulainn encountered an old woman milking a cow,
and did not notice that her leg and eye were bandaged. He
stopped to chat with her, accepted a cup of milk, and blessed
her for her kindness … and this blessing healed Morrigan's
wounds so she could fight him another day. That day arrived
not long after, when Cú Chulainn was on his way to another
battle, and encountered a woman scrubbing blood off a man's
battle armor. He knew this was a bad omen, but he moved
on and engaged in battle with the enemy later that day. Sure
enough, this turned out to be his last day on Earth. Morrigan,
who of course was the woman with the stained armor,
watched in her crow form as her beloved was wounded and
died on the battlefield.

Oozlum

Oozlum

Ouzelum | Weejy Weejy Bird

✳ SYMBOLIC MEANINGS
Circular reasoning; Ridiculous behavior.

🌀 POSSIBLE POWER
Ability to fly up its own backside.

🏛 CULTURE
Australia; Great Britain

🌐 FOLKLORE AND FACTS
British and Australian legends tell us of the Oozlum, a bird
that flies in a spiral of tighter and tighter circles until it
eventually flies right up its own backside. In some versions
of the story, the bird becomes so enamored with the beauty
of its own tail feathers that it chases them until it ends up
in its own rectum. *Brewer's Dictionary of Phrase and Fable*
notes that the Oozlum flies backwards (a thing only a few
hummingbirds can actually do), so it does not know where
it's going, but "it does like to know where it has been."
• Says w.t. Goodge in an 1899 volume, *Hits! Skits! and
Jingles!*: "It's a curious bird, the Oozlum, / And a bird
that's wise, / For it always flies tail-first to / Keep the dust
out of its eyes!" • In the few attempts to provide a visual
representation of an Oozlum, it looks much like a parrot
with a stunted bill, though considerably larger than the
average bird, and perhaps with a topknot or crest. • A
slightly different but equally mythical bird, and perhaps
an Oozlum variant, the Weejy Weejy Bird is said to have
a single wing, so it has no choice but to fly in ever-tighter
circles until it, too, vanishes on the same route as the others.
Another variation, the Oozlefinch, is an Americanization of
the same concept, though this bird flies backwards at speeds
otherwise unknown to aviation. This mascot of the Air
Defense Artillery—a branch of the u.s Army that specializes
in anti-artillery weapons—carries a Nike-Hercules surface-
to-air missile, just in case it needs one.

Phoenix

Phoenix

Bennu | Firebird

✦ COLLECTIVE NAME
The Phoenix is a solitary bird.

✦ SYMBOLIC MEANINGS
Rebirth; Renewal.

✦ POSSIBLE POWERS
Immortality; Rising from the ashes of its own death.

✦ CULTURE
Ancient Greece

✦ FOLKLORE AND FACTS
Exactly how and where we acquired the legend of the Phoenix has been a subject of debate for thousands of years. The best guess is that it began with Herodotus, the Greek historian, who recorded the Egyptian story of a bird named Bennu. This bird died in fire, but a few days later, its young emerged from the ashes. • This tale had its own rebirth in Greek mythology as the Phoenix, an immortal bird who eventually tired of its cushy life in Paradise. Phoenix traveled to the mortal world, where things lived and died—but the bird knew that he would remain immortal. As he watched things live and die around him, he, too, longed for renewal. Phoenix built a nest of twigs, and as he waited for Apollo, the sun god, to arrive, he began to sing. Apollo passed over as morning came, and the sun god so admired Phoenix's song that he actually stopped in midair to listen. As he enjoyed the song, a spark from the sun dropped down onto Phoenix's nest of twigs. The nest ignited, and Phoenix burst into flames, dissolving into ashes. • All was not lost for Phoenix, however. Three days later, the magical bird sprang up from the ashes, young and renewed. The bird realized that he could do this again and again, but he understood that he would have to wait one thousand years before his next renewal. He continues to repeat this cycle of death and rebirth, as he will for eternity. • Other cultures have similar stories of a bird that can regenerate: Native Americans describe the Thunderbird, which can not only renew its own life, but renews the Earth with rain. Chinese mythology has the Fenghuang (No. M003 in this book). Even *Harry Potter and the Chamber of Secrets* describes Fawkes, the phoenix bird that comes to Harry's rescue. The popular motif gives us hope for regeneration or reincarnation, spiritually if not literally.

Roc

Roc

Rokh | Rukh | Rukk

✦ COLLECTIVE NAME
Flock of rocs

✦ SYMBOLIC MEANINGS
Destruction; Strength.

✦ POSSIBLE POWER
Supernatural strength.

✦ CULTURE
Middle East

✦ FOLKLORE AND FACTS
Larger than any living bird of prey, the mythical Roc plays a role in many seafarers' folk tales and Middle Eastern myths. Believed to be a fantastical overstatement of the power of real-life eagles in Arab countries, the Roc is much larger than life, described as able to carry off a human being, or to appear on the horizon with such gigantism that sailors mistook it for a mountain. • The great thirteenth-century Venetian explorer Marco Polo described a bird "so strong that it will seize an elephant in its talons and carry him high into the air and drop him so that he is smashed to pieces." In *One Thousand and One Nights*, the classic Arabic book of fairy tales, Sinbad the Sailor's shipmates abandon him on an island, where he discovers a nest of huge bird's eggs and realizes they must be from a Roc. He devises a way to attach himself to the massive bird and fly off to the mainland— but this only shifts his problems to a new site, as the bird drops him off into a valley filled with giant snakes. The Roc feeds on these snakes, and as Sinbad scrambles away, he discovers that diamonds cover the valley floor. He spots a cadre of merchants there, who tell him that they harvest the diamonds by tossing big chunks of raw meat into the valley, so the Roc and other birds pick up the meat and carry it to their nests. The merchants then make lots of noise and drive away the birds, and pick off all the diamonds that stuck to the meat. Sinbad collects a bag full of diamonds, then straps himself to a piece of meat; the Roc picks him up with the meat and carries him out of the valley.

No. M009

Sanzuwu

Three-Legged Crow

Bird-Sun | Golden Crow | Sun Crow

✿ COLLECTIVE NAME

Flock of sun crows

✹ SYMBOLIC MEANING

Power of the sun.

✺ POSSIBLE POWER

Driving the sun across
the sky.

▥ CULTURE

China

☾ FOLKLORE AND FACTS

The Three-Legged Crow, Sanzuwu or Sun Crow in
Chinese mythology, is one of the Twelve Ornaments with
which high-ranking personages in China decorated their
garments. While described most often as a crow or other
corvid species, the Sun Crow usually is embroidered in
red, or sometimes in gold, giving it the name "golden crow."
• Sanzuwu usually appears at the center of a disc that
represents the sun, implying that the mythical bird actually
lives in or on the sun. • Chinese folklore tells us that there
were ten sun crows, and each took a shift every ten days
to circle the globe in a carriage driven by Xihe, the sun
mother. This went on in a constant relay, with each crow
tagging out when it returned to the red mulberry tree the
sun crows shared as their principal roost, and the next crow
hopping into the carriage and dashing off. • This went on
continuously until sometime around 2170 BCE, when all ten
crows inexplicably came out on the same day and ten suns
rose, setting the entire world on fire. China's best archer,
Hou Yi, shot down nine of the suns, returning the world to
normal—but when the gods sent Yi an elixir in gratitude
that would make him immortal, he declined to swallow it,
choosing instead to stay with his wife, Chang'e, whom he
loved very much. One day, however, one of Yi's apprentices
tried to steal the elixir, and Chang'e swallowed it herself
to keep the boy from getting it. Now immortal, she flew
skyward and chose to live on the moon, so she would still
not be far from Yi. Since then, China's annual Mid-Autumn
Festival has a special day on which people honor Chang'e,
goddess of the moon.

No. M010

Tengu

Tengu

Daitengu | Hanatakatengu | Heavenly Dog | Karsu-Tengu | Konoha-Tengu

✿ COLLECTIVE NAME

Gurupu of Tengu

✹ SYMBOLIC MEANINGS

Demons of war; Mischief; Protection in mountains and
forests.

✺ POSSIBLE POWERS

Friends of Buddhism's enemies; Trickster.

▥ CULTURE

Japan

☾ FOLKLORE AND FACTS

Tengu have made mischief in Japan since ancient times,
though these winged supernatural beings have evolved over
many centuries to look less and less like the bird form they
took in the Middle Ages. In the earliest drawings of Tengu,
the creatures had enormous bird bills, but that—and not their
warlike tendencies or their better-than-thou attitude—turned
out to be over the top for what Japanese worshippers could
tolerate. Somewhere around the beginning of the sixteenth
century, artists morphed Tengu into winged goblins with
human faces and extraordinarily long, red noses, something
people found more relatable, or perhaps easier to hate. One
theory suggests that the new guise resembled the white
foreigners who began to arrive in Japan around that time.
• These demons actually originated in China, where the
concept began as the spirit of a real meteorite that crossed
the sky over China in the year 637. Tengu first showed up
in Japanese folklore as a foxlike character that could cast
spells on people (hence the "heavenly dog" nickname);
over the next 300 or so years, Tengu became more and
more associated with the sky, so the demon grew wings and
took on a birdlike visage. These Tengu were believed to be
allies of the sworn enemies of Buddhism, so Tengu began to
represent war and conflict. Some were even said to be the
reincarnation of resentful priests, now with the power to
cause damage. • The image of a Tengu transformed in the
sixteenth century to the form it takes now, with a bright
red complexion and an elongated proboscis. Today these
creatures can be either good or tricksters, but they maintain
a level of haughtiness that makes them as off-putting as they
ever were.

No. M011

Thoth

Thoth

Asten | Khenti | Lord of Khemennu | Sheps

✤ COLLECTIVE NAME

Thoth is a single being.

✳ SYMBOLIC MEANINGS

Arbitration of disputes; Judgment of the dead.

✺ POSSIBLE POWERS

Control of time and change of seasons; Creator of the universe.

𐄂 CULTURE

Ancient Egypt

☾ FOLKLORE AND FACTS

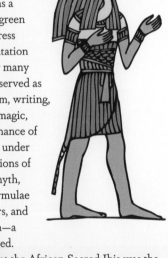

Thoth originated in ancient Egypt, where artwork thousands of years old portrays him as a man with the head of a green ibis, often with a headdress that contains a representation of the moon. Known by many different names, Thoth served as god of the moon, wisdom, writing, hieroglyphics, science, magic, and art, and the maintenance of the universe itself came under his power. In some versions of the Egyptian creation myth, Thoth calculates the formulae to create Earth, sky, stars, and everything they contain—a hardworking deity indeed.

• Egyptians believed that the African Sacred Ibis was the Earthly manifestation of Thoth, so he wore the head of one to denote their importance to the world. The Sacred Ibis eats many creatures that carry parasites that are dangerous to humans, so they performed a tremendous service to ancient Egyptians, who had no other way to combat these toxins (see more on this in entry No. 361). • When in his ibis form, Thoth causes time to move ahead and regulates the change of seasons. Later in Middle Eastern history, drawings of Thoth have the head of a baboon; in this form, he governs equilibrium, a simpler job than running the universe. He maintains balance, prevents catastrophic change, and serves as an advisor to other gods and kings.

WORKS CONSULTED

PRIMARY SOURCES

All About Birds. Cornell Lab of Ornithology, allaboutbirds.org.

Barnouw, Victor. *Wisconsin Chippewa Myths and Tales and Their Relation to Chippewa Life*. Madison: The University of Wisconsin Press, 1977.

Bird Stories. Planet of Birds, planetofbirds.com.

Birds of the World. Cornell Laboratory of Ornithology, birdsoftheworld.org.

Brophy, Hailey. World Birds: Joy of Nature. worldbirds.com

Chamoiseau, Patrick. *Creole Folktales*. New York: The New Press, 1994.

Cocker, Mark, and Mabey, Richard. *Birds Britannica*. London: Chatto & Windus, 2005.

Dave, K.N. *Birds in Sanskrit Literature*. Delhi: Motilal Banarsidass Publishers Private Limited, 1985. https://archive.org/details/BirdsInSanskritLiterature/page/n3/mode/2up?q=garuda.

de Vries, Ad. *Dictionary of Symbols and Imagery*. Amsterdam: North-Holland Publishing Company, 1976. https://archive.org/details/dictionaryofsymboooovrie.

Eyers, Jonathan. *Don't Shoot the Albatross!* Nautical Myths and Superstitions. London: Adland Coles Nautical, 2012.

Grimal, Pierre. *The Dictionary of Classical Mythology*. Oxford: Wiley, 1996.

Higgins, P.J., ed. *Handbook of Australian, New Zealand & Antarctic Birds*. Melbourne: Oxford University Press, 1999.

IUCN Red List of Threatened Species, https://www.iucnredlist.org.

Lake-Thom, Bobby. *Spirits of the Earth: A Guide to Native American Nature Symbols, Stories, and Ceremonies*. New York: Penguin Random House, 1997.

McLeod, Pauline, Francis Firebrace Jones, and June E. Barker. *Gadi Mirrabooka, Australian Aboriginal Tales from the Dreaming*. Englewood, CO: Libraries Unlimited, 2001.

Muhawi, Ibrahim, and Sharif Kanaana. *Speak, Bird, Speak Again*. Berkeley, CA: University of California Press, 1989, new edition 2021.

National Folk Museum of Korea. *Encyclopedia of Korean Folklore and Traditional Culture Vol. II*. Seoul: Gil-Job-le Media, 2014.

"Native American Totem Animals and Their Meanings." Legends of America. https://www.legendsofamerica.com/na-totems

Pritchard, Evan T. *Bird Medicine: The Sacred Power of Bird Shamanism*. Rochester, VT: Bear & Co., 2013.

Stickney, Eleanor. *A Little Bird Told Me So*. Danbury, CT: Rutledge Books,1997.

Tate, Peter. *Flights of Fancy*. New York: Penguin Random House, 2007.

Temple, Olivia and Robert, trans. *Aesop: The Complete Fables*. New York: Penguin Random House, 1998.

Thomas, Taffy. *The Magpie's Nest: A Treasury of Bird Folk Tales*. Stroud, UK: The History Press, 2019.

Warren-Chadd, Rachel, and Marianne Taylor. *Birds: Myth, Lore & Legend*. London: Bloomsbury Publishing, 2016.

ADDITIONAL SOURCES

"VII. Lesser Gods." Hawaiian Mythology Part One: The Gods. Internet Sacred Text Archive, accessed Oct. 9, 2023. https://sacred-texts.com/pac/hm/hm09.htm

"100 of the World's Worst Invasive Alien Species." Global Invasive Species Database, accessed June 22, 2023. http://www.iucngisd.org/gisd/100_worst.php

"200,000 Budgies." The Tree Projects, accessed Nov. 4, 2023. https://www.ourbreathingplanet.com/bee-hummingbird/amp

"About the Yellow-Eyed Penguin." The Yellow-Eyed Penguin Trust, accessed Nov. 3, 2023. https://www.yellow-eyedpenguin.org.nz

Aeschylus. *Eumenides*. https://topostext.org/work.php?work_id=14

"Aetos Dios." Theoi Greek Mythology, accessed Oct. 8, 2023. https://www.theoi.com/Ther/AetosDios.html

Alaska Science Center. "Juvenile Bar-Tailed Godwit B6 Sets World Record." United States Geological Survey, Nov. 3, 2022, accessed Nov. 2, 2023. https://www.usgs.gov/centers/alaska-science-center/news/juvenile-bar-tailed-godwit-b6-sets-world-record

Albert, Daniel. "Ivory Gull: A Birdwatcher's Holy Grail." Life in Norway, Oct. 23 2023, accessed Nov. 7, 2023. https://www.lifeinnorway.net/ivory-gull/

Albuquerque, Carlos. "Eurasian Jay Totem." Ichthyoconodon, July 25, 2012, accessed Oct. 27, 2023. https://ichthyoconodon.wordpress.com/2012/07/25/eurasian-jay-totem/

"Alcyone and Ceyx." Greeka.com, accessed Oct. 4, 2023. https://www.greeka.com/greece-myths/alcyone-ceyx

Allen, Kevin. "8 Things You Need to Know About Honolulu's White Fairy Tern." *Hawai'i Magazine*, Apr. 5, 2019, accessed Oct. 27, 2023. https://www.hawaiimagazine.com/8-things-you-need-to-know-about-honolulus-white-fairy-tern/

"American Indians & Hummers." Operation RubyThroat, July 1, 2000, accessed Nov. 18, 2023. https://www.rubythroat.org/CultureIndianSummary01.html

Andreev, A. V. (2009). "The Blakiston's Fish Owl (*Ketupa blakistoni*) at the North-Eastern Limits of Its Range." *Osnabrücker Naturwissenschaftliche Mitteilungen*, 35: 47–54

Andreoni, Maura. "The Ancient Admiration of Birds: Flamingoes as Masterpieces of Art and Food." Ancient Origins, June 25, 2019, accessed Nov. 9, 2023.

https://www.ancient-origins.net/history-ancient-traditions/flamingos-0012192

"Aosagibi." Accessed Nov. 6, 2023. https://yokai.com/aosagibi/

"Argentine Folklore: The Legend of the Origin of the Carau." Under the Influence! Sept. 5, 2018, accessed Oct. 8, 2023. https://ztevetevans.wordpress.com/tag/limpkin/

Armstrong, Edward A. *Saint Francis, Nature Mystic: The Derivation and Significance of the Nature Stories in the Franciscan Legend*. Berkeley and Los Angeles, CA: University of California Press, 1973.

Ashby, Anne. "Legends About the Kiwi." Oct. 29, 2013, accessed Oct. 8, 2023. http://www.anneashby.com/legends-about-the-kiwi/

Ashliman, D. L. "The Golden Mallard." Golden Fowls, 2019, accessed Oct. 7, 2023. https://sites.pitt.edu/~dash/goldfowl.html#jataka

"Australian Pelican." Australian Museum, Sept. 12, 2020, accessed Nov. 8, 2023. https://australian.museum/learn/animals/birds/australian-pelican/

Avia. "Celtic Animal Signs." Whats-Your-Sign.com, Dec. 16, 2017, accessed Nov. 19, 2023. https://www.whats-your-sign.com/celtic-animal-signs.html#h-celtic-wren-sign

"Barbary Partridge." Visit Gibraltar, accessed Oct. 4, 2023. http://www.visitgibraltar.gi/see-and-do/natural-attractions/barbary-partridge-37

Barton, Allan. "The Legend of the Clay Birds." The Antiquary, accessed Nov. 8, 2023. https://medievalart.co.uk/2008/09/13/the-legend-of-the-clay-birds/

"The Beings of the Skies and Those of the Earth Face Off." Michigan History Series, Michigan News, University of Michigan, accessed Oct. 18, 2023. https://news.umich.edu/the-beings-of-the-skies-and-those-of-the-earth-face-off/

Belaunde, Luisa Elvira. "Parrots and Oropendolas: the Aesthetics of Gender Relations Among the Airo-Pai of the Peruvian Amazon." *Journal de la société des américanistes*, 1994, 80, 95-111. Accessed Nov. 12, 2023. https://www.persee.fr/doc/jsa_0037-9174_1994_num_80_1_1527

"Belted Kingfisher: River Patrol." American Bird Conservancy, accessed Nov. 3, 2023. https://abcbirds.org/bird/belted-kingfisher

Bennet, Taylor. "Black Skimmer Colony Thriving at Freeport Dow Chemical Plant." Gulf Coast Bird Observatory. Accessed Nov. 15, 2023. https://www.gcbo.org/wp-content/uploads/2020/01/Black-Skimmer-Article.pdf

Bergenholtz, Bjorn. "Some Additional Etymological Information." BirdForum, Aug. 17, 2014, accessed Nov. 7, 2023. https://www.birdforum.net/threads/some-additional-etymological-information-–-part-iii.289124/

BirdNote. "People Once Believed Bohemian Waxwings Had an Amazing Superpower." Audubon, Dec. 3, 2018, accessed Oct. 10, 2023. https://www.audubon.org/news/people-once-believed-bohemian-waxwings-had-amazing-superpower

"Birds Caribbean Expresses Deep Concern Over Three Damaging Developments in Grenada." Birds Caribbean, Aug. 28, 2020, accessed Nov. 2, 2023. https://www.birdscaribbean.org/2020/08/birdscaribbean-expresses-deep-concern-over-three-damaging-developments-in-grenada/

"Birds in Q'eqchi' Maya Culture." Community Cloud Forest Conservation, accessed Nov. 7, 2023. https://cloudforestconservation.org/knowledge/community/ethnoornithology/

Bjarnason, Baldur. "The Falcon's Shriek." January 2, 2013, accessed Oct. 30, 2023. https://www.baldurbjarnason.com/2013/01/02/the-falcons-shriek/

Blakey, Heather. "Moola the Pelican." While Waiting for Godot, Jan. 31, 2018, accessed Nov. 8, 2023. https://whilewaitingforgodot.net/2018/01/31/moola-the-pelican/

"The Blue Rock Thrush." *Malta Today*, Oct. 29, 2010, accessed Nov. 5, 2023. https://www.maltatoday.com.mt/environment/nature/5953/58-the-blue-rock-thrush/

Boles, Walter E. The Robins and Flycatchers of Australia. North Ryde, NSW: Angus & Robertson, 1988.

Bonta, Bruce. "Inuit Myth Fosters Purity." INC Greensboro, Oct. 16, 2008, accessed Oct. 26, 2023. https://peacefulsocieties.uncg.edu/2008/10/16/inuit-myth-fosters-purity/

Borrud, Hillary, and Gordon R. Friedman. "Lawmakers Adjourn 2017 Session with Mixed Results for Biggest Priorities." *The Oregonian*, July 7, 2017, accessed Nov. 7, 2023. https://www.oregonlive.com/politics/2017/07/lawmakers_adjourn_2017_session.html

"Bowerbird." San Diego Zoo Wildlife Alliance, accessed Nov. 13, 2023. https://animals.sandiegozoo.org/animals/bowerbird

"Bringing Back the Sharptail." Minnesota Sharp-Tailed Grouse Society, accessed Nov. 19, 2023. https://www.sharptails.org/bringing-back-the-sharptail/

Brown, Cathy. "Meet the Andean Condor, the King of the Andes." World Wildlife Fund, Apr 9, 2022, accessed Nov. 20, 2023. https://www.nathab.com/blog/andean-condor

Bryan, Kenza. "Woman Convicted of Husband's Murder after Parrot Witness Repeats 'Don't Shoot.'" *Independent*, July 21, 2017, accessed Nov. 12, 2023. https://www.independent.co.uk/news/world/americas/woman-murder-husband-parrot-witness-don-t-shoot-convicted-michigan-glenna-duram-a7852476.html

Burton, Richard F., trans. *The Thousand and One Nights*. New York: Limited Editions Club, 1934.

"Bushtit." BirdZilla, accessed Nov. 12, 2023. https://www.birdzilla.com/birds/bushtit/

Carnavon, Anna. "What Does a Yellow Bird Symbolize? Unveiling the Meaning Behind the Yellow Feathered Bird." ColoringFolder, May 18, 2023, accessed Nov. 15, 2023. https://coloringfolder.com/what-does-a-yellow-bird-symbolize/

Carr-Gomm, Philip. "The Swan." Order of Bards, Ovates & Druids, March 9, 2020, accessed Oct. 22, 2023. https://druidry.org/resources/the-swan

Chapman, David. "Wildlife Watch: The Rook." *Saga*, Feb. 1, 2016, accessed Oct. 19, 2023. https://www.saga.co.uk/magazine/home-garden/gardening/wildlife/birds/the-rook

Cheke, Anthony S. "The Dodo's Last Island." Royal Society of Arts and Sciences of Mauritius. Archived (PDF) from the original on 28 March 2016, accessed Oct. 12, 2023. https://web.archive.org/web/20160328040044/http://dodobooks.com/wp-content/uploads/2012/01/Cheke-2004-DodosLastIsland.pdf

"Cherokee Ethnobiology: Red-Tailed Hawk." Cherokee Nation, 2008, accessed Oct. 12, 2023. https://www.cherokee.org/media/pvlj1u0f/redtailedhawk.pdf

Cho, Anjie. "Meaning and Uses of Mandarin Duck Symbols in Feng Shui." The Spruce, Feb 2, 2022, accessed Aug 20, 2023. https://www.thespruce.com/mandarin-ducks-feng-shui-5217709

Chris. "Skylark Spiritual Meaning and Symbolism (9 Omens)." Symbolism and Metaphor, Nov. 17, 2022, accessed Aug. 20, 2023. https://symbolismandmetaphor.com/skylark-symbolism-spiritual-meaning/

Clarke, Philip. *Where the Ancestors Walked: Australia as an Aboriginal Landscape*. Crows Nest, NSW: Allen & Unwin, 2004.

Clifford, Garth C. "Duck Symbolism & Meaning." *World Birds Joy of Nature*, July 20, 2022, accessed Oct. 6, 2023. https://worldbirds.com/duck-symbolism/#east

"Cockatiel History – How the Cockatiel Got Its Name." Cockatiels as Pets, accessed Nov. 6, 2023. https://cockatielsaspets.com/cockatiel-history

"Cockatiel Symbolism." *Cockatiel World*, Aug. 3, 2023, accessed Nov. 6, 2023. https://cockatielworld.co.uk/cockatiel-symbolism

"Common Myna." eBird, Cornell Laboratory of Ornithology, accessed June 22, 2023. https://ebird.org/species/commyn

Connors, Valerie. "Waynaboozhoo and the Great Flood." Accessed Oct. 26, 2023. http://www.uwosh.edu/coehs/cmagproject/ethnomath/legend/legend9.htm

"Conserving Rwanda's Emblematic Gray Crowned Crane." Rwanda Wildlife Conservation Association, accessed Oct. 10, 2023. https://whitleyaward.org/winners/conserving-rwandas-emblematic-grey-crowned-crane/

Copernik Cahiers, Perla. "Roseate Spoonbill: The Flaming Bird." Conservation and Photography, Dec. 31, 2021, accessed Nov. 10, 2023. https://perlacopernikcahiers.com/2021/12/31/roseate-spoonbill-the-flaming-bird/

Couch, Stacey L.L. "Spirit Animals: Great Horned Owl." *Wild Gratitude*, accessed Oct. 11, 2023. https://www.wildgratitude.com/great-horned-owl-symbolism/

"Coyote and the Quails; Coyote and the Fawns." Indian Legends of California and the Southwest. Accessed Oct. 13, 2023. http://www.mythfolklore.net/3043mythfolklore/reading/california/pages/07.htm

Craciun, Adriana. "What a Roving Steller's Sea Eagle May Tell Us about Ourselves." Atlas Obscura, May 22, 2023, accessed Oct. 29, 2023. https://www.atlasobscura.com/articles/stellers-sea-eagle-in-maine

"Cranes and Culture: How These Special Birds Have Shaped Our Histories." Overberg Crane Group, accessed Oct. 8, 2023. https://www.bluecrane.org.za/cranes-and-culture-how-these-special-birds-have-shaped-our-histories/

Crew, Bec. "Australasian Bittern Known as the Bunyip Bird." Australian Geographic, March 5, 2015, accessed Oct. 10, 2023. https://www.australiangeographic.com.au/blogs/creatura-blog/2015/03/australasian-bittern-bunyip-bird/

Crew, Bec. "Oriental Dwarf Kingfisher, a Rainbow by Any Other Name." *Australian Geographic*, May 24, 2014, accessed Oct. 17, 2023. https://www.australiangeographic.com.au/blogs/creatura-blog/2014/05/oriental-dwarf-kingfisher/

"Crocodiles Would Never Eat This Bird!" TrTube, Jan. 1, 2022, accessed Nov. 11, 2023. https://www.youtube.com/watch?v=DcnNeSlOxfk

Crystal. "Discover the Meaning and Symbolism of Mourning Doves." AZ Animals, Oct. 17, 2023, accessed Nov. 20, 2023. https://a-z-animals.com/blog/discover-the-meaning-and-symbolism-of-mourning-doves/

"Cuban Trogon: The National Bird of Cuba." AZ Animals, accessed Nov. 11, 2023. https://a-z-animals.com/blog/cuban-trogon-the-national-bird-of-cuba/

Curtis, Sam. "The Great Gray Owl." *Montana Pioneer*, accessed Nov. 17, 2023. https://montanapioneer.com/the-great-gray-owl/

Datiles, Jen. "Myths in the Museum: The Iron-Eater and the Ostrich Egg." London's Global University, July 4, 2019, accessed Nov. 17, 2023. https://blogs.ucl.ac.uk/researchers-in-museums/2019/07/04/myths-in-the-museum-the-iron-eater-and-the-ostrich-egg/

"A Deadly Toll: The Devastating Wildlife Effects of Deepwater Horizon—and the Next Catastrophic Oil Spill." Center for Biological Diversity, accessed Nov. 8, 2023. https://www.biologicaldiversity.org/programs/public_lands/energy/dirty_energy_development/oil_and_gas/gulf_oil_spill/a_deadly_toll.html

"The Demoiselle Crane." Stories for the Museum Floor, April 27, 2018, accessed Oct. 27, 2023. https://storiesfromthemuseumfloor.wordpress.com/2018/04/27/the-demoiselle-crane/

Dendy, Teresa. "Anna's Hummingbird." Birds Named for Birds, accessed Oct. 13, 2023. https://birdnamesforbirds.wordpress.com/dishonorifics-teresa-dendy/annas-hummingbird-by-teresa-dendy/

Deschermeier, Hanzi. "The 5 Best Tasting Waterfowl." The Meat Eater, Sept. 24, 2020, accessed Oct. 6, 2023. https://www.themeateater.com/hunt/waterfowl/the-5-best-tasting-waterfowl

"Did Benjamin Franklin Want the National Bird to Be a Turkey?" The Franklin Institute, accessed Oct. 28, 2023. https://www.fi.edu/en/benjamin-franklin/franklin-national-bird

"Discover the Unique National Bird of Puerto Rico." Puerto Rico Travel, accessed Nov.16, 2023. https://www.puertoricotravel.guide/blog/the-discover-the-unique-national-bird-of-puerto-rico/

"The Divinity of the Resplendent Quetzal." *The Holbrook Explorer*, Jan. 22, 2014, accessed Nov. 9, 2023. https://www.holbrooktravel.com/blog/birding/divinity-resplendent-quetzal

Dupree, Nancy Hatch. "An Interpretation of the Role of the Hoopoe in Afghan Folklore and Magic." Folklore, 85(3), 1974. Accessed Nov. 20, 2023. https://www.tandfonline.com/doi/abs/10.1080/0015587X.1974.9716553

"Eagle, Hummingbird and Coyote: An Ohlone Creation Myth." Multo (Ghost), accessed Oct. 13, 2023. https://multoghost.wordpress.com/2016/06/29/eagle-hummingbird-and-coyote-an-ohlone-creation-myth/

Eccles, Vanessa K. The Mysterious Red-Winged Blackbird. Fabled Collective, Sept. 30, 2022, accessed Aug. 20, 2023. https://www.fabledcollective.com/the-mysterious-red-winged-blackbird/#:~:text=The%20Red%2Dwinged%20Blackbird%20Symbolism,of%20their%20lore%20and%20symbolism.

"Egyptian Vulture." LIFE Egyptian Vulture Project. Accessed Nov. 5, 2023. https://www.lifegyptianvulture.it/en/

Ellison, George. "The Honest Little Bird." *Smoky Mountain News*, May 10, 2006, accessed Nov. 16, 2023. https://smokymountainnews.com/archives/item/13484-the-honest-little-bird

"Entertainment: Best 100 British Films – Full List." BBC News, Sept. 23, 1999, accessed Oct. 25, 2023. http://news.bbc.co.uk/2/hi/entertainment/455170.stm

Erickson, Laura. "For the Birds Radio Program: Ovenbird." Laura Erickson's For the Birds, May 19, 2016, accessed Nov. 15, 2023. https://www.lauraerickson.com/radio/program/10970/ovenbird/

"Falcon Symbol." Warpath 2 Peace Pipes, accessed Oct. 25, 2023. https://www.warpaths2peacepipes.com/native-american-symbols/list-of-symbols.htm

Finger, Nathan. "The Bird That Doesn't Build a Nest." Creatures, Medium, Aug. 12, 2021, accessed Oct. 27, 2023. https://medium.com/creatures/the-bird-that-doesnt-build-a-nest-14d897d9a948

"Forty-Second Supplement to The American Ornithologists' Union Check-List of North American Birds." The Auk, 117(3), July 2000, 847-858. https://academic.oup.com/auk/article/117/3/847/5561758?login=false

Fox, Florence C. *The Indian Primer*. American Book Company, New York, 1906.

Fox, Leonard (1990). Hainteny: The Traditional Poetry of Madagascar. Bucknell University Press. pp. 261, 422. ISBN 978-0-8387-5175-6.

Free Spirit Meg. "Totem Animal: Blue-Footed Booby." Free Spirit Meg, March 11, 2019, accessed Nov. 17, 2023. https://freespiritmeg.com/2019/03/11/totem-animal-blue-footed-booby

Friedman, Amy. "The Golden Egg." *The Oklahoman*, April 8, 1996, accessed Oct. 23, 2023. https://www.oklahoman.com/story/news/1996/04/08/the-golden-egg/62359012007/

Friedman, Shani. "Owl Myths and Legends." Wild Birds Online, Oct. 16, 2016, accessed August 18, 2023. https://wildbirdsonline.com/blogs/news/owl-myths-and-legends

Frost, Robert. "The Oven Bird." 1916, located on Wikipedia Nov 15, 2023. https://en.wikipedia.org/wiki/The_Oven_Bird

"Galah." Native Symbols, accessed Oct. 24, 2023. https://nativesymbols.info/galah/

Gallagher, Tim. *The Grail Bird*. Houghton Mifflin Company, Boston, 2005.

"Gawai Kenyalang (Hornbill Festival)." The Land of Hornbill's Celebrations, accessed Oct. 11, 2023. https://sharmabelle.wordpress.com/the-gawai-festival/gawai-kenyalang/

Gerard, John. *Generall Historie of Plantes*. London, England, 1597. Accessed on Wikipedia, Oct. 10, 2023. https://en.wikipedia.org/wiki/Barnacle_goose_myth#References

Gertz, Emily. "Scientists Ran World's Most Evolutionarily Distinct Birds." *Popular Science*, Apr 15, 2014, accessed Nov. 16, 2023. https://www.popsci.com/article/science/scientists-rank-worlds-most-evolutionarily-distinct-birds/

Gillard, Ernest Thomas. *Living Birds of the World*. Reprinted by Literary Licensing, LLC, Oct. 29, 2011.

"The Golden Pheasant in Chinese Culture and Tradition." Terra Firma Tourist, Oct. 14, 2012, accessed Oct. 17, 2023. https://www.terrafirmatourist.com/the-golden-pheasant-in-chinese-art-and-culture/

"Gone for 300 Years, Common Crane Comes Home to Rewetted Irish Peatlands." Bord na Móna, accessed Oct. 27, 2023. https://www.bordnamona.ie/gone-for-300-years-common-crane-comes-home-to-rewetted-irish-peatlands

Goodheart, Emily. "East of the Sun and West of the Moon: The Folklore of Arctic Animals." World Wildlife Fund, Feb. 3, 2018, accessed Nov. 14, 2023. https://www.nathab.com/blog/folklore-arctic-animals/

Gosford, Bob. "The Bush Stone Curlew as a Harbinger of Death??? And more." WorldWaders News Blog, Sept. 28, 2010, accessed Oct. 11, 2023. https://worldwaders.wordpress.com/2010/09/28/the-bush-stone-curlew-as-a-harbinger-of-death/

Goulet, Brianna. "Blue-Jay Symbolism and Meaning." *Birdzilla*, May 18, 2023, accessed Oct. 22, 2023. https://www.birdzilla.com/learn/blue-jay-symbolism-meaning/#:~:text=Blue%20Jays%20primarily%20symbolize%20protection,creation%2C%20abundance%2C%20and%20healing.

"Greater Prairie Chicken." The Nature Conservancy, accessed Nov. 19, 2023. https://web.archive.org/web/20110121202756/http://www.nature.org/animals/birds/animals/gprairiechicken.html

Greenspan, Joseph. "What Is a Seahawk, Anyway?" Audubon, Jan. 29, 2015, accessed Nov. 16, 2023. https://www.audubon.org/news/what-seahawk-anyway

"The Guatemalan Symbol of Freedom: The Resplendent Quetzal." Trama Textiles, Apr 8, 2021, accessed Nov. 9, 2023. https://tramatextiles.org/blogs/trama-blog/symbol_of_guatemala_the_resplendent_quetzal

"Gyrfalcon." The Peregrine Fund, accessed Oct. 25, 2023. https://www.peregrinefund.org/explore-raptors-species/falcons/gyrfalcon

Haas, Dieter, and Mundy, Peter. "Vultures Revered in Time and Place." *Vulture News*, 63 (4-13). January 2013, accessed Nov. 18, 2023.

Haines, Bryan. "8 Great Blue Turaco Facts." Storyteller. Travel, Oct. 5, 2023, accessed Oct. 19, 2023. https://storyteller.travel/great-blue-turaco-facts/

Hannemann, Emily. "Do Swallow Bird Sightings Have Special Meaning?" Birds & Blooms, June 20, 2022, accessed Nov. 14, 2023. https://www.birdsandblooms.com/birding/swallow-bird-meaning

Harman, Alex J., et al. "Grasshopper of the Cherokee Nation in Northeast Oklahoma." Oklahoma State University Extension, April 2022, accessed Nov 17, 2023. https://extension.okstate.edu/fact-sheets/grasshoppers-of-the-cherokee-nation-in-northeast-oklahoma.html

Hart, Patrick; Tanimoto-Johnson, Ann; Harriman-Pote, Savannah. "Manu Minute: The Common Myna." Hawai'i Public Radio, Nov. 22, 2021, accessed June 22, 2023. https://www.hawaiipublicradio.org/podcast/manu-minute/2021-11-22/manu-minute-the-common-myna

Hartley, William G. (February 1992), "Mormons, Crickets, and Gulls, A New Look at an Old Story", in Quinn, D. Michael (ed.), *The New Mormon History: Revisionist Essays on the Past*, Salt Lake City, Utah: Signature Books,

Hauck, Anthony. "Why Does South Dakota Have So Many Pheasants?" *Star Tribune*, Dec. 10, 2009, accessed Nov. 9, 2023. https://www.startribune.com/why-does-south-dakota-have-so-many-pheasants/79008327

"Hawaii State Bird: Nene History and Facts." Hawaii Bird Guide, accessed Oct. 11, 2023. https://hawaiibirdguide.com/hawaii-state-bird/

Hawkins, Kristen. Wood Duck Spiritual Meaning, Symbolism and Totem. Spirit & Symbolism, Mar 18, 2023, accessed Aug 20, 2023. https://spiritandsymbolism.com/wood-duck-spiritual-meaning-symbolism-and-totem/

Haxby, Clare. The National Bird of Singapore. ClareHaxby.com, accessed Aug. 19, 2023. https://clarehaxby.com/blogs/news/136990983-the-national-bird-of-singapore-crimson-sunbird

Heimbuch, Jaymi. "6 Myths and Superstitions about Owls." Treehugger, Oct. 24, 2022, accessed Aug. 18, 2023. https://www.treehugger.com/myths-and-superstitions-about-owls-4864542

"The Hell-Diver and the Spirit of Winter." Ojibwe Oral Tradition, Milwaukee Public Museum, accessed Nov. 11, 2023. https://www.mpm.edu/content/wirp/ICW-141

Helleland Ådnanes, Jens. "The Mythical, Wise, and Dangerous Owl." Jan. 24, 2013, accessed Oct. 11, 2023. https://partner.sciencenorway.no/animal-kingdom-forskningno-norway/the-mythical-wise-and-dangerous-owl/1381563

Helmenstine, Anne Marie. "9 Ways Crows Are Smarter Thank You Think." ThoughtCo., June 22, 2019, accessed Oct. 19, 2023. https://www.thoughtco.com/crows-are-more-intelligent-than-you-think-4156896

HIH Princess Takamado. "The Black Kite: a Clever Hawk." BirdLife International, Aug. 5, 2021, accessed Nov. 5, 2023. https://www.birdlife.org/news/2021/08/05/the-black-kite-a-clever-hawk

Hines, Barry. *A Kestrel for a Knave*. Original publication 1968, reprinted by Penguin Classics 2000.

Hose, Charles, and William McDougall. "Chapter 14: Ideas of the Soul Illustrated by Burial Customs, Soul-Catching, and Exorcism." *Pagan Tribes of Borneo*, accessed Nov. 14, 2023. https://web.archive.org/web/20120204074028/http://www.nalanda.nitc.ac.in/resources/english/etext-project/history/paganborneo/chapter15.html

"How the Bluebird and Coyote Got Their Color." Sialis, accessed Nov. 15, 2023. https://www.sialis.org/bluebirdstory.htm

"Huitzilopochtli, Aztec God." Britannica, accessed Oct. 30, 2023. https://www.britannica.com/topic/Huitzilopochtli

Hume, Lucile Bayon. "A Wonderful Bird is the Pelican." Detours Podcast, April 23, 2013, accessed Nov. 8, 2023. https://countryroadsmagazine.com/outdoors/knowing-nature/a-wonderful-bird-is-the-pelican/

Hurst, James. "The Scarlet Ibis." 1960. http://jjett.pbworks.com/w/file/fetch/97072218/The_Scarlet_Ibis.pdf

Hutchins, Lisa. "The Lark Bunting: Underdog State Bird." *Colorado Life*, accessed Oct. 12, 2023. https://www.coloradolifemagazine.com/blog/post/the-lark-bunting-underdog-state-bird

"Iceland: Fire and Ice, Land of Myth." *Nature*, PBS, May 14, 2008, accessed Oct. 25, 2023. https://www.pbs.org/wnet/nature/iceland-fire-and-ice-land-of-myth/3024/

"Iduna." Occult World, accessed Oct. 30, 2023. https://occult-world.com/iduna/

"Is this Bird Smoking? Viral Video of Rare Bare-Throated Bellbird Stuns Internet." *Times Now*, Oct. 18, 2022, accessed Nov. 12, 2023. https://www.timesnownews.com/videos/viral-videos/is-this-bird-smoking-viral-video-of-rare-bare-throated-bellbird-stuns-internet-watch-video-94937385#

Ishmael, Odeen. *Guyana Legends: Folk Tales of the Indigenous Amerindians*. Xlibris Corp., 2011.

Janiart. "Hornbills and Dayaknese Culture." BorneoScape, accessed Nov. 14, 2023. http://www.borneoscape.com/2021/05/helmeted-hornbills-and-dayaknese-culture.html.html

"Javan Hawk-Eagle–*Nisaetus bartelsi*." The Eagle Directory, accessed Nov. 5, 2023. http://eagleencyclopedia.org/species/javan_hawk_eagle.html

Jha, Mrityunjoy Kumar. "Brahminy Ducks: The Chakwa-Chakwi Love Birds of India." Daikiworld,com, May 31, 2021, accessed Nov. 17, 2023. https://www.daijiworld.com/news/newsDisplay?newsID=838703

Jones, Paul Anthony. "Christbird." Haggard Hawks, Jan. 27, 2021, accessed Nov. 3, 2023. https://www.haggardhawks.com/post/christbird

Julien. "Meet the National Bird of Nepal, the Himalayan Monal (Dafne)." Exploration Junkie, accessed Nov. 3, 2023. https://www.explorationjunkie.com/nepal-national-bird/

Julien. "Meet the National Bird of Paraguay, The Bare-Throated Bellbird." Exploration Junkie, accessed Nov. 12, 2023. https://www.explorationjunkie.com/paraguay-national-bird/

Keegan, Jane Linda. *Kororā and the Sushi Shop*. Scholastic New Zealand, 2022.

Kersey, Donna. "The Story of the Hummingbird." God's Other Ways, accessed Nov. 8, 2023. https://www.godsotherways.com/stories/2020/3/25/do-the-next-thing-4baw5-8faz4-8858t-9sdzk-7e82s-8b4j4-5r9gl-r549t

"Kestrel Folklore." Peak Boxes, March 30, 2019, accessed Oct. 25, 2023. https://peakboxes.co.uk/knowledge-learning-blog/2019/3/30/kestrel-folklore

Kitchener, Andrew. "The Tale of the Montserrat Oriole." National Museum of Scotland, accessed Oct. 30, 2023. https://blog.nms.ac.uk/2020/07/22/the-tale-of-the-montserrat-oriole/

"Kookaburra's laughter (An Australian Legend)." *Sun Herald*, accessed Oct. 23, 2023. https://www.sunherald.com/living/article83236122.html

"Kororā: about Little Penguins." Blue Penguins Pukekura, accessed Oct. 24, 2023. https://www.bluepenguins.co.nz/blue-penguins

Kuhnlein, Harriet V., and Murray M. Humphries. "Gulls." Traditional Animal Foods of Indigenous Peoples of Northern North America. Accessed Nov. 2, 2023. http://traditionalanimalfoods.org/birds/shorebirds/page.aspx?id=6466

LaMère, Oliver. "The King Bird." Wisconsin Archaeologist, 1920, accessed Nov. 20, 2023. https://hotcakencyclopedia.com/ho.KingBird.html

Landers, Art. "Art Landers Outdoors: The Distinctive Call of the Yellow-Billed Cuckoo Foretells of Summer Storms." NKY Tribune, Aug. 30, 2019, accessed Oct. 18, 2023. https://nkytribune.com/2019/08/art-landers-outdoors-the-distinctive-call-of-the-yellow-billed-cuckoo-foretells-of-summer-storms/

Langley, William. "The Ruddy Ducks with Nowhere Left to Hide." *The Telegraph*, March 31, 2014, accessed Nov. 7, 2023. https://web.archive.org/web/20140331050056/http://www.telegraph.co.uk/earth/wildlife/10626557/The-ruddy-ducks-with-nowhere-left-to-hide.html

"Largest Vocabulary for A Bird Ever." *Guinness World Records*, accessed Nov. 4, 2023. https://www.guinnessworldrecords.com/world-records/70967-largest-vocabulary-for-a-bird-ever

"Lark Symbolism and Meaning." Symbols & Meanings, accessed Oct. 24, 2023. https://spiritanimaldreams.com/lark-symbolism/

Larson-Wang, Jessica. "The History Behind the Cormorant Fishermen of Erhai Lake". Culture Trip. Archived from the original on 2020-08-16. Retrieved 2019-08-17.

Lartey, Jamiles. "'Don't Shoot': Pet Parrot's Words May Be Used in Michigan Murder Trial." *The Guardian*, June 27, 2016. Accessed Nov 12, 2023. https://www.theguardian.com/us-news/2016/jun/27/parrot-murder-trial-martin-duran-dont-shoot

Laubscher, Cyril. "Maroon-Bellied Crowned Pigeon … A Large Terrestrial Pigeon from New Guinea." AFA Watchbird, 2007, accessed Oct. 27, 2023.

Lee, John J. "Ortolan: The Controversial French Delicacy You'll Probably Never Try." Tasting Table, Nov. 3, 2022, accessed Oct. 24, 2023. https://www.tastingtable.com/1078603/ortolan-the-controversial-french-delicacy-youll-probably-never-try/

"The Legend of the African Crowned Crane." Lexia Learning Resources, accessed Oct. 10, 2023. https://www.lexialearningresources.com/Core5/closereads/CR_SE_L16.pdf

"The Legend of the Hermit Thrush." Oneida Indian Nation, accessed Oct. 16, 2023. https://www.oneidaindiannation.com/the-legend-of-the-hermit-thrush/#:~:text=The%20hermit%20thrush%20remains%20hidden,the%20other%20birds%20fall%20silent.

Leianna. "Trolls on the Isle of Rum." RSPB, Feb. 20, 2012, accessed Nov. 13, 2023. https://community.rspb.org.uk/ourwork/b/scotland/posts/trolls-on-the-isle-of-rum

Leland, Charles G. "How Glooskap Became Friendly to The Loons, and Made Them His Messengers." *The Algonquin Legends of New England*, 1884, accessed Oct. 27, 2023. https://sacred-texts.com/nam/ne/al/al12.htm

Lenfest, Margret. "The Story of the Maple Tree." Swarthmore.edu, accessed Oct. 18, 2023. https://www.swarthmore.edu/SocSci/Linguistics/LenapeLanguageResources/pdf/StAmourLenfest.pdf

Le Roux, M., "Scientists Plan to Resurrect a Range of Extinct Animals Using DNA and Cloning". *Courier Mail*, 23 April 2013. Accessed Oct. 23, 2023. http://www.couriermail.com.au/news/scientists-plan-to-resurrect-a-range-of-extinct-animals-using-dna-and-cloning/story-e6freon6-1226626834888?nk=6a30daade715237f987174b18faf3de7

"Lesser Flamingo." SeaWorld Parks & Entertainment, accessed Nov. 9, 2023. https://seaworld.org/animals/facts/birds/lesser-flamingo/

Lewis, Deane. "Owls in Mythology & Culture." The Owl Pages, accessed Oct. 9, 2023. https://www.owlpages.com/owls/articles.php?=62

Li, Yunqui. "Wildlife of China: The Golden Pheasant." CGTN, Feb 5, 2019, accessed Oct. 17, 2023. https://news.cgtn.com/news/3d3d514d79456a4e30457a6333566d54/index.html

"Lilit Phra Lo." Wikipedia, accessed Nov. 3, 2023. https://en.wikipedia.org/wiki/Lilit_Phra_Lo

Lim Hong Yao and Kit Ho, Jonathan. "*Aerodramus fuciphagus* – Edible-nest Swiftlet." National University of Singapore, Jan 2, 2019, accessed Aug 19, 2023. https://wiki.nus.edu.sg/display/TAX/Aerodramus+fuciphagus+-+Edible-nest+Swiftlet

Limiñana, Arthur. "Why the French Can't Get Enough of This Illegal Bird." *Vice*, Jan. 29, 2017, accessed Oct. 24, 2023. https://www.vice.com/en/article/8qenxv/why-the-french-cant-get-enough-of-this-illegal-bird

Line, Les. "The Puffins Keep Their Secrets." National Wildlife Federation, Aug. 1, 1994, accessed Oct. 26, 2023. https://www.nwf.org/Magazines/National-Wildlife/1994/The-Puffins-Keep-Their-Secrets

Lipske, Michael. "Bermuda's Born-Again Petrels." National Wildlife Federation, Jan 14, 2013, accessed Nov.12, 2023. https://www.nwf.org/Home/Magazines/National-Wildlife/2013/FebMarch/Conservation/Bermuda-Petrels

"Little Owl Folklore." Peak Boxes, March 30, 2019, accessed Oct. 9, 2023. https://peakboxes.co.uk/knowledge-learning-blog/littleowlfolklore

Lowe, Gail. "The Legend of the Phoenix." Phoenix Creative Arts, Sept. 18, 2021, accessed Nov. 9, 2023. https://phoenixcreativearts.co.uk/the-legend-of-the-phoenix/

Lumini, Scoil Rince. "Dance in Irish Mythology, Part 3." *Irish Folklore and Mythology: Volume VII*. July 26, 2021, accessed Oct. 27 2023. https://www.irishdancect.com/news/irish-folklore-and-mythology-volume-vii8908882

Lund, Nicholas. "The Shoebill: Or, the Most Terrifying Bird in the World." Audubon, Aug. 5, 2016, accessed Oct. 10, 2023. https://www.audubon.org/news/the-shoebill-or-most-terrifying-bird-world

Macdonald, Helen. *Falcon*. Reaktion Books, 2016.

MacGregor, Alasdair Alpin. *The Peat-Fire Flame. Folk-tales and traditions of the Highlands & Islands*. The Moray Press, Edinburgh & London, 1937. https://digital.nls.uk/early-gaelic-book-collections/archive/81146179?mode=transcription

"The Magic of the Macaw." Volunteer Latin America, accessed Oct. 9, 2023. https://www.volunteerlatinamerica.com/blog/posts/the-magic-of-the-macaw

"The Magic of the Morepork." Stuff, June 22, 2012, accessed Nov. 6, 2023.

"Magpie Split Five Ways." *Bird Guides*, July 26, 2018, accessed Nov. 10, 2023. https://www.birdguides.com/articles/taxonomy/magpie-split-five-ways/

"Manutara, the Sacred Bird that Still Lives in the Memory of Rapa Nui." Imagina Rapa Nui Easter Island, accessed Nov. 6, 2023. https://imaginarapanui.com/en/manutara-sacred-bird-rapa-nui-easter-island/

"Māori & Birds of Prey / Ruru in Māori Mythology." Wingspan National Bird of Prey Center, accessed Nov. 6, 2023. https://www.wingspan.co.nz/maori_mythology_and_the_ruru_morepork.html

Masanobu, Kagawa. "Tengu: The Birdlike Demons that Became Almost Devine." Nippon.com, Dec. 2, 2022, accessed Nov. 18, 2023. https://www.nippon.com/en/japan-topics/b02507/

Matenga, Edward (2001). "The Soapstone Birds of Great Zimbabwe". Studies in Global Archaeology. 16: 1–261.

Matthews, Mimi. "The Peacock in Myth, Legend, and 19th Century History." Mimi Matthews.com, May 13, 2016, accessed Nov. 8, 2023. https://www.mimimatthews.com/2016/05/13/the-peacock-in-myth-legend-and-19th-century-history/

"The Mayan Fable of the Toh Bird." *Precambrian Tales, Weeds and Wildflowers*, April 18, 2022, accessed Nov. 5, 2023. https://medium.com/weeds-wildflowers/the-mayan-fable-of-the-toh-bird-9f5f40516349

McGrath, Sheena. "Apollo: the Swan-God." We Are Star Stuff, accessed Oct. 22, 2023. https://earthandstarryheaven.com/2015/04/22/apollo-swan/

McIntyre, Judith. "How the Loon Became a Water Bird." *The Common Loon, Spirit of Northern Lakes*, accessed at Journey North.org, Oct. 27, 2023. https://journeynorth.org/tm/loon/Legends.html

McKay, Helen F., ed. *Gadi Mirrabooka: Australian Aboriginal Tales from the Dreaming*. London: Bloomsbury Publishing, 2001.

"Meleager." *Britannica*, accessed Nov. 6, 2023. https://www.britannica.com/topic/Meleager-Greek-mythology

Meneely, Scott. "King Vulture." WhoZoo.org, accessed Nov. 15, 2023. https://whozoo.org/Anlife99/scottmen/newvulture.htm

"Millions of Albatrosses Now Lead-Free on Midway." American Bird Conservancy, Aug. 17, 2018, accessed Nov. 9, 2023. https://abcbirds.org/albatrosses-now-lead-free-on-midway

Minns, Sean. "Rook—Sentinel of the Farmlands." Avibirds, March 25, 2021, accessed Oct. 19, 2023. https://avibirds.com/rook

Misra, P.K. "A Story of Bulbul and Camel." Star of Mysore, Dec. 15, 2018, accessed Nov 13, 2023. https://starofmysore.com/a-story-of-bulbul-camel/

Montgomerie, Bob. "The Sacred Sacred Ibis." American Ornithological Society, Oct. 15, 2018, accessed Nov. 18, 2023. https://americanornithology.org/the-sacred-sacred-ibis

Mostert, Tim. "Know Your nation: Why the Blue Crane Is Honoured amongst Many African Tribes." News24, June 18, 2017, accessed Oct. 8, 2023. https://www.news24.com/life/archive/know-your-nation-why-the-blue-crane-is-honoured-amongst-many-african-tribes-20170618

Muir, John. *The Mountains of California*. Sierra Club Books, March 1989 (re-release of 1894 book).

Muller, Nazma. "On the Wing: Birdwatching in the Caribbean." *Caribbean Beat*, December 2014, accessed Oct. 30, 2023. https://www.caribbean-beat.com/issue-130/on-the-wing#axzz8HdwVg1eY

"Mut." Ancient Egypt Online, accessed Oct. 28, 2023. https://ancientegyptonline.co.uk/mut/

"Mut." *Britannica Kids*, accessed Oct. 28, 2023. https://kids.britannica.com/students/article/Mut/312377

"Myna Bird." AZ Animals, Apr 6, 2023, accessed June 22, 2023. https://a-z-animals.com/animals/myna-bird

"The Myths of Ursa Major, The Great Bear." AAVSO Hands-On-Astrophysics Teaching Manual, accessed Nov. 11, 2023. https://www.aavso.org/myths-uma

Narayan, Shoba. Episode 34: Amazing Bird Species: Brahminy Kite. The Bird Podcast, Feb. 27, 2022, accessed Oct. 29, 2023. https://birdpodcast.com/2022/02/27/episode-34-amazing-bird-species-brahminy-kite/

Narula, Roohi. "Know it 'Owl': Ritualistic Sacrifices of Owls During Diwali." Wildlife SOS, Nov. 10, 2021, accessed Nov. 20, 2023. https://wildlifesos.org/chronological-news/know-it-owl-ritualistic-sacrifices-of-owls-during-diwali/

"Native American Astrology." Two Feathers, accessed Oct. 7, 2023. https://twofeathers.co.uk/pages/native-american-astrology#snow-goose-and-capricorn

"Native American Auk and Puffin Mythology." Native-Languages.org, accessed Oct. 26, 2023. http://www.native-languages.org/legends-puffin.htm

"Native American Bittern Mythology." Native-Languages.org, accessed Oct. 10, 2023. http://www.native-languages.org/legends-bittern.htm

"Native American Blackbird Mythology." Native-Languages.org, accessed Nov. 13, 2023. http://www.native-languages.org/legends-blackbird.htm#google_vignette

"Native American Dance Styles: Shawl Dance." Nanticoke Indian Tribe, accessed Oct. 22, 2023. https://nanticokeindians.org/about/culture/

"Native American Duck Mythology." Native-Languages.org, accessed Nov. 4, 2023. http://www.native-languages.org/legends-duck.htm

"Native American Legends: Wisakedjak." Native-Languages. org, accessed Nov. 9, 2023. http://www.native-languages. org/wisakejak.htm

"Native American Titmouse Mythology." Native-Languages. org, accessed Oct. 10, 2023. http://www.native-languages. org/legends-titmouse.htm

Newberry, Gretchen N. "The Mythos of Nighthawks." Gretchen N. Newberry, Aug. 22, 2017, accessed Oct. 17, 2023. https://gretchennewberry.wordpress. com/2017/08/22/the-mythos-of-nighthawks/

Nielsen, John. *Condor: to the brink and back—the life and times of one giant bird*. New York: HarperCollins, 2006.

"Northern Cardinal Symbolism: Deciphering the Myths and Meanings of This Vibrant Bird." Birdfact, Aug. 18, 2023, accessed Oct. 16, 2023. https://birdfact.com/articles/ northern-cardinal-symbolism

"Northern Shrike." *Birdzilla*, accessed Oct. 31, 2023. https://www.birdzilla.com/birds/northern-shrike/

Nystrom, Siera. "American Dipper: John Muir's Water Ouzel." Sept. 19, 2016, accessed Oct. 18, 2023. http://natural-history-journal.blogspot.com/2016/09/ american-dipper-john-muirs-water-ouzel.html

O'Brien, Patricia J., and Diane M. Post. "Speculations about Bobwhite Quail and Pawnee Religion." Plains Anthropologist, 33(122:1), Nov. 1988, pp. 489-504. https://www.jstor.org/stable/25668799

O'Hara, Keith. "The Morrigan Goddess: The Story of the Fiercest Goddess in Irish Myth." The Irish Road Trip, June 29, 2023, accessed Nov. 10, 2023. https://www. theirishroadtrip.com/the-morrigan/

"Oilbird." Our Breathing Planet, accessed Nov. 16, 2023. https://www.ourbreathingplanet.com/oilbird/

"Old Nog." *Roaringwater Journal*, May 18, 2014, accessed Oct. 9, 2023. https://roaringwaterjournal.com/tag/ folklore-of-herons

"Olonkho." Google Arts and Culture, accessed Nov. 2, 2023. https://artsandculture.google.com/story/ wAUxd1RDHiSUIQ

"One For Sorrow". Bird Spot. 11 November 2020. Retrieved Nov. 9, 2023. https://www.birdspot.co.uk/ culture/one-for-sorrow-magpie-nursery-rhyme

"Orpendola Bird: A Spectacle to Behold." TheGoddessGarden.com, Nov. 22, 2019, accessed Nov. 12, 2023. https://thegoddessgarden.com/the-oropendola/

"Oystercatcher Rattle." Donald Ellis Gallery, accessed Oct. 28, 2023. https://www.donaldellisgallery.com/offerings/ northwest-coast/oystercatcher-rattle-n4337

Pashby, Jim. "Snow Bunting." Montana Outdoors, accessed Nov. 11, 2023. https://fwp.mt.gov/binaries/content/ assets/fwp/montana-outdoors/snowbunting.pdf

Peers, Eleanor. "Dancing With Cranes, Singing to Gods: The Sakha Yhyakh and post-Soviet national revival." Located in Ziker, John P., et al. *The Siberian World*, Mar. 29, 2023. Routledge, London.

"Penelope in Greek Mythology." Greek Legends and Myths, accessed Nov. 3, 2023. https://www. greeklegendsandmyths.com/penelope.html

"The Penguin." The Tawaki Project, accessed Oct. 24, 2023. https://www.tawaki-project.org/the-penguin/

Phan, Hai Dang. "The Seed and the Thrush, and From the Pines." *New England Review*, Middlebury College, 43 (1), 2022. Project Muse, accessed Nov. 19, 2023. https://muse. jhu.edu/article/851387/pdf

Phillipsen, Ivan. "The Hoatzin: A Weird and Wonderful Bird." Wild Latitudes, accessed Nov. 7, 2023. https://wildlatitudes.com/the-hoatzin-a-weird-and- wonderful-bird/

"Phoenix. A to Z Photo Dictionary, Japanese Buddhist Statuary." Accessed Oct. 25, 2023. http://www. onmarkproductions.com/html/ho-oo-phoenix.shtml

Pinch, Geraldine. *Egyptian Mythology: A Guide to the Gods, Goddesses, and Traditions of Ancient Egypt*. Oxford University Press, 2002.

Poppie, Tammy. "Brown-Headed Cowbird Spiritual Meanings & Symbolism – It' s Not All Bad!" On The Feeder, Oct. 28, 2023, accessed Nov. 5, 2023. https://www.onthefeeder.com/brown-headed-cowbird- spiritual-meaning/

Poppie, Tammy. "The Ultimate Guide to Starling Meaning and Symbolism." On the Feeder, Oct. 28, 2023, accessed Nov. 17, 2023. https://www.onthefeeder.com/starling- meaning/

"Prairie Chicken Dance." *Canadian Encyclopedia*, accessed Nov. 19, 2023. https://www.thecanadianencyclopedia.ca/ en/article/greater-prairie-chicken

Profumo, David. "The Folklore of the Mistle Thrush." *Country Life*, Nov. 29, 2014, accessed Nov. 19, 2023. https://www.countrylife.co.uk/country-life/folklore- mistle-thrush-66404

"Puffins in Folklore." Folklore Fun, March 22, 2018, accessed Oct. 26, 2023. https://folklorefun.wordpress. com/2018/03/22/puffins-in-folklore/

"Quail." Greekmythology.Fandom.com, accessed Oct. 21, 2023. https://greekmythology.fandom.com/wiki/Quail

Radko, Gemma. "Meet the Streamertail, the 'Most Beautiful Bird in Jamaica.'" American Bird Conservancy, Sept. 22, 2016, accessed Nov. 19, 2023. https://abcbirds.org/meet-the-streamertail/

Rain, Chloe. "Snowy Owl's Medicine, Meaning, and Spiritual Significance." Explore Deeply, Jan. 26, 2022, accessed Oct. 11, 2023. https://exploredeeply.com/live-your-purpose/appearance-of-the-great-white-snowy-owl-and-its-spiritual-significance-and-meaning-in-our-lives

Rasmussen, Cindy. "The Rufous Hornero: The National Bird of Argentina." AZ Animals, Dec. 12, 2022, accessed Oct. 26, 2023. https://a-z-animals.com/blog/rufous-hornero-the-national-bird-of-argentina/

Rasmussen, Cindy. "Turquoise-Browed Motmot: The National Bird of El Salvador." AZ Animals, Feb. 23, 2023, accessed Oct. 25, 2023. https://a-z-animals.com/blog/turquoise-browed-motmot-the-national-bird-of-el-salvador/

Raye, Lee. "Sea eagles (Haliaeetus albicilla) in 'Canu Heledd' (the Singing of Heledd)." National History, April 27, 2014, accessed Oct. 28, 2023. https://historyandnature.wordpress.com/2014/04/27/eaglesincanuheledd/

"Red-Backed Shrike Is Bird of the Year." SwissInfo.ch, Jan. 30, 2020, accessed Nov. 2, 2023. https://www.swissinfo.ch/eng/society/nature-_red-backed-shrike-is-bird-of-the-year/45527626

"Red-Legged Partridge." New Zealand Birds, 2009, accessed Oct. 4, 2023. https://www.nzbirds.com/birds/redleggedpartridge.html

"Red-Legged Partridge." Purdey.com, Oct. 18, 2022, accessed Oct. 4, 2023. https://www.purdey.com/blogs/a-guide-to-game-birds-1/red-legged-partridge

Reimann, Matt. "This foolish bird lover brought a few sparrows to America, and now there are 540 million of them." Timeline, Medium, Aug. 7, 2017, accessed Nov. 8, 2023. https://timeline.com/sparrows-invasive-species-america-9546e6a9e57e

Retofuerst. "Woodpecker Symbolism." Accessed Oct. 23, 2023. https://retofuerst.com/woodpecker-symbolism/#myth

"Rhinoceros Hornbill." Rangkong Indonesia, accessed Oct. 11, 2023. https://rangkong.org/en/enggang-in-indonesia/rhinoceros-hornbill

Robb, Magnus "Northern Fulmar." The Sound Approach, accessed Oct. 26, 2023. https://soundapproach.co.uk/species/northern-fulmar/

Roberts, Brian L. "Readers' forum: Feeling blue about Pink Floyd." Deseret News, March 26, 2007, accessed Nov. 9, 2023. https://web.archive.org/web/20131004221343/http://www.deseretnews.com/article/660205853/Feeling-blue-about-Pink-Floyd.html?pg=all

Rogers, Jude. "Up Close with the Red Kits in Wales." VisitWales.com, accessed Nov. 5, 2023. https://www.visitwales.com/things-do/nature-and-landscapes/wildlife-flora-and-fauna/return-red-kite

Room, Adrian. Brewer's Dictionary of Phrase and Fable. Cassell, London, 1999.

Rosen, Brenda. The Mythical Creatures Bible: The Definitive Guide to Legendary Beings. Sterling, New York, 2009.

Rotherham, Ian. "The Little Bird That Folk Believed Spoke To The Devil Himself." The Star, April 3, 2020, accessed Nov. 15, 2023. https://www.thestar.co.uk/news/opinion/columnists/the-little-bird-that-folk-believed-spoke-to-the-devil-himself-2528482#

Rowe, Matt. "Famed NYC Red-Tailed Hawk Known as Pale Male has Died at Age 32." Lafaber Company, 2023, accessed Oct. 12, 2023. https://lafeber.com/pet-birds/famed-nyc-red-tailed-hawk-known-as-pale-male-has-died-at-age-32

"A Royal Feather." Nomad, Nov. 27, 2013, accessed Oct. 29, 2023. https://www.nomad-tanzania.com/hub/a-royal-feather

Royer, Erica. "Conserving the Last of Guam's Avifauna: The Recovery of the Guam Rail." Smithsonian's National Zoo & Conservation Biology Institute, Jan. 13, 2020, accessed Oct. 26, 2023. https://nationalzoo.si.edu/center-for-species-survival/news/conserving-last-guams-avifauna-recovery-guam-rail

Sadhwani, Bhavya. "13 Superstitions We Still Believe in and How They Originated." India Times, May 10, 2017, accessed June 22, 2023. https://www.indiatimes.com/lifestyle/self/13-ancient-superstitions-we-still-belive-in-and-how-they-originated-249834.html

Sain, Todd Sr. "Bee Hummingbird." Our Breathing Planet, accessed Nov. 4, 2023. https://www.ourbreathingplanet.com/bee-hummingbird/

"Scarlet Macaws of Palenque." Atlas Obscura, accessed Oct. 9, 2023. https://www.atlasobscura.com/places/scarlet-macaws-of-palenque

Schapera, Isaac (1965). The Khoisan Peoples of South Africa. G. Routledge and Paul. p. 167. ISBN 9780710020819. Retrieved September 22, 2008.

Schueman, Lindsey Jean. "Kagu: the Unique Flightless Bird of New Caledonia that Screams." One Earth, accessed Nov. 14, 2023. https://www.oneearth.org/species-of-the-week-kagu/

"Scissor-Tailed Flycatcher." *The Encyclopedia of Oklahoma History and Culture.* Accessed Nov. 19, 2023. https://www.okhistory.org/publications/enc/entry.php?entry=SC007

Scott, Shelley. "Latin America Passage: The Eagle and the Cactus." Formative, accessed Oct. 16, 2023. https://app.formative.com/library/5d56be1e37180f9a038c59b4

"The Seagulls and the Whisky Jacks." Native Languages, accessed Nov. 2, 2023. http://www.native-languages.org/creestory5.htm

Shanahan, Mike. "Will the Bird that Dodged a Bullet Pay the Price of Peace?" Under the Banyan, Nov. 2, 2017, accessed Oct. 21, 2023. https://underthebanyan.blog/2017/11/02/will-the-bird-that-dodged-a-bullet-pay-the-price-of-peace/

Shaw, Sylvie. "The Sacred Kingfisher." River Stories and Sense of Place, Nov. 7, 2007, accessed Nov. 18, 2023. http://rivercityandsenseofplace.blogspot.com/2007/11/sacred-kingfisher.html

Shelley, Percy Bysshe. "To a Skylark." 1820, accessed Aug 20, 2023. https://www.poetryfoundation.org/poems/45146/to-a-skylark

Shumaker, Heather. "The Phoenix through the Ages." Swarthmore College Bulletin, Oct. 2008, accessed Nov. 9, 2023. https://www.swarthmore.edu/bulletin/archive/wp/october-2008_the-phoenix-through-the-ages.html

Shyloh. "Arctic Terns." BeakingOff, July 15, 2013, accessed Nov. 16, 2023. https://beakingoff.wordpress.com/2013/07/15/arctic-terns/

"Siamese Fireback: 11 Facts About Thailand's National Bird." Culture Trip, accessed Nov. 3, 2023. https://theculturetrip.com/asia/thailand/articles/siamese-fireback-11-facts-about-thailands-national-bird

Siddiqi, Sanaa. "Boreal Owls in Alaska Takvialnguaraq." *Alaska Fish & Wildlife News*, March 2022, accessed Aug. 18, 2023. https://www.adfg.alaska.gov/index.cfm?adfg=wildlifenews.view_article&articles_id=1027

"Significance to Humans Lfa." Bird Watching Blog, Aug. 28, 2023, accessed Nov. 13, 2023. https://www.birdwatchingblog.us/feeding-ecology/significance-to-humans-lfa.html

Simpson, Rick and Elis. "South American Breeding Waders. Lapwings." WaderQuest, Oct. 8, 2021, accessed Nov. 20, 2023. https://www.waderquest.net/wp-content/uploads/2021/08/6-SA-breeding-waders-LapwingsR.pdf

"Skitters: The Black Oystercatcher." Council of the Haida Nation, Nov. 10, 2017, accessed Oct. 28, 2023. https://www.haidanation.ca/skitters-the-black-oystercatcher/

Slack, Tucker. "Wild Thing: Bird of Many Aliases." *TPW Magazine*, Nov. 12, 2012, accessed Nov. 15, 2023. https://tpwmagazine.com/archive/2012/nov/scout5_wildthing_woodcock/

Slaght, Jonathan C. (2020). *Owls of the Eastern Ice: A Quest to Find and Save the World's Largest Owl.* New York: Farrar, Straus and Giroux. p. 26.

"Slithering Settlers: The Story of Aruba's Boa Situation." DCNA, accessed Oct. 25, 2023. https://dcnanature.org/invasive-boa

Souchon, James. "The South African Significance of the Secretarybird." Londolozi Blog, Aug. 17, 2020, accessed Nov. 15, 2023. https://blog.londolozi.com/2020/08/17/the-south-african-significance-of-the-secretary-bird/

"Sound and Vision: The Purple-Crested Turaco." Letting Nature Back In, accessed Oct. 29, 2023. https://naturebackin.com/2019/09/12/sound-and-vision-the-purple-crested-turaco/

"South Carolina State Bird." Netstate, accessed Nov. 18, 2023. https://www.netstate.com/states/symb/birds/sc_carolina_wren.htm

"Species Spotlight: Shoebill." Defend Them All Foundation, July 29, 2021, accessed Oct. 10, 2023. https://www.defendthemall.org/blog/2021/7/29/species-spotlight-shoebill#:~:text=Shoebills

"Spooky Owl Provides Natural Rodent Control for Farmers." UF News, University of Florida, Oct. 28, 1999, accessed Nov. 20, 2023. https://web.archive.org/web/20140307224545/http://news.ufl.edu/1999/10/28/owls1/

"St. Lucia Amazon." World Parrot Trust, accessed Oct. 6, 2023. https://www.parrots.org/projects/st.-lucia-amazon

StarStuffs. "Animal Totems: Dictionary of Birds." Accessed Nov. 10, 2023. https://www.starstuffs.com/animal_totems/dictionary_of_birds.html

Stoller, Marianne. "Birds, Feathers, and Hopi Ceremonies." *Expedition Magazine*, 1991, accessed Oct. 17, 2023. https://www.penn.museum/sites/expedition/birds-feathers-and-hopi-ceremonialism/

Stone, Jennifer. "The Meaning of Sparrows: Symbolism and Identification." Owlcation, July 21, 2022, accessed Nov. 8, 2023. https://owlcation.com/social-sciences/The-Meaning-of-Sparrows-Identification-and-Folklore

"The Story of Kāhu: Bringing a Te Ao Māori Lens to Storytelling." *NZ Herald*, Oct. 18, 2021, accessed Oct. 18, 2023. https://www.nzherald.co.nz/kahu/the-story-of-kahu-bringing-a-te-ao-maori-lens-to-storytelling/
DPEAFYMOSURKQPRINIQNTACNIY

"Story of the Day: How the Lark Got Her Crest." *Mythology and Folklore Un-Textbook*, University of Oklahoma, accessed Oct. 26, 2023. http://mythfolklore.blogspot.com/2019/08/story-of-day-how-lark-got-her-crest.html

"Story of the Duck with Golden Eggs." *World of Tales*, accessed Oct. 6, 2023. https://www.worldoftales.com/European_folktales/Russian_Folktale_9.html#gsc.tab=0

"The Story of the Oriole." Sacred-texts.com, accessed Nov. 7, 2023. https://sacred-texts.com/etc/bnm/bnm26.htm

Stratton, Florence and Bessie Reid. "The Pecan Tree's Best Friend," in *When the Storm God Rides*, Charles Scribner & Sons, 1936. https://sacred-texts.com/nam/se/wsgr/wsgr25.htm

Summerville, Tara. "Red-Winged Blackbird Meaning & Symbolism." Songbird Hub, Apr 20, 2023, accessed Aug 20, 2023. https://songbirdhub.com/red-winged-blackbird-meaning/

Summerville, Tara. "The Meaning of Mockingbird–Symbolism and References." Songbird Hub, April 21, 2023, accessed Nov. 5, 2023. https://songbirdhub.com/meaning-of-mockingbird/

Sundar, KSG; Choudhury, BC (2003). "The Indian Sarus Crane *Grus a. antigone*: a Literature Review". *Journal of Ecological Society*. 16: 16–41. Accessed Oct. 7, 2023. https://archive.org/details/JEcologicalSociety16/page/n15/mode/2up?view=theater

Swick, Gerald. "S-S-S-Smokin'! The Long, Sometimes Humorous Debate over Tobacco." Once in American History, Oct. 7, 2018, accessed Oct. 9, 2023. https://geralddswick.com/s-s-s-smokin-the-long-sometimes-humorous-debate-over-tobacco/

"Swift Folklore." Peak Boxes, March 30, 2019, accessed Oct. 8, 2023. https://peakboxes.co.uk/knowledge-learning-blog/swiftfolklore

Symbols of Conviviality. Andes Amazon Field School, accessed Nov. 12, 2023. http://andesandamazonfieldschool.com/Andes_and_Amazon_Field_School/Oropendolas.html

Taggart, Diane. "Long Island Wildlife Bird of the Week: American Bittern." Fire Island and Beyond, accessed Oct. 10, 2023. https://www.fireislandandbeyond.com/long-island-wildlife-bird-of-the-week-american-bittern

"The Tale of the Red-Headed Woodpecker." Camp Gravatt, July 8, 2019, accessed Nov. 4, 2023. https://www.campgravatt.org/blog/2019/7/8/the-tale-of-the-red-headed-woodpecker

Tan, Jim. "How the UK's Red Kites Came Back from the Brink." *National Geographic*, Mar. 17, 2022, accessed Nov. 5, 2023. https://www.nationalgeographic.co.uk/animals/2022/03/how-the-uks-red-kites-came-back-from-the-brink

Teeuwissen, Jon. "The Story of Swan Lake in Black and White." Detroit Opera, Aug. 13, 2020, accessed Oct. 22, 2023. https://detroitopera.org/the-story-of-swan-lake-in-black-and-white/

"This Fall: Witness the Magic of Chimney Swift Migration." Audubon North Carolina, accessed Oct. 17, 2023. https://nc.audubon.org/news/fall-witness-magic-chimney-swift-migration

Thömmes, Katja. "What Instagram Can Teach Us About Bird Photography: The Most Photogenic Bird and Color Preferences." *Iperception*, March-April 2021, 12(2). Accessed Nov. 11, 2023. https://www.ncbi.nlm.nih.gov/pmc/articles/PMC8073730/

"The Thunder Nation and the Eagle." White Wolf Pack, accessed Oct. 13, 2023. http://www.whitewolfpack.com/2011/08/thunder-nation-and-eagle.html

Tipp, Cheryl. "The Tale of the Seven Whistlers." British Library, Feb 7, 2019, accessed Nov. 6, 2023. https://blogs.bl.uk/sound-and-vision/2019/02/the-tale-of-the-seven-whistlers.html

Toews, Mitchell. "The Seven Songs." Fictive Dream: Short Stories Online. Nov. 26, 2017, accessed Nov. 13, 2023. https://fictivedream.com/2017/11/26/the-seven-songs/

"Toucan Spirit Animal: Meaning and Interpretations." Spirit Animals, accessed Nov. 13, 2023. https://www.spiritanimals.org/toucan/#meaning_of_toucan_in_various_mythologies

"The Towhee Medicine." The Healing Path of the Raven & Wolf, accessed Nov. 4, 2023. https://lifeofwaya.com/2012/05/31/the-towhee-medicine-2/

"Tror Yorng (Giant Ibis): The National Bird of Cambodia." IntoCambodia,org, accessed Nov. 12, 2023. https://intocambodia.org/content/tror-yorng-giant-ibis-national-bird-cambodia

"Turtle Doves in Culture." Operation Turtle Dove, accessed Nov. 16, 2023. https://www.operationturtledove.org/turtle-doves/turtle-doves-in-culture/

Ujorha, Tadaferua. "Crowned Crane: The Sad Story of Nigeria's National Bird." Daily Trust, Feb. 3, 2018, accessed Oct. 10, 2023. https://dailytrust.com/crowned-crane-the-sad-story-of-nigerias-national-bird/

"U.S. Accused in Albatross Chick Deaths." NBC News, Feb. 1, 2010, accessed Nov. 9, 2023. https://www.nbcnews.com/id/wbna35184107

Veit, Lena, and Nieder, Andreas. "Abstract Rule Neurons in The Endbrain Support Intelligent Behavior in Corvid Songbirds." Nature Communications, 4 (2878), 2013. https://www.nature.com/articles/ncomms3878#citeas

Vidal, John. "Hasta la Vista Ruddy Duck." *The Guardian*, May 28, 1993, accessed Nov. 7, 2023. https://www.theguardian.com/theguardian/from-the-archive-blog/2012/mar/08/1993-hasta-la-vista-ruddy-duck

"Video: Sage-Grouse Explained by Vox." Audubon Rockies, accessed Oct. 17, 2023. https://rockies.audubon.org/sagebrush/resources/video-sage-grouse-explained-vox

Wagner, Eric. "What Makes a Whimbrel?" *High Country News*, June 25, 2021, accessed Nov. 6, 2023. https://www.hcn.org/articles/essays-what-makes-a-whimbrel

Wallace, Dr. George. "Tourism Takes the Bird." Terrain.org, 2007, accessed Nov. 2, 2023. https://www.terrain.org/articles/21/wallace.htm

Walsh, James. "The White Stork: An International Symbol of Peace?" Greater Manchester, accessed Oct. 17, 2023. https://gmgreencity.com/the-white-stork

"Wandering Whistling Duck." Kakadu National Park, accessed Oct. 23, 2023. https://parksaustralia.gov.au/kakadu/discover/nature/birds/wandering-whistling-ducks/

Warren, Michael J. "The winter angel." *The Compleat Birder*, Dec. 27, 2016, accessed Nov. 2, 2023. https://compleatbirder.wordpress.com/tag/shrike-folklore/

Warren-Chad, Rachel, and Marianne Taylor. *Birds: Myth, Lore, and Legend*. Bloomsbury, London, 2016.

Waters, Hannah. "How the House Sparrow Conquered the World Is Encoded in Its Genes." Audubon, Aug. 21, 2018, accessed Nov. 8, 2023. https://www.audubon.org/news/how-house-sparrow-conquered-world-encoded-its-genes

Watts, Brian. "Farewell to Hope." The Center for Conservation Biology, Apr 3, 2019, accessed Nov. 6, 2023. https://ccbbirds.org/2019/04/03/farewell-to-hope/

Wee Kek Koon. "What is Edible Bird's Nest and Its Supposed Benefits? Plus How the Popular Myth of Who Introduced It to the Chinese Is Easily Disproved." *South China Morning Post*, July 9, 2023, accessed Aug 19, 2023. https://www.scmp.com/magazines/post-magazine/short-reads/article/3226859/what-edible-birds-nest-and-its-supposed-benefits-plus-how-popular-myth-who-introduced-it-chinese#

West, Kimberly J. "American Redstart Bird Spiritual Meaning: Totem, Symbols, and Folklore." BirdWatchExperts, July 29, 2023, accessed Nov. 15, 2023. https://birdwatchexperts.com/american-redstart-bird-spiritual-meaning/

Whaanga, Hēmi, et al. "Dead as the Moa." University of Waikato, Sept. 7, 2018, accessed Oct. 23, 2023. https://www.waikato.ac.nz/news-opinion/media/2018/dead-as-the-moa

"What Are Edible Bird's Nests? All You Need to Know." Healthline, accessed Aug. 19, 2023. https://www.healthline.com/nutrition/bird-nest-benefits-and-downsides

"What Is a Sacred Site?" Aboriginal Areas Protection Authority, accessed Oct. 23, 2023. https://www.aapant.org.au/sacred-sites/what-sacred-site

"What Is PUKANA?" Pukana Adventure Co., accessed Nov. 6, 2023. https://www.pukanaadventures.com/pages/about-us

"What Is the Casque For?" ZooParc Beauval, accessed Oct. 11, 2023. https://www.zoobeauval.com/en/zooparc/animals/rhinoceros-hornbill

"What Is the National Bird of Nigeria?" World Atlas, accessed Oct. 10, 2023. https://www.worldatlas.com/articles/what-is-the-national-bird-of-nigeria.html

"What Is the State Bird of Georgia? (And Why?)" Birdfact, Jan. 4, 2023, accessed Nov. 18. 2023. https://birdfact.com/articles/state-bird-of-georgia

"When Did 'Chicken' Become Synonymous with Being Afraid?" *Independent*, Nov. 29, 2014, accessed Oct. 27, 2023. https://www.independent.co.uk/arts-entertainment/books/features/when-did-chicken-become-synonymous-with-being-afraid-9887896.html#

White, Lewis. "7 Fascinating Facts about Capercaillie." Discover Wildlife, accessed Nov 18, 2023. https://www.discoverwildlife.com/animal-facts/birds/facts-about-capercaillie

"Why Doves Is a Symbol of Relationship Longevity." Feng Shuied. Oct. 20, 2019, accessed Nov. 16, 2023. https://www.fengshuied.com/the-dove

"Why Oilbirds Are Living in the Dark, Even in Daytime." Planet of Birds, Oct. 20, 2013, accessed Nov. 16, 2023. https://planetofbirds.com/why-oilbirds-are-living-in-the-dark-even-in-daytime

"Why the Black Cockatoo?" Ngaoara, accessed Oct. 13, 2023. https://www.ngaoara.org.au/story

Wiederholt, Ruscena. "The Tale of the Rose-Colored Spoonbill." The Everglades Foundation, accessed Nov. 10 2023. https://www.evergladesfoundation.org/post/the-tale-of-the-rose-colored-spoonbill

"Wigeon, Mareca Penelope." BirdFact, accessed Nov. 3, 2023. https://birdfact.com/birds/wigeon

"Wild Turkey." Navajo Zoo, accessed Nov. 4, 2023. https://navajozoo.org/wild-turkey/

Williston, Teresa Peirce, trans. *Japanese Fairy Tales*. Chicago, New York, and London: Rand McNally and Company, 1904. Accessed June 7, 2024. https://sites.pitt.edu/~dash/sparrow.html#williston

Winding, Teri. "Storks in the Spring." TerriWinding.com, May 20, 2020, accessed Oct. 17, 2023. https://www.terriwindling.com/blog/2020/05/storks.html

Winterman, Denise. "Why Are Magpies So Often Hated?" *BBC News Magazine*, Mar 28, 2008, accessed Nov 10, 2023. http://news.bbc.co.uk/1/hi/magazine/7316384.stm

"The Wirebird." Saint Helena Island, accessed Oct. 17, 2023. http://sainthelenaisland.info/wirebird.htm

Wordsworth, William. "To the Skylark." 1827, accessed Aug 20, 2023 at poetryfoundation.org, https://www.poetryfoundation.org/poems/45561/to-a-skylark-56d225364d1a9

Yallowitz, Charles. "Monster Month: Oozlum Bird." Legends of Windemere, Oct. 26, 2022, accessed Nov. 6, 2023. https://legendsofwindemere.com/2022/10/26/monster-month-oozlum-bird/

Yamamoto, Hiroshi. "On the Cries of the Green Pheasant (*Phasianus colchicus*) Concerned to the Earthquake." *Japanese Journal of Ornithology*, 1971, 20:90, pp. 239-242. Accessed Nov. 9, 2023. https://www.jstage.jst.go.jp/article/jjo1915/20/90/20_90_239/_article

Yeats, William Butler. "The Wanderings of Oisin, Book 1." FamousPoetsandPoems,com, accessed Nov. 7, 2023. http://famouspoetsandpoems.com/poets/william_butler_yeats/poems/10410

"Zimbabwe Bird Flies Home." BBC News, May 14, 2003, accessed Oct. 30, 2023. http://news.bbc.co.uk/2/hi/africa/3028589.stm

ACKNOWLEDGMENTS

Many, many thanks to Amy Lyons for thinking of me for this project, and for introducing me to the folks at The Quarto Group and Wellfleet Press. My editor, Elizabeth You, and everyone at Quarto has made this book a wonderful project, welcoming me into the process and making me feel like I'm on a team that cares about quality and accuracy. I am grateful, as always, to my agent, Regina Ryan, who oversees the contracting process for me and keeps my author career moving in the right direction. Finally, there is no one more integral to my success than my extraordinary husband of thirty-four years, Nic Minetor, who understands my need to spend weeks on end in front of a screen and keyboard and supports all of my creative pursuits—and who is ready with a glass of whisky and a kind word when I need them most.

PHOTO CREDITS

Unless otherwise listed below, all images © Shutterstock.com

The Atlas Object/Creative Market: G, R, T chapter opener

Biodiversity Heritage Library: H chapter opener (Harpia harpyja), 019 (*Amazona imperialis*), 065 (*Burhinus grallarius*), 235 (*Ninox novaeseelandiae*), 387 (*Zenaida macroura*)

Getty Royalty free: Title page opener, How To Use this Book opener, M001 (*Caladrius*)

John James Audobon: A, B, C, E, F, I, L, M, O, P, S chapter openers, 261 (*Pelicanus occidentalis*)

The New York Public Library: D, J, Q, U, V chapter opener (*Quiscalus quiscula*), 261 (*Pelicanus occidentalis*), 334 (*Seiurus aurocapilla*), 368 (*Trochilus polyt*), 386 (*Zenaida aurita*)

Shen Quan: Fanciful & Mythical Birds chapter opener

United States Fish and Wildlife Service: 387 (*Zenaida macroura*)

© EnelEva / Adobe Stock: 024 (*Anas platyrhynchos domesticus*)

About the
AUTHOR

Randi Minetor is the author of more than ninety traditionally published books, with a focus on birds, nature, travel, and America's national parks. Her books about birds cover subjects including backyard birding, bird-friendly gardening, local and regional birding field guides, quick-reference guides to the birds, trees, and wildflowers of New York and the mid-Atlantic states; and the natural history and evolution of birds. She writes for *Birding* and *North American Birds* magazines, and has been published in *Bird Watcher's Digest*. She also serves as president of the Rochester Birding Association in New York. In addition to writing about birds, Randi is best known for her non-fiction books in the Death in the National Parks series, on Glacier, Zion, Acadia, Rocky Mountain, and Everglades National Parks, as well as New Hampshire's Mount Washington and Maine's Mount Katahdin.

Index of
COMMON NAMES

Index of
BIRDS

ACCORDING TO IUCN CLASSIFICATION

Index of
COMMON MEANINGS